Open access edition supported by the National Endowment for the Humanities / Andrew W. Mellon Foundation Humanities Open Book Program.

© 2019 Johns Hopkins University Press
Published 2019

Johns Hopkins University Press
2715 North Charles Street
Baltimore, Maryland 21218-4363
www.press.jhu.edu

The text of this book is licensed under a Creative Commons Attribution-NonCommercial-NoDerivatives 4.0 International License: https://creativecommons.org/licenses/by-nc-nd/4.0/.
CC BY-NC-ND

ISBN-13: 978-1-4214-3050-8 (open access)
ISBN-10: 1-4214-3050-9 (open access)

ISBN-13: 978-1-4214-3051-5 (pbk. : alk. paper)
ISBN-10: 1-4214-3051-7 (pbk. : alk. paper)

ISBN-13: 978-1-4214-3088-1 (electronic)
ISBN-10: 1-4214-3088-6 (electronic)

This page supersedes the copyright page included in the original publication of this work.

PROSODY AND PURPOSE IN THE ENGLISH RENAISSANCE

BY THE SAME AUTHOR

Christian Rite and Christian Drama in the Middle Ages
The Enduring Monument: Praise in Renaissance Literary Theory and Practice
Entering the Maze: Identity and Change in Modern Culture
Toward Freedom and Dignity: The Humanities and the Idea of Humanity

Prosody and Purpose in the English Renaissance

O. B. Hardison, Jr.

THE JOHNS HOPKINS UNIVERSITY PRESS
BALTIMORE AND LONDON

© 1989 The Johns Hopkins University Press
All rights reserved

The Johns Hopkins University Press
701 West 40th Street
Baltimore, Maryland 21211
The Johns Hopkins Press Ltd., London

The paper used in this publication meets the minimum requirements of American National Standard for Information Sciences—Permanence of Paper for Printed Library Materials, ANSI Z39.48-1984.

Library of Congress Cataloging-in-Publication Data

Hardison, O. B.
Prosody and purpose in the English renaissance / O. B. Hardison, Jr.
    p. cm.
Bibliography: p.
Includes index.
ISBN 0-8018-3722-7 (alk. paper)
1. English poetry—Early modern, 1500–1700—History and criticism.
2. English language—Early modern, 1500–1700—Versification.
3. Epic poetry, English—History and criticism. 4. Verse drama, English—History and criticism. 5. English poetry—Classical influences. 6. Renaissance—England. 7. Classicism—England.
8. Literary form. I. Title.
PR535.V4H37   1989
821'.3'09—dc19   88-22598
                                                      CIP

To Kurt & Nora Hertzfeld

Contents

Preface   xi

PART ONE: Contexts

CHAPTER I: Prosody and Purpose   3
Preliminary Concepts. Prosodic Systems. The Syllabic Aspect of English Renaissance Verse. The Metrical Ambivalence of English Verse. Historical Perspective. Music and Prosody.

CHAPTER II: *Ars Metrica*   23
Meter, Genre, Music. Grammar and Prosody (1): Construction and Metaplasm. Grammar and Prosody (2): Standard Approaches Grammar and Prosody (3): Donatus and the Metrical Foot. Diomedes and Poetic Art. Bede and Rhythmic Poetry.

CHAPTER III: Rude and Beggerly Ryming: 43
The Romance Tradition
Ars Rithmica. From Accentual to Syllabic Verse. *Parisiana Poetria*. *L'Art de Dictier*. The Pléiade and the Rejection of Medieval Tradition. Reactions: Tradition and Radical Change.

CHAPTER IV: A Question of Language: Italy and the Shaping of Renaissance Prosodic Theory — 71

Vernacular Eloquence. The Heritage of the Trecento. Courtly Vernacular and Rational Speech. Trissino: Traditional and Classical Prosody. Giraldi Cintio: Classical Form and Vernacular Prosody. Tolomei and Quantitative Verse. A Note on Annibale Caro's *Aeneid*.

CHAPTER V: Notes of Instruction — 92

Esoteric Humanism. Ascham and the Question of English. *Prosodia*: Lily and Brinsley. Palsgrave and Ascham: "Trew Quantitie." Gascoigne: Mother Phrase and Proper *Idióma*. Hard Classicism: Harvey, Webbe, Campion. The Middle Road: Syllable and Accent. Daniel and the Native Tradition

PART TWO: Performances

CHAPTER VI: A Straunge Metre Worthy To Be Embraced — 127

Heroic Aspirations. A Straunge Metre. The Death of Dido. Surrey and His Editors.

CHAPTER VII: Jasper Heywood's Fourteeners — 148

The Seneca Project. Comic and Tragic Verse at Midcentury. *Thyestes*.

CHAPTER VIII: *Gorboduc* and Dramatic Blank Verse, with a Note on Comedy — 171

Imperatives of State and of Performance. Speech as Speaking. Speech as Speeches. A Note on Comedy. Classical Trends. Gascoigne and Comic Dialogue in Prose.

CHAPTER IX: Heroic Experiments — 196

Thomas Phaer and Moderate Classicism. Richard Stanyhurst and the Classical Absurd. Chapman and Homer. Spenser and the Return to Romance. Davenant and the Rational Quatrain.

CHAPTER X: Speech and Verse in Later Elizabethan Drama — 226

Actorly Speech. *Opsis* and Illocution. The Mirror of Custom. Renaissance Comments on Dramatic Verse and on Acting. Marlowe's Mighty Line. Kyd and Shakespeare. Verse and Memory.

CHAPTER XI: True Musical Delight   258
  Music and Muse. Prosody and the Irrational. The Note on
  the Verse of *Paradise Lost*. Tagging the Verse.

Notes   277

Index   329

Preface

This study began as an investigation of the prosody underlying Surrey's translation of the *Aeneid* into blank verse around 1540. The study expanded far beyond its original limits, in large measure because I could not find a treatment of English prosody in the sixteenth century that answered the questions I was asking. I hope what I have done will prove useful to others who ask similar questions, not only about renaissance verse but about English verse of any period.

The first section of this book is subtitled "Contexts" and places English renaissance prosody in the context of those prosodic systems that influenced it in the sixteenth century. These chapters establish a foundation in historical prosody for approaching the subject. They are detailed and may occasionally seem formidable. I do not apologize for this fact. The subject itself is complex. I have tried to be no more complex than the subject demands, and I have concentrated in the text on explication, while relegating controversies and fine points to the notes.

The second major section of this book is subtitled "Performances." It examines only two types of poem—heroic and dramatic—but it attempts an examination of the prosody of these types during the period between Surrey's translation of the *Aeneid* (ca. 1540) and Milton's *Paradise Lost* (1667). The focus on two genres was necessary because of space limitations. However, it is appropriate because heroic and dramatic poetry are especially well defined during the period in question, both in critical theory and through practical experimentation. In addition, the two forms are so closely related in Italian, French, and English prosodies that to treat one requires consideration of the other.

My title is *Prosody and Purpose in the English Renaissance*. Purpose is involved throughout. In the first section ("Contexts"), it is involved, for example, in the relations posited in ancient theory between meter and genre, in the concept of prosodic decorum, in attempts to introduce the ancient strategies of construction into uninflected modern languages, in efforts to make vernacular forms like the hendecasyllabic, the Alexandrine, and the English decasyllabic capable of effects comparable to those of ancient forms, in the relation between romance prosodic conventions and the celebration of cultural roots, and in efforts in the seventeenth century to devise prosodic forms that meet the need of reason to protect itself against imagination.

Music is an aspect of prosody that relates to purpose in special ways, and a concern for the musical aspects of prosody runs through the present book, culminating in the chapter on Milton's *Paradise Lost*. The musical aspect of prosody is often associated with the ability of poetry to be constitutive—that is, to make objective otherwise unimaginable realities rather than simply to imitate what is. In the high Middle Ages, the requirement that language be subordinate to music contributed directly to the development of the syllabic prosody of romance languages and to the elements of romance theory that are corollaries of the idea that poetry is, to use the phrase of Eustache Deschamps, "natural music."

In the second part of the book ("Performances"), purpose is also understood in terms of cultural, political, and professional objectives that shaped individual poems. Among these are the desire to elevate culture by elevating the language and linguistic forms that make thought possible, the need to adapt verse to performance by actors who move and gesture and interact as well as declaim, and the quest for a verse form able to present undistorted communications from an invisible source of truth.

In the course of this study several important generalizations about prosody have emerged. The first is the importance of what ancient grammar called "construction" to an adequate theory of prosody. Construction is the control of syntax and syntactical rhythms and hence of the grammatical forms that shape vocal performance. It can be considered a part of grammar, a part of rhetoric, or a part of prosody. It is especially relevant to heroic poetry and drama—heroic poetry because epic seeks forms of expression elevated above common speech, and drama because dialogue aims at forms that are like speech and capable of shaping intonation when a passage is vocally performed. Construction cannot be excluded from the study of prosody in the period under consideration. Indeed, as modern studies of intonation show, it is relevant to the prosody of any period, including the present. It is considered in the following pages both in relation to ancient prosodic theory and in relation to aspects of vocal performance, illocution, and actorly speech that are discussed in their proper places in the "Performances" section.

A second important general point is the dominance of syllabic concepts of prosody in the period covered. Some years ago Edward Weismiller remarked in a review of theories about Milton's versification that "the devices [Chaucer] used—or such of them as were not ruled out specifically by changes in language—seem to recur in the syllable counting verse of the 16th and 17th centuries. . . . This may be coincidental. It may, on the other hand, suggest the possibility that the technique of Chaucer's French-Italian line . . . was better understood in the 17th century . . . than we supposed." The present study is in full agreement with Professor Weismiller's position. Syllabic concepts are dominant in English discussions of prosody in the sixteenth and seventeenth centuries. As the "Performances" section shows, English verse of the same period is best understood in terms of this tradition, with important special features arising from Latin and Italian as well as French influence, and from renaissance as well as medieval models. Here again, purpose is involved. The syllabic tradition is itself complex. Different poets emphasize different elements of the tradition depending on what they want their poetry to do, and the same poet may use different prosodic strategies for different kinds of poems.

It should be added immediately that the present study makes no claim to having finally "solved" the outstanding problems of English prosody. As I observe in chapter 1, certain problems are forever beyond a simple solution because of the many diverse influences, linguistic as well as poetic, that have shaped the English language. English prosody will always involve apparent contradictions and ambivalence, quite aside from the fact that individual authors vary from one to another because of talent, personality, background, and the like.

The foundations of modern historical prosody were established for English verse between 1880 and 1910 by Jakob Schipper, George Saintsbury, and Robert Bridges. Very substantial progress has been made since their work, and studies now abound for specific authors and literary periods. Progress has not, however, brought consensus, and there continue to be deep divisions regarding the historical as well as the applied aspects of prosody.

I acknowledge here special obligations to Derek Attridge's *Well-Weighed Syllables* (1974), Susanne Woods's *Natural Emphasis: English Versification from Chaucer to Dryden* (1985), and the prosodic essays contributed by Edward Weismiller to the *Variorum Commentary on the Poems of John Milton* (1972, 1975). Among works that have treated Continental prosodic traditions, Georges Lote, *Histoire du vers français* (1949–56), and Mario Pazzaglia, *Il Verso e l'arte della canzone nel 'De vulgari eloquentia'* (1967), have been especially valuable. T. V. F. Brogan's *English Versification, 1570–1890* (1981) remains for me, as for all others who venture into this field, an indispensable guide and resource.

I have found contemporary work on applied prosody stimulating but less immediately relevant than the historical studies to the issues I have examined. Especially useful among applied prosodic studies have been the series of articles on English renaissance poets by George T. Wright. These articles combine historical understanding with sensitivity to the sound of verse in ways that are, if not unique, at least exemplary, and no one working in the field can fail to learn from them. Unfortunately, his book *Shakespeare's Metrical Art* had been announced but had not appeared at the time my own book was being prepared for press.

I also acknowledge my obligation to the concept of relative stress defined in 1900 by Otto Jespersen and incorporated by George L. Trager and Henry Lee Smith, Jr., into *An Outline of English Structure* (1951), and to the theory of generative prosody outlined by Morris Halle and Samuel J. Keyser, Jr., in *English Stress: Its Form, Its Growth, and Its Role in Verse* (1971). Although different systems of generative prosody have been offered since 1970, principally those of Karl Magnuson and Frank Ryder (1970, 1971) and Paul Kiparsky (1975, 1977), the work of Halle and Keyser remains the basic statement of the position. Finally, for reasons explained above, I have drawn on efforts to integrate syntax into the study of prosody as illustrated especially by the work of David Crystal (*Prosodic Systems and Intonation in English* [1969]) and D. W. Harding (*Words into Rhythm: English Speech Rhythm in Verse and Prose* [1976]).

At different points in the following pages I have used the conventions of quantitative, syllabic, and accentual scansion to reveal details of prosodic technique. For quantitative scansion, I have used "⏑" to indicate a short syllable and "–" to indicate a long syllable. For accentual scansion, "x" indicates a light stress, "/" a heavy stress, and "\" a secondary stress. This three-stress system should not be taken as a rejection of the idea that proper treatment of many passages of English verse requires four degrees of relative stress, an idea with which I agree. An asterisk ("*") is regularly used to mark a caesura. A straight line ("|") is used to separate feet.

For lines scanned in terms of syllabic conventions, I have adopted the system outlined by Jean Suberville (*Histoire et théorie de la versification française* [rev. ed., 1946; rpt. 1968]) and refined by Clive Scott (*French Verse-Art: A Study* [1980]), except that I use an asterisk (*) for the caesura. Measures are indicated by number of syllables and separated by a plus sign (+). Thus the string [2+4*4+2] indicates a conventional Alexandrine with no extrametrical syllables, having two measures in each half-line and the caesura after the sixth syllable. An apostrophe following a number indicates that the measure ends with an extrametrical unstressed syllable. An Alexandrine with an epic caesura would be shown as [2+4'*4+2]. Primary accents in syllabic lines are indicated by a ("/") above the accented vowel.

Quotations of renaissance verse are from original editions or twentieth-century old-spelling editions. Except in a few passages in which it seems to me important for aesthetic reasons to retain the original usage, *u*, *v*, *i*, and *j* are normalized. For convenience, English renaissance critics are quoted as far as possible from G. Gregory Smith (*Elizabethan Critical Essays* [1904; rpt. 1950]) and J. E. Spingarn (*Critical Essays of the Seventeenth Century* [1907; rpt. 1957]).

Foreign language quotations are translated in the text. When such quotations involve sensitive definitions or have aesthetic qualities important to the discussion, the originals are included in the notes. Otherwise, the originals are omitted in order to save space.

My interest in the *ars metrica* dates from the early 1960s, when I drew on some of its concepts to clarify the relation between poetry and grammar in late classical and medieval theory in *The Enduring Monument* (1962; rpt. 1973). Two of the chapters in this book (6 and 9) include materials published in different form in articles in *Studies in Philology* and the *Shakespeare Quarterly*.

Like many students of the history of English renaissance prosody, I owe a large debt to Professor Edward R. Weismiller. Since I became aware of his work, I have been happy to consider myself one of the "tribe of Ed." Professor Weismiller generously took time from a busy schedule to read a draft of this book in manuscript. His meticulous and expert suggestions were invaluable. I owe another considerable debt to Professor T. V. F. Brogan, who also read the book in manuscript and also offered many helpful suggestions. Neither Professor Weismiller nor Professor Brogan is responsible for whatever deficiencies may appear in the following pages, but the present book is the better for their generous and expert attentions.

I wish to express my thanks also to Joy Sylvester of the University of North Carolina at Chapel Hill for reading the sections of the book that deal with French prosody, and to the staffs of the Lauinger Library of Georgetown University and the Folger Shakespeare Library for generous assistance in many of the tasks of research. My thanks also to Mary V. Yates for her expert editorial contributions to preparing this manuscript for publication.

My greatest debt has been, as in the past, to my wife, Marifrancis.

PART I

Contexts

CHAPTER I

Prosody and Purpose

The discussion of prosody depends on concepts that may at first appear to be simple but turn out on closer inspection to be complex and difficult. If certain prosodic concepts can be defined at the outset, the chances for later confusion will be reduced.

Syntax is central to verse as well as to prose. It has a determining effect on the way a given text is enacted by the speaking voice and creates what speech act theory calls the illocutionary aspect of the text. The Latin term for the use of figures that shape syntax is *constructio*—"construction" in English. The Greek term *syntaxis* is also common in sixteenth-century grammars. This aspect of prosody is recognized—and, indeed, emphasized—by romance and classical prosody, both of which strongly influenced English prosody during the sixteenth century.

In the syllabic prosody of the romance languages, accent arises from phrase and clause units—that is, units of meaning—rather than from natural accents of words arranged so they objectify a succession of units called feet. In *French Verse-Art,* Clive Scott remarks, "Generally the position of rhythmic accents in the French line is determined by its syntax and semantic intention, and these will usually be indistinguishable from one another."[1]

Classical prosody is also much concerned with "syntax and semantic intention," and renaissance discussions of ancient versification are fully aware of this fact. In ancient grammars, treatment of *constructio* immediately precedes and leads to treatment of verse. Construction produces rhythms that are found in prose as well as verse and is thus at least as important to versification as meters and strophes.

An effort to recover the ancient theory of construction and apply it to vernacular poetry is evident in Dante's *De vulgari eloquentia*. The effort was continued in the analysis of syntax by Latin-oriented humanists of the fifteenth century. The work of these scholars has been outlined by Aldo Scaglione in *The Classical Theory of Composition from Its Origin to the Present* and Jean-Claude Chevalier in his *Histoire de la syntaxe*. It was encouraged by Erasmus, and it is evident in such works as the *Syntaxis* of Joannes Despauterius (1515) and the *De emendata structura Latini sermonis* (1524) of Thomas Linacre, both influenced by Erasmus. Testimony on the priority of syntactic rhythms to meter in verse is given by sixteenth-century grammarians who observe that only schoolchildren read poems in a way that gives precedence to meter. Experienced readers emphasize meaning—in other words, their reading is shaped by construction. Renaissance musical literature also recognizes the importance of construction. In the *Sopplimenti musicali* (1588), for example, Gioseffo Carlino, distinguishes between "rhetorical accent," which is created by syntax, and other accent patterns created by meter and music.[2]

The importance of construction is also recognized by twentieth-century students of intonation and speech rhythm, of whom David Crystal and D. W. Harding are representative. These twentieth-century theorists are generally unaware of the precedent for their approach established both by the ancient theory of construction and by the traditions of syllabic versification. However, to argue, as they do, that the important rhythms of English verse are not metrical but phrasal is to argue that the models provided by the theories of construction and of syllabic prosody are at least as helpful in explaining English verse as the models provided by accentual prosody. Whatever the relevance of this position to English verse after Milton, it accords well with the shaping influence of French and Italian verse on English verse from Chaucer to Milton and also with the powerful upsurge of interest in ancient grammar and prosody at the beginning of the sixteenth century.

Preliminary Concepts

To approach English prosody in the sixteenth century, one needs to define several basic concepts. The first is accent. In the *Ars major*

(I, v), the fourth-century grammarian Donatus distinguishes among three elements in pronunciation: tone, breath, and time.

"Tone" (*tonus*) refers to pitch, which is high, low, or intermediate. "Breath" (*spiritus*) refers to aspiration; for example, standard English "how" versus Cockney "'ow." It is more relevant to Greek than to Latin or English, but it is retained by renaissance grammarians because Donatus included it. "Time" (*tempus*) refers to the "times" that were said to comprise each of the standard metrical feet.

"Time" is the basis of Greek and Latin prosody. The long and short "times" of the metrical feet in a line of poetry are objectified by the long and short vowels of the words that make up the line. A long syllable was customarily said to have exactly twice the duration of a short syllable.

"Tone" is considered a form of accent by Donatus and his followers, but it arises from pitch rather than from stress. Donatus uses three marks—*acutus* (/), *gravis* (\), and *circumflexus* (ˆ)—to designate three kinds of tone.[3] As the accent marks used by Donatus show, the acute accent is associated with a rising of the voice. It is often called *levis* ("light") for this reason. The grave accent is associated with a falling pitch of the voice. The circumflex is ambivalent, a point shown graphically by a mark that combines the acute and grave marks (ʌ). It is an anachronism in Latin, a survival from Greek prosody. In chapter 5 we will encounter English prosodists who translate *gravis* as "heavy" and equate it with stress in the sense of loudness. "Loudness," however, is different from "tonal lowness," and, in fact, stressed vowels in English tend to have an acute ("high" or "rising") tone.

All romance languages adopt some of the accent marks used by Donatus, and French adopts all of them. In French, the acute accent still identifies a high (i.e., "rising") pitch and the grave accent a low (i.e., "falling") pitch.[4] A syllable bearing an acute accent is called "tonic." Tonic accent occurs on the final syllable (oxytonic) or, in words with an unaccented (*atone*) final syllable, on the next-to-last, or penultimate, syllable (paroxytonic). Modern, linguistically inclined theorists argue that medieval French verse had a definite stress accent,[5] but for most of the history of French prosody, it has been accepted that stress accent is weak or negligible and that the basic verse unit is the line, which has a terminal accent and is articulated by phrases that divide it into measures. Clive Scott explains:

> French words do not have inbuilt claims on accent (stress) as most English words do. . . . The French word has only a *potential* accent. . . . But when

the words appear in grammatical groups in a syntactical system, they yield their individual accent-potential to the group, and the group accent falls on the last accentable syllable of the last word of the group. Rhythm and syntax thus go hand-in-hand in French verse, and in scanning French lines, we discover the rhythmic measures and accents associated with them by identifying the principal grammatical groups.[6]

PROSODIC SYSTEMS

A rich source of complication in the study of English renaissance prosody is that four different systems were influential and to some degree conflated during the period. Three of these—accentual-alliterative, quantitative, and what I will call accentual foot meter—can be described briefly. The fourth—syllabic—will require more attention. To complicate matters further, none of the four systems is adequate to explain fully what was actually being written. The standard term to describe what was being written is "accentual-syllabic." The term accurately suggests that the verse is a mixture of elements. This being the case, it is best discussed after a review of the four less complex systems.

The most prominent aspect of accentual-alliterative meter is stress, and in this, the system utilizes an element inherent in the Germanic roots of the English language. A line of Old English poetry normally has four heavy stresses, two per half-line separated by one to three lightly stressed syllables. Many prosodists believe that later English poetry conceals a still-dominant four-stress pattern beneath its other, apparently more regular rhythms.[7] Normally, at least three of the stressed syllables are alliterated so that the alliteration links the two half-lines.

No sixteenth-century English poet wrote alliterative verse pure and simple. However, decasyllabic lines that have four heavy stresses and a fifth stress, which is "promoted" but remains secondary, are common in the sixteenth century. Frequently such lines seem to divide into half-lines separated by a pause, each with two heavy stresses. When the stressed syllables have prominent alliteration, one may suspect a kinship with the alliterative tradition. The kinship may be unconscious, or it may arise from intentional archaism. Thomas Sackville's "Induction" in *A Mirror for Magistrates* provides many examples. Sackville was perfectly capable of writing decasyllabic lines without heavy alliteration. One therefore suspects intentional archaism when it appears. Line 3, for example, is a four-stress line with a promoted fifth syllable ("with"). There is strong alliteration, although it does not link the half-lines in the Old English fashion:

```
x    /   x /   x * [\]  x   / x  /
And old Saturnus with his frosty face.
```

Alliterative linkage of half-lines is illustrated a few lines later:

```
       /      /  *  /              /
The soil that erst so seemly was to seen.
```

George Gascoigne's blank verse satire *The Steele Glas* has many such lines, in part because Gascoigne's prosody alludes to *Piers Plowman* and is thus intentionally archaic. Similar effects can be found in English verse of the 1590s—for example in Edmund Spenser's *Faerie Queene*, where they are complemented by archaic spellings and vocabulary.

Quantitative—or classical—prosody gained currency in England through the influence of humanism. The terms used to explain it were adopted throughout Europe during the Renaissance to explain vernacular prosody.

The most direct result of the prestige of quantitative prosody in England was a movement to write quantitative verse in the vernacular. A considerable body of English quantitative verse survives from the sixteenth century. This verse and the theories behind it are reviewed by Derek Attridge in *Well-Weighed Syllables*.

Quantitative poetry goes against the grain of the English language, and most of the poems written according to its formulas have only historical interest. Quantitative theory, however, exerted an influence well beyond quantitative poems. To use classical terms to describe English verse is to encourage the assumption that the practices for which the terms stand define the way English verses are or should be made. Latin prosody helped to establish the idea—or the beginning of the idea—that words should be arranged in a line of English verse so that they can be divided into feet—especially disyllabic feet—in which the natural pattern of unstressed and stressed syllables formed by the words expresses a pattern like the one expressed by long and short syllables in quantitative verse.

This leads to the third system of prosody that influenced English versification in the sixteenth century—accentual foot meter.

This system must be approached with caution. In the first place, it exists primarily as a theory, and English sixteenth-century verse constantly resists its limitations. This is not surprising—English is not Latin. In the second place, the theory appears in sixteenth-century English treatises only tentatively and in combination with other theories. It was, in other words, a theory trying to be born rather than a fully articulated system. The theory did not emerge in something like its modern form until the later eighteenth century.[8] Once it emerged, however, it quickly became dominant and remains so today. Modern prosody offers several alternatives, but the classical terms and concepts remain entrenched. The central chapter of Joseph Malof's excellent *Manual of English Meters* (1970) is a presentation of what Malof calls "foot verse" using the classical terms and concepts.

If practice is distinguished from theory, verse that can be scanned as accentual foot meter appeared in England well before *The Canterbury Tales*. Since English is a stressed language, poets who wrote in regular patterns of light and heavy stresses were merely doing what came naturally. On the other hand, if they had been asked to explain their prosody, they would have spoken of syllable count and line types rather than metrical feet, and their terminology would have echoed that of the French poets who influenced them. Neither accentual nor syllabic terminology quite works. Medieval English verse is more inclined to regular stress patterns than medieval French verse, but it is not as easily segmented into regular units as the norm posited by accentual foot meter. Much English sixteenth-century verse is also more irregular than one would expect if it had been written according to the formulas of accentual foot meter.

The fourth prosodic system to be considered here is romance, or syllabic, prosody. It entered England from France after the Norman Conquest and was sophisticated by Chaucer through a combining of French with Italian prosodic conventions. Although the main features of syllabic prosody are probably less familiar to modern readers of English poetry than classical theory, their influence extends from the Middle Ages to the age of Dr. Johnson. One of the most influential eighteenth-century works on English prosody, Edward Bysshe's *Art of English Poetry* (1702 and later editions), is unabashedly syllabic, and is, in fact, largely a translation of a French treatise by Claude Lancelot—*Quatre traites de poësies* (1663).[9]

Syllabic prosody places its chief emphasis on line length as determined by syllable count. It is in this sense a prosody of number. The standard romance lines are named by the number of syllables they have rather than by a dominant foot. A French poem is thus described as in "octosyllables" or "decasyllables" rather than "iambic tetrameter" or "iambic pentameter."[10] As we will see, when the term "foot" is used in medieval and renaissance discussions of syllabic prosody, it has a range of meanings including "syllable" (e.g., Deschamps, Sidney) and "part of a stanza" (Dante).

Although syllable count is strict, license is permitted under a variety of well-defined conditions. An epic caesura is one with an uncounted (weak or mute) syllable just before the pause. A weak or mute syllable at the end of the verse is also uncounted. The following fourteen-syllable line from the *Jeu de saint-Nicolas* (13th c.) is an acceptable Alexandrine. The first extra syllable creates an epic caesura and the second is an uncounted extrametrical syllable. Merging of terminal and initial vowels (synaloepha) is another kind of license. It occurs in the contraction *m'en* and is pronounced when the line is read:[11]

```
        /      *                    /
Vez les armes reluire toz li cuers m'en esclaire.
 1   2    3     4    5  6[7] 1  2    3     4   5   6[7]
```
[6'*3 + 3']

In a decasyllabic line:

```
       /       *              /
Molt larges terres de vos avrai conquises.
 1     2     3    4 [5] 1  2   3   4  5    6[7]
```
[4'*6']

In syllabic verse, each line type has a pause or division (caesura) near its center, with the qualification that Italian hendecasyllabic verse varies the caesura more freely than the French decasyllabic or Alexandrine and may omit the caesura entirely. In the Alexandrine, the division usually comes after the sixth syllable. In the decasyllabic line, it usually comes after the fourth or the sixth syllable. A normal (masculine) caesura has an accented syllable before the pause. There are two kinds of feminine caesura. A lyric caesura has a counted unaccented syllable just before the pause and is an even-numbered syllable. The epic caesura has an uncounted weak syllable before the pause and is an odd-numbered syllable. Feminine caesura is common in English as well as French verse, but in English the unaccented syllable is pronounced rather than mute, and, to quote Jakob Schipper, "sometimes even two or more unaccented syllables follow upon the last accented one before the pause takes place."[12]

Wherever the caesura comes, the two half-lines (hemistichs) created by it are marked by prominent terminal accents, which are either oxytonic (on the last syllable) or, in the case of feminine caesura or line-end, paroxytonic (on the penultimate syllable). In the line from *Saint-Nicolas* ("Vez les armes"), both accents are paroxytonic. The end of the second division, which is also the end of the line, is further marked by rhyme, of which more later.

Syllabic lines are subdivided into measures. The longest sustainable measure is six syllables,[13] but a measure can have more than six syllables if the rules permit some to be uncounted. The most common measures are of four or two syllables, although one-, three-, and five-syllable measures are also used. Each measure ends with an accent. The term *coup* is sometimes distinguished from *caesura* and used to indicate the secondary pause following a measure that does not coincide with either the midline or the end-line pause. Technically speaking, when a pause occurs, it immediately follows the accented vowel and trailing consonants are included in the next measure.

In the twelve-syllable line, four accents are usual, but only the two at the caesura and line-end are mandatory. The Alexandrine usually has four accents. Decasyllabic lines usually have three or four accents. It may be noted that an English decasyllabic line with four primary accents resembles a four-accent line of the type considered above in relation to Old English prosodic survivals.

Although syllabic verse does not have regular metrical feet, its measures and accents give it a strong syntactic rhythm. Clive Scott explains, "French rhythms are essentially phrasal, that is to say, that there is a marked coincidence of emphasis and pitch-change. . . . Certainly French accents have nothing to do with beat, and very rarely are French rhythmic patterns a surface laid over the line . . . as English meters can so easily seem to be."[14] As Scott indicates, "scansion" in the sense of dividing the line into feet and marking the light and heavy syllables is irrelevant to syllabic verse. Syllabic prosody uses a marking system based on syllable count, caesura, measures, and terminal accents.

Italian prosody is syllabic but differs from French in several ways. It expresses accent more freely than French and is in this respect somewhat closer to English prosody. It also allows a broader range of merging and coalescence of vowels and is less prescriptive about when they are and are not used. Moreover, although French elisions are usually pronounced when a verse is read, Italian elisions can be used to justify syllable-count but ignored when a verse is read.[15]

Syllabic prosody is illustrated by the following passages, which also include some of the special strategies mentioned above. The first is a group of three Alexandrines from Emilie's speech at the beginning of Corneille's *Cinna* (I, i, 48–52).[16] Since the third line is divided into two measures of six syllables each, it has only two accents:

    /   / * /   /
Montre-toi genereux, souffrant qu'il te surmonte;   [3 + 3*2 + 4′]

/   / * /   /
Pluus tu lui donneras, plus il te va donner,   [1 + 5*1 + 5]

         /*   /
Et ne triomphera que pour te couronner.   [6 + 6]

A second illustration is provided by two decasyllables from the Old French *Vie de saint Alexis* (11th c.).[17] The first line has three emphatic accents, the second, four:

 / *   /   /
De la dolor que demenat li pedre   [4*4 + 2′]

/   / *   /   /
Grant fut la noise, si l'entendit la medre.   [2 + 2′*4 + 2′]

Syllabic verse is marvelously flexible. Its basic unit is the line rather than some smaller element. Each Alexandrine or decasyllable is an artful adjustment of a set number of syllables into measures, with two major accents (at caesura and line-end) fixed by position, and from zero to two additional accents fixed not by position but by phrasing. A mathematical calculation of variations is possible for each standard line: there are thirty-six possible variations on the Alexandrine.[18]

Because French verse respects the line as a formal unit, enjambment is infrequent, and when it is used it tends to occur in semiformal patterns defined by the technical terms "rejet" and "contre-rejet," which refer respectively to the portion of the thought unit "run over" the initial line, and to the portion in the initial line. Enjambment of this sort is relatively common in late medieval French and was used in the sixteenth century, but it was attacked by Malherbe and was largely abandoned in the seventeenth century.

Even in French medieval poetry, enjambment is less prominent than in the verse of Dante and other Italian poets of the Trecento. The reason for this is plain from the discussion of artful syntax in Dante's *De vulgari eloquentia* and from the intricate syntax of the lyrics given by Dante as examples of expressive poetry. Word order in French medieval verse tends to be standard, and syntax generally respects the units established by measure, caesura, and line. Dante, however, is already touched by the ideal of classical imitation. He has read the discussion of syntax in the *Rhetorica ad Herennium,* and he appreciates the contribution of construction to the poetry of Vergil and Statius. He is interested in applying what he has learned to Italian poetry, and he bequeathed this interest to Petrarch. Its influence can be seen in the intricate counterpoint of syntax and rhyme scheme in the Petrarchan sonnet.

Rhyme is a key factor in syllabic verse. The word is derived from the Latin *rithmus,* and the derivation nicely expresses the close association of rhyme with rhythm. The rhythm of the syllabic line is established by its accents. The principal accent is the terminal one, which defines the line itself. Hence the medieval practice of defining the entire line by the "foot" created by the rhyme word. Rhyme is also called "cadence."

If accent falls on the final syllable of the rhyme word, the rhyme is masculine, if on the next-to-last, it is feminine. Italian verse allows the accent to fall on the third-to-last syllable (*sdrucciolo*). French verse carefully distinguishes between degrees of rhyme.[19] In English discussions of rhyme, considerable emphasis is placed on the need for exact correspondence of "cadences" and the evil of "falsifying" accent or changing the spelling of a word to create a rhyme.[20] This close relation between word accent and rhyme explains why Sir Philip Sidney, discussing the difference between "Auncient" (i.e., classical) and "Moderne" prosody in his *Apology for Poetry,* states that "the chiefe life of [modern poetry] standeth in that lyke sounding of the words, which wee call Ryme" and adds, "Nowe, for the ryme, though wee doe not observe quantity, yet wee observe the accent very precisely." Sidney means that although English verse is careless about regular foot patterning in the classical manner ("quantity"), it is careful to use exact rhymes—that is, rhyme words with the same accent form. He notes that French has masculine and feminine rhymes and Italian has rhyme with accent on the third-to-last syllable, while "English hath all three, as *Due, True, Father, Rather, Motion, Potion.*"[21]

Arrangements of rhyming lines, beginning with the couplet, create stanzas. The stanzas can have a single line length throughout or the line lengths can vary, and the rhyme scheme can repeat or change, as happens between the octave and sestet of an Italian sonnet. A treatise on romance prosody commonly includes sections on rhyme, on standard lines as determined by syllable count, and on stanza types. The format remains consistent from late medieval treatises on vernacular prosody to the discussion of "ryming" forms of poetry in book 2 of Puttenham's *Arte of English Poesie*, published in 1589.

THE SYLLABIC ASPECT OF ENGLISH RENAISSANCE VERSE

In general, syllable count appears today to be the primary and rhyme the secondary feature of romance prosody; but for medieval and renaissance critics, rhyme was the most obvious feature, and the term "rhyme" was often used to stand for the whole romance prosodic system. Alternatively, rhyme was associated with "number" in the sense of the number of syllables (in contrast to the number of feet) in a line.

This association is illustrated by Sir Philip Sidney's complaint in a manuscript note to *Arcadia* about "those rimes we commonly use observing nothing but the number of syllabes, as to make of it viii, x, or xii feete (saving perchance that some have some care of the accent)."[22] Sidney is using the term "foot" in the romance way to mean syllable (or, as the note has it, "syllabe"), since there are no English lines of eight, not to mention ten or twelve, metrical feet. Evidently the term "rime" refers to line types as determined by syllable count rather than end-rhyme per se. Equally instructive is the sharp distinction made by Gabriel Harvey between the forms of poetry based on "meter," meaning classical quantitative meter, and those based on "number": "In the next seate to these hexameters, adonickes, and iambicks I sette those that stand upon the number, not in meter, sutch as my lorde of Surrey is sayde first to have putt forth in prynte."[23]

English renaissance critics regularly refer to English verse as though it is syllabic and to be understood in relation to romance prosodic tradition. It is also clear that the most common English line forms have close parallels in romance poetry. This is obvious in the case of octosyllabic and decasyllabic lines in couplets and in crossed-rhyme quatrains. Cases have also been made for derivation of the fourteener and of poulter's measure from medieval Latin or romance forms or a combination of both.[24]

How does one determine whether a given poem should be understood in syllabic terms? An obvious sign is careful accounting of syllables. English renaissance poets seem to have been very careful—though not compulsive—about observing "numbers."[25] Regular placement of caesura in positions approved by syllabic poetry and a tendency for a decasyllabic line to have four primary stresses with one at the caesura and one at line-end also suggest romance influence. Also suggestive is the regular use of various kinds of poetic license, or metaplasm, to justify lines that are in technical violation of a proper syllable count. Accounting of syllables and use of licenses permitting merging and coalescing of syllables form the basis of Robert Bridges's demonstration that the verse of *Paradise Lost* is syllabic and of later arguments that it is influenced by Italian *versi sciolti*. Epic caesura and one or more unstressed syllables at line end are further indicators of romantic influence.

Other characteristics also suggest romance influence. They are less subject to testing, but they are important. It is the coincidence of grammatical phrase, measure, and terminal accent that creates the syntactic emphasis of syllabic verse. In some English lines, accent as determined by meaning consistently seems to ignore or override patterns that would be required if the arrangement of the words was intended to objectify a regular meter. Such lines obviously lean toward syllabic verse. Since French verse is more respectful of the line unit than Italian, heavily enjambed English verse—for example, the verse of *Paradise Lost*—is likely to be influenced by Italian sources and may, at times, be considered in rebellion against the more regular tradition of French prosody.

The idea that meaning should take precedence over meter is especially relevant to sophisticated dramatic verse, but it also applies to nondramatic verse. A considerable body of prosodic theory exists that insists speech rhythm—"intonation"—rather than meter is the governing principle of English verse. In "Intonation and Metrical Theory," David Crystal comes to a conclusion identical with that of syllabic prosody—namely, that the fundamental unit of verse is the line. D. W. Harding (*Words into Rhythm: English Speech Rhythm in Verse and Prose*) is less theoretical than Crystal but makes a similar point. Natural speech rhythm should always determine the sound of a verse: "The notion that our reading should . . . be some kind of 'compromise' between metre and natural speech is indefensible."[26] Although Crystal and Harding are apparently unaware that there is historical precedent for their position, they argue, in effect, that English verse is best understood in relation to the tradition of romance prosody. If so, much English verse written between 1370 and 1700 can be considered a form of syllabic verse that emphasizes speech rhythms and observes romance rules for rationalizing variations in syllable count.

Rhyme is associated specifically and emphatically throughout the Renaissance with the romance tradition. Obviously, the use of rhyme does not show that a given poem conforms in other ways to romance conventions. However, certain complex stanza forms have powerful and overt romance associations. These include lay, rondeau, ballade, triolet, villanelle, and douzain, among French forms, and sonnet, sestina, ottava rima, terza rima, and canzone among Italian forms. Rhyme royal is the most distinctive stanza form that England adds to the list.

Since these observations are abstract, it will be useful to provide examples of syllabic scansion of English verse. The first consists of two decasyllabic lines from Chaucer's "Balade de bon conseyl":

/ / * / /
Flee fro the prees, and dwelle with sothfastnesse,

[1 + 3*2 + 4']

/ / * /
Suffyce unto thy good, though it be smal.

[2 + 4*4]

Here regular syllable count requires merging of vowels (synaloepha: "dwelle-with"; "suffyce-unto"). The final *e* in "sothfastnesse" is uncounted by convention. If these variations are allowed, the lines can be understood as well-formed decasyllables with masculine caesuras. Since the analysis does not assume regular meter, the initial heavy stress on "Flee" does not have to be "explained" as trochaic substitution. Accents come at the caesura and at the end of the line. The accent on "sothfastnesse" is somewhat ambiguous, but the case for a romance (paroxytonic) accent is made very strong by the internal ("Leonine") rhyme with "prees." Each measure also ends with an accent, and the accents reinforce syntactical meaning. If one accepts the placement of the primary accent of "sothfastnesse" on the penultimate syllable, the rhythm of the two lines is four accents followed by three. The accented words are thematic, although the effect is not especially striking. The lines avoid enjambment, and there is no accented alliteration to give the lines the flavor of alliterative meter. In general, the syllabic model fits very well. For comparison, note the French decasyllabic line quoted by Chaucer in "Le Pleintif countre Fortune":

/* / /
Jay tout perdu mon temps et mon labour.

[4*2 + 4]

A second illustration comes from the sixteenth century. It is the last line of the first stanza of *The Faerie Queene,* scanned here as romance verse rather than accentual meter:

Fierce warres and faithfull loves shall moralize my song.

[2+4*4+2]

Seen from the romance point of view, Spenser's line is a classic Alexandrine. There are twelve syllables and no elisions. If we assume that the *e* of "Warres" and "loves" was no longer pronounced in the sixteenth century, there are no extra syllables. The caesura comes after the sixth syllable, and within the half-lines the measures are arranged symmetrically, as mirror images of each other. Each half-line has two accents.

Three accents come at the ends of the measures where they appear. In the exception ("moralize"), two unstressed syllables follow the stressed one. As Schipper observes in a comment already quoted, this is acceptable in English syllabic verse. Alliteration ("fierce/faithfull"; "moralize/my") is present but muted by the fact that both cases involve unaccented or weakly accented syllables. As in a well-made French Alexandrine, the balance within and between the half-lines is thematically expressive. In the first half-line, "warres" and "loves" are singled out, in the second, "moralize" and "song." When the line is considered as a whole, "warres" is paired with "moralize" and "loves" with "song." Finally, the line is emphatically a unit. The line preceding it ends with a colon, and the line itself, being the last in the stanza, ends with a period. A later line (II, x, 60) nicely illustrates the formula of an Alexandrine with lyric caesura. As in the previous line, the thematic pairing of accented words is emphatic:

So settled he his kingdom and confirmed his right.

[4+3*3+2]

Two swallows do not make a summer, but romance scansion fits these lines very well.

The Metrical Ambivalence of English Verse

Let us step back for a moment. Chaucer stands at or just before the beginning of the renaissance tradition, and Milton stands at the end of it. How should Chaucer's verse be described? George Saintsbury is a powerful advocate of regular accentual meter. He is followed by Paull Baum in *Chaucer's Verse* and by Jack Conner in *English Prosody from Chaucer to Wyatt*. In *English Stress*, Halle and Keyser offer rules for generating well-formed lines based on "positions" rather than "feet." When applied to Chaucer, however, their system encourages conclusions like those of classical metrical analysis: Chaucer writes a form of iambic pentameter.

Edward Weismiller is a knowledgeable advocate of understanding Chaucer's verse and that of many later English poets as shaped decisively by French and Italian models. John Fisher and Susanne Woods generally agree.[27] Still other scholars, represented by Ian Robinson (*Chaucer's Prosody* [1971]), advocate reading Chaucer's verse in terms of phrasal accent. In Robinson's opinion, neither foot pattern nor syllable count is primary. Instead, the verse follows contours defined by semantic and syntactical features, or measures. Although Robinson rejects all theories attempting to explain Chaucer's prosody on the basis of foreign models, emphasis on measure and syntactical units is, as we have seen, characteristic of romance verse, and one wonders whether Robinson would not have been more persuasive if his work had begun with a review of medieval French prosody.[28]

The debate about the place of syllabic principles in English verse occurs again in criticism of John Milton's *Paradise Lost*. Robert Bridges does not consider Milton's poetry in relation to romance tradition, and he is fully aware of the role of stress in English verse. However, he argues in *Milton's Prosody* that the central principle in Milton's verse is syllable count. This is not enough for F. T. Prince who not only argues in *The Italian Element in Milton's Verse*, that Milton was following Italian models but criticizes Bridges for being unconsciously wedded to disyllabic feet and thus unable to appreciate fully the significance of his discoveries about Milton's verse.[29]

Sir Philip Sidney's reference to "those rimes we commonly use observing nothing but the number of syllabes . . . (saving perchance that some have some care of the accent)" shows that the most distinguished English critic—and one of the most acute prosodists—of the sixteenth century considers the norm for English poetry to be syllabic and also understands "accent" primarily in relation to cadence—that is, the terminal accent of the line that defines the rhyme type.

This, however, is too simple. The fact is that the "norm" changes in the sixteenth century from poet to poet because different poets understand their work in different ways. Some are self-consciously classical and imitate Latin or Italian renaissance practices. Some are self-consciously medieval and imitate French and Middle English models. Many are simply following the lead of earlier English poets.

There is another important factor to consider. The reason for disagreement among scholars as to how certain works should be scanned is that the works themselves often support two approaches. English is not free, as a language, from internal tensions. It remains essentially Germanic, but it has been deeply influenced by French.

Since English renaissance verse always has stress and the stresses tend to be regular, most octosyllabic and decasyllabic verse of the period can be scanned as either syllabic or metrical without fundamental violation of its expressiveness. If it is considered metrical, variations from the norm can be understood as substitutions. Decisions as to which system of analysis is proper therefore depend to a considerable degree on the person doing the scanning and the number of variations from the norm permitted by the scansion system or the flexibility of the generating rules.[30]

The possibility must also be recognized that the English heard syllabic verse as a succession of light and heavy stresses. Even when English poets state that "number" is their guiding principle, their verses have stress, and the stresses tend to occur at regular intervals. It follows that when they read French and Italian poetry, whether in the fourteenth or the sixteenth century, they may have heard English-style stresses. Jack Conner makes just this suggestion in *English Prosody from Chaucer to Wyatt:* "English being a language of strong and weak stress, the English heard strong and weak stresses in Old French whether or not the stresses really occurred."[31] Thus, for example, an English poet might have heard the line quoted above (p. 11) from the *Vie de saint Alexis* as a kind of iambic tetrameter:

```
x \ x /   x / x / x / [x]
De la dolor que demenat li pedre.
```

It is also possible that Chaucer heard the following pattern in the French line he quotes in "Le Pleintif countre Fortune":

```
x /   x / x /   x \   x /
Jay tout perdu mon temps et mon labour.
```

In the same way, the first line of the *Divine Comedy* might become:

```
x  / x \ x  / x / x /x
Nel mezzo del cammin di nostra vita.
```

The same problem confronts the modern student of prosody. Chaucer's "Balade de bon conseyl" has already been quoted (p. 15) to illustrate syllabic scansion. It can also be scanned using the conventions of accentual foot meter:

```
 /   x    x  /   x    / [x] x    /  x  \ x
Flee from the prees, and dwelle with sothfastnesse,
 x / [x]x \  x  /    x   \  x   /
Suffyce unto thy good, though it be smal.
```

The same approach can be applied to the last line of the first stanza of Spenser's *Faerie Queene:*

```
 \     /    x  /  x /    x    / x \   x  /
Fierce warres and faithfull loves shall moralize my song.
```

Perhaps the debate is really about models and labels rather than versification. The object is to describe lines of poetry; does it matter which labels are used? The answer is yes, it does matter, because a Heisenberg effect operates in prosody. The assumptions with which one begins—usually objectified in the labels one uses—influence how one writes if one is an author and how one understands verse if one is a reader or a critic.

My own feeling is that the more open system—the syllabic—provides the best starting point for interpretation of sixteenth-century prosody. It is consistent with the romance terminology that is so often used by English renaissance critics when they discuss English "rhyming" verse. It also permits emphasis on meaning rather than meter and is thus in accord with the position taken by David Crystal and D. W. Harding, as well as with what is known about the way Latin verse was read in the sixteenth century. It is not, however, a panacea. It does not change the fact that English words carry stress and that their stressed and unstressed syllables tend, in verse, to form regular patterns. Nor does it change the fact that sixteenth-century English critics often refer to classical feet, especially the iambic foot, in English poems.

Historical Perspective

If we consider Old English poetry a foundation almost totally obscured by the sixteenth century, the next prosodic tradition that contributed to the shaping of English renaissance verse was French. In the later fourteenth century, Chaucer's reading of Dante and his adaptations of Boccaccio's *Filostrato* (*Troilus and Criseyde*) and *Teseida* (*The*

Knight's Tale) resulted in the introduction into English of Italian practices. In the early sixteenth century a second phase of Italian influence began with the imitation of Petrarch, Serafino Aquilano, Luigi Alamanni, and other Italians. Translation and imitation of poems were complemented by an awareness of the lively debates about the nature of literary language that were carried on in Italy throughout the first half of the sixteenth century and by discussions of specific verse forms and their appropriateness to various poetic tasks.

Classical influence also began to assert itself at the beginning of the sixteenth century. The immediate source of this influence was Erasmian humanism, which was primarily Latin and was disseminated through the school curriculum.

An important cultural result of the revival of classical theory was to make renaissance poets aware of two distinct bodies of poetry—the one Latin and classical, the other vernacular and medieval—each with its own aesthetic, its own themes, and its distinctive prosodic traditions. What seemed in the early sixteenth century to be traditional poetry was medieval and influenced by romance traditions. Conversely, during the first half of the century, the "new" poetry was classical and influenced by Greek and Latin traditions or by Italian imitations of these traditions.

The traditional and the new poetry objectify cultural tensions that are also evident in discussions of language. In Italy the debates began in the early sixteenth century with Castiglione's *Book of the Courtier* and Pietro Bembo's *Prose della volgar lingua*. In France, the key document was Joaquin DuBellay's *Deffence et illustration de la langue francoyse*, published at midcentury. In England the question of language was examined at midcentury by John Cheke, Roger Ascham, and Thomas Wilson, among others. The discussion was partly about internationalism, partly about nationalism and cultural roots, and partly about the relationship between language and thought.

Toward the end of the sixteenth century, the gap between the romance and the classical tradition widened perceptibly. In *The Shepheardes Calender*, and again in *The Faerie Queene*, Edmund Spenser powerfully reasserted the vitality of romance themes and techniques. In spite of his own efforts and those of such resolute imitators as Giles and Phineas Fletcher, within twenty years after the publication of *The Faerie Queene*, Ben Jonson was proclaiming the triumph of vernacular classicism, and by the second half of the seventeenth century, neoclassicism had all but defeated its rivals. Milton's ability to combine classical formalism with Spenserian sensuousness was unique to Milton.

Not until the later eighteenth century did the neoclassic canons—long hardened into "rules"—give way to a renewed Gothicism that was called "romantic" in recognition of its affinities to the romance tradition.

Music and Prosody

Underlying all theories relating prosody to genre is a relation that varies in particulars but is consistent from ancient Greece to the end of the seventeenth century. It is the relation between poetry and music. Poetry begins with music in Greek mythology: Orpheus and Amphion are the earliest singers as well as the earliest poets, and the first command that Homer gives his Muse in the *Iliad* is "Sing." Hebrew poetry also recognizes its affinity with music: the Psalms are among the most brilliant poetic moments in the Old Testament. In practical terms, rhythm belongs to music, and, as Aristotle admits in the *Poetics*, the meters are part of rhythm. Underlying the legends and primitive traditions, there is a concept that music bequeaths to ancient prosody: art is not imitative but constitutive. It makes possible the perception of realities that would be unknowable without it.

We have seen that construction is an aspect of prosody. It is also related to music. Quintilian makes the musical aspect of construction explicit when he explains in the *Institutio oratoria* (I, x, 22–25) that its purpose is to create musicality of the sort found in poems and songs through "regular structure and smooth combination of words." An aspect of construction that links it directly to meter and that especially interested Cicero is the theory of *clausulae*—the metrical clause terminations that, in simplified form, became the *cursus* of the Middle Ages.

In late antiquity, the tradition relating poetry and music was reasserted in the *De musica* of St. Augustine. The close relation between poetry and music in ancient thought is shown by the fact that the *De musica* is primarily about rhythm, meter, and metrical proportions and says little about what would today be considered "musical subjects." In the ninth century, a new form of poetry emerged that was intimately linked to music. "Proses"—also called "sequences"—take their form from the melodies for which they were written and are in this sense subordinate to music. For reasons we will examine in chapter 3, they are initially unmetrical. Later, they begin to be written in regular meter. This development is again connected with music—specifically, with the new "measured music" of the early twelfth century. The effect of the renewal of the alliance between music and poetry is apparent in the earliest northern French treatise on prosody, the *Art de dictier* by Eustache Deschamps (1392), which opens with the statement that poetry is "natural music."

Much renaissance discussion of music and verse is, one feels, conventional. Much, however, is not. Musical poetry in sixteenth-century England can be said to begin with poems like Sir Thomas Wyatt's "My Lute, Awake," which continues the tradition of the courtly poetry of the *trouvères* into the reign of Henry VIII. By midcentury, Protestants were singing hymns written in common meter, and at the turn of the century, the English school of lutenist-songwriters, led by Thomas Campion, achieved a marriage of poetry and music that remains impressive today. Campion also sought deeper harmonies in quantitative poems that attempt to revive the ancient alliance between poetry and music.[32]

In Italy, interest in the musicality of classical forms contributed to the emergence of a new genre—opera. In England a similar interest encouraged the masque and the lyric harmonies of Ben Jonson and Robert Herrick, as well as the richer music of Milton's great experiments. Milton was a competent amateur musician as well as a poet. Like Homer, he begins by commanding the epic Muse to sing; and the infinitely varied music of that song continues until the departure of Adam and Eve from Paradise at the end of book 12 of *Paradise Lost*. Since the Muse sings of "things invisible to mortal sight," the poem is, among other things, a powerful reassertion of the ancient theory that poetry is constitutive and that its power comes to it through music.

The relation between poetry and music is thus a basic theme in the history of renaissance prosody. In the following chapters we will often have occasion to observe corollaries of this fact. For the present, we merely note its importance to the subject before us.

CHAPTER II

Ars Metrica

METER, GENRE, MUSIC

Aristotle's *Poetics* shows that by the later fourth century B.C. the main features of the system of classical meters had been established. Aristotle knows that dactylic hexameter is proper for heroic verse, iambic meter for abusive satire, and trochaic meter for poetry associated with dance. He also knows that comedy adopted iambic verse at an early stage in its development because iambic verse is close to speech.

Tragedy was slower to take up the form, but eventually the natural affinity between iambic verse and speech made it do so:

> By developing away from a satyr-play . . . tragedy achieved, late in its history, a dignified level. Then the iambic meter took the place of the tetrameter. For the poets first used the trochaic tetrameter because their poetry was satyric and very closely associated with dance; but when dialogue was introduced, nature itself discovered the appropriate meter. For the iambic is the most conversational of the meters—as we see from the fact that we speak many iambs when talking to each other, but few [dactylic] hexameters, and only when departing from conversational tone.[1]

There are brief references in the *Poetics* to elegiac verse, dithyrambs, and choric odes. The lack of interest in choric odes reflects the fact that Aristotle ranks "melody" sixth in the list of the six parts of drama in chapter 6[2] and implies that the chorus is becoming superfluous. Sophocles, we are told, treated the chorus as "part of the plot," but Euripides writes choruses simply to impress the public. In fact, some of the choruses of Euripides are interchangeable. Agathon further debased the chorus by inserting odes for decoration even though they had nothing to do with the play.[3]

Aristotle rejects emphatically the popular habit of labeling the poet through the meter being used: "The public at large by joining the term 'poet' to a meter gives writers such names as 'elegiac poets' and 'epic poets.' Here the public . . . completely misses the point that the capacity to produce an imitation is the essential characteristic of the poet."[4]

For Aristotle, poetry is a kind of "making," a point suggested by the root meaning of the verb *poiein*, "to make." It is not "writing in meter" but "imitation" in the sense of "imitating actions by making plots." To make the argument as strong as possible, Aristotle asserts that although Empedocles wrote *On Nature* in hexameters, the work is philosophy, not poetry; and he later adds that the *Histories* of Herodotus would be history and not poetry even if they were written in verse.[5]

The attitude rejected by Aristotle is the basis of what Latin antiquity would call the *ars metrica*. The *ars metrica* makes the use of meter the fundamental characteristic of poetry.

The *Poetics* shows that the basic concepts of the *ars metrica* were already supported by "the public at large" in Aristotle's Greece. They proved remarkably hardy. The *ars metrica* became a standard basis for understanding poetry in later antiquity, and in somewhat simplified form, it was accepted throughout the Middle Ages. In the early Renaissance, it was taught in the schools as a part of the grammar curriculum under the label *prosodia*.[6] Not until the middle years of the sixteenth century, when the *Poetics* became a central critical document, were its assumptions challenged.

As the terms "lyric," "melic," "ode," and "chorus" suggest, much poetry was intended to be sung before it was regarded as separable from music. The relation derives in part from the use of song in worship.[7] It persists because the relation of poetry to music is a real relation. The earliest Greek metrical theory occurs in connection with music. Aristotle acknowledges this fact when he remarks in chapter 4 that meters are "part of the rhythms."[8] By the time Aristotle wrote the *Poetics*, however, metrical theory had diverged along two paths. Those who dealt with meter in relation to music were called *rhythmikoi*, and those who dealt with it in terms of grammar, *metrikoi*.

After Aristotle, treatises on music continued to discuss rhythm and number and meter. Treatises on grammar dealt with the same topics but with less emphasis on their relation to music and more on orthography, accent, standard foot and line types, and strophes. The distinction is implicit in the different labels assigned the musical and grammatical treatises: *ars rithmica* and *ars metrica*. The *De musica* of St. Augustine preserves the sense that poetry is an expression of music and that metrical proportions are essentially musical.[9] Most late classical treatments of prosody, however, are in the tradition of the *ars metrica* and are related to grammar, including treatments by Hephaestion, Donatus, Diomedes, Victorinus, and Servius.

Even in the grammatical treatises a consciousness of the relation between meter and music survives both in terminology and in comments on specific poetic effects.[10] To identify poetry with "writing in meter" is to assert that a musical element—sound—is the defining characteristic of poetry. It is to assert further that there is an essential rather than a conventional relation between meter and genre. According to the *ars metrica*, Aristotle is wrong and the public is right to name poets by their meters. Epic hexameter, for example, is intrinsically heroic. Even Aristotle admits that the rich music of dactylic hexameter is as remote as possible from the sound of everyday speech: "It is the stateliest and most dignified meter, and therefore it is especially receptive to strange words and metaphors."[11] Iambic verse is hospitable to standard words (e.g., 49a15–28) and suited to action: "The iambic and the trochaic tetrameter are expressive of motion, the latter being a dance meter and the former displaying the quality of action (*to de' praktikon*)."[12]

Interpreted in this way, meter is what makes poetry work. Each of the standard meters has a generic sound and is hospitable to a special kind of language. More than meter is needed, but a generic sound is, from the point of view of ancient prosodic theory, the first condition for the establishment of a genre. In a suggestive study of Horace's influence on renaissance poetics titled *La Formación de la teoría literaria moderna: La topica horaciana en Europa*, Antonio Garcia Barrio remarks that classical prosody establishes "complementarity and propriety in the assignment of each meter to a corresponding genre [and] objective status and independence of the genres, each one having its special character and proper vocabulary."[13]

Let us carry this line of thought a step further before turning to specifics. From the point of view of the *ars metrica*, poetry does not represent or "imitate" a pre-existing reality. It is, rather, a medium adapted to the "bodying forth" of a kind of reality that cannot otherwise be bodied forth, and meter is the element that makes the bodying forth possible. As we have already seen from the *Poetics* and will see in more detail presently, certain meters are hospitable by "nature itself" (*aute e physis*, 49a24) to language that complements the generic sound of the meter. The appeal to "nature itself" suggests not a casual but a fundamental and pre-existing relation between the meter and the reality it bodies forth.

Because each of the chief classical meters is distinctive, each permits the bodying forth of a unique kind of reality or sense of reality—heroic, epic, tragic, comic, satiric, elegiac, and so forth. The theory of genres in the *ars metrica* is parallel to the idea that the modes of Greek music—Dorian, Lydian, Phrygian, and so forth—are naturally related to specific emotional states. The point has practical implications for versification. W. R. Hardie observes in *Res Metrica* that ancient metrical forms cannot be understood apart from the genres in which they are used: "An epic hexameter is different from a lyric hexameter, and both are different from the hexameter of satire. So it is, too, with iambic verse."[14]

Many additional elements—plot, episode, ornament, character, and the like—must be coordinated if the bodying forth is to be successful. Assuming success, the resulting poem is not an imitation of a pre-existing reality so much as a model that sets norms for a category of experience. Barrio considers the idea that poetry is a constitutive activity a definitive achievement of classical theory: "One of the most brilliant and . . . modern doctrines of classical literary theory [is] the correspondence between signifier and signified—the continuity and complementarity between the presence of phonetic-rhythmic materials and the nature of the sensations and sentiments associated with them."[15]

It is through their establishment of norms for "sensations and sentiments" that poets can be, in Shelley's phrase, "unacknowledged legislators of mankind"; and it is because such norms become models of reality within the culture that accepts them that poetry can be understood as didactic in more than a superficial sense. The relation of the Homeric poems to Greek culture and of the Pentateuch to Hebrew culture are cases in point. In both, literature is the mirror by means of which society forms its conceptions of itself.

Barrio argues that the constitutive ideal of ancient poetic theory gives way in the Renaissance to a theory of poetry as imitation of a pre-existing reality. The result is an art that gives "priority in the causal order to the natural objectivity of themes, characters, and the social quality of style rather than to structural and rhythmic-formal considerations."[16]

This is unquestionably right for the poetics to which Barrio ultimately looks—neoclassical poetics. However, renaissance poetic theory explicitly recognizes the constitutive aspect of poetry when it invokes the ideas of inspiration and "making," and when it touches on the ancient relations between poetry and music. The following comment, from a gloss to Edmund Spenser's *Shepheardes Calender,* asserts the kinship of making, inspiration, and music but says nothing about "imitation" in Barrio's sense:

> At [that] time an infinite number of youth usually came to theyr great solemne feastes called Panegyrica . . . some learned man being more hable then the rest, for speciall gyftes of wytte and Musicke, would take upon him to sing fine verses . . . At whose wonderful gyft al men being astonied and as it were ravished, with delight, thinking (as it was indeed) that he was inspired from above, called him vatem: which kinde of men afterwarde framing their verses to lighter musick (as of musick be many kinds, some sadder, some lighter, some martiall, some heroical: and so diversely eke affect the mynds of men) found out lighter matter of Poesie also . . . and so were called Poetes or makers.[17]

Ancient treatises on the *ars metrica* make no effort to be eloquent in the manner of this passage. They tend to be derivative and heavily freighted with jargon. Since many were textbooks, their narrowness is understandable. However, in spite of their limitations, they offer a view of poetry that must be taken seriously. It is a view that becomes more reasonable the more one understands literature as constitutive rather than imitative. This is the idea at the center of the *ars metrica.* It is implicit in the equation of poetry with making verses, in the linking of meter to genre, and in the emphasis on the close relationship between poetry and music.

Grammar and Prosody (1): Construction and Metaplasm

Whether or not they treat poetry in detail, ancient comprehensive grammars[18] devote extended attention to closely related subjects: purity of language (*Latinitas*), clarity (*explanatio*), errors of style (barbarism, solecism), metaplasm, figures of diction (*schemata lexeos*), figures of thought (*schemata dianoias*), and tropes like metaphor and synecdoche. These topics are treated in rhetoric as well as grammar, and they apply to prose as well as poetry.[19] Complex strategies are used for ornate (*ornatus*) rather than standard writing (*communis sermo*) and are more common in poetry than in prose. Book 2 of Diomedes' *Artis grammaticae libri III* (4th c. A.D.) illustrates the point. It treats syllables, accent, *Latinitas*, rhetorical schemes, vices and virtues of style, effective ordering of phrases and clauses, and prose rhythms. Its material applies to prose, but it also introduces the discussion of poetry, which is the subject of book 3.

Artful syntax is a large and very important topic, both for classical theory and for critics of the Renaissance who sought to recreate in the vernacular the musicality they associated with Latin poetry. It is called *synthesis* or *syntaxis* in Greek and *conpositio*, *constructio*, and *collocatio* in Latin. Since the terms are more or less synonymous and none is free of ambiguity, here and below, I will use *constructio* and English "construction" for the complex of ideas associated with this subject.

In its most elementary form, *constructio* means "grammatical construction." Construction in this sense is the joining of many separate words into a single grammatical unit. It is used in this way for the subject matter of the last two books (bks. 17, 18) of Priscian's massive *Grammar*, and it often reappears in the same restricted sense in elementary grammars of the sixteenth century, sometimes under the Greek label *syntaxis* and sometimes under the label *conpositio*.[20]

It also has a larger sense that is an extension of the elementary one. The *Rhetorica ad Herennium* explains (IV, 12, 18), "Construction of words (*verborum constructio*) . . . makes all parts of a discourse equally elegant." More specifically, construction is the ordering of syntax for euphony, emphasis, and ornament. Euphony is a musical concept. It includes sound effects (rough, melodious, etc.) created by word choice; sentence rhythms created by phrase (*comma*, *articulus*), clause (*colon*, *clausula*), and period (*periodos*, *ambitus*); and metrical clause terminations (*clausulae*). Since it produces rhythms, construction is a kind of prosody that relates equally to prose and verse. Since its rhythms arise from the grammatical level of the sentence, construction is more fundamental than meter.

Construction provides general formulas for different styles and stylistic effects. The *Rhetorica ad Herennium* explains (IV, 11, 8) that the grand style consists of "smooth and ornamental ordering (*constructio*) of impressive words." Control of word order was always considered an important stylistic device, and in the Middle Ages the theory of word order was formalized. Word order is either "natural" (*ordo natu-*

ralis) or "artificial" (*ordo artificialis*). *Ordo artificialis* is artistic (*ornatus*) in itself and associated with elevated writing. In certain renaissance grammars, the two kinds of ordering are called *ordo grammaticus* and *ordo rhetoricus* or *ordo Ciceronianus*, the latter term making explicit the link between artful construction and Ciceronian imitation. Formulas for different prose styles can be (and were) applied to poetic genres. The theory of the grand style, for example, is directly relevant to the theory of epic and influenced much renaissance discussion of that form.

The mechanics of construction depend on the figures of diction (*schemata lexeos*). Donatus lists seventeen figures in book 3 of the *Ars major*, including zeugma (a single verb with multiple subjects), hypozeuxis (a separate verb for each clause), anaphora (clauses beginning with the same word), epanalepsis (clauses beginning and ending with the same word), polysyndeton (multiple connectives), asyndeton (suppression of connectives), paronomasia (like sounds, including puns), and homoeoteleuton (like endings, a weak form of rhyme). Missing from the list given by Donatus are figures based on illocution (apostrophe, interrogatio), and periodic sentence structure (continuatio) and such related strategies as inversion (anastrophe), balance (isocolon), contrast (antithesis), and climax (gradatio).[21] Renaissance interest in these and related figures is illustrated by John Stockwood's *Progymnasma scholasticum* (1597), which shows 450 ways to vary a single elegiac distich.[22]

The essay *Peri syntheseos* (*On Composition*) of Dionysius of Halicarnassus shows the scope of the ancient concept of construction. It begins with an extended discussion of the relation between construction and music. He then considers prose cadences (the *clausulae* of Latin rhetoric) and supplements the comment with an analysis of the prosody of Homer's description of Sisyphus (*Odyssey*, XI, 593–98). Dionysius asks what the difference is between art prose and poetry and concludes that prose comes close to poetry when it is regular, and poetry comes close to prose when it ignores natural metrical units through the practice, for example, of enjambment.

Ultimately, construction leads to the theory of the three (or four) styles because it provides the strategies that objectify the styles in language. For Dionysius the styles are "austere," "ornate," and "mixed." The austere style, illustrated by Pindar and Thucydides, is rough in sound, curt in its use of words, irregular in phrasal rhythm, and unstudied: "No unnecessary words are added to round off the sentence or clarify the meaning; no care is taken to end the period with ostentatious smoothness." The ornate style, illustrated preeminently by Isocrates, is euphonious, rhythmical, rich in vocabulary, and periodic in structure—"the clauses . . . are well interwoven and . . . all ends with the period."[23]

To achieve its special kind of rhythm, poetry needs licenses of spelling and pronunciation. Donatus explains that such licenses are "barbarisms" in prose but ornaments in verse.[24] The general term for these licenses is "metaplasm." Under metaplasm are included ways to alter a word by addition, removal, or transposition of letters or syllables. Donatus lists fourteen types. Today, the most familiar of these types are apocope (omitting letters at the end of a word: *mage* for *magis*); syncope (omitting in the middle: *extinxti* for *extinxisti*); and synaloepha (merging a final vowel with the vowel of the next word: *ill'ego* for *ille ego*). Ecthlipsis is the omission of a vowel plus *m* as in *mult'ille* for *multum ille*. Synaeresis is making a single vowel of a diphthong (*dinde* for *deinde*), and diaeresis is creating two vowel sounds from one (*dissoluenda* for *dissolvenda*).[25] Shorter grammars treat the subject by listing three or four of the most common terms.[26]

Grammar and Prosody (2): Standard Approaches

In antiquity, specifically prosodic lore was presented in three ways: (1) as part of the treatment of grammar, (2) in separate treatises on the subject, and (3) in essays on special topics. The *Artis grammaticae libri III* of Diomedes illustrates the first approach. It is a comprehensive grammar, and its third book is devoted to poetry. The treatises by Terentianus Maurus (fl. A.D. 175), Aelius Aphthonius (fl. A.D. 275), and Marius Victorinus (fl. A.D. 350) illustrate the second approach. They are limited to prosody but treat the whole subject. The third approach is illustrated by essays by Servius (4th c. A.D.) on the meters of Horace and by Priscian (6th c. A.D.) on the meters of Terence.[27]

Latin discussions of prosody rely on Greek antecedents. Two authors of the second century A.D. account for most of the influence. Heliodoros is described by Victorinus as "standing out among the Greek writers on that art as either first or unique."[28] He is the main source of the lost Latin author Juba (ca. A.D. 200), who, in turn, influenced several of the extant Latin grammarians. The second important Greek author is Hephaestion, who wrote a treatise on meter in forty-eight books later abridged to a one-volume *Handbook* (*Encheiridion*) that survives today.²⁹

Heliodoros and Hephaestion organized their treatises around meters and poetic lines. They taught that there are eight (or nine) prototypical meters (*metra prototypa*) and that all other meters are derived from them.³⁰ The *Musical Encyclopedia* of Aristides Quintilianus treats metric art as a subdivision of the theoretical aspect of music. He codifies the discussion under five headings: (1) letters, (2) syllables, (3) feet, (4) meters, and (5) types of poem. Following Hephaestion, he lists nine rather than eight prototype meters.

Roman contributions to prosody begin with the *De lingua Latina* of Varro (1st c. B.C.).³¹ This work strongly influenced later grammatical and metrical thought. About one-fourth of it survives. In contrast to the Greek theorists, Varro considers all meters to be "derived" from two archetypal forms, the dactylic meter of epic and the iambic meter of comedy. Latin treatments of meter before the third century A.D. follow Varro. After the Greek theory of prototype meters was introduced at the beginning of the third century, Latin treatments tend to combine Greek and Roman theories.³²

Varro also differentiates between Greek and Latin metrical practice. Instead of calling the comic line "iambic trimeter" and thus recognizing the Greek tradition of dipodic feet, he calls it *senarius,* a six-footed line. Longer lines are called *septenarius* (seven-footed) and *octonarius* (eight-footed). Varro also identifies a Latin verse form that predates Greek influence. It is the Saturnian, and it is characteristic of the poetry known as Fescennine verse, a rough, accentual verse form somewhat like "common meter" in English.

By the fourth century, the Latin treatment of prosody is standardized. A typical full-scale *ars metrica* has three parts. The first explains rhythm, metrical feet, and the "meters," meaning the line forms created by uniform and mixed groups of feet. The second gives the forms of poetry as established by prototype meters, and the third, the forms of poetry that use composite meters, often ending with an essay on the meters of Horace.

The sequence of topics in the first part varies, but a pattern is usually visible under the differences. It is a movement from general to specific. Rhythm is the most basic element of poetry and links it to music. In general, it is presented as a segmentation of time (*modulatio*) into determinate units by a marker called an ictus.

A "foot" is a patterning of syllables that objectifies rhythm in a specific form. The various feet give their names to the "meters," which are forms of poetic line and, by extension, the sort of poetry that uses the line. "Meter" in this extended sense is analogous to the modern word "genre." "Number" refers to the number of feet in a line—for example, dimeter, pentameter, hexameter. "Verse" is sometimes used more or less synonymously with "meter" and sometimes distinguished from it. The term includes the proper names used to identify certain types of line: *epos, elegiac verse, scazon*. Simple verse patterns are based on one meter. Complex forms occur in units of two lines (elegy) or strophes (Sapphic, Anacreontic).

Grammar and Prosody (3): Donatus and the Metrical Foot

Because of the prestige of Donatus during the Middle Ages and Renaissance, the definition that he gives of a metrical foot was enormously influential. Although it is brief, it is succinct, and it includes the key terms and concepts.[33]

According to Donatus, a metrical foot is "a definite number of syllables and of time. Every foot has arsis and thesis, a set number of syllables, time [i.e., duration], resolution, figure, and meter. There are four disyllabic feet, eight trisyllabic feet, and sixteen double [i.e., dipodic] feet."[34] Since all of the terms in this definition are central to prosodic theory, it will be well to consider them carefully.

A metrical foot in classical prosody objectifies a pattern of "times" through an arrangement of long and short syllables. There are three standard categories of metrical feet—those consisting of two syllables, those consisting of three syllables, and those consisting of four syllables. Certain four-syllable feet are considered dipodic—that is, they consist of two feet of two syllables each. There are twenty-eight possible two-, three-, and four-syllable feet. The four disyllabic feet are the pyrrhic (two short syllables: ⌣⌣), the iambus (a short followed by a long: ⌣–), the trochee (a long followed by a short: –⌣), and the spondee (two long: ––). The eight trisyllabic feet are the tribrach (⌣⌣⌣), anapest (⌣⌣–), dactyl (–⌣⌣), amphibrach (⌣–⌣), amphimacer, or cretic (–⌣–), bacchius (⌣– –), antibacchius (⌣– –), and molossus (– – –). The sixteen four-syllable feet are illustrated by the choriambus (–⌣⌣–) and the diiambus (⌣–⌣–), which is the basis of iambic trimeter. More complex feet are "mixed" or "composite" (*syzygiae*).[35]

Classical prosody is complicated by the distinction between

rhythm and meter.³⁶ Quintilian offers a helpful illustration. Rhythm, he says, is dependent strictly on time intervals. It "only measures the length of time, so that the same space of time regularly elapses from arsis to thesis."³⁷ Meter adds to regular time intervals a fixed "order" (*ordo*) of syllables.

Ancient poetic feet consist of time durations rather than heavy and light stresses. The rhythm of a line of verse is objectified by the durations of the feet into which the line is divided. The feet are themselves subdivided into units. In Latin the basic time unit of a metrical foot is a *mora* or *tempus*. A short syllable (◡) consists of one *mora* and a long (–) of two *morae*. A dactylic hexameter line, for example, is divided into five equal units of four *morae* each, plus a sixth (final) unit in which the last syllable can be either short or long (*anceps*, "ambivalent"). Thus the first line of Vergil's *Aeneid* ("Arms and the man I sing, who first from the shores of Troy . . .") is conventionally scanned as follows:

– ◡ ◡ | – ◡ ◡ | – – | – – | – ◡ ◡ | – ˘
Arma virumque cano Troiae qui primus ab oris.

Although critics like Dionysius of Halicarnassus knew that the duration of vowels varied considerably, it was conventional to consider short syllables exactly one-half the duration of long syllables.³⁸ Under certain well-defined circumstances, ancient prosody allows a long syllable to be replaced by two shorts. This is called "resolution." Conversely, two shorts can be replaced by—are equivalent to—one long. Given the convention that one long equals two shorts, this kind of substitution preserves the durations of the feet in which it occurs and thus has no effect on the rhythm of the line or its total "time."

Two additional points are relevant. Ancient prosody recognizes that the reader must sense the units in a line in order to recognize that it has rhythm. This means the units must be separated by an identifiable marker. The marker is called the "ictus." Since the root meaning of "ictus" is "blow" or "stab," stress seems to be involved. Theoretically, this is not the case. The ictus is compared to a blow in the sense that it "marks time." It is also symbolized by reference to dripping water³⁹ or a regular percussive noise (*percussio*) like the fall of a blacksmith's hammer or finger taps, the latter image being Quintilian's.⁴⁰ The duration of each unit of the rhythm is objectified by the time that elapses between one ictus and the next. In accentual meter, stress accent coincides with the ictus, so that there is a literal *percussio* marking the rhythm in the verse itself. In quantitative prosody, the *percussio* is psychologically rather than phonetically defined. In something of the same way, the tapping of the foot can mark the rhythm of a fiddle tune but does not constitute its rhythm.

The situation is complicated by the fact that Latin words have accent as well as vowel quantity. Since the primary accent of a Latin word frequently coincides with the ictus, it is possible to conclude that classical feet are more or less (even if not perfectly) coordinated with accent. This is incorrect. The word *dŏmĭnă*, for example, is accented on the first syllable, but that syllable is short. *Domina* can therefore not be used as a quantitative dactylic foot (–⌣⌣), although it can be used in accentual poetry as an accentual dactyl (/xx).

Let us now return to Donatus and, in particular, the terms "arsis" and "thesis." In Greek prosody arsis ("lifting up") and thesis ("setting down") refer to the upbeat and downbeat of a melodic line and are related by etymology to the uplifting and placement of the feet during a dance. The Romans, however, came to equate arsis and thesis with "raising" and "lowering" of the voice. Priscian, for example, explains that the *tu* syllable of *natura* is the arsis, because it requires a "lifting up" of the voice, while the *ra* syllable is the thesis because it involves a lowering of the voice. Since the "lifting up" of the voice is a way of "marking time" and thus of defining a rhythmic interval, arsis (rather than thesis) is associated with ictus.

Arsis (i.e., "raising") can come in the first or the second half of a standard foot or the first or second unit of a dipodic foot. If it comes in the first half, the rhythm is falling; if in the second, it is rising. Since metrical feet merely objectify rhythms, if the rhythm of a line is "rising" the feet should be conformable to that pattern. Thus, although an iambus and a trochee have the same "times," an iambus (rising) is not interchangeable with a trochee (falling), nor is a dactyl (falling) interchangeable with an anapest (rising), although exceptions do occur. Certain feet like the spondee (– –) and the tribrach (⌣⌣⌣) fit either type of rhythm. Normally, substitution preserves both rhythm and "time." It therefore does not change a meter, even though when it is used, a foot is created that differs from the normative foot. For example, a line of six feet consisting mostly of spondees has as much right to be called "heroic meter" as a line of six feet consisting mostly of dactyls.[41] Patterns of substitution in other meters—for example, comic iambic trimeter—are more complex.

One further point. Although substitution does not change the rhythm of a line or the name of its meter, it does have an aesthetic effect. "Figure" is the term for the specific pattern of the line with its substitutions. There are thirty-two possible figures for the dactylic hexameter line. The simplest—which is rare—is a line consisting entirely of spondees.[42] Placement of caesura also affects the feeling of a line. Other aesthetic considerations include use of elision (metaplasm) and "quality." "Quality" refers to the positions in the line that permit substitutions and the feet allowed in them. It is a feature of regular meters in contrast to strophes like the Sapphic that are compounded from different meters.[43]

DIOMEDES AND POETIC ART

Diomedes is a more interesting figure than Donatus in the history of critical theory. Although he used some of the same Greek sources as Donatus, he probably did not know the latter's work.[44] His treatment of poetry begins with accent and poetic feet, but it quickly broadens out into a consideration of genre concepts and literary aesthetics.

Book 1 of the *Artis grammaticae libri III* treats basic grammar: letters, words, parts of speech, and inflections. Book 2 explains *Latinitas*, vices of style, virtues of style, and "composition," with emphasis on phrase, clause, and period and on prose rhythm. Book 3 is devoted to poetry and ends with a discussion of the meters of Horace.

For Diomedes, poetry is "a metrical structure of fictional or true narration in appropriate rhythm and foot, proper for utility and pleasure."[45] Since Empedocles and Lucretius write in meter, Diomedes considers them both poets. His category of narration thus admits verse treatises as well as historical and fictional "stories."

The definition includes rhythm, meter, and foot. Rhythm involves regularity of time but not the specific pattern (*modus*)[46] of the feet in the line. Definitions of rhythm and meter are given in parallel form: "Rhythm is a joining of feet and times with ictus and without specific pattern of feet; or, as others say, rhythm is the structured form of a verse retaining syllable count (*servans numerum syllabarum*) and often having arsis and thesis of syllables."[47] The essential element of rhythm is regular units of time. The units are defined by arsis, which in Latin usage is associated with "raising of the voice" and, hence, with ictus. The internal structures of the metrical feet that make up the line are not significant for rhythm as long as all the feet have the same duration. A metrical line, conversely, is "a joining of feet fixed in respect to number and pattern. Or this: meter is putting together of feet moving along in an established ordering and retaining a specific pattern of arsis and thesis."[48]

Lines in meter can be "biotic" or "poetic" or common to both. The distinction goes back ultimately to Aristotle's observation in the *Poetics* that dramatic verse is like speech. A biotic metrical line is one that occurs "in everyday life and conversation." It is thus one that has a strong illocutionary quality. Diomedes shows his understanding of this implication of the term by observing that biotic lines are proper for comedy, which uses iambic meter because that meter is "like speech."[49] Poetic lines, conversely, use artfully created metrical patterns. They are different from speech—that is, ornate and musical.

After a treatment of two-, three-, and four-syllable feet, Diomedes turns to poetic genres. He follows the system based on the role played by the author that is introduced by Plato (*Republic*, III, 392C) and elaborated by Aristotle in chapter 3 (48a19–24) of the *Poetics*. There are three possibilities. The author can speak entirely in his own person, or through his characters, or sometimes in one way and sometimes in the other.

These different manners produce the dramatic, narrative, and "mixed" genres respectively.[50] The dramatic genre is "active or imitative, which the Greeks call dramatic or mimetic." "Active" (*activum*) specifically relates drama to action in the sense of dramatic performance, a point complementing Horace's comment in the *Ars poetica* (l. 82) that iambic verse is suited to action.[51] Diomedes recognizes four types of drama, each with different prosodic norms: tragedy, comedy, satyr play, and mime. He also lists specifically Roman types: *praetextata* (historical plays), *tabernaria* (low comedies), *atellana* (farces), and *planipes* ("shoeless," i.e., base plays).[52]

The narrative genre divides into sententious, historical, and didactic (*angeltice, historice, didascalice*) types. The third type is philosophical in the manner of Empedocles and Lucretius and Vergil's *Georgics*. Aristotle had rejected Empedocles from the ranks of poets because Empedocles does not imitate. Since Diomedes makes "writing in verse" the basis of his definition of poetry, he is quite willing to call Empedocles a poet. His "mixed" genre includes the heroic manner of Homer and the lyric manner of Archilochus and Horace.

Diomedes now turns to specific forms. Epic is in heroic meter and treats "divine, heroic, and human events." Later it is called "first in dignity."[53] Elegy is alternate hexameter and pentameter. It is for love lament or mourning the dead.

The name for iambic verse comes from the Greek word *iambizein*, "to lampoon" (Latin, *maledicere*). Archilochus first used iambics for angry personal attacks on the vices and crimes of his enemies. Hipponax also used the form to create the *scazon*, or "limping iambic," named from the fact that a spondee or trochee is substituted for the iambus normal in the sixth foot of the regular iambic line, making the line seem to "limp." Satire was domesticated into Latin poetry by Lucilius. It is called "satire" from "satyr" because "ridiculous and shameful things are said in this sort of poem."[54]

After commenting briefly on pastoral, Diomedes returns to drama.[55] Although his discussion is extended, it offers nothing that cannot be found in other sources. Tragedy deals with the fortunes of heroes and kings and ends in disaster. Comedy deals with private characters and characters from the middle and lower classes, and it never ends in death. The subjects of tragedy are wars and affairs of state; of comedy, love intrigues and elopements. Roman comedies do not have choruses, but they do have dialogue sections (*diverbia*) and scenes that include song (*cantica*). Diomedes later comments on the laxity of Latin iambic verse, but he has less to say on that subject than several other authors of the *ars metrica*.

The discussion of poetry ends with several technical chapters. There are three types of hexameter line—pure dactylic, iambic, and mixed dactylic. The third type, which uses spondees as well as dactyls, is the heroic or epic line. The standard enumeration of the thirty-two metrical "figures" (i.e., mixtures of dactylic and spondaic feet) possible in the epic line is given. Additional variety is provided by different placements of the caesura. Verses can be integral (*integrae*), disjunctive (*iniuges*), balanced (*aequiformae*), mixed (*partipedes*), incremental (*fistulares*, or "piping"), antithetical (*aequidici*), or sonorous (*sonores*). Poems can be "finite," with all the lines in the same meter, as in the *Iliad*, or "nonfinite," as in the Sapphic stanza.[56]

While discussing meters Diomedes repeats the theory of Varro that all are "derived" from dactylic hexameter and iambic trimeter. He also lists the nine "prototype" meters of Hephaestion, and he ends with a discussion of the meters of Horace.[57]

Before we leave Diomedes, it will be useful to review once again his definition of poetry: "A metrical structure of fictional or true narration in appropriate (*congruens*) rhythm and foot, proper for utility and pleasure." In addition to identifying poetry with "writing in meter," the definition stresses the relation between meter and subject matter. The key word is *congruens*, here translated "appropriate." The concept is a corollary of "construction"—that is, the creation of a syntax and rhythm appropriate to the subject.

Another term suggested by *congruens* is "decorum." Decorum of meter is the choice of musical forms complementary to the subject. In poetry, choice depends on three factors—topic (or "argument"), social status of characters represented, and genre. Heroic poetry deals with great affairs of state and the lives of princes and heroes. Its meter is called the "stateliest and most dignified meter" by Aristotle (*Poetics*, ch. 24); fit for "deeds of kings and generals and the sad events of war" by Horace (*Ars poetica*, l. 73); and proper for "deeds of heroes" and "battle lines and slaughters" by Mallius Theodorus.[58]

The concept of metrical decorum is enlarged by the importation into poetic theory of the "three styles" of Roman rhetoric. The names for the styles in the *Rhetorica ad Herennium* are "high" (*gravis*), "middle" (*mediocris*), and "low" (*adtenuata*),[59] and each requires a special sort of composition in the sense of the deployment of vocabulary, rhythms, and figures. In the later Middle Ages, subject matter, social class, genre, and style were combined in the "wheel of Vergil."[60] Vergil's *Eclogues* deal with trivial events (the loves and disappointments of shepherds) and lower-class figures. They are therefore in a low style except when they touch on issues of state. In the *Georgics* Vergil speaks in his own (middle-class) voice as a teacher and moralist. The *Georgics* are in the middle style. The *Aeneid* is in the high style. The "wheel of Vergil" is not a new medieval doctrine but a visual codification of a traditional theory of the relation between composition and genre.

There are innumerable minor traditions about prosodic decorum to be culled from Diomedes and other authors of the *ars metrica*. The hexameter line should have a dactyl in the fifth foot (although there are exceptions), and the caesura is normally in the third foot (penthemimeral). Many spondees make a heroic line "heavy" and "sonorous"; dactyls make it "light" and "swift." At the caesura, metrical diaeresis (coincidence of the end of a foot with the end of a word) is harsh, but after a dactyl in the fourth foot, it is "bucolic" because it is common in pastoral poetry. Each classical foot has a "proportion" based on the ratio of arsis to thesis. The dactyl, for example, has a proportion of one to one; the iamb of two to one. Various metrical "proportions" express mystical harmonies. St. Augustine's *De musica* explores this subject in great detail. In chapter 12 of book 5, the doctrine of half-lines is explored. Vergil's first line ("Arma virumque cano . . .") has the caesura after the fifth half-foot (*ca | no**; penthemimeral caesura). The line divides by half-feet into the proportion of five plus seven. The result is an unexpected harmony. Five squared is twenty-five. Seven is the sum of three and four, and the sum of three squared and four squared is—*mirabile dictu!*—twenty-five. The two parts of the line, which seem unequal when first examined, have a hidden equivalence.

The iambic trimeter line should always end with an iambus (if it ends with a spondee, it is a *scazon*). Otherwise, it admits frequent substitution, in keeping with its relaxed, "speech-like" quality, the tragic form being more formal than the comic. The Roman form is especially relaxed. In the first, the third, and the fifth foot, a spondee, anapest, dactyl, or tribrach can be substituted. In the second and the fourth foot, a tribrach is permitted. Satiric verse should be rough in both sound effects and meter. The elegiac distich seeks elegant formal arrangements of words within each line and encourages the play of one line against the other. The Pindaric is "labyrinthine" because Theseus invented it after slaying the Minotaur. Short lyrics should be "musical," "harmonious," and "polished," in contrast to epic verse, which should be "swelling."

Many of the definitions of the *Artis grammaticae libri III* were repeated in medieval encyclopedias and manuals of poetry, and its influence continued to be significant in the Renaissance. The only ancient work of criticism that had comparable influence is the *Ars poetica* of Horace, and the fate of Horace in the early sixteenth century is closely linked to that of Diomedes. The popular and frequently reprinted commentary on the *Ars poetica* by Badius Ascensius, first published in Paris in 1500, begins with a summary of the theories of Diomedes about the triple decorum of poetry and its kinds. As Badius moves through the text, he continuously invokes Diomedes to explain Horace's lines.

BEDE AND RHYTHMIC POETRY

According to C. B. Kendall, Bede's most recent editor, the *De arte metrica* was composed in A.D. 701 or 702.[61] It draws on several late classical grammarians, including Diomedes, Donatus, Servius, and Marius Victorinus, and Mallius Theodorus. Its most famous passage is chapter 24, which is the earliest extant definition of Latin accentual meter. Another important feature is its use of Old Testament and Christian poetry to illustrate metrical forms.

The essay consists of twenty-five chapters. The first eight are entirely grammatical, dealing, respectively, with letters, syllables, including introductory, middle, and terminal syllables of nouns and verbs, and the vowel quantities of conjunctions. Chapter 19 identifies the standard four disyllabic, eight trisyllabic, and sixteen tetrasyllabic feet. All other feet are composite. Chapters 10 through 12 treat dactylic hexameter and pentameter, the combination of the two lines in the elegiac couplet, the beauties of the heroic line, and caesura. These are followed by chapters on elision (synaloepha), expansion (diaeresis), poetic license, and the meters. The work ends with chapters on rhythm and on the dramatic, narrative, and mixed forms of imitation.

Discussion of the meters begins with dactylic hexameter: "It is called heroic because in it are sung most especially the deeds of heroes, that is, of brave men, [and] it is more excellent and more beautiful than all the other meters."[62] The origin of the form with the Delphic Oracle and the use of the term "Pythian" to identify it are noted, and a new suggestion is added. Jerome says the Book of Job is in hexameter verse, so heroic meter has precedents in—perhaps was derived from—the Old Testament.[63] We also learn that Deuteronomy and at least two psalms (118, 144) are in elegiac meter. The Song of Songs is dramatic in form, and Ecclesiastes is "mixed" like the *Odyssey*. The idea that Greek and Latin verse forms were derived from the Hebrews was familiar to St. Jerome and was commonplace by the time Bede wrote his treatise. The *De arte metrica* may, however, have helped to popularize it in the later Middle Ages.

Bede approves of enjambment: "In hexameter poetry joining of several verses is most pleasing. . . . You find . . . often that there are seven or even more verses mutually related."[64] The verse welcomes ornamental words and proper names and variety. These points are illustrated by spirited and sustained "verse paragraphs" from Arator and Sedulius. Bede recognizes, however, that different genres require different styles. He praises Ambrose for writing hymns with end-stopped lines that are adapted to antiphonal singing.

Dactylic pentameter is presented as a variant of hexameter, to which it is joined in the elegiac couplet. Bede makes the standard observation (here echoing Isidore, *Etymologiarum*, I, 39, 14) that elegy is for lament: "The structure of this kind of poem is fitting for the lament of wretches, where the first verse is a hexameter, the second a pentameter."[65] He adds that the author should respect the couplet form and complete the sense of the verse either in each line or at the end of the pentameter line of each couplet. The Sapphic stanza is illustrated (ch. 18) by a hymn for St. Felix by Paulinus of Nola, and the Anacreontic (ch. 22) by a quotation from Prosper of Aquitaine.

Bede has little to say about iambic trimeter, which he correctly calls *senarius* (ch. 20). This meter is associated primarily with satire and drama, and Bede does not show much knowledge of either form. Later, in chapter 25 we are told that drama "means 'fable' in Latin" (*drama enim Latine fabula dicitur*).[66] The comment echoes the explanation given by Diomedes in the *Artis grammaticae: fabula* is from *fatibula* and alludes to the fact that Latin comedies regularly include songs, or it is from *faciendo*, meaning "doing" and thus "acting." Bede is, however, vague about the difference between drama and narrative. Instead of citing instances from drama, he illustrates the *senarius* (ch. 20) from the proemium of Prudentius's narrative poem *Psychomachia*.

The famous chapter on rhythm (ch. 24) recognizes what C. W. Jones calls "isosyllabic stress meter."[67] Rhythm is defined as "a measured arrangement (*compositio*) of words, governed not by metrical rule but by the number of syllables, as determined by the ear, in the fashion of the unlearned poets."[68]

Rhythmic verse, in Bede's sense, is created by constructions that place words so the natural accent of each word coincides with the ictus of the metrical foot in which it is placed. Dag Norberg explains, "Bede appears to have been the first [theorist] to identify verse rhythm with the natural accents of words."[69] The use of natural accent means that anyone who knows how to pronounce words correctly can sense the rhythm of the verses in which they appear by a simple "judgement of the ear." By the same token, metrical errors caused by failure to coordinate word accent with ictus are immediately obvious "even to the unlearned."

This kind of poetry composes its feet with lightly and heavily accented syllables. As Bede explains matters, it does not consider length and shortness of syllables because these elements create "meters" rather than "rhythms." If the accentual feet are regular, the number of syllables will be the same for every line with the same meter and the same number of feet. The result is a prosody fundamentally different from the quantitative system. The quantitative system allows resolution of two short syllables, for example, into a long syllable. Conversely, in accentual meter, a modification that changes the number of syllables will destroy the rhythm of the line and is therefore a defect.

Bede's realignment of metrical rule foreshadows a new era of European poetry. The path to the new poetry is, however, anything but direct. To follow it, we will need to consider the place of the sequence in the development of vernacular prosody. Sequences are shaped in part by construction and in part by musical influences, and they do not, initially, have regular meters of the sort envisaged in Bede's chapter on rhythmic verse.

Chapter 25, Bede's concluding chapter, summarizes the theory of the three genres as defined by the relationship of poet to poem. It is drawn almost verbatim from Diomedes. However, Bede cites Ecclesiastes and Wisdom along with the *Georgics* to exemplify the didactic (narrative) form, in which the author speaks in his own person, and Job (which Bede explains is partly in meter and partly in "rhythmic prose") along with the *Odyssey* and the *Aeneid* to exemplify the mixed form. The dramatic form is illustrated by the Song of Songs, in which Solomon, the author, never speaks and the interlocutors are Christ and the Church.

Bede is one of the earliest critics to confront directly the problem that vernacular poets of the Renaissance confronted; namely, how to apply the terminology and concepts of ancient prosody in a new cultural and linguistic environment. He is dealing with Latin rather than a vernacular language, but it is a Latin already different from the Latin the earlier writers of the *ars metrica* had assumed. It is using accentual meter in spite of the fact that classically trained writers know the practice is "unlearned." And it has assimilated works and styles radically different from those of Greek and Roman literature.

Initially these works and styles were Hebrew, but by the time Bede undertook his treatise, the Hebraic aesthetic had been thoroughly assimilated into Christian Latin poetry. In the process, the concept of the "Latin" literary tradition was enormously broadened. When Bede looked back, he saw not only Cicero and Vergil and Horace, but also Jerome's Vulgate and St. Augustine's *City of God* and the poetry of Prudentius and Paulinus of Nola. A complementary broadening is evident in the meaning of classical rhetorical terms as they are applied in Bede's *On Schemes and Tropes* to the figurative language of the Old Testament. To the degree that terms are defined by their referents, the meaning of the whole system of terms of classical rhetoric is changed fundamentally in Bede's treatise.

By introducing the subject of rhythmic poetry, Bede announces that the Latin language has changed along with the literary aesthetic. It not only says new things and uses new sorts of imagery, it is beginning to have a new sound. This observation leads directly to the prosodic innovations that are the subject of the next chapter.

CHAPTER III

Rude and Beggerly Ryming: The Romance Tradition

When Roger Ascham complained in 1570 in *The Scholemaster* about English poets who use "our rude and beggerly ryming, brought first into Italie by *Gothes* and *Hunnes*," he was recognizing a fact about English poetry. It began with alliterative verse of the sort used in *Beowulf* and, in Middle English, in *Piers Plowman*. During the centuries following the Norman Conquest, alliterative verse gave way to lines regulated by syllable count and linked by rhyme. These lines adopt prosodic conventions that first appear in medieval Latin and that are also the basis of romance prosody. Not until the sixteenth century was the romance tradition challenged. As Ascham's comment shows, humanism produced a violent reaction against it. In spite of this reaction, however, it continued to influence the way poems were written and the way poets talked about their art.

ARS RITHMICA

The Ambrosian hymns of the fourth century are in iambic dimeter, a classical Latin form. However, their syllables are often so arranged that the natural accent of each word coincides with the mandatory long syllable—and hence the ictus—of a quantitative iambus, and each lightly accented syllable corresponds to the syllable of the iambus that is normally short. Most scholars agree that the Ambrosian hymns can often be scanned in two ways—as regular quantitative lines, and as lines composed of accentual feet.[1]

This prosodic ambivalence is illustrated by the Ambrosian hymn "Aeterne rerum conditor." It is given below, first with a quantitative scansion and then with an accentual scansion.[2]

Quantitative:

```
_  _|  ⏑  ⏑|_    _|  ⏑  ⏑
Aeterne rerum conditor
_  _  |  ⏑_|    ⏑    _|  ⏑  ⏑
Noctem diemque qui  regis
_  _|  ⏑  _|  _   _|  ⏑  ⏑
Et temporum  das tempora,
⏑  ⏑|⏑  _|  _   _|⏑⏑
Ut alleves  fastidium.
```

As noted in chapter 2, the Venerable Bede defines accentual meter as "a measured arrangement of words governed not by metrical rule but by number of syllables, as determined by the ear."[3] In this meter, a natural word accent marks the ictus of the foot. Secondary accent is permitted (though not mandatory) in words of more than two syllables (e.g., "cónditòr").[4] Using this license, accentual scansion of the first stanza of "Aeterne rerum" produces three lines that are regular iambic (ll. 1, 3, and 4) and one that is irregular.

Accentual:

```
x  /| x  /|x    / | x \
Aeterne rerum conditor
/  x  x/    x    x / x
Nocte diemque qui regis
x  /   x \    x  /    x \
Et temporum das tempora,
x  /|x \ |  x  /|x\
Ut alleves  fastidium.
```

Both quantitative and accentual scansions "work" for the regular lines. There is, however, a marked difference in the implications of the two systems.

Latin quantitative verse is based, as we have seen, on equal time units. It is thus isochronic. Latin accentual verse is based, conversely, on equal numbers of syllables. It is thus isosyllabic. Since every syllable is counted, every line in the same meter and with the same number of feet must have the same number of syllables unless extra syllables are permitted by poetic license. Even though—regarded accentually—the Ambrosian hymns do not limit themselves to iambics, they consist of lines having eight syllables, with a norm of four feet to each line. Both metrical irregularity and isosyllabic lines are illustrated by "Aeterne rerum conditor." Further symmetry is introduced by the division of the Ambrosian hymns into two long lines for antiphonal singing.[5]

By the ninth century, Latin poems appear that are acceptable from an accentual point of view but unacceptable from a quantitative point of view. An example is provided by the following stanza written in the early tenth century by Hartmann of St. Gall.[6] The poem tends to the norm of quantitative iambic dimeter, but in six cases words are used that have a short syllable where quantitative rules would call for a long syllable. The vowels of the incorrect syllables (i.e., those with "false" quantities) are italicized in the first scansion that follows:

Quantitative:

$-\ \cup|-\ \ -|\cup\ \ -|\ \cup\ \ -$
Sic vo*l*untatis integrae

$-\ \ -|\ \cup\ \ \cup|-\ \ \cup|\ \cup\ \cup$
Perfecta n*i*tent *o*pera

$-\ \ \cup|\ \cup\ \ -|\ \cup\ \ -|\ \cup\ \ -$
Terr*a*que cord*i*s optimi

$-\ \ -|-\ \ \cup|-\ \ \cup|\ \cup\ \cup$
Centenum refert n*u*merum.

Accentual scansion of the same stanza reveals a regular pattern of iambic feet:

Accentual:

x /|x /|x / |x \
Sic voluntatis integrae

x /| x /|x / |x \
Perfecta nitent opera

x /| x /| x /| x \
Terraque cordis optimi

x /|x   /|x   / | x \
Centenum refert numerum.

There is general agreement that accentual foot verse was created intentionally as early as Commodian (ca. A.D. 250), who apparently used it for mnemonic purposes in connection with acrostics in poems called *Instructiones* for lower-class Christian converts.[7] As we have seen, Bede considers quantitative poetry learned and accentual poetry "popular." Later, the quantitative type is often called *versus* or *metrum*, and the accentual, *rithmus* or *modulatio*.

Why did accentual Latin verse become popular? One answer to this question is that after the high tide of the Empire, Latin gradually reverted to its natural accentual form. Michel Burger suggests that as formal Latin became progressively more difficult for the less educated, the ability was lost to "hear" quantity. Accent took over by a natural and evolutionary process, first in the provinces and then in urban centers: "Accent increased in intensity; among uncultured groups, people no longer sought to read quantitative verses with the rules of quantity, but by letting themselves be guided by the rhythm of Latin of their age, that is to say . . . accented syllables."[8]

Another factor, suggested by the Ambrosian hymns, may have been the desire of the Church for poetry that could be sung easily by uneducated people. Accentual rhythms are, as Bede notes, easier for the uneducated to understand than quantitative ones. Theories abound, and even when scholars agree on larger issues, they often disagree on particulars. What seems beyond dispute is that accentual meter first appeared in conjunction with quantitative meter, but that in the earlier Middle Ages, the two strategies produced two different kinds of poetry. As popular poetry gained favor, a reaction occurred that is evident in the considerable body of classicizing verse written by self-consciously "learned poets" during the Carolingian renaissance.

From Accentual to Syllabic Verse

According to the school of thought originated by Wilhelm Meyer and advocated today by Michel Burger, between the fourth and the ninth century, accentual writers imitated quantitative meters and stanza forms. Imitation resulted in various line types that became the basis of both the Latin and vernacular poetry of the later Middle Ages. Beginning from the position that "verse has a structure which is proper to it and independent of music," Burger argues, for example, that classical iambic trimeter is the basis of the French decasyllabic line, that dactylic hexameter leads to the hendecasyllabic, and that double iambic dimeter underlies the French Alexandrine. According to Burger, the major romance verse forms had taken shape before the emergence of the various romance languages.[9]

This position cannot be rejected. It is in accord with the fact that accentual poetry using the old quantitative patterns continued to be written in the later Middle Ages. By the twelfth century, accentual equivalents of many of the standard ancient meters were being composed, and it is not illogical to speculate that these underlie vernacular forms. Among the learned forms, hexameters, elegiacs, and Sapphics were especially popular, but other meters and strophes were common. It is entirely possible that ancient quantitative line types were prototypes of some of the line types that became standard in the prosodies of European vernaculars. On the other hand, what might be called the "metrical" school of medieval prosody, in contrast to the "musical" school, fails to account in a satisfying way for the apparent shift in romance languages from meter to syllable count and from unrhymed verse to rhymed verse.

Rhyme is centrally important in Latin and romance prosodies of the high Middle Ages. Why? Burger does not integrate his analysis of metrical forms with an analysis of the development of rhyme. An alternative approach is taken by Eduard Norden, who sees rhyme as a combination of rhythmic prose with (in the Latin Middle Ages) the extensive use of like endings (homoeoteleuton).[10] The currently dominant theory, however, is that the proximate source of rhyme is accentual poetry rather than rhythmic prose.[11] We will return to rhyme, but first we need to note the appearance of a new type of poetry in the eighth or ninth century.

Much medieval Latin poetry cannot be neatly divided into feet, whether quantitative or accentual. Georges Lote argues that the sole consistent feature of this verse is that it is careful about syllable count. Lote's syllabism has been challenged, but the most recent review of the many thorny questions raised by the emergence of rhymed syllabic forms concludes that he is closer to the truth than his critics.[12] It is non-metrical syllabic verse rather than verse in accentual meters that is the most likely precedent for the syllabic versification characteristic of romance languages.

In the Mass, there are chants between the Epistle and the Gospel. One of these, the "Alleluia," was customarily extended by the addition of a melody sung while holding the final *a*. The added melody was called a *jubilus* or—because it followed the official chant—a *sequentia*. Because the added melodies were long and intricate, verbal texts were created to be sung to them as aids to memory. These texts were called "proses" because they were not in regular meters, and also "sequences," like the melodies to which they were matched.

Sequences are closely associated with the monk Notker Balbulus of St. Gall (ca. 840–912).[13] Notker describes the syllabic basis of the sequence in the introduction to his *Liber hymnorum*. The long melodies of the *jubilus* were hard to remember. After seeing some verses from the monastery at Jumièges, Notker decided to try his own hand at composing words for the melodies. His master Iso explained that each note ought to have a separate syllable, and this is the principle he followed. In the resulting poems, each note of the music corresponds to one—and only one—syllable of the text. We know today that Notker's account is a considerable simplification and that the sequence was already a well-established form by the time he became interested in it. Nevertheless, his account is useful because it shows that the syllabic aspect of the sequence was well understood at a relatively early period.[14]

Since melody precedes text, text must follow melody. The melodies are not, however, simple compositions. In the first place, they are subdivided into phrases or measures (*clausulae*).[15] The text of a sequence is constructed so that it falls into grammatical units reflecting the phrasing of the melody. Verses subdivided into two units are standard, but verses having three or more units are common. A melody of two units produces a text of two phrases, usually expressed visually as two lines.

In the second place, the melodies are chanted antiphonally. This means that the texts accompanying the melodies are written in paired line groups or strophes. All of the text of a melody must be sung before the melody repeats. Because of the one-note/one-syllable rule, each line must have exactly the same number of syllables as its sibling. In other words, the lines must be isosyllabic. A melody having two measures of unequal lengths produces a text with two lines having unequal numbers of syllables. A pause marks the transition from the first to the second line, another pause marks the transition from the first text to its antiphonal twin, and a still more emphatic pause marks the point where one melody ends and a new melody, with new text, begins. Typically the text is constructed so that the pauses coincide with standard syntactic units—comma, colon, and period.

The result is a dynamic blend of uniformity and change. Since the musical phrasing shapes the text, its dynamic is mirrored in the verbal *clausulae*, which are further ornamented by rhetorical devices associated with construction. William of Lô (d. 1349) writes admiringly of the use of these devices by Adam of St. Victor: "He made many proses . . . which are composed (*componunter*) with most appropriate schemes (*schemata*) so they progress neatly and by clausula (*clausula-*

tim), subtly decorated with a pretty marriage of words, ornamented (*picturatae*) with wonderful flowers of learning (*flosculae scientiarum*)."[16]

The following sequence ("Psallat ecclesia") is reputed to be the first successful sequence that Notker composed.[17] The paired units are isosyllabic and are based on a melody having three measures:

Unit		Syllables	Total
A-1	Haec domus aulae	5	
	caelestis	3	
	probatur particeps	6	14
A-2	in laude regis	5	
	caelorum	3	
	et ceremoniis	6	14
B-1	et lumine continuo	8	
	aemulans	3	
	civitatem sine tenebris	9	20
B-2	et corpora in gremio	8	
	confovens	3	
	animarum quae in caelo vivunt.	9	20

A German sequence of the tenth century, "Cantemus cuncti melodum," illustrates a type of sequence that has a refrain.[18] In it the word "Alleluia" is repeated at the end of each complete unit. The device is of interest because of the frequency with which refrains are used in later medieval poetry:

Unit		Syllables
A-1	Nunc vos, o socii,	6
	cantate laetantes	6
	Alleluia	
A-2	et vos pueruli	6
	respondete semper	6
	Alleluia	

A major change in sequence texts occurred in the twelfth century. It is related to the emergence of the new, metrically regular form of music associated with the composers Leoninus and Perotinus. Leoninus is credited with introducing "measured" music based on the analysis of the rhythmic qualities of poetic meter by St. Augustine in the *De musica*. There were six basic measures, but only three were generally useful—iambic, trochaic, and dactylic.[19] These "rhythmic modes," as they were called, became the basis of melodies based on strict measure—*musica mensurabilis,* in contrast to the older form called *musica plana*.

The advent of melodies using the rhythms of metrical feet encouraged the creation of texts in regular meters. The "regular" sequences associated preeminently with Adam of St. Victor are in trochaic meter with one or more octosyllabic lines followed by a line of seven syllables and ornamented by disyllabic rhyme. The strophes are always paired, and the strophe forms change, but the changes are irregular. In Adam's sequence "Zyma vetus expurgetur," for example, four three-line strophes are followed by two seven-line strophes, followed by two three-line strophes like the initial four, followed by four six-line strophes, and so forth. The changes in strophe form signal changes in melody. The regular sequences have also abandoned the conventional isolated introductory and concluding strophes. Some later compositions called sequences are, in fact, poems with simple stanzas repeated from beginning to end—for example, the "Dies irae" (ca. 1250) and "Stabat mater" (ca. 1275).

Because of their use of disyllabic meter and their preference for the octosyllabic line, regular sequences appear to have a kinship with the Ambrosian hymns. An obvious difference is the fact that they do not have to retain a single repeated stanza form. Whatever their relation to earlier hymnody, they establish the precedent for a flowering of Latin poems, profane as well as sacred, in accentual iambic and trochaic meter. Some of these poems retain irregular strophes, now standardized in formulas for complex stanzas such as those used in the lay and the ballade.

Lote believes that there is no relation in the earlier sequence between the movement of the notes in the melody and either stress or pitch accent in the words. If this is true (it has been questioned), it is not surprising. The melodies came first. The job of the poet was to fit the words to them, not to make elegant metrical forms that might claim to have sufficient phonetic value in their own right to influence the shape of the melodies. The basic regulating principle of the sequence is therefore syllable count and (with one very important exception) syllable count only.[20]

The exception to the indifference of the sequence to accent occurs at the end of each line unit in the text, and this brings us back to rhyme. The line-ends of the sequence are marked by rhyme. Initially, the rhyme is assonant. Since the sequence probably originated from melodies extending the final *a* of "Alleluia," it is not surprising that in early French sequences the rhyme letter is often *a*—as, for example, in the first unit of a sequence that evidently predates Notker's compositions:

> Qui regis sceptra
> forti dextra
> solus cuncta.[21]

The weak rhymes of "Qui regis" remind us that rhyme needs accent to achieve its full effect. Hence the later sequences show a concern for accent at the end of the line that is not evident elsewhere in the line. Is this concern for accent related to the prose *cursus*—and is rhyme really a development of the rhythmic endings of *clausulae*? Perhaps, but the jury is out at this point, and there is no need to speculate. The result of the introduction of rhyme in the sequence is clear. Rhymes are normally of one or two syllables, and the accents occur in either trochaic or iambic patterns. Normal Latin rhyme is feminine (paroxytonic) and disyllabic (*Maria/via; scandit/pandit*). It is called "spondaic rhyme" in medieval poetry manuals. It is typically encountered in trochaic meter and in iambic meter with an extra terminal syllable. True masculine rhyme is possible but rare in Latin (*flos/vos*). The standard kind of masculine rhyme uses trisyllabic words with a promoted final syllable. It is called "iambic" or "dactylic" rhyme in the manuals. It is used most frequently in accentual dactylic verse (*glória/transitória*), and, with a promoted final foot, in iambic verse (*prodíins/exíins*). The term "leonine rhyme" can refer either to internal rhyme within a line or to trisyllabic rhyme (*gemina/semina*), considered highly ornamental.

Lote believes that the complex rhyming stanzas, or strophes, of medieval Latin and French poetry were end-products of various arrangements of line and rhyme in the sequence. Although Dag Norberg agrees that the sequence is important, he and others maintain that other factors are involved.[22] Simple, repetitive rhyming stanzas are created on analogy to the regular sequence of the twelfth century, while obviously classical forms (e.g., accentual Sapphics) imply continuation of experiments that began with Commodian's accentual hexameters.

Brilliant use of rhyme is evident in the well-known sequence "Victimae paschali laudes," written by Wipo (d. 1048), Chaplain to Emperor Henry III.[23] The lines selected are of special interest because they were appropriated soon after being composed by writers of the Latin liturgical plays known by the generic title of *Visitatio sepulchri*. In other words, the antiphonal mode of chanting, which is innate to the form, has affinities with dramatic dialogues that were recognized by medieval dramatists:

Unit		Syllables	Total
A–1	/x Dic nobis Maria	6	
	/x Quid vidisti in via?	7	
	/ x Sepulchrum Christi viventis	8	
	/ x Et gloriam resurgentis,	8	29
A–2	/ x Angelicos testes	6	
	/ x Sudarium et vestes.	7	
	/x Surrexit Christus spes mea;	8	
	/x Praecaedet suos in Galilea.	8	29

Here we have something like two "stanzas" of four lines each, rhymed in couplets: *a a, b b | c c, d d*. The rhymes have the pattern of accentual trochaic feet, but the lines in which these rhymes occur have no regular metrical pattern. They are "proses." The demarcation between "stanzas" occurs at the transition between units A–1 and A–2, at which point the melody repeats even as the two stanzas remain joined by artful grammatical linking. Since the syllable count of the lines comprising the stanzas is the same, the stanzas are isosyllabic. Each partial line ends with a rhyme based on repetition of stressed vowels. Vowel rhyme is illustrated by *mea/Galilea;* two-syllable rhyme involving consonants is illustrated by *viventis/resurgentis* and *testes/vestes*.

A pair of trochaic strophes from Adam of St. Victor's Easter sequence "Zyma vetus expurgetur" completes the set of examples.[24] Note the truncation in the fourth lines:

Unit

A–1   / x / x /   x / x
           Mors et vita conflixere
           resurrexit Christus vere
           et cum Christo surrexere
             / x / x   / x/ [x]
             multi testes gloriae.

A–2   Mane novum, mane laetum
           vespertinum tergat fletum;
           quia vita vicit letum,
             tempus est laetitiae.

Whether the text of a sequence is regular or irregular, the connection between melody and form remains close. If two strophes have lines of the same number of syllables and the same rhyme scheme, the same melody is implied. In a vernacular stanza form like the sonnet, the two four-line units at the beginning can thus be understood to have the same "melody," and the melody can be said to change with the volta, or turn, that marks the change from octave to sestet. The formula for the French lay requires paired stanzas (called *couples*) with the same number of syllables in corresponding lines and the same rhyme scheme. If the stanzas of a poem are identical, they imply that a single melody is repeated from beginning to end.

The earliest formal poem in French, the "Cantilène de sainte Eulalie," was written around the year 880 to commemorate the discovery of the bones of that saint in Barcelona in 878. It looks like a rough sequence with lines arranged in couplets. Although there are irregularities, the basic difference between the "Cantilène" and the early, pre-Notkerian sequences is that the caesuras are irregular. Both Wilhelm Meyer and Georges Lote believe the "Cantilène" confirms the link between the sequence and the development of romance prosody.[25] This conclusion has, however, been challenged.[26]

The point to be made here is accepted by all parties. The verse combining syllable count and rhyme that emerged in the high Middle Ages and became standard for the romance languages differs from early medieval accentual verse. Lote's explanation is persuasive. Romance verse probably derives its reliance on "number" from the fact that its verses were written to pre-existing melodies according to a formula that required one syllable for each musical note and that divided verses into measures ending with accented syllables and, eventually, rhyme. Only after this development—and following the emergence of a new musical style—was there an outpouring of Latin lyrics that combined the rhymes of the sequence with regular accentual feet. Even after this happened, the new accentual stanzas retained the fondness of the sequence for doubling and for complex variations of stanza form.

In French poetry, syllabic lines came to be characterized by an accented syllable or syllable group at the end of a partial line, followed by a caesura and another partial line-ending with an accented syllable or syllable group and a pause. French rhyme, both internal and terminal, makes use of these elements. Initially assonance was the rule. Early narrative poems (chansons de geste) were written in irregular groups of lines (*laisses*) united by having the same assonant rhyme. When true rhyme began to be used in the twelfth century, masculine rhyme predominated. Feminine (paroxytonic) rhyme arrived late in French poetry and was initially used timidly.[27] The types most commonly cited have analogues in Latin rhymes. Although terminologies differ, in general, rime suffisante requires a vowel and a consonant (*cité/beauté*). Rime riche requires three elements (vowel and two consonants: *arche/marche, rêve/trêve*). Rime Léonine has two syllables and is occasionally called très riche or rime double (*divers/univers*). Rime équivoque is punning rhyme using the same sounds but different meanings (*Dante en/d'antan*).

In France, narrative came to prefer couplets (rimes plates) and quatrains (rimes croisées—crossed rhyme of the form *a b a b;* or rimes embrassées—of the form *a b b a*), which the late Middle Ages liked with alternating masculine and feminine rhymes. Although syllable count was fixed, there were licenses. A feminine line-ending was permitted, resulting in an extra final syllable, which was not counted although it was still pronounced in Old French. In "epic caesura," an extra unstressed syllable precedes the caesura.

Many of these characteristics, including license, are illustrated by the following line from the "General Prologue" of Chaucer's *Canterbury Tales*. Assuming "Caunterbury" to have four syllables, the line has an epic caesura and can be described as a twelve-syllable decasyllabic:

```
      / x*               / x
To Caunterbury with ful devout corage.
```

[4'*6']

In medieval French poetry, merging of terminal with initial vowels (synaloepha) is standard. In the line that follows, these licenses are illustrated by the merging of the final *e* of "droughte" with the *o* of "of." The *e* of "Marche" is probably also merged with the *ha* of "hath." There is an extra unstressed syllable at the end of the line:

      /   /   *   /   / x
The droughte of Marche hath perced to the roote.
        U   U

[2 + 2*2 + 4']

Note that both of the lines quoted from Chaucer can be scanned either as syllabic or as iambic pentameter. If scanned as iambic pentameter, the second line has a promoted syllable ("to"):

x /   x / x* x   /   x /   x / x
To Caunterbury with ful devout corage.

And:

x   /   x   /   x   / x \   x / x
The droughte of Marche hath perced to the roote.

Rhyme in the early lines of *The Canterbury Tales* includes rime suffisante ("licour/flour"), rime riche ("roote/soote"), and rime équivoque ("seke/seeke").

PARISIANA POETRIA

Numerous high medieval treatises on the *ars rithmica* have survived.[28] Among these are the *Laborintus* (ca. 1230) of Everardus Alemannus and the *Parisiana poetria de arte prosaica, metrica, et rithmica* (ca. 1220) by John of Garland.[29] According to its editor Traugott Lawler, the *Parisiana poetria* is "the only thorough attempt we have to gather three distinct areas of the medieval arts of discourse (*ars poetica, ars rithmica,* and *ars dictaminis*) under a single series of rules."[30] It treats rhetoric, including the three styles—high, middle, and low (chs. 1, 2, 4, 5); the classical genres, including epithalamium, epitaph, bucolic, eclogue, lyric, and ode, plus tragedy and comedy understood as narrative forms (chs. 4, 5); the classical meters, including the meters of Horace (ch. 7); and the *ars rithmica* (most explicitly, ch. 7, ll. 466–1366). Of considerable interest is the assumption that prose and poetry are complementary. The rhythm of prose is determined by *clausulae*—that is, by the strategies of composition. At the beginning of the treatise, "rhythms" are illustrated by reference to "proses of the liturgy"—that is, sequences, although this definition is not repeated in the discussion of poetry proper, where "rhythms" are interpreted as having accentual meter as well as having rhyme.[31]

The discussion of rhythmic art forms a unit. In Lawler's opinion, it was written as an independent treatise and later combined with the *Parisiana poetria*. Since the readers to whom the book is addressed are called *pueri*, it must have been intended as a schoolbook. Its subject matter shows that in spite of its extended discussion of rhetoric, it was used in the grammar curriculum.[32] In this respect it is like the *Ars versificatoria* of Matthew of Vendôme and the *Poetria nova* and *Documentum de arte dictandi et versificandi* of Geoffrey of Vinsauf, which also contain much rhetorical lore, even though they are intended for the grammar curriculum.[33]

In spite of their rhetorical bias, the first six chapters include a good deal of prosodic material. Chapter 5 lists poetic blemishes including hiatus and the addition and subtraction of letters. Chapter 6 discusses case rhyme (*similiter cadens*), as in *sanus/probus*. True rhyme (*similiter desinens*) is said to be "what prompted the invention of leonines and syllabic verse."[34] It is disyllabic rhyme with like sounds in stressed syllables, as in *veni/leni* and *Maria/via*.

Rhythmic verse (*rithmus*, translated by Lawler as "rhymed poetry") is introduced in a passage stressing its relation to music: "*Rithmus* is a branch of the art of music. For music is divided into the cosmic, which embraces the internal harmony of the elements, the humane, which embraces the harmony and concord of the humours, and the instrumental, which embraces the concord evoked by instruments. This includes melody, quantitative verse, and *rithmus*."[35] The link acknowledged here between poetry and music is both historical and contemporary. As John of Garland himself has noted, high medieval poetry is influenced by the sequence, which is arranged in measures related to the melodies for which the poetry was originally composed.

Moving from the large subject of poetry and music to more specific topics, John of Garland takes up the relation between *rithmus* and rhyme: "The art of rhythmic poetry (*rithmica . . . ars*) is that which teaches how to compose a rhymed poem (*rithmum*)." A rhymed poem is a harmonious arrangement of words with like endings, "regulated not by quantity but by number of syllables."[36]

This is a concise and apparently adequate definition. The key element is "number of syllables." It "regulates" the poem. Rhyme is assumed—rhythmic art exists to teach how to compose rhyming poems—but it does not "regulate" the poems.

The quantitative terms "iambic" and "spondaic" are used for the "feet" (*pedes*) created in syllabic verse by ictus (*percussio*). The use of classical terminology for quite unclassical poetic strategies is confusing. In the first place, in John's system, a line has only one "foot"—the combination of accented and unaccented syllables at its end. The line derives its name from its terminal "foot," which is also its rhyme. The definition refers logically to lines that resemble those of a "prose" in having no fixed metrical pattern except at the end. However, John uses verses in accentual meters to illustrate the definition.

In the second place, John's metrical terms are themselves misleading. A foot created by an accent on the next-to-last syllable in a line is called "spondaic"—we would call it trochaic. *María* is spondaic in this system. The alternate type of foot, created by an accent on the third-to-last syllable, is called "iambic." *Caeléstia* is iambic. Although the last vowel (*a*) can be scanned as a weak syllable, we have already noted when discussing rhyme in the sequences that it can be "promoted" so that it, too, can have accent (*caeléstià*).[37]

A line can have anywhere from two to eight syllables, and lines can be rhymed in couplets or quatrains or in more complex ways. A "simple" poem is all in one "foot"; a "composite" (*compositus*) poem is a mixture of spondaic and iambic *rithmi* (here, "rhymes"). The ground rhythm of the poem is determined by the first line. According to John, alternation of the two-line forms enriches the music of the poem, producing *consonancia*—"consonance" or "harmony." This is not a vague general observation about "musicality." It is an observation derived from the fact that in the sequence a line with a given number of syllables is linked to a specific melody. To vary the number of syllables is to vary the melody. The observation anticipates and helps explain later French fondness for alternating masculine and feminine rhymes. Lines can also be considered half-lines, so that two six-syllable lines can be understood to produce a dodecasyllabic line, while combinations of four- and six-syllable lines can be understood to produce decasyllables.

Different types of line linked by rhyme into stanzas produce differing "proportions" (*proporciones*), a concept that is still current in renaissance discussions of stanza forms. The term refers to the variants of rhyme scheme that are mathematically possible for a given number of lines. A couplet has only one "proportion" (*a a b b* etc.). A quatrain has two proportions (*a b a b* and *a b b a*); the third possibility (*a a b b* etc.) is simply a couplet. A five-line stanza has seven proportions, and so forth.³⁸ John gives examples of eighteen (later nineteen) types of *rithmici*, ending with ten-syllable iambic, followed by sixteen "variations," and forty-four kinds of stanza, including stanzas with "tails" (*caudata*).

The chapter turns to quantitative forms. Leonine verses are in this category in spite of their use of rhyme. After a digression back to *rithmici* John reviews three "quantitative" forms used for hymns: Asclepiad, Sapphic, and iambic dimeter, the form of the Ambrosian hymns. The examples given follow quantitative metrical patterns but are accentual rather than quantitative and use rhyme. They are followed by a listing of the meters of Horace. The treatise ends with a list of the twenty-eight classical feet and forty-four different lines and variations on lines.

L'Art de Dictier

For anyone interested in English versification, the most important French treatise of the Middle Ages is Eustache Deschamps's *L'Art de dictier*, written in 1392.³⁹ Chaucer probably knew this treatise. Although it appeared too late to influence his style, it summarizes the concepts he absorbed from the French poetry that he imitated in his lyrics and in his octosyllabic and decasyllabic verse.

Since Deschamps is writing on vernacular poetry, he ignores the quantitative tradition. The distinctive feature of his treatise is that it begins with a review of the seven liberal arts. It is, in other words, touched by the medieval humanism that appeared in the twelfth century and continued to vie with scholasticism in thirteenth- and fourteenth-century France. Deschamps passes rapidly over grammar, rhetoric, and logic, the three areas to which poetry was most commonly related in medieval Latin treatises on poetry. Geometry and arithmetic receive more attention, and music is treated in some detail.

Like John of Garland, Deschamps stresses the link created by rhythm between music and poetry. The latter is "musique naturelle" in contrast to the former, which is "musique artificielle," the making of tunes. The distinction is based on the notion that poetry cannot be learned by someone who lacks a natural capacity for it, whereas music is made according to rules that can be summarized in an "art" and learned. Poetry is produced by the mouth rather than by instruments: "It is called 'natural' because it cannot be learned by a person unless he has a natural talent for it, and it is a verbal music that produces words in meter."[40]

Deschamps promises to explain the various types of poem, the nature of vowels and consonants, the art of writing in meter (*metrifiant*, by which he means syllabic poetry), rules for elision, types of rhyme, and the variety of ballades and other forms. The discussion of vowels and consonants recalls the *ars metrica* and has a similar aim. The letters determine the rules for elision. A review of poetic forms follows. Deschamps is not concerned with epithalamia, epitaphs, odes, elegies, and the like, but with ballades, rondeaux, cengles et doubles, chancons balladées, virelays, lays, and serventois.

The emphasis on ballade evidently represents the taste of the author. Deschamps wrote over a thousand of them with innumerable variations, many of which are listed and illustrated in the treatise: "balade de .VII. vers couppez," "balade de .IX. vers tout leonim," "balade equivoque, retrograde et leonim," and so forth. The emphasis is significant in view of the possibility that Chaucer derived rhyme royal from the ballade. Special attention is also given to the lay. It is created in paired stanzas (*couples*), with the form normally varying after each pair. A typical lay has twelve units, making twenty-four stanzas, and begins and ends with a unique stanza. The emphasis on duplication of units may be a heritage from the sequence.

The first example of a "balade" is in ten-syllable lines, but because of its end-word, the first line has "xi. piez." The next line has "dix piez," and the fifth is truncated (*coppé*). The use of the word "foot" to refer to syllables in the line (as in "dix piez") should be noted because it crops up in renaissance discussions of syllabic versification. Just as John of Garland advocates alternating "spondaic" and "iambic" lines, Deschamps favors mixing masculine and feminine rhyme and thus producing lines of regularly alternating length. The simplest form of rhyme is "consonans" (called "rime pauvre" by other authorities), meaning assonance, or vowel rhyme. "Sonante" is true rhyme based on like vowel sound followed by like consonant sound (*monde/onde*). Disyllabic rhyme is "Leonim" (of the form *dolente/presente; concepcion/ constellacion*). "Equivoque" (punning rhyme) is rhyme in which the same word or sound takes two different senses, as in *dolente/lente*. This type of rhyme is later equated by Deschamps with "rime riche," in which a single word has two meanings ("deus scens sur une diction").

RUDE AND BEGGERLY RYMING / 59

However, the usual meaning for "rime riche" is disyllabic rhyme. A device without precedent in the *Parisiana poetria* is the envoy, the short end-stanza, or reprise.

L'Art de dictier marks the dominant trend in French poetic theory from the time of its composition until the time of the Pléiade. In W. F. Patterson's words, "The treatises before 1544, the date of Jacques Peletier's *L'Art poétique d'Horace,* continue with but slight change the tradition of the fourteenth century."[41] The emphasis is on syllable count, rhyme, and stanza forms and their variations. During the period in question, a conventional terminology develops to describe the content of treatises on poetry. "First rhetoric" is rhetoric of the sort offered in the *Rhetorica ad Herennium* and Cicero's *De inventione*. It is the rhetoric of invention, arrangement, delivery, and, above all, style and the rhetorical figures. "Second rhetoric" (*seconde rhétorique*) deals with poetic techniques and is a vernacular equivalent of the *ars metrica*. When English poets between Chaucer and Wyatt looked to France, they encountered second rhetoric both as a theory and as the shaping element in the poetry of writers like Mellin de Saint-Gelais and Clément Marot.

A full survey of the prosodic theories of the second rhetoric is not by any means without interest for students of English poetry of the fifteenth century. Authors like Jacques Legrande, Jean Molinet, Regnaud Le Quex, and Pierre Le Fère offer many intriguing variations and refinements on the definitions offered by Deschamps. In general, they are more concerned than Deschamps with minutiae of syllable count, caesura, rhyme, and stanza and less with the relation between poetry and music. The memory occasionally surfaces, but as the name "second rhetoric" indicates, it is less important than the treatment of poetry as a verbal art. As we approach the sixteenth century, narrative forms are considered more fully. There is also a broadening of interest to include dramatic forms like morality play and farce, and in larger poetic concerns, including decorum. For present purposes, however, we will turn from Deschamps directly to the treatise that marks the decisive shift from medieval to renaissance prosodic concerns, the *Art poétique françoys* (1548) of Thomas Sebillet.

Sebillet's *Art poétique françoys* is the high point of second rhetoric and, at the same time, a decisive break from it.[42] It was not sufficiently decisive, however, to satisfy DuBellay, who made it the occasion for the first manifesto of the Pléiade, the *Deffence et illustration de la langue francoyse,* and its reputation has been adversely affected by this fact.

In spite of its bad press, the *Art poétique françoys* is the first critical treatise on French vernacular poetry with a pronounced classical flavor. It is indebted to Horace's *Ars poetica* and reflects the interest generated by the publication in 1544/45 of Jacques Peletier's version of that work.[43] The influence of Horace on French critical thought begins with the elaborately annotated Latin edition of the *Ars poetica* (1503) by Badius Ascensius and continues throughout the century. However, the *Art poétique* is the first French critical treatise to make Horace the basis of a comprehensive theory of poetry, even though its assimilation of Horace is imperfect; and it is the first French treatise to commingle the practical, down-to-earth attitudes of Horace with the exotic theories of Italian Neoplatonism about divine inspiration. Unlike their Italian counterparts, French sixteenth-century critics make little use of Aristotle's *Poetics*.

Sebillet begins with a Horatian distinction between poets and rhymers ("Poetes qui sont mieuz appeléz ainsi que rymeurs"). The passage recalls the old medieval distinction between learned and popular poetry. It is a rejection not of rhyming poetry, but of the concept of poems as elaborately rhymed trivialities shaped by the formulas of second rhetoric. It would be repeated by members of the Pléiade, with the implication that Sebillet is one of the rhymers. Sebillet's own answer to the sterile formalism of the rhymers is to turn to Plato and the idea that the poet is a visionary and prophet.

The body of Sebillet's work contains much that is conventional. Book 1 is specifically rhetorical and grammatical. It deals with invention, line forms by syllable count, rhyme, caesura, and orthography. Like Deschamps, Sebillet refers to syllable count with the term "foot" ("nombre de piedz"), but he also understands the difference between syllabic verse and "long and short times of syllables." Book 2 deals with stanza forms and genres. He understands that many medieval forms are dying or defunct—rondeau, for example, "belongs to the past" rather than the present. However, in several chapters he betrays a confused notion of the difference between classical and romance standards. Classical epigram (II, i) is equated with witty verses by Marot; ode (II, vi) is linked with chanson; Juvenal's satires are linked with the rough satirical form called "coc a l'âsne," a position ridiculed by DuBellay. Chapter 14 was especially irritating to the new generation of French poets. It treats the *Romance of the Rose* as a great literary work comparable to the epics of Homer and Vergil.[44]

Errors of judgment aside, Sebillet is a reasonable critic. He believes there are excellent French poets—especially Mellin de Saint-Gelais and Clément Marot. He insists the French language must seek its own forms of versification because it is different from Greek and Latin. He remains preoccupied, like his predecessors and successors, with metaplasm. The epic caesura is to be avoided at all times (I, vi), as is the "coupe feminine," which places a mute *e* just before the caesura and a vowel after it, thus inviting a slurring over of the pause.

Sebillet is interested in narrative as well as lyric forms. The decasyllabic line is still "héroïque" for Sebillet, but the Alexandrine is also well suited, in his opinion, for serious poetry: "It cannot be properly used except for very serious subjects, such as the ear finds weighty" (I, v). He takes note of French experiments with quantitative verse ("vers mesurés") but calls them "very strange in our French poetry." Blank verse is also noticed, only to be rejected. It is cold and spiritless, "like a corpse without blood or soul."[45]

When Sebillet reviews the genres of poetry in book 2, his weakness is painfully evident. The basic problem is an indiscriminate mingling of medieval and classical forms. Although he has read his Horace, he seems unaware that a cultural revolution has occurred and that as a result, criticism must recognize two distinct bodies of poetry, each with unique rules and aesthetic standards. Instead, he mixes medieval and ancient forms as though they were variant offshoots of a single tradition. This is why he can compare chanson and ode and the *Romance of the Rose* and the *Aeneid,* and why he considers medieval morality plays more or less equivalent to classical tragedies. His failure to recognize cultural change probably was as infuriating to DuBellay as his admiration of the much-maligned Clément Marot.

Sebillet's list of genres begins with epigram defined as a short, pointed poem in verse. It then moves to sonnet and then back to standard French forms: rondeau, ballade, chant royal, chanson. Next, it considers classical forms—verse epistle, elegy, and eclogue—and then tragedy, which is equated with morality plays: "The French morality play is in certain respects equivalent to Greek and Latin tragedy in that it treats serious actions and princes."[46] The morality play is also like farce, only graver. An apparent classical reminiscence enters the comment on morality play dialogue. It is often written in prose by the moderns because prose is close to speech. Sebillet may be influenced here by Italian experiments in prose comedy. If so, he has a somewhat hazy concept of performance, which he seems to equate with recitation: "The excellent composers of that sort of comedy, wishing verse to have the liberty of speech and the decorum of certain phrases, loved much better to recite their comedies in elegant prose (in order better to express their purpose and meaning) than to subject themselves to [the restraints of] rhythm [= 'rhyme']."⁴⁷

On the subject of epic Sebillet stresses the need to improve the French language by translation (II, xiv) and mentions as illustrations Salel's *Iliad* (1545) and Peletier's *Odyssey* (1547). Ovid's *Metamorphoses*, translated by Marot in 1533, is also considered "epic." In short, Sebillet is informed but indiscriminate. He is unable to fully assimilate cultural changes that were already well advanced as he was writing his essay.

THE PLÉIADE AND THE REJECTION OF MEDIEVAL TRADITION

After Sebillet, we enter the flood tide of humanistic poetics. The motive of reforming the language so that it will be adequate to support an enlarged and elevated culture is the foundation of Joachim Du-Bellay's *Deffence et illustration de la langue francoyse* (1549).⁴⁸ This work is in part a manifesto written in haste to distinguish the point of view of the "new poets" of the Pléiade from that of Sebillet and in part an assertion that the French vernacular has come of age. Much of Du-Bellay's discussion of language is drawn from the *Dialogo delle lingue* of Sperone Speroni and is thus a French outcropping of the Italian debate about the "question of language." However, DuBellay is not advocating subservience to Italian culture. As Franco Simone has pointed out, he is a nationalist interested in advancing the cause of French culture against the claims of Italian culture.⁴⁹ Moreover, he is by no means wholly dependent on Italian critical theory. Among the other sources on which he relies, the *Ars poetica* looms large.

DuBellay was tutored by the eminent Greek scholar Jean Dorat. He knows that a fundamental change has occurred in the way the French understand their cultural heritage. There are two bodies of literature. Far from being complementary, they are antithetical. One announces the exhaustion of a tradition and the other a future that is being created even as he writes.

DuBellay accepts the difference between French and the ancient languages, but he rejects the traditional romance forms and with them the work of most of his predecessors. The famous advice that begins book 2, chapter 4, comes with an echo of Horace's advice to the Pisos (*A.P.*, 268–69) about studying Greek sources: "Read and reread first of all (O future poet) and handle lovingly, night and day, the Greek and Latin exemplars; and leave aside all those old French poets to the games of Tolouse and the contest of Rouen—such as rondeaux, ballades, virelays, chants royal, chansons, and other such groceries, which corrupt the taste of our language and serve no purpose except to advertise our ignorance." [50]

In place of trivialized forms inherited from the Middle Ages, there are the great ancient genres—epigram, elegy, verse epistle, satire, ode, eclogue, tragedy, comedy. The French can also adopt forms that have been perfected by the Italians, most notably for DuBellay and Ronsard, the sonnet.[51] Finally, there is the epic (II, v). French poets can use the stories of Lancelot or Tristan as subject matter since Vergil used legendary Roman history for the *Aeneid;* but they must achieve true epic elevation so the result will be "for their immortal glory, the honor of France, and the great improvement of our language." The advice is interesting because it so emphatically distinguishes between subject matter and style. True elevation is a matter not of the poet's historical or legendary sources but of the verse forms he selects and the devices used to make them ornate.

The later chapters of the *Deffence* are devoted to language proper. DuBellay argues that the French language needs to be enriched by new words, that it must use more complex and sinuous constructions based (ch. 9) on Greek and Latin, and that it must cultivate rhetorical embellishment. Antonomasia (using the attribute for the thing, as in "virgin huntress" for Diana) is especially recommended. Rhyme is acceptable to DuBellay. He considers it an ornament of French verse as pleasing aesthetically as quantity in classical verse. It falls within the French equivalent of the ideal of *Latinitas,* and it should be cultivated. He rejects équivoque rhyme as affectation, and he notes that Luigi Alamanni uses unrhymed verse with success. Perhaps French is capable of a similar form.[52]

The *Deffence* is a strong and partisan argument for the new poetry. The *Art poétique* of Jacques Peletier (1555) is more moderate and more comprehensive.[53] Peletier had published an important version of Horace in 1544/45. As we have seen, it influenced Sebillet. At about the same time, he met Ronsard and DuBellay and later received the dedication of DuBellay's sonnet sequence *L'Olive* (1549). He was also an advocate, like Jean-Antoine de Baïf, of reformed spelling and—incidentally for our purposes—a mathematician.

His *Art poétique* is a balanced treatment of the subject, although its commitment to the program of the Pléiade is unequivocal. Book 1 discusses general topics: the divine origin of poetry, the dignity of the poet, art versus nature, poetry and rhetoric, imitation. Most of these topics had been treated by Sebillet and DuBellay, but they were still novel, and Peletier's discussion is more thoughtful than that of his predecessors.

Book 2 begins with material familiar to second rhetoric. Chapter 1 deals with rhyme, which it approves. Chapter 2 treats French verse forms, classifying them in the usual way by the number of syllables in the line. Peletier anticipates the future triumph of the Alexandrine. Although it is "fort rare," it is better suited to heroic subjects than the decasyllabic line. An emphatic shift occurs as Peletier turns from romance forms to the new classical forms, which he calls simply "the genres" (*genres d'ecriere*). They include epigram, sonnet, ode, elegy, and the rest. When discussing comedy, Peletier suggests, as Sebillet had done before him, that the French equivalent of ancient drama (in this case, comedy rather than tragedy) is the morality play. This is a curious exception to the understanding shown elsewhere in the essay of the classical genres and doubtless reflects the lag in the development of drama in France when contrasted to Italy or England. The book ends with a discussion of poetic license and a peroration on the nobility of poetry.

Ronsard's *Abbregé de l'art poétique françois,* published anonymously in 1565, is in some ways a companion piece to Peletier's *Art*.[54] Its motto is from Horace's *Ars poetica:* "Scribendi recte sapere est et principium et fons." Ronsard mentions Aristotle when considering "poetry in general," but his treatise is innocent of the theories of the *Poetics*. He agrees with Horace on the subjects of imitation, the greatness of the ancients, and such specifics as the need to avoid "fantastic inventions," to revise constantly, to being *in medias res,* and the like. The *Abbregé* is more moderate than DuBellay's *Deffence* in that it deals with the medieval heritage by polite neglect rather than scornful rejection. It also devotes considerable attention to details of versifying in the French language, and while so doing, it touches on many subjects that were dealt with in treatises of second rhetoric, among these, rhyme, alternating masculine and feminine rhyme, and the poetic treatment of mute *e*.

Ronsard praises the Alexandrine. The decasyllable is "vers commun." It was used by "les vieux poëtes françois," and modern poets are advised to amuse themselves with it prior to going on to the Alexandrine. Ronsard claims to have "mis en honneur" the Alexandrine—that is, to have been the first French poet to recognize its full potential. He devotes a section of the *Abbregé* ("Des vers Alexandrins") to proving that "Alexandrines have the place in our language of heroic verse among the Greeks and Latins."

A debt to the *ars metrica* tradition, probably via Horace, is evident in Ronsard's association of form with genre. This is evident from his use of the term *altiloque* (high-sounding), which is simply a transliteration from Latin, to describe the form: "The composition of the Alexandrine should be very grave, elevated, and (so to speak) high-sounding." Ronsard does not follow up the implications of "composition" and "high-sounding" by reviewing Latin prescriptions for elevated syntax, nor does he consider the prescriptions of Latin rhetoric for the grand style. He does, however, observe that since the Alexandrine can sound like prose if not handled well, it needs rich ornamentation through vocabulary and "very rich rhyme" (*ryme assez riche*).[55]

In the *Abbregé*, "vers commun," the decasyllabic, is the French equivalent of ancient elegy. A poet should try such verse before going on to more serious forms. As for prosody pure and simple, epic caesura is not permitted, and sense should, in general, coincide with natural verse units. Alternation of masculine and feminine rhyme is encouraged on the basis of ancient precedent and also because its musicality complements the ancient association of poetry with music: "Make your verses [alternately] masculine and feminine as far as possible, in order to agree more with music and the concord of instruments by whose favor it seems Poetry was born, since Poetry is not agreeable without instruments or the grace of one or more voices."[56]

Ronsard used the Alexandrine with great success in his *Hymnes* (1555), but (as he admits in the *Abbregé*) he did not use it for the *Franciade*. In a preface to the *Franciade* issued posthumously in 1587, he explains that in his youthful enthusiasm he overpraised the Alexandrine, equating it with both heroic verse and the *senarius* of tragedy: "In my youth, out of ignorance, I thought [Alexandrines] held in our language the status of heroic verses, considering them—although they correspond more to the *senarii* of Tragedy than to the magnanimous verse of Homer and of Vergil—better suited to magnificent arguments [i.e., subjects] and the most splendid spiritual conceptions than the decasyllabic line."[57] He now realizes that they are too prosy, too "enervated and flaccid," and that they baffle readers because of their excessive length. The discussion broadens out into a remarkably thorough review of the requirements of epic, illustrated by copious quotations from Vergil. In the course of the discussion he warns against aping Latin syntax, since French depends on word order for its clarity, and he retracts his earlier reservations about the use of enjambment—Vergil used it to grand effect, and so can the French.

Ronsard's interest in the relation between poetry and music is important, complex, and well recognized by Ronsard scholars. It occurs in the context of a renewed interest in ancient music and the Platonic doctrine of *musica mundana* and the sympathetic emotional force of ancient musical modes. It is therefore more philosophical and more self-consciously "classical" than the older tradition. It is not, however, less practical. Ronsard was an accomplished musician and was fascinated by the beauty of the human voice singing a melody or expressing the melodic qualities of verse in speech.

REACTIONS: TRADITION AND RADICAL CHANGE

Shortly after its publication, DuBellay's *Deffence* was attacked in an anonymous critique, the *Quintil Horatian* (1550), now known to be the work of Barthelémy Aneau (1500?–60), friend of Marot and professor of rhetoric at Lyons.[58] Aneau criticizes DuBellay's flat rejection of the French literary past. To DuBellay's scorn for older French authors the *Quintil* replies, "You make a grievous error in accusing most ungraciously the ignorance of our elders which in your ninth chapter you less rudely call 'simplicity.' But our ancestors certainly were neither simple nor ignorant, either of things or of words."[59] The critique is political as well as aesthetic. DuBellay has turned his back on the national heritage.

In one sense the point is valid. The classical ideal is international, even though it may be expressed in a vernacular language. Since the fall of Rome, Corydon and Phyllis, Aeneas and Dido, and Mars and Venus have belonged to all cultures and all ages equally. Therefore they cannot belong to any specific culture or express its unique values. In another sense, however, the critique is unjust. DuBellay wants to enrich French culture. He is a nationalist and a modern. When he contemplates the ruins of Rome, he knows its glory is past. It has become an "other" to be mourned or idealized but not recovered. The moderns of the Renaissance are condemned—or privileged—to make their own worlds in what Thomas Greene has called their "historical solitude." However, this does not mean they can ignore the ancients. Ancient ideals, expressed movingly in a noble style, can be revived in France if French poets can learn the secrets of that style.

The conflict between the medieval and the classical aesthetic continued in the following decades. The *Quintil* looks forward to Etienne Pasquier's *Recherches de la France* (1560–1611), a collection of essays on the history and literature of the French people.[60] Although Pasquier believed Ronsard to be the premier French poet, "à qui la France fait hommage," in the course of his work, he praises the Troubadours and French writers like Guillaume de Lorris and Jean de Meun, and he extends the favorable review to the much-despised poets of the fourteenth and fifteenth centuries. In Book 8 he includes an appreciation of the French farce *Maître Pathelin*. Pasquier, and also Jean Vaquelin de la Fresnaye, whose *Art poétique* (1574) draws on Pasquier for some of its insights into French medieval literature, were on the losing side of the argument. After the turn of the sixteenth century, French poetry would be resolutely classical and rationalist along the lines defined by Malherbe.

At the opposite pole from Pasquier and Vaquelin stand Jacques de la Taille and Jean-Antoine de Baïf. Both writers are interested in imitating not only the genres of classical poetry but their quantitative meters as well.

W. F. Patterson has argued that the chief impulse behind their hard-edged classicism was the *Poetices libri septem* of Julius Caesar Scaliger (1561).[61] Scaliger's work was enormously influential throughout Europe and deserves much of the credit—if credit is the right word—for creating the mix of Horace, Aristotle, and rhetorical criticism that is the foundation of neoclassic practical criticism.

Scaliger takes two positions that are important for the history of prosody. In the first place, he lends his considerable prestige to the idea that the defining characteristic of poetry is verse, the idea at the center of the *ars metrica*. His *Poetices* begins with a definition of poetry: "The name 'poet' does not come from 'feigning' (*fingendo*) (as many believe) in the sense that poets create fictions, but from 'making' (*faciendo*) verses."[62] The assertion that poetry is not "feigning" is a rejection of the theory of poetry as "making of fictions" advocated by renaissance students of Aristotle's *Poetics*. By the same token, the linking of poetry with "making verses" reasserts the supremacy of the *ars metrica*. Scaliger follows out the implication of his definition by dividing poetry into its material and its formal cause. The material cause is discussed in book 2 ("*Hyle*"), which is simply three chapters of generalization followed by fifty-four chapters in which classical prosody is explained.

In the second place, nowhere in the *Poetices* is the romance tradition recognized, and nowhere are its rules and conventions described. For Scaliger it is invisible; it does not exist.

Given Scaliger's classicism and his emphasis on *ars metrica* concepts and formulas, it is not surprising that several poets began asking whether French could not be reshaped in the image of Greek and Latin. Had not the Romans reshaped their language in the image of Greek? It was a question asked in Italy and England as well as France. The Pléiade had renewed many of the ancient genres, but was that enough?

Jacques de la Taille's *La maniere de faire des vers en françois, comme en grec et en latin* (1573) concludes that French poetry is "completely degraded and bastardized by slavish imitators."[63] The path of reform is to abandon rhyme for quantitative verse—"vers mesurés a l'antiquité"—and de la Taille provides an elaborate set of rules for creating such verse. His treatise begins with position, accent, vowel quantity, and consonants, and continues with a description of the standard metrical feet. The concluding section reviews various kinds of metaplasm. The rules need not detain us—they are the French equivalent of rules for quantitative verse devised in many other European countries in the sixteenth century. De la Taille offers them so poets will have an alternative to the verse forms of popular literature and of the school of Clément Marot: "Morality plays, ballades, farces, chants royal, rondeaux, lais, virelais, Coqs à l'Ane, and all these rhyming trivialities."[64]

The high point of the French quantitative movement is the *Etrenes de poézie fransoeze an vers mesurés* (1574) by Jean-Antoine de Baïf. Baïf, who shared Jean Dorat as a tutor with DuBellay, experimented with "vers mesurés" and composed chansons in quantitative meter. Like his friend Ronsard—and also like Thomas Campion in England—he was a musician as well as a poet. He was convinced there is a close relation between classical meters and music that cannot be duplicated by rhyming poetry. His "vers mesurés" are in French quantitative meter on the lines advocated by de la Taille. Their two distinguishing features are that they use a reformed spelling intended to make their phonetic principles clear, and that they are composed to bring out the musicality of the words. Following a tradition that is also recalled by de la Taille in his *Maniere*,[65] Baïf decided that the Psalms were originally in meter and translated them into "vers mesurés."

Baïf and the musician Joachim Thibault de Courville founded an Académie de Poesie et de Musique in 1571. Parallel to Baïf's academy was the Camerata of Florence, which took an intense interest in the relation between music and words sung (or recited) by a single voice.[66]

The translations made by Wyatt of poems by Marot and Mellin de Saint-Gelais and Grimald's translation of Theodore Beza's Latin poem on the death of Cicero show that English writers of the age of Henry VIII were interested in developments in France. However, in the first half of the sixteenth century, French vernacular poetry was still dominated by second rhetoric. It offered few lessons that English poets could not learn from their own native tradition. This was not the case in the second half of the century. After the emergence of the Pléiade, English poets are increasingly aware of French critical theory and increasingly interested in the work of contemporary French poets.

CHAPTER IV

A Question of Language: Italy and the Shaping of Renaissance Prosodic Theory

Vernacular Eloquence

The greatest medieval treatise on vernacular poetry is not French but Italian. It is Dante's *De vulgari eloquentia* (ca. 1305). The *De vulgari* is written in Latin, but its subject is the Italian language and the verse forms appropriate to various kinds of expression in that language. The first printed edition of the *De vulgari* was a translation from Latin into Italian issued in Venice in 1529 by Giangiorgio Trissino. The work was not published in Latin until 1577, and then in France rather than Italy.[1]

Trissino's edition was published less out of piety toward Dante than out of interest in the debates about language of the first quarter of the Cinquecento. The debates initially centered on the value of the vernacular in comparison to Latin. However, they soon moved to the questions reviewed by Dante in book 1 of the *De vulgari*. Should "Italian" be a synthesis of all regional dialects (Dante's solution), or should it be "Tuscan" or "Florentine" or something else? As the debates continued they moved into areas considered by Dante in book 2. What is the source of literary greatness? Can vernacular poetry achieve the elevation of ancient poetry? If "imitation" is the solution to the problem, how should one go about imitating? A new element was added by the prestige of the poets of the Trecento—especially Petrarch—in the early sixteenth century. Should Italian poets imitate their great ancestors? Is the terza rima of the *Divine Comedy* a proper narrative form? Can the rhymed eleven-syllable (hendecasyllabic) verse of the

Divine Comedy and Petrarch's sonnets be adapted to the needs of unrhymed verse (*versi sciolti*)? Are the sonnet and the canzone proper lyric forms?

It is uncertain today whether Dante undertook the *De vulgari* as preparation for writing the *Divine Comedy* or to review Italian literary forms or out of patriotism. Whatever the case, his ideas were directly relevant in the atmosphere of national ferment and literary experiment that characterized the first half of the Cinquecento. Trissino underscored their relevance by dedicating his translation to Cardinal Ippolito de'Medici, well known for his interest in the question of language, and later a patron of experiments in *versi sciolti* and quantitative meters.[2]

At the beginning of the *De vulgari* Dante asserts his originality: "I have not found anyone before me who has treated the question of vernacular eloquence." He admits, however, at the end of this sentence that he will draw ideas "not only from my own genius but also accepting and drawing from others."[3] Dante is obviously well grounded in both the *ars metrica* and the *ars rithmica*. He also used Horace's *Ars poetica* and the *Rhetorica ad Herennium*. He appears to have known the *Parisiana poetria* of John of Garland and one or more minor essays on Troubadour poetry, and he drew on the *Tesor* of Brunetto Latini.[4]

In the *De vulgari,* as in the *ars metrica* tradition, poetry is defined as language in verse, and Italian poets are "those who versify in the vernacular." Dante reviews the nature and forms of syllabic versification and the lines (by numbers of syllables), rhyme schemes, and stanzas that it generates. Given Dante's subject, the emphasis falls naturally on forms used by the Troubadours and the *stilnovisti*. In this respect the *De vulgari* resembles the French treatises on rhyming poetry examined in the last chapter. Dante also shows his awareness of romance tradition through heavy emphasis in book 2 on the close relations between music and poetry. The debt of the *De vulgari* to the musical poetics (*ars rithmica*) of the Middle Ages has been thoroughly reviewed by Mario Pazzaglia.[5]

On the other hand, Dante is fully justified in his claim to originality. The *De vulgari* is not a compilation of material from earlier treatises like the medieval *artes poeticae* collected by Edmond Faral or a handbook of literary forms like the *Summa artis rithmici* (1332) by Antonio da Tempo.[6] It is an analytical treatise, and it has the originality of perspective that characterizes all of Dante's work. The originality is announced by the bold claim in its opening chapter that the vernacular is not merely acceptable but is nobler than "grammatical" language simply because it is "natural"—"naturalis est nobis."

If the work is compared to French treatises on poetry, the obvious source of Dante's originality is his analysis of the rhetorical basis of poetry. Roger Dragonetti remarks that the *De vulgari* is distinguished from the French works by its effort to formulate "a technique of verbal orchestration more refined than that of the traditional lyric."[7] Pazzaglia is more precise. He speaks of a "syntactic-architectural ideal" and concludes that "the original and distinctive feature of the *De vulgari eloquentia* is syntax in the double sense of articulation of discourse . . . and organization of the stanza."[8] As these comments suggest, construction is a central concept in Dante's work.

Book 1 of the *De vulgari* is a survey of Italian dialects intended to define the proper language—"illustrious, cardinal, courtly, and curial"—for the Italian poet.

Book 2 is devoted to literature per se. It begins with a review of the triple decorum of poetry that recalls the "wheel of Vergil." The poet must, in the first place, be equal in both talent and learning to the task he has undertaken. Second (ch. 2), he must choose a proper subject. The subjects worthy of the highest kind of poetry are love, virtue, and arms, although Dante knows of no Italian poet who has treated the latter subject. Third (ch. 3), the form of the poem must be fitting. For the highest subjects, the canzone is the only adequate vernacular form. It needs only itself, whereas the chief competing form, the ballad, needs "dancers to keep time." The comment strikes the modern reader as odd, but it is a reminder that in spite of his originality, Dante is a medieval author for whom etymology remains an important category of thought.

Chapter 4 turns to practical matters. Great poets write "according to rules." These are the Latin poets who have an established metrical system. Vernacular poets have no such rules and normally write by "chance" (*casu*), meaning something like "instinct." They can, however, improve this situation by imitating the ancient poets. There is the germ here of the theory of imitation that would be so extensively developed by Petrarch. It is significant because Dante offers not a bland injunction to imitate, but specific prescriptions on how to go about imitating.

There are three styles—the low (elegy; *stylum miserorum*), the low-middle (comedy), and the high (tragedy). The doctrine is familiar. As in the *Rhetorica ad Herennium*, each style is associated with specific qualities. Poetic lines in the tragic mode should be "proud," meaning that they should be varied but should favor the hendecasyllabic, the most elevated of all Italian lines. A special virtue of the tragic line is its hospitality to complex constructions and noble words. Canzoni use many different line lengths, but the hendecasyllable is the most excellent: "It seems the most elevated of all [lines] . . . both for its duration and for its hospitality to aphorisms, constructions, and [ornamental] words." The comment is technical: "constructions" refers to syntax—specifically, the figures of diction.

The *Divine Comedy* uses the hendecasyllabic line exclusively, and unrhymed hendecasyllabics are *versi sciolti*. These observations help to explain why, quite aside from its celebration of the vernacular, Dante's analysis appealed to sixteenth-century Italian poets. It appears to anticipate their own equation of hendecasyllabic verse with ancient heroic and dramatic verse. In fact, both Dante and the poets of the Cinquecento have a point. The hendecasyllable is more flexible than the French decasyllable because of its lack of a mandatory strong caesura and its tolerance for enjambment.[9] This is another way of saying that it is more hospitable to fluid—hence Latinate—constructions than French verse. Dante both understands the potential of the form and anticipates its uses in the Cinquecento.

The theory of construction is invoked again in relation to style. It is defined (after Priscian) as "a joining together of words" and divided into the simple requirement of grammatical agreement and the more complex requirement of a construction "filled with urbanity" (*urbanitas*). Such construction produces three virtues of style. A style without it—illustrated by the plain vocabulary and syntax of "Petrus amat multum dominam Bertam"—is "insipid" (*insipidus*). The first virtue of a refined style is "savor" (*sapor*), which comes from the use of artificial rather than natural word order. Savor arises from the use of figures of diction to create pleasing departures from standard syntax and to ornament the sentence with the terminal rhythms of the *cursus*.[10] The second virtue is "charm" (*venustas*), which arises from figurative language such as personification and simile. The third is "elevation" (*elevatio*), which arises from an ornamental and elevated vocabulary. The aesthetic aspects of vocabulary, including the sounds associated with different kinds of words and the effects of various phonetic combinations, are outlined in the following chapter (ch. 7).

Of special interest at this point in the *De vulgari* is a list of eleven poems that illustrate various aspects of construction. They cannot be analyzed here, but the precision of Dante's system can readily be demonstrated. The second stanza of the first poem ("Si per non . . ."), for example, is sixteen lines neatly divided six/ten into two periodic sentences. Similar adjustments of syntax to rhyme scheme and to the "turn" (*volta*) between the first and second major units of the poem are found in the other poems cited. Figurative language ("charm") is also common, though, in general, the vocabulary seems less "elevated" than one would expect from Dante's comments on the subject. Perhaps this is because the poems are all love lyrics. At the end of the discussion of construction, Dante cites ancient writers who are proper guides to the art. Half are poets—Vergil, Ovid, Statius, Lucan—but half are prose writers—Livy, Pliny, Frontinus, Orosius. The list is a reminder that construction is an art halfway between prose and poetry and applies equally to both.

The later chapters (II, x–xiv) discuss the forms of stanza, line, and rhyme. The emphasis is on structural elements. These elements complement the poem's construction in ways that are illustrated by Dante's eleven-poem anthology. The basic unit is the stanza (*stantia*), which is "a mansion or receptacle able to contain all art" (II, ix, 2). The stanza may (but need not) have a *diesis,* that is, a "turn" (Italian, *volta*). Here there are obvious memories of the relation between romance prosody and musical form. Dante equates the *diesis* with a change of melody, because the meter (i.e., the syllable count of the lines) changes. We recall the similar behavior of the verbal units of the early Latin sequence, and of the precedence in this tradition of melody over text.[11] A change in melody results in a change in the form of the text. In an artful poem the "turn" in the stanza will therefore be complemented by a turn in thought.

Dante explains that *diesis* separates the introductory section (*frons*) of the canzone from the concluding section (*cauda* or *sirma*). If a rhyme scheme is repeated in the first section, making it bipartite, the repeated units are called "feet" (*pedes*). The term is potentially confusing because a "foot" in Dante's sense is not a metrical foot like an iambus but one or more lines taken as a unit. One recalls the equation of the line with the meter of the final "foot" in the *Parisiana poetria*. Dante remarks that in Latin verse the line is made up of feet, while in romance verse the feet are made up of lines (II, xi, 12). If units are repeated after the *diesis,* they are called *versus.* An alternate form, illustrated by Arnault Daniel's poem in hendecasyllabic lines "Sols sui qui sai . . . ," is unrhymed. Although medieval unrhymed hendecasyllabics are sometimes considered forerunners of renaissance *versi sciolti*, they do not involve conscious imitation of classical verse forms and should therefore probably be considered a different species.

The Heritage of the Trecento

Consideration of Dante has already brought us from the Trecento to the early Cinquecento. The transition is less abrupt than it may seem in the abstract. Although several minor treatises on Italian vernacular poetry and one major one (the *Summa* of Antonio da Tempo) were written after Dante, the main emphasis of Quattrocento poetics was on Latin rather than the vernacular, and on philosophic questions about poetic art rather than the *ars metrica*.[12] Lorenzo de'Medici, Poliziano, Serafino Aquilano, and Ariosto showed that brilliant vernacular poetry could be written, but the poetry lacked a sophisticated critical rationale. Conversely, in the Cinquecento, the ideas about the vernacular introduced in the *De vulgari* are suddenly and dramatically pushed to the forefront of Italian critical thought.

The question of language ranged Latinists generally against advocates of the vernacular; but at its center was the question raised by Dante: given the variety of Italian dialects, what should be considered the official vernacular, the language to be used by the poets who would forge the new national consciousness?[13] Machiavelli, Pietro Bembo, Benedetto Varchi, and Giambattista Gelli argued in favor of the Florentine dialect. Was it not the dialect of Petrarch and Boccaccio? Muzio, Castiglione, and Trissino followed Dante, arguing for an eclectic language—"courtly Italian"—drawing on all of the better Italian usages. Claudio Tolomei and Lodovico Dolce take a compromise position in favor of "Tuscan," which is a broader dialect than Florentine but not as comprehensive as "Italian."[14] One result of this analysis of language was a renewal of interest in the poetic forms used by Dante, Petrarch, and other poets of the Trecento. Another was the creation of a series of dictionaries of Italian (1535, 1536, 1543, and 1546). Yet another, anticipating *Finnegans Wake* by four centuries, was the surrealistic pastiche language invented by Teofilo Folengo for the successive versions, each retitled, of *Baldus* (1517–52).

In terms of date of composition, Baldessar Castiglione's *Book of the Courtier* was an early contribution to the question of language, since the first draft was composed around 1515. However, for various reasons, including a compulsion to revise, Castiglione delayed publication until 1528, a year before his death.

The first decisive published contribution to the question of language, and the most important treatment of the century, is Pietro Bembo's *Prose della volgar lingua* (1525). In this dialogue Bembo speaks through the mask of his brother Carlo. On the one hand, Bembo is a liberal: Latin no longer meets the needs of Italian letters, and Italians must use their native language. On the other, however, he is a conservative: Italians cannot simply use the language custom has provided for them; they must establish models of linguistic purity and formal excellence and must imitate these models in the same way that those seeking to write elegant Latin must imitate Cicero. Petrarch and Boccaccio are Bembo's models for Italian letters. Not only must they be imitated, but the Florentine dialect in which they wrote must be considered the literary language of Italy. Bembo recognizes Dante's greatness, but Dante lived before the dawn of humanism. He is politely ignored.

Defending Petrarch and Boccaccio involves Bembo in two difficulties. Proposing Florentine as the standard literary language means rejecting the more generalized "courtly Italian" advocated by Dante. This amounts to claiming Florentine hegemony in matters of language. The claim may have seemed proper to Florentines, but it irritated citizens of other city-states. Second, Bembo advocates what he himself (in the person of Carlo) recognizes is a vernacular equivalent of Latin Ciceronianism. Petrarch and Boccaccio must be followed in all things. Yet they use many archaic words and constructions that are corrupt or unknown outside of Florence. Moreover, many words have entered the Italian vocabulary since they wrote. If they are followed in all things, literary Italian will become as artificial as Ciceronian Latin. Dictionaries will have to be made of approved words and usages. Terms invented long ago by Varro to describe *Latinitas* gain new currency in this debate. Current habits will have to be changed, and "use" (i.e., usage) and "custom" will have to yield to "authority." Bembo was willing to accept the implications of this position, and his own *rime* are careful imitations of Petrarch.[15]

Trissino deeply admired Bembo, but he followed the lead of Dante and Castiglione. His three central statements on the subject all appeared in 1529. The first, his translation of the *De vulgari*, has already been considered. The second is his dialogue *Il Castellano*, which defines the ideal language as "courtly" (*lingua cortegiana*). The term means "language as spoken at noble courts" or the "language used by good courtiers" or simply "cultivated language." It is derived ultimately from Dante but most immediately from Castiglione's *Book of the Courtier*. It establishes the ideal of a national language drawing on all dialects and emphasizing current usage rather than being restricted to a language already two centuries old.

The third is the *Poetica*, which is essentially an analysis of the versification and verse forms used by the poets of the Trecento. Its apparent conservatism is, however, misleading. It is not an eclectic summary of all recognized verse forms in the manner of Antonio da Tempo's *Summa*. Rather, it is a selective discussion of a few forms, with heavy emphasis on those used by Petrarch and Boccaccio. In this respect it complements Bembo's call for a return to the Italian poetry of the Trecento. In another respect, however, it goes beyond Bembo. Trissino believes that Italian needs to develop new verse forms. He promises in the *Poetica* to supplement the sections on Italian forms with two sections (not published, however, until the 1560s) on the great classical genres.[16]

Language reform seemed to certain other critics to require Italian quantitative verse, while still others felt that Italian poetry could safely go its own way. In their later phase, the debates between the advocates of traditional Italian prosody and the classicists merged with debates about the merits (or demerits) of Dante and the Gothic imagination and of Ariosto and medieval romance. The question of language also gave rise to debate about dialect words, archaisms, and neologisms, and to questions as to whether, in language, "authority" or "art" or "custom" should determine usage. Inevitably, spelling became an issue. Trissino believed that reform of language requires the reform of spelling, and eccentric spellings, including the use of the Greek omega, make Cinquecento editions of his books look extremely odd.

All of the theories about language reform found in French and English criticism of the sixteenth century are found first in Italy, with two reservations. In the first place, the Italian arguments are sometimes more sophisticated and almost always more fully elaborated. In the second, the Italians were attempting to create a unified culture on the basis of a common—or more or less common—language while they were divided politically and subject to divisive foreign pressures. The issues were further complicated by rivalry among the city-states. France and England were already unified politically, and in spite of the continued importance of dialects, both had established standard national languages by the time they began to consider the questions raised in the Italian debates. The political aspects of the question of language therefore had a greater sense of urgency and cut deeper in Italy than in France or England.

COURTLY VERNACULAR AND RATIONAL SPEECH

A substantial introduction to the question of language was accessible to sixteenth-century English readers in Sir Thomas Hoby's translation of Castiglione's *Courtier* (1561). Castiglione's spokesman in book 1 is Count Lodovico of Canossa. "Count Lewis," as he is called in Hoby's translation, advocates "courtly language," but he argues against equating it with the language of Petrarch and Boccaccio. Florentine is only a dialect, and many Trecento words have become archaic or precious. The position is directly contrary to that taken by Bembo. Castiglione summarizes the case for an eclectic "courtly language" in a dedication to Bishop Michel de Silva. In Hoby's translation:

> It was not meete I should have used many [words] that are in Boccaccio. . . . Neyther would I binde my self to the maner of the Tuscane tunge in use now a dayes, bicause the Practicing emonge sundrye Nations, hath alwayes bene of force to transport frome one to an other . . . new woordes, which afterward remaine or decaye, according as they are admitted by custome or refused . . . and bicause (in mine opinion) the kinde of speache of other noble Cities in Italy . . . ought not altogether to be neglected for the woordes which in these places are used in commune speach. . . . Besides this in Tuscane they use many woordes cleane corrupte from the Latin, the which in Lumbardye and in the other partes of Italy remaine wholl and without any chaunge at al. . . . assuredly as it may be called a rash presumption to take in hand to forge new wordes, or set up the olde in spite of custome: so it is no lesse, to take in hande against the force of the same custome to bring to naught and (as it were) to burye alive such as have lasted nowe many yeares.[17]

One other treatise on the subject of language should be mentioned because it brings together the opposing views and sets the stage for a debate that would intensify at the end of the sixteenth century. Sperone Speroni's *Dialogo delle lingue* (1542)[18] has four major speakers. Lazaro Bonamico argues that Latin is the only language suited to noble subjects because it is timeless and universal and is the language of the greatest writers. Rome owes more, he says, to Cicero than to Caesar. Bembo disagrees: the vernacular is potentially just as noble as Latin and provides excellent models for modern writers. The supreme models are, of course, Petrarch and Boccaccio. The problem is that

Bembo's position is antiquarian. The third important speaker is called simply "Cortegiano." He is obviously Castiglione, but he apparently also represents Speroni's point of view. "Cortegiano" favors "courtly language." Such a language must avoid archaisms, be current and readily understood, be national rather than a dialect, and be hospitable to new words.

In general, Speroni agrees with "Cortegiano," but he had been deeply impressed while a student at Bologna by the philosopher and freethinker Pietro Pomponazzi. The fourth important speaker in the dialogue is a "scholar" who summarizes Pomponazzi's thoughts on language. They are rational and unsentimental. All languages are equally capable of expression if cultivated. The sooner the great works of philosophy are translated, the sooner the gap will be closed between learned and popular culture. The purpose of language is to express the truth of things, not to produce eloquence for its own sake. The position anticipates the philosophical argument common at the end of the sixteenth century that things are more important than words, and that humanism wasted much of its energy on words.[19]

Speroni's dialogue had a greater influence than that of many of its predecessors. As noted in chapter 3, it is an important source for DuBellay's *Deffence et illustration de la langue francoyse*. Whether or not Speroni was an influence on Bacon, the ideas about language expressed by his "scholar" are found in the *Novum organum* and reverberate throughout English seventeenth-century discussions of the style appropriate for a rational and scientific age.

In spite of Pomponazzi's theories, the national heritage was a far more important concern in the early Cinquecento than the relative merits of words and things, and there is a striking contrast between the Italian sense of the national heritage and the sense of the national heritage elsewhere in Europe. When the Italians looked back, they were not ashamed of what they saw. They saw Dante, Petrarch, and Boccaccio. Dante was somewhat problematic because he was associated with what humanists considered an age of Gothic darkness. However, Petrarch and Boccaccio were heroes of the humanist cultural revolution. As Bembo argued, they had established norms for vernacular poetry, most especially the canzone, the sonnet, terza rima (Petrarch's *Trionfi*), and ottava rima (Boccaccio's *Teseida*).

In addition to perfecting their verse forms, these poets had made the hendecasyllabic an extraordinarily flexible line and provided brilliant examples of the sort of complex, Latinate construction that Dante advocated in the *De vulgari*. Their work therefore embodied rhetorical qualities humanists of the Cinquecento admired. One of the recurrent conclusions of these critics was stated initially by Bembo: Italian poets could—and should—imitate their predecessors as well as the ancients. To cite only the most obvious contrast, when DuBellay looked back at the French literary heritage, he did not see imposing models. He saw medieval banalities and the camp followers of Marot.

The English "courtly makers" of the age of Henry VIII were more ambivalent than the poets of the Pléiade. They recognized the greatness of English medieval poets—most obviously, Chaucer—but they were clearly searching for new directions, and they looked especially to Petrarch and Petrarchan imitators like Serafino Aquilano for guidance. Only in the later sixteenth century, when the new style was irreversibly established, was there an affirmation of the English national heritage comparable to the affirmation of the Italian heritage by Bembo, Castiglione, and Trissino.

TRISSINO: TRADITIONAL AND CLASSICAL PROSODY

As we have seen, Trissino is a pivotal figure in the development of Italian ideas about prosody. The four divisions of his *Poetica* (1529) constitute the most detailed treatise of the early Cinquecento on vernacular poetry.[20] Trissino also experimented with Italian forms equivalent to ancient forms: *Sophonisba*, a tragedy in mixed meters with *versi sciolti* for its dialogue (1524), and *Italia liberata da Gotthi*, an epic in *versi sciolti* (1547).

A continuation of the *Poetica* was published in 1562. It has two "divisions." In them, the romance bias of the first four divisions is replaced by ideas about tragedy and comedy drawn from Aristotle's *Poetics*. It is often said that Trissino abandoned his earlier, theoretically conservative position because of the rediscovery of the *Poetics* between 1530 and 1550. However, the fact that *Sophonisba* was complete by 1524 (and written earlier) shows that many of Trissino's apparently Aristotelian ideas date from the 1520s. Evidently, his critical thinking matured early and changed less decisively than is usually thought.

The object of the 1529 *Poetica* is announced in its first section. The ancient poets contributed to the perfection of men in antiquity; used properly, poetry can work its magic again on contemporary society. Since classical poetry has been treated thoroughly by ancient writers, Trissino will deal with rhyming poetry in Italian. His two precedents are Dante and Antonio da Tempo. From the former he derives his preference for a courtly Italian rather than a Tuscan literary language. From the latter he derives much detail about the machinery of medieval rhyming poetry.[21]

The first of the four divisions deals with language. In a Latin treatise it would be understood as a discussion of *Latinitas*. In addition to advocating Italian in contrast to Tuscan, Trissino praises the use of standard words and the ideals of clarity, greatness, beauty, truth, and artifice. Metaphors (*trasportazioni*) are useful but should not be strained.

The second division considers varieties of rhyme. Like his medieval predecessors, Trissino equates rhyme with rhythm: "Rhyme is that which the Greeks called 'rhythm' and the Latins 'number,' and you can therefore say that rhyme, rhythm, and number are more or less the same thing."[22] Given this definition, it is not surprising that Trissino understands the metrical foot in relation to rhyme, and rhyme, in turn, as the element that defines the rhythm of the line.

A discussion of accent follows that is refreshingly sophisticated if compared with French and English comments on the subject. The elements of the syllable are listed as they are in Donatus: time, breath, and tone. Italian depends on tonic accents, that is, on acute, grave, and circumflex. Trissino observes that the quantitative feet of ancient prosody are not important for Italian. The feet (i.e., the terminal rhythms) of Italian lines are composed of arrangements of tonic accents: "Just as the [ancient poets] made the first syllable of the iambus short and the second long, in the same way, we make the first syllable of the iambus 'grave' (*grave*) and the second 'acute' (*acuta*) as in 'Amór'."[23] Lines can be complete or can lack a syllable (*sceme*) or two (*amezzate*). Thus a hendecasyllabic is counted as such even though it has ten syllables—a situation that is the reverse of the French practice of ignoring extra unaccented syllables. Although trisyllabic feet are seldom used, dipodic feet on the model of Greek iambic meter are common. A diiambic, for example, is scanned \/ \/and a choriambus / \\/. Three kinds of elision are permitted.

Division 3 treats the line combinations that rhyme establishes, beginning with couplets. Couplets that do not rhyme are "discordant" (*discorde*); those that do are "concordant." The other standard forms are terza rima, quatrains, *quinarii*, and *senarii*, the label being determined by the number of lines interlaced by rhyme. All other line arrangements are combinations of simpler ones. When lines of differing length are used, the poet must take care to maintain consistent alternation. In the fourth division, the *Poetica* moves to stanza forms. Sonnet comes first and is examined most elaborately. Later sections consider *ballate, canzoni, madriali* (madrigals), and *serventesi*. The treatise ends with the promise of additional divisions to cover the classical genres of tragedy, comedy, and epic.

As already noted, the second part of the *Poetica* (1562) draws on Aristotle's *Poetics*. Almost all of the comment on versification in the first part of the *Poetica* is technical—concerned with vocabulary, accent, rhyme, line arrangement, and stanzas. Conversely, the emphasis of the comments in the second part is on decorum. Little is said about the syllabic aspect of *versi sciolti,* but a great deal is said about their suitability to various poetic forms and subjects. The emphasis on decorum shows that Horace's *Ars poetica* was at least as important for Trissino as Aristotle's *Poetics*.

Ancient hexameter verse, Trissino says, is well suited to elevated subjects and is hospitable to metaphors and all other figures. Italians have found that the best form for these purposes is the unrhymed hendecasyllabic. He admires the use of rhymed form of the line by Dante and Boccaccio, but he complains that rhyme forces the poet to write in standardized units that interfere with the continuity of the narration. Therefore, he kept the line but eliminated the rhyme:

> I wanted to abandon terza rima and likewise the ottava rima of Boccaccio because they did not seem adapted to continuous [i.e., narrative] material, if not . . . because of the [like] endings, from which there grows a certain uniformity of figures, then because with such endings it is proper always to maintain a relation from two verses to two [others], or from three to three, or four to four . . . and the like, and that is totally contrary to the continuous development of the material and the interweaving (*concatenazione*) of the meanings and of the constructions (*construttioni*). Therefore I dropped rhyming endings and kept the verse form, that is the hendecasyllable. . . . For the hendecasyllable is . . . superior to all other verse forms . . . and they say *versi sciolti* are . . . splendidly adapted to dramatic poems. This verse form will therefore be the one that, in my opinion, best fits the heroic poem.[24]

Of special interest is Trissino's emphasis on "continuous development of the material and the interweaving of the meanings and of the constructions." It implies both complex syntax and enjambment and suggests that both are contrary to the elegant partitioning that is typical of French narrative poetry and complemented by rhyme. Construction is at least as important to the "new verse" as freedom from rhyme and, in fact, complementary to that freedom.

However, Trissino is not entirely comfortable with unrhymed verse. In the same passage in which he denigrates rhyme, he repeats that he is writing on vernacular poetry and must therefore write about rhyme. In spite of the fact that rhyme is associated with the Middle Ages, in which "not merely literature but all the fine arts were brought down to the lowest point," it is, he admits, sweet and attractive and "not to be given up."

Classical practice requires different forms—dactylic hexameter and iambic trimeter—for epic and tragedy. Heroic verse tends to be elevated and musical, dramatic verse "like speech." Trissino notes that Italian uses the same verse form for both.

Even though Trissino was a mediocre poet, the comments that he makes in the prefaces to his tragedy and his epic have a special interest because they draw on experience as well as theory. Both prefaces relate verse form to syntax, but the basis of the relationship is different in each case.

Commenting on *Italia liberata* in a preface addressed to the Emperor Charles V, he stresses the need for *enargia*. The term comes from the essay *On Style* by Demetrius Phalarion.[25] *Enargia* is vividness (Latin *evidentia*). It is essential to epic and is created by the particularizing of descriptions. Particularizing depends on verse form and syntax. It requires flexible units that can be expanded and contracted to match the subject: "Speaking with care, one creates every detail of the actions, and nothing is left out, and no periods that are spoken are truncated or shortened."[26] *Versi sciolti* allow the subject to be developed according to its own demands, not the demands of a stanza. As Trissino remarks in the *Poetica,* the result is "continuous development of the material and the interweaving of the meanings and of the constructions." In a verse essay (in *versi sciolti*) titled *Tre libri di arte poetica* (1551), Girolamo Muzio makes the same point when contrasting the lyric charm of tercets (i.e., terza rima) and stanzaic poems to the trumpet blast of *versi sciolti:*

> More apt by far for lyre than for the trumpet,
> The tercet and the stanza: in both forms
> It suits me well to close in numbered verses
> My careful thought; I know that I must end
> The thought and line together or I fail. . . .
> [But when] we wish the style to move along
> Without a lag or fall, in that same place

> Where old poets wrote in six dactylic measures,
> We use verse without rhymes. These shine
> More brilliantly and far surpass the others.[27]

The freedom of *versi sciolti* recommended them for dramatic verse as well as epic. In drama, *versi sciolti* permit natural word order in contrast to artificial order. In his preface to Agostino Ricchi's comedy *I Tre tiranni* (1533), Vellutello makes the point explicit:

> The author . . . sought to distance himself from prose as little as possible. To do this he has proceeded in a natural manner without transposition of words . . . and with continuation of the sentences from one verse into the other, and with the ends of the replies not ever coincident with the end of the verse. This is because otherwise it would be hard for the sound of the verse not to interfere with the natural speech—and that is the situation chiefly to be avoided in the [comic] style of writing.[28]

In the case of epic, then, *versi sciolti* contribute to a noble elevation; in drama they make possible a conversational style.

To return to *Italia liberata,* after commenting on *versi sciolti*, Trissino notes that epic *enargia* requires the use of "comparisons and similes and images," and that Homer's verse has a "marvelous spaciousness" (*meravigliosa largheza*) as well as "sonorousness" and "elevation."[29] All of these qualities come directly or indirectly from Aristotle's prescriptions for heroic verse. Unfortunately, Trissino's verse is notoriously flat. It did, however, catch the attention of the age. For many years a consideration of *versi sciolti* was mandatory in any Italian discussion of the technique of epic poetry.

Trissino also experimented with *versi sciolti* in the dialogue sections of *Sophonisba*. The dedication of that work to Pope Leo X says nothing of *enargia*. Instead, Trissino lectures his patron on the adaptability of the form to expression of suffering. The argument is a variation on the appeal to natural order already seen in Vellutello's preface to *I Tre tiranni*. Strong emotion produces spontaneous expression. Since tragedy requires strong emotion, it requires a form that does not imply studied artistry. This idea is more sophisticated than the usual comment that the verse of drama should be "like" prose or everyday speech. It relates tragic emotion (*pathos*) and "manner of imitation" to the formulas of construction:

> I really do not believe it can be called a defect that the verses are in Italian and do not have the customary rhyme but are unrhymed in many places. The reason I made the poem in this way is that it is better and more noble—and perhaps far less easy—to create successfully than is sometimes

thought. And it is not only very useful for narration and speeches, but necessary for the arousal of pity. This is because speech that arouses pity is born from sorrow, and sorrow does not express itself in carefully considered words, and for that reason rhyme, which shows careful thought, is truly antithetical to pity.[30]

GIRALDI CINTIO: CLASSICAL FORM AND VERNACULAR PROSODY

Giraldi Cintio was also committed to the ennoblement of the Italian language. His hero was Pietro Bembo: "This language . . . was almost reborn through [Bembo's] efforts . . . and it also owes [him] much for having enriched it so successfully."[31] Cintio announces his allegiance to Bembo's efforts to purify the language in a poem titled "The Tragedy to Whoever Reads It" added at the end of the 1543 edition of his tragedy *Orbecche*. As a well-disciplined follower of Bembo, he has restricted his vocabulary to words used by Petrarch and Boccaccio. He will await the judgment of his drama by Bembo, Trissino, Molza, Tolomei, and Alamanni:

> . . . divine Bembo . . .
> Bembo the divine, who rescued the vulgar language
> From wandering in the shadows and the dark kingdom
> Of Pluto, with lyre happier than the one
> That Orpheus used for his longed-for wife.
> And gentle Trissino, who with his song,
> Brought tragedy, before anyone else, from Tiber
> And Ilissus to the waves of the Arno. And great
> Molza. . . .
> And good Tolomei, who has led Italian poetry to Latin
> Numbers and the Roman fashion with his new method of writing,
> And . . . Alamanni. . . .[32]

Cintio wrote another tragedy, *Didone*, shortly after *Orbecche* and gave a public reading of it in 1543. To his surprise, an unidentified auditor raised a question: why did he not write the tragedy in prose rather than in verse? As we have seen, there was agreement early in the century that *versi sciolti* are well suited to tragedy. They are like everyday speech ("parlare d'ogni dì") and thus equivalent to classical iambic trimeter, and they are also verse. Even as it was being established, however, this position was challenged from two directions. Ariosto had originally written his comedies in prose, and Agostino

Michele argued in his *Discorso in cui si dimostra come si possono scrivere le tragedie e le commedie in prosa* (1532) that far from being second-best, prose comes closer than *versi sciolti* to the ancient prescriptions and the real needs of drama.

At the other extreme, Sperone Speroni wrote *Canace* (1542) in lines of irregular length, irregularly rhymed. The play was immediately attacked for being undramatic. Who, after all, speaks in irregular rhymed lines? Speroni replied that the Italian hendecasyllabic line is not like the ancient iambic trimeter but more like ancient dactylic hexameter. It is too grand for dramatic dialogue. The proper modern verse form for tragedy will be varied to suit the different speakers and will use rhyme on occasion to point up important moments. To which the detractors replied, "Nonsense." Speroni's modern editor, Christina Roaf, comments: "The discussion always returns to fix on the same requirements: although grave and sublime, tragic verses should be, above all, apt for representation; for that reason they should be natural, should observe decorum, and should be verisimilar."[33]

In the *Apology* that follows *Didone*, Cintio sides with Trissino and against Michele's prose and Speroni's rhyme. He argues that Aristotle assumed dramas are in verse and that having composed his comedies in prose, Ariosto recognized the error and rewrote them in verse even though the verse leaves much to be desired. Trissino took the right path: "He wrote his *Sophonisba* in the verse form that he, before anyone else, created . . . in place of [ancient] Iambic verse, doing this because such verses were like the familiar speech of our own time and fell, like Iambics, from the tongue of people engaged in common discourse. And Rucellai sided with the opinion of this excellent tragedian in his *Rosmonda*, which appeared with great praise shortly after *Sophonisba*."[34]

Cintio broadens the argument in his *Discorsi intorno al comporre de i romanzi, delle commedie, e delle tragedie* (1554). Rhymed verses are too artificial for drama—"farther from everyday speech than any of the other kinds."[35] Rhyme is appropriate for the chorus and "the moral and affective parts" (i.e., aphorisms and moments of intense pathos).[36] For the most part, however, tragedy should be written in "complete verses without rhyme" (i.e., *versi sciolti*). In fact, "complete verses with rhyme are no longer used by the Italians."[37] Nor are *sdruccioli* of the sort used by Ariosto acceptable: "If unrhymed verse is appropriate for drama because it is very much like everyday speech, the *sdrucciolo* is most inappropriate, being a meter that has not a bit of similarity to the conversations that arise from day to day among men."[38]

Although Cintio agrees with Trissino about the appropriateness of *versi sciolti* for drama, he disagrees on the subject of heroic poetry. He believes heroic poetry needs the added ornamentation of rhyme, because rhyme "carries with itself sweetness of sound and gravity accompanied by number and other elements that suggest elevation. These things do not exist and cannot exist in the verses their modern inventor, Trissino, called 'free' (*sciolti*)."[39]

In Cintio's view, the use of rhyme in epic and its abandonment in drama differentiate between the two forms. To Aristotle's suggestion that epic and tragedy have much in common, Cintio replies that the hexameter of epic is fundamentally different from the iambic trimeter of drama. Iambic meter has elevation (*grandezza*), but it is entirely different from heroic verse.[40] Apparently, Tasso agreed with Cintio. Although he experimented with *versi sciolti* in his *Le Sette giornate del mondo creato*, his masterpiece, *Gerusalemme liberata*, is in ottava rima.

Two uses of *versi sciolti* may have directly influenced English poetry of the early sixteenth century. Luigi Alamanni began composing eclogues in *versi sciolti* in 1519, and his *Rime Toscane* (1533) contain "*Selve*" imitating the *Silvae* of Statius. His *Coltivazione*, imitating Vergil's *Georgics*, made him famous as a classical innovator. DuBellay mentions it, and scholars have speculated that Alamanni may have met (and influenced) Surrey during one of Surrey's visits to France. Alamanni reaffirmed his classicism in 1549 by composing his comedy *Flora* in classical *senarii* and *octonarii*, in the manner (he claims) of Plautus and Terence.[41]

Another use of *versi sciolti* that may have influenced English thinking about versification is the translation of the *Aeneid* by several authors, published in Venice beginning in 1539. The list of translators includes several well-known literary figures, among them Bernardino Borghesi, Ippolito de'Medici, and Alessandro Piccolomini. Each book was published separately, dedicated to a prominent lady. The books were then published in pairs and in larger groups. The first six books appeared in 1540: *I sei primi libri del Eneide di Vergilio, tradotti*. . . . .[42]

The most important English renaissance translation of the *Aeneid* is the blank verse version by Henry Howard, Earl of Surrey, completed around 1540. Whether or not Surrey met Alamanni or read the *Coltivazione*, he must have known of the Vergil translation. If he did, its use of *versi sciolti* would have encouraged his decision to use blank verse for his own work. It was much discussed and went through many printings in various forms. Because of its presentation of the greatest of Latin authors, outside of Italy it was no doubt far more visible than the work of Trissino and Cintio.

TOLOMEI AND QUANTITATIVE VERSE

Claudio Tolomei (1492–1555)—the "buon Tolomei" included in the list of literary mentors at the end of Cintio's *Orbecche*—was the founder and leader of the Accademia della Nuova Poesia in Rome. The name of the academy identifies the interest of its members in quantitative verse. Tolomei's chief contribution to the history of prosody is the poetry he inspired and the list of rules in *Versi, et regole de la nuova poesia Toscana*, published in 1539.[43]

The volume is a collection of poems in Italian quantitative meters. They were all inspired by Tolomei, and one of the requirements for inclusion seems to have been the composition of a poem in his praise, usually as the wise shepherd Dametas. The predominant verse form in the volume is classical elegiac verse, but hendecasyllabics and several lyric forms are also used. Quantitative scansion is usually provided by the editor whenever a new meter or stanza form is introduced. The object of the volume is explained in a prefatory letter by Cosimo Pallavicino. The poems are admittedly modest, says Pallavicino, but Vergil himself began with pastoral poetry. What they show is that the classical genres—epigram, ode, elegy, eclogue, and epithalamium—can be written in Italian measures: "We are setting out for a walk along the beautiful ancient streets."[44]

The last four pages of the volume contain the "rules" to which the title of the volume alludes.[45] They are a series of observations on monosyllables, caesuras, and Italian syllable quantity. Combined with the scansions preceding various poems, they are a primer for writing quantitative poetry. They are not, however, a full-scale textbook. A publisher's endnote explains that they are gathered from discussions held over the year preceding the volume. They will be amplified, we are assured, when Tolomei publishes an explanation of the new poetry, which he is actively preparing.

In his dialogue *Il Cesano,* Tolomei advocates "Tuscan" in contrast to those who would make Florentine the standard vocabulary of Italy and those who argued for a national (i.e., "Italian") vernacular.[46] This fact is less significant than his uncompromising advocacy of a vernacular equivalent of quantitative poetry. He questions the value of *versi sciolti* for Italian heroic verse. In spite of the use of this form by Trissino and Alamanni, it seems prosy to him. He can also be generous in his praise of accomplishment. In a letter to Alamanni he states that the *Coltivazione* is a "light and ornament" to the Italian language and will lead others along the path to excellence.[47]

Tolomei's system of revised spelling should be noted because it is a common strategy of advocates of quantitative prosody in the vernacular. His interest in minor genres like elegy and ode is also significant. It points in a direction that would be explored with increasing frequency as the century progressed by poets seeking classical forms different from—and more personal than—the great public genres of epic, tragedy, and comedy.

Although Tolomei may be compared as an advocate of quantitative verse to Jean-Antoine de Baïf in France and Thomas Campion in England, he is less significant as a literary figure than either. Samuel Daniel makes a slighting reference to him in the *Defence of Ryme* in connection with quantitative verse: "Nor could this very same innovation in the Verse, begun amongst them by C. Tolomei, but die in the attempt, and was buried as soone as it came borne, neglected as a prodigious and unnaturall issue amongst them."[48]

A Note on Annibale Caro's *Aeneid*

The imitation of classical forms continued in Italy throughout the sixteenth century. Gabriello Chiabrera made pioneering experiments at the end of the century in the vernacular Pindaric. His work is only the most visible of many contributions to the effort to domesticate into the Italian vernacular the full range of classical forms, together with the diction and vocabulary appropriate to each. We can conclude the present review by noting that one of the most successful of the earlier experiments was the result of yet another attempt to translate Vergil.

Annibale Caro (1507–66) was a member of the circle associated with Cardinal Ippolito de'Medici and Claudio Tolomei, and a friend of Francesco Molza. He is included in Giraldi's list of prominent experimenters in classical forms. He is of interest in the present study because, although he had no influence on English writers of the sixteenth century, he is one of the Italian experimenters in *versi sciolti* who, along with Torquato Tasso, may have been known to Milton.

Caro admired Bembo and Varchi extravagantly and wrote sonnets to Molza. It was Caro who remarked of Trissino's rather flat verses, "Paiono da vero fatti co'piedi"—"they seem truly made with feet."

His own work was more artful. His *Aeneid* translation (1563–66) is generally considered to be the finest example of *versi sciolti* from the Cinquecento. Francesco Flora calls it "the first convincing example of the legitimacy in this form of poetry without rhyme. . . . [Caro] was not a translator obsessed by the letter; rather, he adjusted his own subtle poetry to that of Vergil."[49] The translation is elevated, musical, and sustained. It is exactly what was needed to vindicate the theories of Trissino.

After Caro's *Aeneid*, the most important Italian experiment using heroic *versi sciolti* is Tasso's *Le Sette giornate del mondo creato* (1593). This work was clearly an influence on Milton's *Paradise Lost*, although, like Caro's *Aeneid*, it came too late to be significant for sixteenth-century English poetry. When it was published, France was already well on the road to recognizing the Alexandrine as the standard form for epic and drama. In England, the key experiments in blank verse had already been made. In the seventeenth century, Milton returned to the Italian poets of the Cinquecento for instruction, but he was almost alone. When his contemporaries looked abroad, most of them looked to France.

CHAPTER V

Notes of Instruction

Prosodic theory entered sixteenth-century England in several ways: through study of the *prosodia* in grammar schools, including analysis and imitation of ancient poetry; through explanations of versification in editions of major Latin poets such as Horace, Vergil, Terence, and Seneca; through Italian, French, and English treatises on versification; through efforts to reproduce the qualities of ancient poets in vernacular translations and imitations; and through the influence on later poets of successful imitations and translations.

Without question the influence of successful poems was the most important means whereby prosodic traditions were absorbed into English poetry. Chaucer undoubtedly learned more from reading and translating Eustache Deschamps and Giovanni Boccaccio than from reading such treatises on prosody as may have been available to him, and Chaucer's contemporaries and immediate successors learned from him. At the beginning of his career, Shakespeare learned far more from Kyd and Marlowe than from such theorizing about dramatic verse as he may have encountered in grammar school.

Initially, however, English renaissance poets had to learn from Latin and Continental poetry and from such theory as they could locate. They also sought to adapt to native poetry the terminology and values of the Latin prosody they had studied as schoolchildren. Along with the Latinate values and terms came both conscious and unconscious assumptions about the nature of literary language.

Esoteric Humanism

Prosodic questions were complicated in England by the ideal of cultural reform that the humanists of the age of Henry VIII inherited from Petrarch and the Italian civic humanists of the Quattrocento. Initially, the ideal was a reform so broad it included all of Europe. The earlier humanists considered themselves members of an international community of intellectuals, unified by the common language of Latin and by the cultural traditions for which that language was a vehicle.

Such a broad program could not hope to succeed in a single generation, and in the fifteenth century, humanists increasingly came to regard educational reform as the path to success. Inevitably, the humanist curriculum focused on Latin and included much material that had been familiar in medieval education. What was new was the insistence by humanist educators like Guarino da Verona and Vittorino da Feltre on teaching the full range of ancient thought and expression. Among other aspects of the new system, its emphasis on mastery of Latin style—and through that, mastery of communication—was especially significant for poetry.[1]

Desiderius Erasmus (1466–1536) has always been recognized as the chief spokesman for humanism in northern Europe. His influence in England was deep, and it lasted throughout the sixteenth century.

Today he is best known for *The Praise of Folly* and his edition, with Latin translation and notes, of the Greek New Testament. In England, however, his most influential works may well have been his contributions to education: the *De pueris instituendis,* the *De duplici copia verborum ac rerum,* the *Adagia,* and the *Colloquia,* among others. One of the chief vehicles of his influence was a grammar book written primarily by his English disciple William Lily. It is called the Royal Grammar because throughout the sixteenth century it was officially approved by the Crown for use in schools throughout England. It thus helped to shape the concept of style of every Englishman of the age who attended an approved grammar school.

Here a distinction will be useful. Two kinds of humanism can be observed in sixteenth-century Europe. The first can be called exoteric because it is centered on Latin and is international in its outlook. Erasmus is a prime example of an exoteric humanist.[2] The second type of humanism is esoteric because it is centered on the vernacular and looks inward to the national culture. Exoteric humanism supports the ideal of a community of European nations united by a common language—

Latin—and a common religion—Catholic Christianity. In spite of its emphasis on a common culture, esoteric humanism tends to identify its interests with those of the state.

After the Reformation, exoteric humanism became, in effect, a myth sustained by the school curriculum rather than reality. Meanwhile, esoteric humanism flourished. Long after English humanists had given up the dream of an international community, they still sought to improve English culture through education and assimilation of the classical tradition into the vernacular. In the process, they reviewed many of the topics first explored in Italian debates about the question of language, and it is within the context of this review that sixteenth-century English theories of prosody are best understood.[3]

Ascham and the Question of English

Roger Ascham (1515–68), tutor and, later, Latin secretary to Elizabeth, provides the most explicit sixteenth-century statement of the linguistic ideals of the esoteric humanists. In *Toxophilus* (1545), he explains that he writes in English rather than Latin in order to benefit his countrymen: "Though to have written . . . in an other tonge had bene bothe more profitable for my study, and also more honest for my name, yet I can thinke my labour wel bestowed yf with a little hynderaunce to my profyt and name maye come any fourtheraunce to the pleasure or commoditie, of the gentlemen and yeomen of Englande, for whose sake I tooke this matter in hande."[4]

Ascham's *Scholemaster* is directly concerned with education. The centerpiece of his new style of education is to be the imitation of the ancient classics.[5] Much of the book is devoted to a detailed analysis of how to go about "imitating." Along the way, a good deal of attention is devoted to literary matters.

Imitation is far more for Ascham than acquiring the literary style of long-dead authors. Those who learn a crude language can only repeat its crudities: "If ye would speake as the best and wisest do, ye must be conversant where the best and wisest are: but if yow be borne or brought up in a rude countrie, ye shall not chose but speake rudelie."[6] Although some speak wisely, even in the rudest tongue, the best policy is to imitate the best languages, which are Greek and Latin: "In the Greeke and Latin tong . . . we finde alwayes wisdome and eloquence, good matter and good utterance, never or seldom a sunder."

If language is crude, Ascham suggests, thought will inevitably be crude also; conversely, if language is elevated, thought will be elevated. The theory posits complementarity between language and the thought that language makes possible. It anticipates the theory that language is the framework within which the world is conceptualized developed by Ernst Cassirer in *The Philosophy of Symbolic Form*, which is to say it is sophisticated and serious. In the sixteenth century the debate hinged on the distinction between things and words—*res et verba*. Language in the humanist view is not a collection of names for things but the means by which things are known. To develop an elevated and harmonious style is to reshape culture so that it, too, becomes elevated and harmonious.

Ascham supports his argument by reference to the contrast between ancient and medieval culture. The contrast is basically a humanistic contrast between classical and medieval Latin, sharpened by Ascham's anti-Catholicism. However, the fact that its outlines are familiar does not make it superficial. Ascham felt that history testifies to the close relation between good language and good thinking, or, as later participants in the debate would have it, between things and words:

> They be not wise therefore that say, what care I for a mans wordes and utterance, if his matter and reasons be good. . . . Ye know not, what hurt ye do learning that care not for wordes but for matter, and so make a devorse betwixt the tong and the hart. For marke all aiges: looke upon the whole course of both the Greeke and Latin tonge, and ye shall surlie finde that, whan apte and good wordes began to be neglected, and properties of those two tonges to be confounded, than also began, ill deedes to spring: strange maners to oppresse good orders, newe and fond opinions to strive with olde and trewe doctrine, first in Philosophie: and after in Religion: right judgement of all thinges to be perverted, and so vertue with learning is contemned, and studie left of.[7]

A properly elevated language is rich in literary forms as well as words. As we have seen, such forms were thought to be constitutive by ancient prosodic theorists. They are the means whereby certain kinds of vision are "bodied forth." Without them the vision cannot be objectified. English culture must either reproduce these forms or discover equivalents for them. Ascham focuses on prosody near the end of book 2. Recalling discussions with Thomas Watson and John Cheke about "our new English Rymers," he remarks that men of discernment prefer quantity to rhyme. By "ryme" he means the whole romance literary tradition, which he considers both a symptom and a cause of the debased quality of medieval culture:

> As *Vergil* and *Horace* were not wedded to follow the faultes of former fathers ... we Englishmen likewise would acknowledge and understand rightfully our rude and beggerly ryming, brought first into Italie by *Gothes* and *Hunnes*, whan all good verses and all good learning to were destroyd by them.... But now, when men know the difference, and have the examples, both of the best and of the worst, surlie to follow rather the *Gothes* in Ryming than the Greekes in trew versifying, were even to eate ackornes with swyne, when we may freely eate wheate bread emonges men.[8]

Sir Thomas Hoby agrees with Ascham but thinks that the Italians, who led the way in restoring their language and culture by imitating the ancients, can provide models as worthy as the Greeks and Romans. His translation of Castiglione's *Book of the Courtier* (1561) is intended to be a contribution to the larger effort. The relationship in *The Book of the Courtier* between an elevated culture and a courtly style makes the work directly relevant to the concerns of esoteric humanism. Hoby remarks concerning the labor of translation, "As I ... have to my smal skil bestowed some labour about this piece of woorke ... I wishe, with al my hart, profounde, learned men in the Greeke and Latin shoulde make lyke proofe, and everye manne store the tunge according to hys knowledge and delite ... that we alone of the worlde may not bee styll counted barbarous in oure tunge, as in time out of mind we have bene in our maners."[9]

In the preface to his *Discourse of English Poetrie* William Webbe observes that great progress has been made in the reform of "our English tongue." Only one area of language—poetry—lags behind:

> It is to be wondred at of all, and is lamented of manie, that where as all kinde of good learning have aspyred to royall dignitie and statlie grace in our English tongue, being not onlie founded, defended, maintained, and enlarged, but also purged from faultes, weeded of errours, and pollished from barbarousnes, by men of great authoritie and judgement, onlie Poetrie hath founde fewest frendes to amende it.

The explanation for the inadequacy of English poetry is "the canckred enmitie of curious custome," and the prescription is "some perfect platforme or *Prosodia* of versifying."[10]

Finally, writers like William Webbe relate the civilizing power of poetry to specific classical genres. The power is symbolized in myths of the raising of the walls of Thebes by the songs of Amphion and the charming of the beasts by Orpheus, and by references to the "golden world" of Edenic perfection revealed by inspired poets. Webbe writes:

> To begin therefore with the first that was first worthelye memorable in the excellent gyft of Poetrye, the best wryters agree that it was *Orpheus*, who by the sweete gyft of his heavenly Poetry withdrew men from raungyng uncertainly and wandring brutishly about, and made them gather together and keepe company, make houses, and keep fellowshippe together, who therefore is reported (as *Horace* sayth) to asswage the fiercenesse of Tygers and moove the harde Flynts. After him was *Amphion*, who was the first that caused Citties to bee builded, and men therein to live decently and orderly according to lawe and right.[11]

It was, then, with a high sense of mission that English humanists set about finding English equivalents of the ancient literary forms.

PROSODIA: LILY AND BRINSLEY

The "prosody" section of a renaissance Latin grammar is an abbreviated version of a Latin *ars metrica*. By far the most important Latin grammar for England between 1540 and 1650 is the grammar that William Lily wrote for the boys at St. Paul's School. This grammar was still so popular in the seventeenth century that at least four commentaries on it appeared between 1625 and 1641.[12]

The work is divided into two sections. The first has the title *A Shorte Introduction of Grammar*. It is in English because it is for children who as yet know no Latin at all. It explains the eight parts of speech. The second part is in Latin: *Brevissima institutio seu ratio grammatices cognoscendae*. It has four major subsections. "Orthographia" deals with letters, spelling, and pronunciation. "Etymologia" is an expanded treatment of the eight parts of speech already presented in the *Shorte Introduction*. "Syntaxis" includes "concordance" (agreement), "figures of words," and "construction." Figures of words are certain kinds of metaplasm: prosthesis, aphaeresis, epenthesis, syncope, paragoge, apocope. "Construction" includes many of the ancient figures of diction: apposition, evocation, syllepsis, prolepsis, zeugma, synthesis, antiposis, and synecdoche.[13]

The fourth section is "Prosody, which teaches the right pronunciation of words" ("Prosodia . . . quae rectam vocum pronuntiationem tradit"). Following Donatus, it divides the subject into "tone," "breath," and "time."

Lily's introductory definition is followed by sections describing the nature of a poetic foot and types of feet. The types are the four two-syllable types and eight three-syllable types familiar from the *ars metrica*. Four types of metaplasm are added to the types listed previously in connection with figures of words: synaloepha, ecthlipsis, synaeresis, and diaeresis. The caesura is defined, and four types, depending on placement in the hexameter line, are distinguished.

In the next section ("De generibus carminum") verse types are specified. Lily carries over intact the ancient traditions relating prosody to function. The verse types are heroic, or hexameter, elegiac, Asclepiad, Sapphic, and Phalaecean. Iambic verse is associated with Archilochus. The Greek dipodic tradition is preserved in the division of iambic verse into dimeter (two units of two feet) and trimeter (three units of two feet). Treatment of genres is followed, in turn, by an extended discussion of vowel quantity in beginning, midword, and terminal syllables. The reason for the detail is that the first and most critical task of students who are beginning the study of Latin verse is to distinguish between long and short vowels. Various rules, drawn from the *ars metrica*, are given. They have been examined thoroughly and their limitations described by Derek Attridge in *Well-Weighed Syllables*, and they need not detain us.[14] The book is rousingly concluded with a reprint of Erasmus's essay on the proper course of study, *De ratione studii*, which alludes in its title to a youthful essay (now lost) by Varro on education.

The discussion of prosody extends in the 1567 edition of Lily's grammar to fifteen pages. Whatever the merits of its rules in an absolute sense, teachers and students believed they were valid. They were thought to define strategies that made Greek and Latin poetry uniquely artistic. They had become second nature to many educated Englishmen by the time they had reached adolescence. Not surprisingly, they formed an important part of the conscious—and unconscious—perspective within which Englishmen understood vernacular poetry. In the second half of the sixteenth century, classical terms began to be used to describe English verse, and the vocabulary of English prosody continues to be heavily classical even today.

John Brinsley's *Ludus literarius, Or the Grammar Schoole* (1612) is a textbook on how to teach Latin in grammar school. It is heavily indebted to Roger Ascham and credits him by name for its method of double translation. Much of it can be readily understood within the outline of an ancient comprehensive grammar. After such preliminaries as orthography and basic grammar, it turns (ch. 10) to "composing, or right placing of the words . . . which you know is a principal matter in writing pure Lataine." "Composing" transliterates Latin *compositio*, a synonym, as we have seen, for construction. The discussion begins with a contrast between "plaine naturall order" and "to compose or place finely; which belongeth to Rhetorick." The basic contrast is the medieval distinction between *ordo naturalis* and *ordo artificialis*. Brinsley's humanist heritage is evident in terms that he considers synonymous. "Natural order" is called *ordo grammaticus* in contrast to *ordo Ciceronis*, later (ch. 11) glossed as "the Artificiall order of composing or placing the words according to Tully and the purest Latinists."

We see clearly here the relation between renaissance interest in construction and the doctrine of imitation. Brinsley quickly explains the specifics of composition. Five pages of examples of "Rhetoricall order" are given. They include purely grammatical devices and devices that use the figures of diction (e.g., verb placement at the end to create periodic structure). We have already observed that Latin treatments of construction usually include prose rhythm. Brinsley ends this section of the *Ludus* with a discussion of the prose rhythms used by Cicero. It may be added that his suggestions for exercises in construction are liberally developed in the appendix of a commentary on the Royal Grammar by one "R. R. Master in Arts" published in 1641. "R. R." includes a lengthy appendix "Of Parsing," which provides examples of how to drill students in "naturall" and "artificiall and rhetoricall" word order.[15]

Chapter 13 ("Of Versifying") provides a detailed sketch of how versification was taught.[16] "The making of a verse," Brinsley informs his reader, "is nothing but the turning of words forth of the grammaticall order, into the Rhetoricall, in some kinde of metre, which we call verses." The ancient tradition that composition is equally relevant to prose and poetry is recalled in this comment. Poetry is prose with all of the ornaments of *syntaxis* plus the added ornament of fixed meter.

For Brinsley's students, training in versification begins with daily sessions of reading poetry aloud. Their curriculum includes Ovid's *Tristia* and *Metamorphoses* and Vergil's poems, plus a sampling of other poets from *Flores poetarum*, a massive anthology compiled early in the sixteenth century by Octavianus Mirandula.[17] After the poems have been read, they are translated. Points of grammar and scansion are discussed. When the students have become thoroughly familiar with the rules of scansion, they select a poem of Ovid and reduce it to a list of its original words. They then compose poems of their own using the words. They read their compositions to each other. A friendly rivalry develops. In no time, Brinsley assures his readers, the students are writing verse as easily as they write prose.

Once beyond elementary rules the students are encouraged to imitate models and thus to become familiar with genre conventions. Brinsley recommends the progression hallowed by Vergil's career: first simple poetry like eclogue, then poetry in a middle style, like the *Georgics,* and finally epic. For technical assistance Brinsley particularly recommends "*Smetius* his *Prosodia.*" He also recommends "M. Stockwood, *Progymnasma scholasticum.*" This latter work is of some importance historically. It is an update of a collection of Latin translations from the *Greek Anthology* made by Erasmus and others and published originally by Stephanus. Stockwood includes the Greek along with the Latin texts. He also includes modern "sentences" and provides illustrations of how the originals can be varied. Brinsley praises him for showing 450 ways to vary the word order of a single elegiac distich.[18]

In a later chapter (ch. 18) Brinsley discusses the correct reading of verse. The chapter is of special interest because it contrasts reading that emphasizes scansion with skilled reading, which observes construction and implies something like vocal enactment. Although beginners read verse to bring out the meter, Brinsley advises advanced students "to utter every dialogue lively, as if they themselves were the persons who did speake in that dialogue." When they prepare to recite Vergil's *Eclogues* they should memorize the text in order "still more lively, in saying without booke, to express the affections and persons of shepheards, or whose speech soever else, which they are to imitate."

The point is quickly generalized: "So in all Poetry, for the pronuntiation, it is to be uttered as prose; observing distinctions and the nature of the matter; not to be tuned foolishly or childishly after the manner of scanning a Verse, as the use of some is."[19] The advice to read verse "as prose" does not mean it is not poetry. It means that in a proper reading, the speaker should seek to express the living motives underlying the verse, and these take precedence over a reading intended simply to express meter. The word "tuned" makes an explicit contrast between singsong recitation and expressive reading. Brinsley's advice is interesting in relation to all genres of renaissance poetry. As the remarks about eclogue indicate, it is especially relevant to verse that has dramatic qualities.

Taken together, Lily's Royal Grammar and the *Ludus literarius* give a clear picture of the sort of training in prosody that an English schoolboy would have received between 1500 and 1650. Among the striking details are the emphasis on composition, the recognition that composition controls vocal enactment of the poetic line, and the preference for enactment in contrast to creating a verbal "tune" by emphasizing meter. All of these tendencies are based on classical precedent, but they suggest that when read during the Renaissance, Latin verse might have sounded very much like syllabic verse. It is curious that Brinsley recommends supplementing his material with more sophisticated treatments of the subject like Smetius and Stockwood but does not mention annotated editions of the classics like the Badius Ascensius edition of Horace. However, a competent master would doubtless have supplied these.

Palsgrave and Ascham: "Trew Quantitie"

Two essays from the first half of the sixteenth century throw additional light on interest in prosody. They both reflect the influence of Erasmus, and both point in the direction of hard classicism.

John Palsgrave's translation (1540) of the Latin prodigal son play *Acolastus* by Guilelmus Gnapheus (Willelm de Volder) contains an extended discussion of comic meter.[20] Palsgrave was an enthusiastic Erasmian humanist, an educator, and a Protestant to whom the Lutheran flavor of *Acolastus* was attractive. He dedicated the translation to Henry VIII with the observation that the king has already "wylled one self and uniform maner of teachynge of all those Gramaticall ensygnements, to be used through out all your hyghnes dominions"—a reference to royal approval of Lily's *Grammar*.[21] The overt reason for his translation is to improve English by encouraging the "kynd of spekyng used of the latyns, whiche we use not in our tonge, but by other wordes expresse the sayde latyn maners of speakinge, and also Adages, metaphores, sentences, or other fygures poeticall or rhetoricall."[22]

The translation will aid teachers of Latin who know their subject but are "not able to expresse theyr conceyte in theyr vulgar tongue."[23] A little of the fire of the great humanists can be felt in Palsgrave's hope that it will set an example to others: "I shall thinke my selfe not onely very well suffised, but also moche fortunate, if this myne enterprise, or at the least fyrst settynge on, maye gyve occasion unto other your graces wel lerned clerkes, to fal in hande with suche of the latyne auctours, as in the judgement of all men be most excellent. . . . So that by theyr dilygente labours may be made suche an establyshed mariage, betwene the two tonges, as may be . . . an incredible furtheraunce to atteyn the pure latynitie by."[24]

The translation is in prose, but like the editors of Latin editions of Roman plays, Palsgrave identifies the meter of each scene at the beginning. The prologue is in *senarii*, with the gloss, "This prologue is made, *Ex versu iambico Senario*, that is to say, of syxe fete, accounting .ii. syllables, to make a foote .i. of .xii. syllables, and sometyme mo."[25] The labels are discussed at length in an essay sandwiched between the first and second scenes of act I: "A briefe Introductory to have some generall knowledge of the dyvers sortes of meters used of our auctor in this Comedye."[26]

Here, a technical vocabulary is introduced: *senarii, septenarii, octonarii, trimetri, tetrametri, trochaici*, and *trochaici catalectici*. Palsgrave also offers "some generall preceptes belongynge to the arte metricall" drawn from appropriate authors in the tradition: "Diomedes, Phocas, Servius, Donatus, Terentianus, Priscianus, Aldus, and Despauterius." In addition, "there be nowe at these dayes a great number of clerkes, whiche have travayled in this arte metricall."[27]

The list includes the major writers on the *ars metrica*. It is also significant in connection with English knowledge of developments on the Continent. Palsgrave mentions Aldus and Despauterius and refers to a "great number" of other writers who have dealt with the subject.

There follow competent, though pedestrian, explanations of the terms. Definitions are also given of the four two-syllable feet. *Scazontes*, or limping meters, are iambic but end with a spondee. Because of elision and quantitative equivalence, many Latin verses are irregular in syllable count but acceptable by the rules of classical prosody. Palsgrave distinguishes between Latin versification and the "juste number of syllables" of the syllabic versification with which his readers are (presumably) familiar: "It is also . . . to be noted, that there may divers thinges cause, that a verse shall not have his juste number of syllables." As the author of a remarkable analysis of the French language, *Lesclarissement de la langue francoyse*, Palsgrave must have been particularly sensitive to the differences between Latin and syllabic prosody.

Three line types are recognized: acatalectic, or perfect; catalectic, or lacking a syllable; and hypercatalectic, or having an extra syllable. Palsgrave observes that ecthlipsis and synaloepha "cause ever one vowel to be drowned so often as they chance in a verse: and yet shal the verse have his just number of syllables never the lesse." The passage concludes with an example of how a Latin verse of twelve syllables can be scanned by being divided into feet, with proper elisions. The verse is first spelled out (with elided vowels dropped) in single syllables, then the syllables are grouped in iambic feet, and finally they are grouped in "iii. syngle meters, by reason whereof they be called *Versus Trimetri*."[28]

After Palsgrave, the next essay in English that attempts a theoretical treatment of prosody is Roger Ascham's *Scholemaster* (1570). Having divided the art of communication into poetry, history, philosophy, and oratory, Ascham subdivides poetry into four genres: comic, tragic, epic, and lyric (*melicum*). The key to imitating these genres is decorum, and understanding decorum depends on familiarity with Aristotle's *Poetics* (which Ascham sees through a glass darkly) and Horace's *Ars poetica* (which he knows well).

Two English authors of Latin tragedy have written well: Thomas Watson, author of *Absalom*, and George Buchanan, author of *Jephtha*. Their plays are exceptional. More typical of the imperfect artists of the period is an unnamed Cambridge scholar who "began the *Protasis* with *Trochoeis Octonariis*: which kinde of verse, as it is but seldome and rare in Tragedies, so is it never used, save onelie in *Epitasi*: whan the Tragedie is hiest and hotest, and full of greatest troubles." Watson was far more circumspect than this anonymous blunderer. He refused to allow his *Absalom* to be published "onelie bicause, in *locis paribus* [in the even feet], *Anapestus* is twise or thrise used in stede of *Iambus*." Since anapest is a rising rhythm like iambus, this is "a smal faulte" and one that the Italians and French would probably ignore, but it is, nonetheless, a fault. Greek tragedy allows an anapest in the first foot but not in the even feet. The iambic measures of Roman comedy are almost without rules, but since *Absalom* is a tragedy, Watson was right to be concerned.[29]

Ascham calls the meter of Plautus and Terence "verie meane, and not to be followed."[30] Like many other renaissance critics, he interprets Horace's advice in the *Ars poetica* about studying Greek originals as a reference to learning correct use of iambic meter: "Horace . . . namely *propter carmen Iambicum* . . . referreth all studentes herein to the Imitation of the Greeke tong, saying, '*Exemplaria Graeca / nocturna versate manu, versate diurna.*'" The point is interesting because it underscores the difference between the sixteenth-century emphasis on prosody in the *Ars poetica* and modern interpretation, which tends to emphasize philosophy and history. In Ascham's interpretation, the line is a recommendation to Roman dramatists that they follow the restrained prosody of Greek iambic verse rather than the license of the Romans.

Mention of Greek models leads Ascham to the deficiencies of English poets. Many strive to equal the ancients, but they are committed to rhyme and to the syllabic prosody associated with it. In book 1 of *The Scholemaster,* Ascham had called for an English heroic line using quantitative dactylic hexameter. His example was often quoted by later English critics. It is by Thomas Watson:

> All travellers do gladly report great prayse of Ulysses,
> For that he knew many mens maners, and saw many Cities.[31]

In book 2 Ascham softens the earlier position. English is different from Latin. Dactylic hexameter lines "rather trotte and hoble, than run smothly in our English tong."[32] Ascham suggests that *carmen Iambicum*—the iambic line—is the proper English heroic meter. The position is a step toward the moderate stance of those who argued that even as it "reformed," English should preserve its native forms and idioms. However, Ascham remains a hard-liner rather than a moderate.

His position is illustrated by his criticism of Surrey's translation of the *Aeneid.* Although he praises Surrey for avoiding rhyme, he complains that Surrey's iambs are imperfect. Surrey has not "fullie hitt perfite and trew versifying," and his feet "be feete without joyntes, that is to say, not distinct by trew quantitie of sillabes. And so, soch feete, be but numme feete, and be even as unfitte for a verse to turne and runne roundly withall as feete of brasse or wood be unweeldie to go well withall."[33] The problem is apparently that Surrey has tried to be quantitative and failed. The ictus does not regularly coincide with a long vowel, dividing the line into isochronic units. The verses are therefore "without joyntes" and are "not distinct by trew quantitie of sillabes." They are clumsy experiments rather than true poetry.

Having made these observations, Ascham moves into a long and heated digression against rhyming. He is complaining about verse written according to syllabic conventions. Because he cannot accept the romance prosodic tradition, he ends by dismissing the main figures of Italian as well as English poetry. They have undeniable charms, but they miss true greatness: "And you, that be able to understand no more then ye finde in the *Italian* tong, and never went farder than the schole of *Petrarke* and *Ariostus* abroad, or els of *Chaucer* at home, though you have pleasure to wander blindlie still in your foule wrong way, envie not others, that seeke, as wise men have done before them, the fairest and rightest way."[34]

GASCOIGNE: MOTHER PHRASE AND PROPER *IDIÓMA*

Five years after *The Scholemaster*, George Gascoigne's *Certayne Notes of Instruction* was published. It should be understood as part of the general English concern between 1540 and 1570 with the "question of language." Gascoigne's position is moderate. On many subjects he agrees with the classicists who apply to English the criteria of *Latinitas* defined by Varro, Cicero, and Quintilian. The moderate classicists support use of native English idiom rather than importation of foreign words and syntax. Ascham is following this tack when he vows in the introduction of *Toxophilus* "to speak as the common people do" and avoid "strange words, as Latin, French, and Italian [which] do make all things dark and hard."[35]

After its use by Thomas Wilson in *The Arte of Rhetorique* (1553),[36] the phrase "inkhorn terms" was used widely in arguments in favor of keeping English pure. In *Certayne Notes* Gascoigne rejects terms that "smell of the Inkehorne." He also rejects attempts to sophisticate English verse with Latinate syntax. This is an argument against imitation of what Brinsley calls "artificial order" and "Ciceronian order." Gascoigne's linguistic ideal is defined in a formula: "mother phrase and proper *Idióma*."[37] Varro would have approved.

Gascoigne is not opposed to imposing the rules of Latin composition on English. His ideal is a syntax and a prosody that fits the English language. Unfortunately, there is no standard vocabulary for discussing the subject. Gascoigne often borrows terminology from the romance tradition, but he also draws freely from the *ars metrica*. The result is often cloudy, but the confusion is itself instructive for anyone interested in sixteenth-century English poetry.

"Emphasis" is an important word for Gascoigne, and the confusions in his *Notes* begin with his attempt to define it: "In your verses remember to place every worde in his natural *Emphasis* or sound, that is to say, in such wise, and with such length or shortnesse, elevation or depression of sillables, as it is commonly pronounced or used."[38] Clearly, "emphasis" in this passage means something like "natural word accent." The reference to "elevation or depression" confirms that interpretation. Confusion sets in because Gascoigne also seems to equate emphasis with "length or shortnesse." "Length" and "shortnesse" have nothing to do with accent. They are quantitative concepts and relate to duration. Either Gascoigne is aware that quantity and accent are different but considers them equivalent in effect, or he is unaware of the distinction, which would be surprising but not impossible.

The most exotic product of the informal equation of quantity with accent is a passage that implies Chaucer is a quantitative poet:

> Also our father *Chaucer* hath used the same libertie in feete and measures that the Latinists do use: and who so ever do peruse and well consider his workes, he shall finde that although his lines are not always of one selfe same number of Syllables, yet, beyng redde by one that hath understanding, the longest verse, and that which hath the most Syllables in it, will fall (to the eare) correspondent unto that which hath the fewest sillables in it: and like wise that whiche hath in it fewest sillables shalbe founde yet to consist of woordes that have suche naturall sounde, as may seeme equall in length to a verse which hath many moe sillables of lighter accentes.[39]

Is this to be taken literally, or is it a roundabout statement that Chaucer's verse follows the Old English strategy of counting accents but allowing variable numbers of unstressed syllables?

To invoke the Old English model is to say that Chaucer's verse is *not* isosyllabic in the romance manner. Perhaps that is the main point of Gascoigne's comment. He is, after all, outlining an improved system of versification. Perhaps the reform requires modification, if not outright rejection, of the syllabic tradition. But the statement seems more overtly classical than that. To say Chaucer uses "the same libertie in feete and measures that the Latinists use" suggests strongly that Chaucer's verse is isochronic in the manner of quantitative meter; that is, it allows substitution of two short syllables for one long and vice versa. Confusion is compounded by the fact that the statement ends with a reference apparently equating "light accent" (*levis*) with short vowel quantity.

Let us return to Gascoigne's "emphasis." Gascoigne uses three accents to mark "emphasis." These are the same accents given in a typical treatise of the *ars metrica* under the heading of "tone." Gascoigne probably borrowed his accents from Lily's Royal Grammar, but since the accent system is commonplace, other sources are entirely possible. There is one significant variation from Lily in Gascoigne's terminology: instead of calling the rising tone *acutus*, he calls it *levis*.

He translates *gravis* as "long," *levis* as "short," and *circumflexa* as "indifferent." *Gravis* is marked by (\), *levis* (Lily's *acutus*) by (/), and *circumflexa* by (ˆ).⁴⁰ What, really, do these accents mean?

Gravis, *levis*, and *circumflexa* can be related to French, where *gravis* would be equivalent to *grave*, *levis* to *aigu*, and *circumflexa* to *circonflex*. In this case *gravis* should be understood as a "falling" and *levis* as a "rising" tonal accent. Perhaps Gascoigne is thinking of English verse in romance terms rather than in terms of Latin prosody.

The possibility of a romance interpretation is reinforced by two other elements in *Certayne Notes*. In spite of his interpretation of Chaucer's verse as isochronic, Gascoigne normally refers to verse forms in terms of number and measure. "Number" means number of syllables in a line. "Measure" is an ambiguous term because it can be used for quantitative as well as syllabic prosody. In the following comment, a syllabic understanding is indicated because of the close linkage of "measure" with syllable count: "I say then, remember to holde the same measure wherewith you begin, whether it be in a verse of sixe syllables, eight, ten, twelve, etc."⁴¹ The case for a romance interpretation is strengthened by yet another fact. Although a few metrical forms listed by Gascoigne are native English (e.g., poulter's measure, rhyme royal), most are French.⁴² Finally, like French prosodists before him, Gascoigne equates rhyme with "rhythm" when he refers to "Rithme royall," and he repeats a distinction as old as Bede's *De arte metrica* when he complains that "our Poemes may justly be called Rithmes, and cannot by any right challenge the name of a Verse."⁴³

In spite of these romance elements, Gascoigne's is emphatically not a treatise in the tradition of second rhetoric. If his system of accents seems to point toward France, his explanations of the system point in two quite different directions, one minor and the other major.

Let us consider the minor direction first. According to one translation in *Certayne Notes*, *gravis* means "long" and *levis* "short." In other words, the terms refer not to tone but to duration. The translations violate the most elementary understanding of the grammatical works from which the terms were borrowed, but there they are. Given their thrust, the third term—*circumflexa*, translated "indifferent"—might be understood to refer to an ambivalent (*anceps*) syllable in quantitative prosody. This is absurd but consistent with the quantitative interpretation.

Gascoigne is not, however, offering a quantitative system of English prosody. Coming, as it does, only five years after Ascham's *Scholemaster*, *Certayne Notes* is best understood as anti-quantitative or at least an attempt to find an alternative to Ascham's quantitative theories. This leads to the second—major—thrust of the terms that refer to accent.

In spite of the translation of *gravis* as "long" and *levis* as "short," Gascoigne's primary concern is stress. Balancing *levis* against *gravis* implies a contrast not between short and long but between "light" and "heavy" understood in relation to stress. This interpretation makes sense out of Gascoigne's equation of *gravis* with "long," in spite of the fact that *gravis* originally means "falling" tonal accent. The mandatory "long" syllable of a quantitative iambic foot coincides with the ictus and can therefore be considered correlative to the "heavy" syllable of an accentual iambic foot.

Unfortunately, there is another problem. If *gravis* is interpreted as "heavy" in contrast to "light," the *gravis* mark (\) should logically designate the "heavy" (stressed) syllable of an accentual foot. Gascoigne does not use it in this way. One page after the *gravis* mark is introduced, it is used to designate lightly stressed syllables, and the mark assigned to *levis* (/) is used for heavily stressed syllables. The following scansion is reproduced exactly as it appears in *Certayne Notes*:[44]

\ / \ \/   \ / \ \ /
Unlesse he beleve, that all is but vayne.

In other words, according to Gascoigne's system of scansion marks, *levis* is heavy and *gravis* is light. This is comprehensible in terms of the Latin equation of *levis*—hence "light" in the sense of "rising"—with voice intonation and with arsis. Since in Latin (in contrast to Greek) terminology, arsis coincides with ictus, the result is probably as close as we can come to Gascoigne's intention. *Gravis* thus refers to thesis and (by implication) light accent; *levis* to arsis and strong accent or "emphasis." The poet's task is to line the light and strong accents up in an order analogous to the pattern of feet in a line of quantitative verse.

Where does the "circumflex" accent fit into this system? It might be understood to refer to English words—notably monosyllables—that can be stressed or unstressed in accentual meter, or words that can bear secondary stress. Alexander Gil, Milton's teacher, seems to have understood it in this way.[45] Perhaps it means nothing at all and is present merely because it was always part of the discussion of *tonus* in the *ars metrica*. There is no way of knowing, because Gascoigne never uses the circumflex in his sample scansions. One point, however, is clear. The thrust of Gascoigne's discussion of various kinds of "emphasis" is against syllabic versification.

Although Gascoigne's rules apply in theory to poems written in all of the possible meters, he observes that in the poetry of his age only one meter is used—the iambic:

> We use none other order but a foote of two sillables, whereof the first is depressed or made short, and the second is elevate or made long; and that sound or scanning continueth throughout the verse. . . . And surely I can lament that wee are fallen into such a playne and simple manner of wryting, that there is none other foote used but one. . . . But, since it is so, let us take the forde as we finde it, and lette me set downe unto you suche rules or precepts that even in this playne foote of two syllables you wreste no woorde from his natural and usuall sounde.[46]

In spite of inconsistencies in terminology, Gascoigne comes close to the concept of English meter as a series of regular feet—or more precisely, a series of stressed and unstressed "positions" independent of the particular poem. In *The Founding of English Metre*, John Thompson calls this aspect of *Certayne Notes* "one of the major stages in the development of English poetic techniques." He believes that Gascoigne formulated the concept of an abstract metrical pattern to which the natural accents of the words in a line should be matched, with meter having precedence: "When language and the metrical pattern come together . . . it is metrical pattern that rules."[47] "Understand," for example, must be used so that the stressed position of the foot corresponds with the natural accent: "understánd" rather than "únderstand."

One imagines that "fitting words to meter" was familiar to Elizabethans from their grammar school exercises in writing Latin verse and seemed quite unremarkable. This sort of "fitting" is clearly implied in the instructions for teaching versification found in Brinsley's *Ludus literarius*. Students reduce a Latin poem to its words, remarking their quantities as they enter them in their notebook. They then create a new poem by making the words fit the dual patterns of grammar and meter. The difference between writing Latin and English verse would have been that the English words are fitted by matching accents rather than vowel quantities.

Gascoigne ends the discussion of meter by repeating the accent rule: match natural word stress with the pattern required by the meter. The rule is rigid. The ideal is a line in which every foot consists of a light syllable followed by a heavy (stressed) one, and in which meter coincides throughout with a natural word stress. The word "treasure," for example, should always be treated as trochaic (the natural stress) and should never be placed in a position that calls for a heavy on the second syllable.[48] Gascoigne does not allow substitution by suggesting, for example, that a trochee can sometimes be used in place of an iambus without injury and on occasion with considerable benefit to the line. His example of an ideal line is syllabically and accentually regular:

> x / x / x / x / x /
> I understand your meaning by your eye.

Insistence on natural word accent is a corollary of Gascoigne's approval of standard and unaffected English. The same bias leads him to several positions that were opposed by classicists. He approves, for example, of English monosyllables: "The more monosyllables that you use the truer Englishman you shall seeme, and the lesse you shall smell of the Inkehorne." Clearly, he does not share Ascham's feeling that monosyllables are undesirable because they make it difficult to "interlace" words in the classical manner, so that foot ending does not coincide with word-ending (diaeresis).

He is also in favor of natural (i.e., grammatical) construction and explicitly criticizes inversions based on Latin syntax: "You shall do very well to use your verse after thenglishe phrase, and not after the maner of other languages. The Latinists do commonly set the adjective after the Substantive . . . but if we should say in English a woman fayre, a house high, etc. it would have but small grace."[49] It is interesting that one of Brinsley's examples of "artificial order" in *Ludus literarius* (ch. 11) is also noun-adjective inversion, although Brinsley is discussing Latin rather than English. Brinsley's approval of artificial order is indicated by the fact that he calls it "Rhetoricall" and "Ciceronian" and associates it closely with the process of creating verse. Gascoigne's position requires rejection of this view, along with experiments in the use of artificial order in English verse by Wyatt, Surrey, and Jasper Heywood, among others. He would permit some nonstandard phrasing, however, by poetic license, "for in some places it may be borne, but not so hardly as some use it." His comments suggest that the principal justification for such license is facilitating end-rhyme.

Mention of poetic license leads to metaplasm. Gascoigne appears to accept classical precedent: "This poeticall licence is a shrewde fellow, and covereth many faults in a verse; it maketh wordes longer, shorter, of mo sillables, of fewer, newer, older, truer, falser; and, to conclude, it tokeneth all things at pleasure, for example, *ydone* for *done*, *adowne* for *downe*, *orecome* for *overcome*, *tane* for *taken*, *power* for *powre*, *heaven* for *heavn*...and a numbre of other."[50]

Certayne Notes also explains stanza forms. Here, if not elsewhere, it closely resembles French treatises of second rhetoric. Gascoigne may be recalling Sebillet's *L'Art poétique* or an earlier French treatment.[51] At any rate he has the same tendency to conflate vernacular and classical traditions. There was, however, no DuBellay in England to take him to task for insensitivity to cultural change.

He begins with "Rithme royall," which is "best for grave discourses." Then comes "ballade," followed by "rondolet," "sonnet," "dyzaynes," "syxaines," "ver layes," and poulter's measure. "Ballade" is defined as having a six-line stanza with lines of six or eight—or occasionally ten—syllables. In spite of the obvious fondness of his contemporaries for the fourteener, Gascoigne does not list it as a standard form, though he notes that poets often set out to write in poulter's measure but "fal into xiiii. and fourtene, *et sic de similibus*, the which is either forgetfulnes or carelesnes."[52] This is hardly a recommendation of the fourteener. Gascoigne commends the "ryding rime . . . such as our Mayster and Father *Chaucer* used in his Canterburie Tales." By "ryding rime" he may mean Chaucerian irregular decasyllabic couplets with strong enjambment, or he may mean Chaucer's decasyllabic interpreted as a rough four-beat line.[53] There is another possible interpretation. Puttenham used the term "riding rime" a few years later in his *Arte of English Poesie* to mean verse that is "licentious" and uses "unshapely wordes" that allow "no convenient Cesure."[54] If Gascoigne understands "ryding rime" in this way, he is being inconsistent with his earlier comment that Chaucer writes isochronic verse resembling Latin verse. Near the end of *Certayne Notes*, he returns to poulter's measure. It is "now adayes used in all Theames" and is especially suited to psalms and hymns.[55]

For Gascoigne, rhyme is an attractive ornament, but not an excuse for complex (hence unidiomatic) word order: "Do rather search the bottome of your braynes for apte wordes than chaunge good reason for rumbling rime."[56] Here the ideal is "perspicuity"—Latin *perspicuitas*. "Perspicuity" is a quality associated with *Latinitas* and means "easy clarity." Gascoigne links it to advice "to use your verse after thenglishe phrase, and not after the maner of other languages," another warning against Latinate construction. The comment on "perspicuity" is followed by the injunction, "frame all sentences in their mother phrase and proper *Idióma*."[57] "English idiom" includes natural order and an English vocabulary free of foreign words and inkhorn terms.

Gascoigne's poetry helps to clarify his purpose. The regularity of his lines in terms of syllable count and accent has already been noted. As we might expect from a poet wedded to "mother phrase and proper *Idióma*," he avoids complex syntax, inversion, and Latin-derived polysyllables. His rhyme schemes are simple, and as a substitute for other kinds of complexity he regularly invokes simple rhetorical formulas such as those given for different types of oration in elementary rhetoric books to provide structure for his lyric poems.[58]

Hard Classicism: Harvey, Webbe, Campion

Between 1579 and 1583, discussions of prosody became highly technical because of the interest of Thomas Drant, Edmund Spenser, Gabriel Harvey, Sir Philip Sidney, and Richard Stanyhurst in quantitative meter.[59] Although quantitative English verse was a doomed cause, the movement often seems to point in the direction of a theory of accentual foot meter, and for this reason its significance may be greater than at first seems to be the case. It also heightened the awareness of English authors of the difference between the poetry of the "ancients" and that of the "moderns." In the process, it sharpened awareness of the linguistic and aesthetic characteristics of both.

Some of the most interesting points are made in correspondence between Spenser and Harvey. The correspondence refers to a literary society called the *Areopagus* that has a special interest in quantitative verse. Whether or not such a society actually existed (it probably did not), the idea for it must have come from Continental academies of poetry like those of Tolomei and Baïf. Among the alleged members are Sidney and Spenser. The important fact about these two members is that when forced to choose between quantitative and romance versification, they both chose the romance tradition. Sir Philip Sidney wrote a pastoral novel adorned with quantitative poems, but his most famous poem is *Astrophil and Stella,* which is a sonnet sequence and includes sonnets in Alexandrines as well as in decasyllabic lines. And in 1579, at almost exactly the time that the correspondence referring to the Areopagus was going on, Edmund Spenser presented himself officially to the literary world in a series of eclogues making ostentatious—and brilliant—use of romance forms.

In spite of these facts, Spenser writes in 1579 that he is "more in love wyth my English Versifying than with Ryming," repeating the old distinction between quantitative verse (*versus*) and syllabic poetry (*rithmus*). He is especially proud of his quantitative iambics and provides an extended example of "*iambicum trimetrum.*"[60] In contrast to these, English rhymes are "Toyes."

Harvey approves. However, he complains that two of Spenser's lines have extra syllables "unlesse happly one of the feete be sawed off with a payre of SYNCOPES."[61] If metaplasm is intended, he says, it should be indicated by the spelling; for example, "Heavnli Virginals" for "Heavenli Virginals." The defect is, however, acceptable in a "mixte and licentious IAMBICKE." The reference is to the poetic license traditionally granted writers of comedy. Because Spenser's "English Comicall Iambickes" are "common and licentious," he has the right to almost any variation on the basic meter that he decides to use. On the other hand, Harvey remarks, Spenser boasted he was following the rules even more strictly than Thomas Watson, who refused to publish his *Absalom* merely because in a few places he used an anapest in place of an iamb. Spenser can use license but must not claim he is following the rules.

Replying, Spenser praises the English hexameters Harvey has sent him and quotes six of his own. He is distressed by the difficulty of accommodating the natural accent of English words to quantitative meters. The word "carpenter," for example, is naturally accented on the first syllable; but since the *e* comes before two consonants, it should be long by position. The implication is that if it is long, it should also be accented. Thus, in an English line written according to Latin rules, "carpenter" ought to be accented on the second syllable. Again, "Heaven" is pronounced as one syllable ("Hev'n") but treated in verse as having two syllables—"stretched out with a *Diastole* . . . like a lame Dogge that holdes up one legge."[62]

Harvey understands the problem. English does not sound quantitative, and when it is written, it does not look quantitative. He surmises that reformed versifying will be impossible without reformed spelling: "ONE AND THE SAME ORTHOGRAPHIE, in all pointes conformable and proportionate to our COMMON NATURAL PROSODYE."[63] As we have noted, reformed spelling was proposed in Italy by Tolomei and in France by Baïf for the same reason and with the same futility. Recalling the freedom allowed to the first versifiers in Greece and Rome, Harvey is comforted by the belief that as innovators, he and Spenser have freedom to experiment. They will, in turn, be regarded as authorities by future generations. More quantitative verses follow, succeeded by detailed consideration of problems of accent in several English words and further comments on "prosodie" and "orthographie." The most interesting feature of these comments is Harvey's emphatic support for native English pronunciation: "You shal never have my subscription or consent . . . to make your *Carpenter*, our *Carpenter*, an inche longer or bigger than God and his Englishe people have made him. Is there no other Pollicie to pull down Ryming and set uppe Versifying but you must . . . against all order of Lawe, and in despite of Custome, forcibly usurpe and tyrannize uppon a quiet companye of wordes . . . ?" He reinforces the point by reminding Spenser that in the *Ars poetica* (l. 72), Horace urges the poet to follow custom and normal usage.[64]

Harvey's sensitivity to the technique of quantitative verse leads to a sharp distinction, made in his letter-book, between verse using "meter" and verse based on "number." The passage clearly identifies the dominant poetic mode of the age as syllabic: "In the nexte seate to thes hexameters, adonickes, and iambickes I sett those that stand uppon the number, not in meter, sutch as my lorde of Surrey is sayde first to have putt forthe in prynte, and my lorde Buckhurste and M. Norton in the Tragedye of Gorboduc, M. Gascoygnes Steele Glasse."[65]

The experiments of Richard Stanyhurst and several lesser writers of quantitative prosody can be ignored here. They all seek to reproduce in English the noble effects of Greek and Latin originals and advocate quantity because they feel the effects cannot be produced without the verse forms.

William Webbe is more interesting. His *Discourse of English Poetrie* (1586) is a general discussion of the subject with a strong classical bias that recognizes clearly the indifference of most English authors to quantitative experiments. The classical bias extends to an appendix consisting of a paraphrase of Horace's *Ars poetica*. In the treatise proper, Webbe reviews the standard classical genres, beginning with "*Hexametrum Epicum*," and provides examples of several forms. He strongly advocates "reformed" versification and marvels at the greatness English poets could attain "if English Poetrie were truely reformed, and some perfect platforme or *Prosodia* of versifying were . . . ratified and sette downe."[66] Evidently, he believes that Surrey attempted to translate the *Aeneid* into quantitative verse but failed for lack of understanding of "true quantity of sillabes."

Webbe admits freely that "the most usuall and frequented kind of our English Poetry hath alwayes runne upon and to this day is observed in such equall number of syllables and likenes of wordes [i.e., rhyme] that in all places one verse either immediately, or by mutuall interposition, may be aunswerable to an other both in proportion of length and ending of lynes in the same Letters."⁶⁷ The description is explicitly syllabic. The relation of syllabic poetry to music is recalled in an observation that rhyme only works if "one meeter or verse be aunswerable to an other, in equall number of feete or syllables, or proportionable to the tune whereby it is to be reade or measured."⁶⁸ The equation of "meeter" with line is a characteristic of romance prosody, and we have already observed the equation of syllables with "feet" in medieval French treatises on poetry and in comments on prosody by Sir Philip Sidney. The close relation between syllable count and melody—a feature of syllabic verse since the sequence—is significant in this comment, as is the assumption that a syllabic line will have a "tune whereby it is to be reade or measured."

When Webbe describes syllabic lines and rhyme schemes, his terminology is again unambiguously syllabic. The longest verse is "sixteene syllables, eache two verses ryming together." He mentions the octosyllabic couplet using cross rhyme, the fourteener, and several forms used in *The Shepheardes Calender:* decasyllabic couplets, nine-syllable couplets, seven-syllable couplets, irregular stanzas, twelve-syllable lines printed as half-lines, and "round" or rondelay.

Yet Webbe also uses classical terminology to describe English verse. He remarks, for example, that "the naturall course of most English verses seemeth to run upon the olde Iambicke stroake."⁶⁹ Having introduced the iambic foot, Webbe immediately gives several examples of lines scanned "according to right quantitie"; for example:

Ĭ that mў slĕnder oaten pĭpe ĭn verse wăs wont tŏ sounde.

This scansion is really based on accent. When Webbe refers to "long" and "short" syllables, he assumes, like most of his contemporaries, that long syllables have natural accent (or stress) in polysyllabic words. As the scansion shows, the result can look at times like the product of a theory of accentual foot meter. Like Gascoigne, Webbe warns against allowing natural accent in positions that the meter would make light. It is a "foule disgrace" and a "wonderful defacing" of the words. He is also opposed to "overthwart placing or rather displacing" of words, whether for the sake of rhyme or from a misguided notion of eloquence.

Thomas Campion is the premier English champion of reformed versifying. Like Baïf in France, he was an accomplished musician. He advocates quantity because he believes it is inherently musical:

> In joyning of words to harmony there is nothing more offensive to the eare then to place a long sillable with a shorte note, or a short sillable with a long note, though in the last the vowell often beares it out. The world is made by Simmetry and proportion, and is in that respect compared to Musick, and Musick to Poetry: for *Terence* saith, speaking of Poets, *artem qui tractant musicam*, confounding Musick and Poesy together.[70]

Campion's *Observations in the Art of English Poesie* (1602) is studiously classical, but the immediate source for its exposition of prosody may have been English. Jane K. Fenyo has shown that his analysis closely follows the "Prosodia" section of Lily's Royal Grammar.[71] After rejecting rhyme (in spite of the fact that some of his most beautiful lyrics are in rhymed stanzas), Campion demonstrates the possibility of creating the standard classical forms in English. He is particularly fond of the "*Iambick* licenciate," which he correctly traces to the metrical freedom of Plautus and Terence. In comic verse, he explains, "In the third and fift place we must of force hold the *Iambick* foote, in the first, second, and fourth place we may use a *Spondee* or *Iambick* and sometime a *Tribrack* or *Dactile*, but rarely an *Anapestick* foote, and that in the second or fourth place."[72]

Of special interest is Campion's observation that in English the same form (iambic pentameter) is destined to be used for two genres that were given different meters by the ancients:

> These [quantitative iambic pentameters] are those numbers which Nature in our English destinates to the Tragick and Heroik Poeme: for the subject of them both being all one, I see no impediment why one verse may not serve them both, as it appeares more plainly in the old comparison of the two Greek writers, when they say *Homerus est Sophocles heroicus*, and againe *Sophocles est Homerus tragicus*, intimating that both Sophocles and Homer are the same in height and subject, and differ only in the kinde of their numbers.[73]

Turning to comedy, Campion adds: "The Iambick verse in like manner being yet made a little more licentiate, that it may therby the neerer imitate our common talke, will excellently serve for Comedies."[74]

The statement that epic and tragic verse forms are "the same in height" would be surprising if Campion were not attempting to justify a situation that he cannot change—namely, that in English, iambic meter has to do for both epic and tragedy. Campion must show that the form is up to the two tasks or concede that English verse cannot produce the full range of poetic effects found in ancient poetry. In general, renaissance critics followed the tradition of the *ars metrica* and identified epic as the supreme genre. Occasionally, on the basis of the *Poetics*, arguments were made that tragedy is the nobler form, but they made scant headway in spite of the popularity of Aristotle. On one point, however, all parties could agree. At its climactic moments, tragic verse is elevated and musical, and in this sense approaches the norm of epic. This is the base on which Campion rests his argument. The argument is strengthened by his implicit recognition in the remarks about comedy that dramatic verse can be relaxed—like "our common talke"—when this is appropriate.

The remainder of Campion's essay consists of chapters on various classical forms: dimeter, trochaic, elegiac, ode, and Anacreontic. The work ends with a chapter on English quantities that considers position, elision (i.e., metaplasm), and orthography.

The Middle Road: Syllable and Accent

Quantitative prosody aside, the two major treatises of the latter quarter of the sixteenth century are Sidney's *Apology for Poetry* (ca. 1580–85) and Puttenham's *Arte of English Poesie* (1589). Both works follow the pattern set by Webbe. They admit that the dominant tradition of English poetry is syllable count or "number" and rhyme. The tendency to waver between syllable count and classical concepts is also evident. They list both native forms and the major classical genres, and they treat the quantitative movement respectfully. In these particulars they resemble the more sophisticated sixteenth-century Italian and French treatises on vernacular poetry.

Sidney's *Apology* devotes a section to the "works" of poetry, meaning its unique ability to teach practical morality. This section is followed by a treatment of poetry's "parts," meaning classical genres: pastoral, elegy, satire, comedy, tragedy, Pindaric, hymn, and epic. The discussion closely associates form and function in the manner of the *ars metrica*.

Sidney is an Aristotelian rather than a follower of the theory equating poetry with writing in meter. He considers poetry imitation in the sense of "making fictions," and he is willing to call a prose work like the *Ethiopian History* of Heliodorus a poem: "It is already sayde (and, as I think, trulie sayde) it is not ryming and versing that maketh Poesie. One may bee a Poet without versing, and a versifyer without Poetry." Scaliger, Sidney adds, is wrong to make verse the defining characteristic of poetry. On the other hand, verse is a delightful musical embellishment and therefore "an inseparable commendation" to poetry.[75]

Sidney wrote competent, even distinguished quantitative verse as well as verse based on syllable count and rhyme. In the section of the *Apology* that considers English poets, he contrasts the "Aunciente" practice of marking "the quantitie of each silable" with the "Moderne" practice of considering "onely number (with some regarde of the accent), the chiefe life of [which] standeth in that lyke sounding of the words, which wee call Ryme."[76] Both techniques are musical, and English is fortunate because it is suited to both.

More significant is the fact that Sidney understands the principles of "Moderne" verse to be derived from the syllabic system of romance prosody. This is evident from the central place he assigns to syllable count and from the way he associates accent with rhyme. His remark that English shows "some regarde of the accent" as well as number is an allusion to the importance of terminal accent—or cadence—in creating the rhymes that close romance verses.

All of the threads of earlier prosodic thought are brought together in the most comprehensive English poetic treatise of the sixteenth century, George Puttenham's *Arte of English Poesie*. In his first book (chs. 6–7) Puttenham relates the history of rhyme. Like all other renaissance critics who write on the subject, he associates rhyme with the fall of Rome and the coming of the barbarians. In chapters 11–30 he lists the ancient genres. They are epic, lyric, elegy, epigram, comedy, tragedy, satire, and several occasional forms drawn from epideictic rhetoric: encomium, lament, birthday song, epithalamium. No reference is made to vernacular forms until the chapter on English poets (ch. 31). This chapter is itself a heavily biased account of the liberation of English from "our rude and homlie maner of vulgar Poesie" by "the first reformers of our English meetre and stile."[77] The reformers are chiefly Wyatt and Surrey, and Puttenham emphasizes their debt to Italy. Since neither poet used quantitative measures, they presumably elevated the "rude and homlie maner" of English poetry by changing its sentiments and rhetoric rather than its prosody. Puttenham adds that the work of the pioneers was complemented by the midcentury translations of Phaer and Golding and reached full flower in the work of poets of the eighties, particularly Sir Walter Raleigh and Sir Philip Sidney.

Book 2 is devoted entirely to prosody. It is complex and sophisticated, although marred by the confusions of terminology found in other critics of the age. A discussion of the "Cesure" (ch. 5) is of special interest because it relates construction to line integrity. Puttenham understands the relation of sentence articulation to meaning. Speech uses pauses "bicause it goeth by clauses of severall constructions & sence." He recognizes three degrees of pause, related to three sentence units of increasing importance—comma, colon, and period.

Pauses are used in poetry as well as prose. Many lines have medial and all have final pause. In an Alexandrine, the pause comes after the sixth syllable. The same is true for a hendecasyllabic. In a decasyllable, it comes after the fourth syllable. Many a poet, however, "delights not in many stayes by the way, and therefore giveth but one *Cesure* to any verse." This is particularly true of "aunciont rymers, as *Chaucer, Lydgate, & others*." All verses, however, require a caesura at the end. This requirement is a corollary of the delight that we take in rhyme "because the Poets chief Musicke [lies] in his rime or concorde, to heare the Simphonie." The emphasis on line rather than metrical foot recalls romance prosody, but the traditional romance correlation between phrase and measure is ignored. Puttenham complains that the pauses in verse are less related to meaning than to musical effect: "Every verse is as it were a clause of it selfe, and limited with a *Cesure* howsoever the sence beare, perfect or imperfect, which difference is observable betwixt the prose and the meeter."[78]

Like Webbe, Puttenham treats vernacular and classical forms separately. The main vernacular forms are defined in chapter 4 of book 2. They are called "meeters," but they are based on syllable count, which Puttenham consistently recognizes as the traditional and true principle of English verse. The chapter begins with "short" meters (two and four syllables). It proceeds through six- and seven-syllable lines to lines of ten and twelve syllables, the latter properly identified as "Alexandrines." The fourteen-syllable line is criticized as "tedious, for the length of the verse kepeth the eare too long from his delight."[79]

The explanation of stanza forms (ch. 11) is also influenced by romance tradition. It moves forward in the manner of treatises of second rhetoric from couplets to quatrains to longer, more complex forms, including the canzone and the *seizino* (sestina). The "proportions" of the various stanzas are also enumerated: two for the quatrain, ten for the *sixain,* eight for the *huitain.* The chapter on verse forms is followed by a discussion (ch. 12) of shaped verse and six chapters (chs. 13–18) on reformed (i.e., quantitative) versifying.

In spite of this syllabic terminology, Puttenham has a clear idea of accent in English verse. He consistently refers to the heavy accent of classical tradition as "sharp." This translates Latin *acutus* and is far less confusing than Gascoigne's term "light." For example, he offers the following line:

Salomon Davids sonne, king of Jerusalem.

The line is acceptable, he says, but it would have been better if the first word had been "a disillable or two monosillables, and not a trisillable: having this sharpe accent uppon the *Antepenultima.*" The natural conclusion is that Puttenham wants a word with an accent that fits an iambic metrical scheme—that is, that he has accentual foot meter in mind. This is not the case. The reason that "Salomon" is unsatisfactory is that it moves too fast and "makes the verse seem but of eleven sillables." The terminology blends syllable count with duration—a quantitative concept—and resolutely refuses to use the terminology of accentual meter. This is true in spite of the fact that the line Puttenham gives (with scansion) to show a proper Alexandrine looks very much like a regular iambic hexameter with "to" and "-em" promoted:[80]

/   /   /   / /   /
Restore king Davids sonne unto Jerusalem.

Two other passages show that Puttenham consciously rejected the concept of accentual foot meter. These are interesting because they suggest how close he came to the concept and how alien it was to his mind set. The first passage is a comment on "*rythmos,* whence we have derived this word ryme." Modern verse is a kind of *rythmos,* and it differs from ancient verse precisely in the fact that it does not use feet: "We have no such feete or times or stirres in our meeters."[81] Puttenham means that English "meeters" use syllables in the French manner, as "a certaine musicall numerositie." Accordingly, he limits his discussion of accent within the line to "cadence." His concepts could have been taken directly from a French prosody manual. Cadence is "the fal of a verse in every last word with a certaine tunable sound, which, being matched with another like sound, do make a *concord.*" It is related to rhyme ("every last word") rather than to the idea of a line divided into metrical feet, and it can involve one, two, or three syllables (ultimate, penultimate, or antepenultimate).[82]

The second time Puttenham comes close to the idea of accentual feet only to reject it is when he discusses English quantitative verse. Like other writers on English quantity, he assumes that the long syllable in an English polysyllable is also normally the accented syllable. It should have "one long time of necessitie, which should be where his sharpe accent falls in our owne *ydiome* most aptly and naturally." Monosyllables can be long or short depending on convenience. These rules permit accentual equivalents of the most common feet (iambus, trochee, dactyl, etc.), but they fail to explain how a polysyllable can take the form of an entirely long or short foot (pyrrhic, spondee, molossus, etc.). For example, "holie" is scanned as two short vowels (a pyrrhic) in spite of the fact that it is accented on the first syllable, and all of the vowels of "permitting" are said to be long (a molossus) in spite of the fact that only one is naturally stressed. Further problems are created by the position rule that makes a vowel long before two or more consonants. The *u* in "sepulchre," for example, must be long because of the consonant cluster following it, and this requires Puttenham to treat it as though it is accented on the middle syllable. In sum, whatever Puttenham's rules allow, they are in direct conflict with the requirements of accentual foot meter.[83]

Although he shows sympathy for English quantity while discussing it, at the end of the discussion Puttenham rejects it as "vaine & superstitious" and announces that there is no similarity between its strategies and traditional English versification. Unfortunately, the announcement creates problems even as it promises to solve them. After Puttenham clearly and unambiguously calls English verse syllabic and rejects the idea of feet, he seems to recommend using feet. Perhaps the reference is simply to the natural accent patterns of words and is not intended to imply that they will be arranged according to regular metrical patterns when placed in a line of verse. Another possibility is that the comment is intended to apply only to rhyme words, which are regularly described in metrical terms in syllabic prosody. Whatever the explanation, Puttenham dismisses quantity with the following comment: "I . . . rather wish the continuance of our old maner of Poesie, scanning our verse by sillables rather than by feete, and using most commonly the word *Iambique* & sometime the *Trochaike*, which ye shall discern by their accents, and now and then a *Dactill*, keeping precisely our symphony of rime without any other mincing measures, which an idle inventive head could easily devise, and the former examples teach."[84]

Book 3 of the *Arte* corresponds to the section on figures associated with construction in classical treatments of prosody. It is so extended that it amounts to a presentation of the rhetorical topic of *elocutio*. Figures of diction are presented under the rubric of "auricular figures" in chapters 11 to 16. These figures are said to cause "alternation to the eare onely and not the mynde."

Daniel and the Native Tradition

Much more could be said about English discussions of prosody in the sixteenth century. After Puttenham, however, there is no major new contribution to theory. The great debate at the turn of the century is between Thomas Campion and Samuel Daniel. It is the last and most interesting of the English debates about quantity and rhyme. It is also the last English debate that recalls Italian arguments about the question of language. Since Campion's essay has already been considered in relation to quantitative prosody, we can concentrate on Daniel.

The *Defence of Ryme* (ca. 1603) opens with one of those majestic statements that demand to be quoted in full:

> We could well have allowed of [Campion's] numbers, had he not disgraced our Ryme, which both Custome and Nature doth most powerfully defend: Custome that is before all Law, Nature that is above all Arte. Every language hath her proper number or measure fitted to use and delight, which Custome, intertaininge by the allowance of the Eare, doth indenize and make naturall. All verse is but a frame of wordes confined within certaine measure, differing from the ordinarie speech, and introduced, the better to express mens conceipts, both for delight and memorie. Which frame of words consisting of *Rithmus* or *Metrum,* Number or measure, are disposed . . . according to the humour of the Composer and the set of the time.[85]

Campion admitted that the best English verse is iambic and that decasyllabic iambic verse is most natural. He is therefore not offering anything new, Daniel says, but "the plaine ancient verse" that English poets always wrote. Daniel believes that so-called reformed iambics are really accentual iambics in a new dress. Campion is giving "onely what was our owne before, and the same but apparelled in forraine Titles."[86]

Daniel continues by discussing his own experiences as an English poet. He dislikes couplets for long poems because they are "tyresome" and monotonous: "They run on with a sound of one nature and a kinde of certaintie which stuffes the delight rather then intertaines it."[87] This is a comment on both French poetry and the considerable body of poetry in decasyllabic couplets that had been written in English by 1600. Blank verse is much superior for both long narrative poems and drama, although rhyme can be used for the tragic chorus and to point aphorisms (*sententiae*). Enjambment beguiles the ear in English blank verse as much as in the verse of Homer and Lucan. For the verse epistle of the sort that Daniel writes, "cross rhyme"—quatrain verse of the form *a b a b*—is best.

In the course of defending custom and nature, Daniel finds, like many of his Italian and French predecessors, that he must also defend medieval culture. Rhyme may be standard in English, but it is associated with the Middle Ages, which meant, as far as humanists were concerned, Gothic barbarians and the dark night of Popish superstition. Daniel rejects this understanding of the Middle Ages. Only a fool, he complains, would say that Europe "lay pittifully deformed in those lacke-learning times from the declining of the Romane Empire till the light of the Latine tongue was revived by Recline, Erasmus, and Moore."[88] The Venerable Bede lived in those lack-learning times, as did Walter Map, Roger Bacon, William of Occam, St. Thomas Aquinas, and Duns Scotus. So did Petrarch, the teacher of all Europe. Daniel's comment shows an awareness of authors not generally thought to have been popular among Protestant writers of the sixteenth century.

The new century thus begins with the suggestion of a Gothic revival complemented by an attack on the couplet and a praise of blank verse and quatrain verse. Critical interest in things Gothic is brilliantly complemented by Spenser's *Faerie Queene*. However, in spite of the "school of Spenser" and excursions into "Gothicism" by the young Milton, the Middle Ages failed to catch the imagination of major English poets of the seventeenth century. Quatrain verse also failed to fulfill the promise Daniel felt it had in spite of its use by William Davenant. Blank verse died out with the closing of the theatres. It would not be revived for heroic poetry until Milton's *Paradise Lost* (1667) and for tragedy until Nathaniel Lee's *Rival Queens* (1677). The couplet, the form specifically rejected by Daniel for longer poems, was the form destined to catch the imagination of the poets of the Age of Reason.[89]

Under the combined influence of Erasmian humanism and English nationalism, English intellectuals set out to purify and elevate the language. An important part of this task was the creation of vernacular literary forms having the nobility of ancient forms.

Hard classicists insisted that ancient nobility can only be achieved by refashioning the language itself. Moderate classicists followed the lead of Trissino in Italy and DuBellay in France, seeking accommodation between the English language and the new classical and Italian forms. In various ways, members of this group appealed to the doctrines of linguistic purity and observance of natural idiom treated in ancient discussions of *Latinitas* and Italian treatises on the question of language. The more radical theorists advocated imitation of classical forms in accentual meters. The more conservative ones sought classical effects but were willing to gain them by reworking traditional forms. A third group continued to assert the validity of the romance tradition. This group took a position resembling the one taken in Italy by defenders of romance like Giovanni Battista Pigna and Giraldi Cintio and by defenders of Dante like Jacopo Mazzoni. It also echoed the endorsement in the *Quintil Horatian* of medieval French traditions.

The Spenser-Harvey correspondence shows the importance of prosody to the practical concerns of renaissance poets, no matter what system they followed, and the treatises of Webbe, Sidney, and Puttenham show its importance for critical theorists. If the discussion is lively, however, it is also confused. Critics talk about English poetry using terms like number, measure, syllable count, rhyme, stanza, and "proportion"—namely, terms derived from the romance tradition. This is unquestionably the dominant position of the theorists, and it must say important things about practice as well as about theory. But the theorists also talk about iambs and caesuras and "emphasis" and the need to match natural accent and meter. Evidently, fully consistent theory of vernacular prosody existed in England in the sixteenth—or for that matter, in the seventeenth—century. The closest approach to rationalizing the problem was to divide the treatment of poetry into a discussion of classical forms and prosody and a discussion of romance forms and prosody. This is the approach taken by Webbe and Puttenham and—to a lesser degree—by Sir Philip Sidney. However, the approach did not eliminate confusion, and the barriers between "classical" and "romance" poetics were always permeable.

PART II

Performances

CHAPTER VI

A Straunge Metre Worthy To Be Embraced

One of the more interesting facts about English blank verse is that it was invented. The evidence suggests it was the result of a self-conscious effort by Henry Howard, earl of Surrey, around 1540, to create a vernacular English form equivalent to the dactylic hexameter of classical epic. It is thus a contribution to the efforts of English esoteric humanism to reproduce in the vernacular the great genres and effects of ancient literature. Surrey clearly derived much inspiration from Vergil, but he was also influenced by what he learned from Italian literature.

Surrey appears to have understood his blank verse as a syllabic form. The fifteenth-century heritage would have pointed in this direction. But Surrey was also clearly dissatisfied with that heritage and seeking a way of either escaping it or transforming it. For the creating of a verse form without rhyme—almost an impossible paradox in view of the time-honored and universal association of "rhyme" and "rhythm"—Italian experiments would have provided essential guidance. These experiments would also have suggested how to use construction to sophisticate the play in the verse of meaning against line.

The irregularity of Surrey's verse, if judged by the criteria of accentual meter, tends to confirm the rightness of understanding his prosody as syllabic. That the irregularity was apparent to Surrey's contemporaries—and disturbed some of them—is shown by Tottel's edition (1557) of books 2 and 4 of the *Aeneid* translation. Throughout the edition, punctuation, spelling, vocabulary, and syntax are changed in order to regularize the verse. This does not mean that Tottel (or his editor) considered Surrey's verse accentual. The evidence offered here suggests it was considered rough syllabic verse and that the changes were intended to correct what appeared to be irregular syllable counting.

Heroic Aspirations

The background of Surrey's effort has been illuminated by the studies of such scholars as Emrys Jones, Alan Hagar, and David Richardson.[1] Heroic poetry is the most important of the large, public literary forms. As Sir Philip Sidney writes in the *Apology for Poetry*,

> [It] doth not onely teach and move to truth, but teacheth and moveth to the most high and excellent truth; [and] maketh magnanimity and justice shine throughout all misty fearfulnes and foggy desires. . . . The Heroicall . . . is not onely a kinde, but the best and most accomplished kinde of Poetry. For as the image of each action styrreth and instructeth the mind, so the loftie image of such Worthies most inflameth the mind with desire to be worthy, and informes with counsel how to be worthy.[2]

The problem of discovering a poetic form complementary to the heroic vision therefore seemed especially urgent. As we know, however, there was no English verse form available to Surrey remotely comparable to Vergil's dactylic hexameter. There are moments of heroic elevation in Chaucer—in the *Knight's Tale*, for example; but the changes that had occurred in the English language during the fifteenth century made it impossible for Surrey to reproduce Chaucer's effects. In fact, he could understand them only imperfectly. When he is closest to Chaucer, as in his sonnet "The soote season that bud and bloom furth brings," his verse has the quality of conscious anachronism. Beyond Chaucer, he had two possible native models: Caxton's prose *Eneydos* (1490), which is translated from the French and would have appeared to Surrey both clumsy and false to the original, and Gavin Douglas's translation of the *Aeneid* into decasyllabic couplets, completed in 1513, though not printed until 1553.

It is clear that Surrey knew Douglas's translation and drew on it. How much he drew on it is unclear. Henry Lathrop concludes that he owes Douglas "nothing fundamental or inspiring. Douglas is diffuse, Surrey is terse; Douglas is familiar, Surrey dignified; Douglas is clumsy, Surrey aims at elegance."[3] On the other hand, Florence Ridley, a more recent student of the subject, concludes that Surrey's debt was deep and continuous.⁴ Perhaps the best answer is that Surrey consulted Douglas as one might consult a Loeb translation today to check the quality of his own work and to pick up any ideas Douglas might have to offer. This is the conclusion of Douglas's chief modern student, Priscilla Bowcutt: "It is possible to over-estimate Surrey's indebtedness to Douglas. . . . I think Surrey consulted Douglas in the first place as an aid to understanding the *Aeneid*. . . . Surrey's aims as a translator were very different from Douglas's. He sought to match Virgil's compression and to 'imitate' many of the more striking formal qualities of the *Aeneid*."⁵

The difference between Douglas and Surrey—and it is an absolutely crucial difference—is that Surrey saw Vergil in terms of style as well as content. Construction is a key to the different effects of the two poets. Douglas uses a standard, frequently colloquial vocabulary, and his narrative moves along using the generally loose syntax, natural order, and closed couplets of the Middle English tradition inherited from Chaucer. The natural order makes his Vergil sound quite English, which is to say that it makes Vergil sound quite un-Vergilian. Surrey, on the other hand, had heard the music of Vergil's Latin. He often heard suggestions of this music in Douglas, and when he did, he used them. When he did not, he created his own music. In the process, he invented a true English equivalent of sustained heroic verse.

We know that Surrey considered Wyatt his master in English poetry. Wyatt introduced him to the new poetry of Italy and to the possibility of a new kind of English. We know too that Surrey's verse is considerably more modern, in the sense of being more regular, than Wyatt's.⁶ In his well-known epitaph on Wyatt, Surrey remarks that Wyatt's hand taught "what might be said in rhyme" and "reft Chaucer the glory of his wit."

Both points are relevant. Wyatt is interested exclusively in rhyming forms of poetry, whether native or foreign. Like Bembo in Italy, Wyatt seems to have regarded the poetic forms of the Trecento as alternatives to the romance forms associated with medieval French (and thus English) poetry. He contributed to the development of the new poetry by his use of terza rima for satire and the sonnet for lyric poetry. His sonnets are of special interest, for they are the outstanding examples in Tottel's *Miscellany* of poems written "in small parcels" in which syntax is brilliantly coordinated with line and rhyme scheme. Wyatt manages, perhaps better than any later English writer, to create an equivalent of Petrarchan construction in his sonnet translations. No later English writer is more successful in uniting phrase, image, line, and rhyme unit in (to use Tottel's phrase) "small parcels" like those of the Italian originals. A like sensitivity to new tonalities is evident in Wyatt's translations of the sonnets of Serafino Aquilano and Luigi Alamanni's satires.[7] Surrey must have learned a great deal about construction from Wyatt. Wyatt had shown "what might be said in rhyme." Surrey would be the first English poet to show what might be said without it.

George Saintsbury considers it "gratuitous futility" to argue that Surrey did not derive the concept of blank verse from the Italians. He is right, but he offers no suggestions about specific influences. F. M. Padelford suggests Niccolò Liburnio, who published a Vergil translation in 1534, or the translation by several hands that Aristotile Zoppio began to issue in 1539. The Zoppio edition is a probable influence because it was well known. Books 2 and 4 were published in 1539–40, at just the time when Surrey was probably setting to work. These are the books that he translated. The Italian translation of book 2 is by Cardinal Ippolito de'Medici and of book 4 by Bartolomeo Piccolomini. Edwin Cassidy suggests that Surrey was influenced by the *versi sciolti* in Luigi Alamanni's *Rime Toscane* (1533), which was published in France at the time when Surrey was in Paris. Another figure whose work was probably known to Surrey is Giangiorgio Trissino. Trissino's interests parallel Surrey's closely. In view of Trissino's prominence in the earlier sixteenth century, it is hard to see how Surrey could have missed him.[8]

A Straunge Metre

Until the twentieth century Surrey's translation was known only through Tottel's edition of 1557. This edition is apparently the source of a few scattered references to Surrey's *Aeneid* in the sixteenth century.[9] Today two other versions of Surrey's *Aeneid* are known that are independent of Tottel. Both are of book 4 alone. The more familiar one is preserved in Hargrave manuscript 205, which dates from the 1560s. This version is reprinted parallel to Tottel's version in the edition (rev. 1928) of Surrey's poems by F. M. Padelford.[10]

The less familiar version is *The Fourth Boke of Virgill* published around 1554 by the printer John Day for William Owen, who was "orator" for Surrey's son, Thomas, duke of Norfolk. Owen tells us in his preface that the text is based on a manuscript "in the authors owne hande" which has been collated by Owen with two other manuscripts, so that it is "both to the latyn most agreeable, and also best standing with the dignity of that kynde of myter."[11]

"The dignity of that kynde of myter" apparently means "the dignity of heroic meter." Owen is echoing the traditional equation in the *ars metrica* of heroic meter with elevated themes. Specifically, he is claiming Surrey's verse is the English equivalent to ancient heroic verse, and his term for the special quality of the meter is "dignity." The term simply translates the Latin *dignitas*, which is used, for example, by Badius Ascensius when discussing heroic poetry in his edition of the *Ars poetica:* Horace "speaks first of the heroic poem because it is accepted as foremost both in dignity (*dignitas*) and in uniformity."[12]

The Day-Owen edition includes another comment about Surrey's meter that reveals much about the state of English prosodic experiments in the 1550s. The title page announces that Vergil has been "translated into English and drawne into a straunge metre . . . worthy to be embraced."

One's natural instinct is to think, "How odd that Owen should consider blank verse 'straunge.'" Even though no English blank verse had been published before 1554, decasyllabic lines, usually joined in couplets or rhyme royal, had been standard for narrative poetry since Chaucer and were also commonplace in the early Tudor period. In *Well-Weighed Syllables* Derek Attridge attributes the word "straunge" to the fact that English readers, trained on classical prosodic rules, lacked a vocabulary to discuss (perhaps even to think about) their native verse.[13]

But perhaps "straunge" may not mean "unfamiliar." Another meaning of the term, common in sixteenth-century as well as Middle English, is "foreign," as in Chaucer's description of palmers who "seken straunge strondes, / To ferne halwes kowthe in sondry londes."[14] If Owen is using "straunge" to mean "foreign," the reference is to Continental—specifically, Italian—models. As we have seen, these models had the avowed purpose of creating an alternative to the rhymed syllabic forms that had been traditional for narrative since the Middle Ages. Moreover, Surrey's interest in developments on the Continent is well attested. His tutor John Clerk commended Surrey in the dedication to *A Treatise of Nobility* (1543) for "the excedyng great paynes and travayles susteyned by yourself in traductions as well out of the Laten and Italien as the Spanyshe and Frenche."[15]

Here we encounter a paradox. Although the "straunge metre" of

Surrey's *Aeneid* is an epoch-making discovery, it has received a distinctly mixed press. Tottel may be responsible for this situation. Although none of the three surviving versions of Surrey's translation is completely trustworthy, Tottel's is the least so. As Henry Lathrop remarks, "All of the early verse printed by Tottel was carefully edited to smooth out metrical irregularities, to correct syntax, and to improve expression according to the taste of the day."[16] The number of changes is considerable, and their effect on the impression the verse makes is, curiously, even greater than their number might suggest in the abstract. The reason is not far to seek. By normalizing the verse, Tottel has obscured the relation between the rhythm of Surrey's lines and their construction.

Tottel's version has helped to create an impression that Surrey's blank verse is "primitive" or "wooden" or "mechanical"—a commendable first effort but unworthy to stand beside later achievements in the form. Tucker Brooke, for example, remarks that "a generation passed before this meter was fully domesticated into England,"[17] and C. S. Lewis, ever prepared to justify his characterization of the early English Renaissance as a "drab age," calls Surrey's verse "too severe, too cold . . . it is Vergil in corsets."[18] Florence Ridley adds, "If one thinks in terms of the resounding majesty of Marlowe, the flexibility of Shakespeare, or the close-textured, effortless movement of Milton, Surrey seems amateurish, awkward, even monotonous."[19] In view of the context within which the *Aeneid* translation occurred and its high sense of purpose, a closer look at the poem is needed before these conclusions are accepted as final.

The Death of Dido

To appreciate Surrey's achievement, we need to examine the translation in detail using the Day-Owen text rather than Tottel or Hargrave. Since it is impossible here to examine the whole work, I offer an examination of a twenty-line passage from Vergil followed by an examination of the same passage in Surrey's translation.

The passage selected comes at the end of book 4 and describes the final agonizing moments of Dido's death on her funeral pyre. It has always been recognized as one of the finest in the Latin original and must have posed a special challenge to its translator. It is not offered as representative of Surrey's translation as a whole, merely as an example of what Surrey is like at his best.

First, we need to recall the Latin original. The following passage is from the Latin edition of Badius Ascensius (1519), which Surrey probably knew.[20] Like other editions of the classics published by Badius, it includes commentaries, in this case, the ancient commentaries by Servius, Tiberius Claudius Donatus, and Probus, and the renaissance commentaries by Badius himself and Philippus Beroaldus. The original punctuation, including the colons, is retained. In Badius, a colon indicates a caesura. Periods mark full stops but not necessarily the ends of sentences. Modern scansion marks have been added over each line:

Tum Iuno omnipotens longum miserata dolorem.
Difficilisque obitus: Irim demisit olympo.
Quae luctantem animam: nexosque resolveret artus.
Nam quia nec fato: merita nec morte peribat.
Sed misera ante diem: subitoque accensa furore. 5
Nondum illi flavum Proserpina vertice crinem
Abstulerat: Stygioque caput damnaverat Orco.
Ergo Iris croceis per coelum roscida pennis.
Mille trahens uarios aduerso sole colores.
Deuolat: et supra caput adstitit. Hunc ego Diti 10
Sacrum iussa fero: teque isto corpore soluo.
Sic ait: ex dextra crinem secat: omnis et una
Delapsus calor: atque in uentos uita recessit.[20]

In the Loeb translation by Fairclough:

Then almighty Juno, pitying her long pain and hard departure, sent Iris down from Olympus to release her struggling soul from the imprisoning limbs. For since neither in the course of fate did she perish, nor by a death she had earned, but hapless before her day, and fired by sudden madness, not yet had Proserpina taken away from her head the golden lock and consigned her to Stygian Orcus. So Iris, all dewy on saffron wings, flits down through the sky, trailing athwart the sun a thousand tints, and halted above her head. "This offering, sacred to Dis, I take as bidden, and from thy body set thee free": so she speaks, and with her hand shears the lock; and therewith all the warmth ebbed away, and the life passed away into the winds.[21]

Without attempting a complete analysis of the artistry of the Latin, we can note a few prominent aspects that would interest any translator.

Vergil's Latin consists of five units—periods—each of which has its own internal structure created by grammar and the figures of diction. Vergil's devices are "artificial." They combine construction with rhetorical ornaments, including metaphor and simile.

Among figures of diction, zeugma is prominent, especially the variety that places a word applied to two constructions between those constructions; thus *miserata* in line 1 and *resolveret* in line 3. Verbs are withheld until the ends of clauses (*demisit, resolveret, peribat, abstulerat*), and participial phrases and subordinate clauses are used at the beginning and for interruption in order to achieve periodic structure. The result is unusual word order (hyperbaton, ll. 6, 9, 10–11). Balanced phrases (isocolon) occur in lines 3 and 4. Contrast between them (antithesis) is nicely underscored (l. 4) by caesura. In one case (l. 9) a participial construction neatly packs an image cluster into a single line unit. In another, staccato clauses (*brevitas*) divide a line into three parts (l. 12). End-rhyme (homoeoteleuton) is used twice in connection with a caesura (ll. 8, 11) and twice in lines without medial caesura (ll. 10, 12). Throughout, figures of diction are complemented by figures of thought, including metaphor (ll. 3, 5), antonomasia (l. 7), and periphrasis (l. 13).

The constructions play artfully against the line and caesura structures. Only four times (ll. 3, 7, 11, 13) does the grammatical unit end with the end of the line. All other lines are grammatically enjambed. However, there are two levels of enjambment. Badius places periods after lines where there is no close grammatical linkage (e.g., noun-adjective) from one line to the next. Lines that have such linkage seem more "enjambed" to him, and they lack periods (ll. 6, 10, 12). The frequency of strongly enjambed lines near the end of the passage enacts the sense of dissolution conveyed by the words (*soluo, delapsus*). The same rules hold for caesura. A colon marks the caesura of a line in which there is no strong grammatical linkage between half-lines. Lines without a colon have such linkage and are therefore more "continuous" (ll. 6, 8, 9). The effect in line 9 nicely reinforces the brilliant visual imagery (*enargia*) associated with Iris and the compaction of this imagery into a single line by the participial construction (*trahens*).

On the level of prosody, the caesura tends to the normal position in the third foot (penthemimeral). Two lines (ll. 10, 12) have two caesuras, and in these cases the caesuras coincide with foot-end (diaeresis). To discuss the metrical variations in detail would be digressive. However, it should be noted that frequent and often mimetic variation of dactyls and spondees is maintained. Synaloepha is used effectively (e.g., ll. 1, 3, 5). Substitution and elision complement each other in line 5. The key word is "sudden" (*subito*). According to the *ars metrica*, dactyls make a line move rapidly, and the line has four dactyls. The caesura is also "rapid," since it occurs in a dactylic rather than a spondaic foot. There are also two occurrences of elision in the line, making the psychological effect still more "sudden."

We now turn to Surrey. Since his verse can be approached accentually as well as syllabically, alternate scansions are given for several lines. Accentual scansions use a simple system of three marks for light (x), heavy (/), and secondary (\). Romance scansions follow the system used earlier in the present book, with one innovation. Because English verse is stressed, even when it is inclining to syllabic norms, I have often used a bar (|) to mark secondary accents in lines scanned according to the romance system. Such accents are secondary only in the technical sense of being in positions other than at the ends of measures. They can be primary when the sense makes this appropriate, a point relevant, for example, to the phrase "long paynes" in Surrey's line 2.

The use of these secondary accent marks for verses scanned syllabically is more than a convenience. As we have noted, stress is natural and inevitable in English verse. The question is not whether it is involved but how it is involved. A further consideration applies. Surrey's free use of enjambment and his differentiation between syllable count and pronunciation suggest Italian rather than French precedents for his verse. This is not surprising in view of his interest in Italian poetry. Italian is more "accentual" than French, and an Italian model would have encouraged Surrey to use accent creatively.

Since his translation has more lines than Vergil's original, one might conclude that he expands, as Gavin Douglas regularly did. This is not the case. Discounting elisions, Vergil's 13 hexameters have some 200 syllables. Surrey's 20 lines of iambic pentameter have perhaps 210. The numbers point to an important feature of Surrey's translation. It neither expands nor contracts. Instead, it is extraordinarily faithful, both to the literal sense of the original and to its artistry.

Latin accommodates itself easily to complex and inverted constructions because the inflectional endings of verbs, nouns, and adjectives show which words belong together. What is easy in Latin, however, is difficult, even "unnatural," in English. Being uninflected, English depends on natural word order to keep grammatical relations clear within the sentence. Surrey wants to escape from the limitations of traditional English construction. His lines reveal an effort to reorder English so that it can have the richness of Latin construction while remaining reasonably transparent to a reader.[22]

The result of Surrey's construction is a form of verse in which the basic unit is the phrase, and the largest unit, which determines the rhythm of the whole, is the period. Within these lower and upper limits, the caesura is variable and enjambment common. When the form realizes its full potential, as in the present passage, units are created that are different from, and often larger than, the decasyllabic line. A sixteenth-century reader, struggling to describe the effect with a vocabulary inherited from the *ars metrica*, might have said that Surrey's verse is somewhat "like prose." It is also highly figured and rhythmic—formal and ritualistic rather than colloquial.

Let us now turn to the passage from Surrey as it appears in the Day-Owen text:

Unit 1	Almyghty Iuno hauyng ruthe by thys	
	Of her long paynes, and eke her lyngryng death,	
	From heauen she sent the Goddesse Iris downe,	
	The thrallyng spiryte, and ioynted lymmes to loose.	
Unit 2	For that neyther by lot of desteny,	5
	Nor yet by naturall death she peryshed:	
	But wretchedly before her fatal daye,	
	And kyndled with a sodayne rage of flame:	
	Proserpyne had not yet from her head berefte	
	The golden heare: nor iudged her to hell.	10
Unit 3	The dewye Iris thus wyth golden wynges,	
	A thousand hues shewyng agaynst the sunne,	
	Amyd the skyes then dyd she flye adowne:	
Unit 4	On Didos heade, where as she gan alyght,	
	Thys heare (quoth she) to Pluto consecrate.	15
	Commanded I bereue, and eke thy spiryte unloose	
Unit 5	From thys body: and when she had thus sayd,	

> With her right hand she cut the heare in twayne:
> And therewyth al the naturall heate gan quenche,
> And into wynde the lyfe foorthwyth resolue.   20

The first thing to recognize about this verse is that it owes a good deal to Gavin Douglas. The debt is to the word choice and in some cases to the rhythmic arrangements of Douglas's translation. However, Douglas wanders in and out of focus. Surrey has taken the best Douglas has to offer and transmuted it.[23]

In Douglas, the line is dominant and the couplet subdominant. The poetry, that is, is decasyllabic in the romance sense. In Surrey the unit is shaped by construction before it is shaped by syllable count. As in the Latin original, a clause unit sometimes corresponds neatly with a line-end (e.g., l. 18), but usually the phrases and clauses are united by being imbedded in the larger grammatical structure of a periodic sentence that extends over several lines. Note also that structure is by no means rigidly framed by the line, a point illustrated by line 17, in which a sustained unit comes to an end in midline (the colon).

Caesura tends to occur in the passage in the location that is favored in decasyllabic verse—after the fourth syllable. However, there are expressive variations from this norm. Caesura can be marked by strong punctuation (colon, ll. 10, 17) or light (comma, ll. 2, 14, 16) or no punctuation. One line (l. 15) has two pauses marked by parentheses. Prosodic effects include syncope, both indicated by spelling ("lyngryng," 2) and implicit ("heauen," l. 3; "spiryte," l. 4), lyric caesura (l. 1) and hiatus (l. 17). In addition, the constant enjambment prevents the lines from dividing repeatedly into half-lines marked off by strong terminal accents in the French manner.

For convenience, the major units of the passage from Surrey have been indicated in the left margin. The first is a periodic sentence extending over four lines. The subject of the Latin original (*Iuno omnipotens*—"Almyghty Iuno") is placed first, exactly as in Vergil. It is followed by a participial phrase ("hauyng ruthe . . .") that occupies one and one-half lines and thus creates a considerable separation, or interruption, between the Vergilian subject ("Iuno") and its verb ("sent"). The verb is further distanced from "Iuno" by the adverbial phrase "from heauen" (l. 3), which would follow rather than precede the verb in normal English word order.

At this point we note a departure from Vergil. In Surrey's English, "sent" is immediately preceded by a subject—"she," referring to Juno.

If "she" is the subject of the verb, "Almyghty Iuno" in line 1 begins to look like the first two words of an independent participial phrase for which there is no precedent in the Latin.

Why did Surrey make his sentence not less but more complicated—more Latinate one might say—than Vergil? The answer is evident. In largest outline, the sentence reads "Almyghty Iuno . . . she sent." In other words, "Iuno" is, in fact, the subject, and "she" is tautological. The motive for the tautology is clarity. The length of the interval between "Almyghty Iuno" and its verb is, as we have already remarked, considerable. It is greater than anything that Surrey's readers would have been used to in English, and the extra subject—"she"—is evidently intended to prevent confusion. The same strategy is used in lines 11–13 ("The dewye Iris . . . then dyd *she* flye adowne)." The need for the strategy may further explain why the title page of the edition refers to Surrey's meter as "straunge." The syntax must have made the translation seem "straunge" in the sense of "foreign and difficult" to English readers accustomed to late medieval stylistic conventions.

The first period is extended further by inversion in line 4. The infinitive "to loose" follows its objects in line 4 rather than preceding them. Since the infinitive phrase modifies (or, perhaps, complements) the verb "sent," it completes the sense of the sentence and brings the period to a neat conclusion at the end of the line. We note in passing that Surrey translates Vergil's *Olympo* as "heauen" (l. 3). This is not significant in itself but becomes so when related to the substitution of "hell" for "Stygian Orcus" in line 10, a point discussed below.

Surrey's rhythm is contrapuntal. The initial period is four lines, or forty (perhaps forty-one) syllables. The sense is incomplete until "sent" in line 3 and not fully resolved until "loose" at the end of line 4. The syntax cuts across the division of the sentence into four equal units separated by the line-ends. However, within the sentence there are subunits. "Almyghty Iuno," for example, is followed by a pause, which is followed by two units consisting of fifteen syllables, divided themselves by a pause after the word "paynes." Because the rhythm is contrapuntal, line 2 can be a rhythmic subunit even as the period asserts grammatical supremacy over the whole. Balance, underscored by *l* alliteration, is created in line 2 by the contrast between "long paynes" and "lyngryng death." This contrast invites enactment in the stress patterns of the verse. Syllabic scansion fits nicely. It properly identifies the strong caesura and marked terminal accents separating the balanced phrases, and it also matches the phrase emphasis of the Latin ("longum . . . dolorem / Difficilisque obitus"). Conversely, to read the line as regular accentual meter tends to convert it into a complicated mixture of primary and secondary accents:

$$\text{Of her long paynes, and eke her lyngryng death.}$$
[4*6]

Versus:

$$\text{Of her long paynes, and eke her lyngryng death.}$$

The word "spiryte" in line 4 is also interesting. Both Tottel and Hargrave give "sprite"—a one-syllable word—here. This regularizes the line. The Day-Owen "spiryte" may be a misprint, but the same spelling occurs in line 16. Perhaps the word was pronounced as one syllable in spite of the spelling. If Tottel and Hargrave took the trouble to substitute "sprite" for "spiryte," however, the motive was most probably to iron out the verse, and this strongly suggests they regarded "spiryte" as defective—that is, as having more syllables than appropriate. Evidently, Surrey is following the Italian convention, later followed by Milton, that licenses can be used for syllable count but do not need to affect pronunciation. Tottel's revision is not an attempt to make Surrey's line "accentual," but an attempt to make it decasyllabic in the literal (and French) sense of having ten syllables.

An argument can be made that the sense of the line is better served by the extra syllable authorized in the Day-Owen text than the neat regularity of Tottel and Hargrave. The phrase "lyngryng death" (in which the syncope [i.e., "lyng'ryng"] is reflected in the spelling and therefore presumably to be pronounced) emphasizes drawn-out torment, and the extra syllable in "spiryte" nicely resonates with that idea. A "regular scansion" (given accentually) is followed below by a syllabic scansion with syncope assumed for syllable count but not for pronunciation:

$$\text{The thrallyng sprite and ioynted lymmes to loose.}$$

Versus:

$$\text{The thrallyng spiryte and ioynted lymmes to loose.}$$
[4'*4+2]

Whatever the status of "spiryte," since the infinitive at the end of line 4 completes the sense of the sentence, it resolves the syntactic as well as the metrical tension of the period. The fact that inversion forces the sentence to end with the word "loose" nicely underscores the sense of tension released. It may be added that the technique of adjusting the syntax to permit ending both line and period on a thematic word is evident in lines 10, 13, 16, 19, and 20.

Although Surrey requires four lines for Vergil's three, he respects the syntactical divisions of his original. Surrey's first two lines translate the first one and one-half lines of Vergil. Line 3 begins exactly where Vergil has placed the caesura in his line 2. It translates the Vergilian half-line, ending where the half-line ends. Line 4 then exactly translates Vergil's line 3. Similar respect for Vergil's line-endings and caesuras can be observed throughout the passage.

The second unit in the passage is six lines long. Its structure is obscured for the modern reader by heavy punctuation (i.e., the colons in ll. 6, 8, and 10), and it is helpful to refer to the Latin original to be sure of what Surrey intends.

The sentence consists of a compound adverbial clause of four lines ("For that neyther . . . Nor yet . . . But wretchedly . . . And kyndled . . .") modifying the main verbs "berefte" and "iudged." The subject of the sentence ("Proserpyne") occurs in line 9. From a syllabic point of view, the first half-line resists separation into measures because of the elision of the final *e* in "Proserpyne." From an accentual point of view, with elision of "Proserpyne," the line is regular until the fourth foot, but the fifth foot is irregular:

```
 |        / *        /       /
Proserpyne had not yet from her head berefte.
          ∪
```

$$[6*3+2]$$

Versus

```
          x x   /
  x /  x    /  x  /  x   x  /  x /
Proserpyne had not yet from her head berefte
[The golden heare: nor iudged her to hell].
```

However it is scanned, the line is saved from metrical isolation by the enjambment that forces the reader to continue to the object of the verb in the next line: "The golden heare."

The second half of line 10 — "nor iudged her to hell" — is associated with the main clause as the second half of a compound predicate (i.e., "not berefte . . . nor iudged . . ."). The colon at midline is misleading to the modern reader. It is a relic of the punctuation used in Latin editions of Vergil and indicates only a pause. Surrey's language here is also significant. Vergil's term for the underworld is "Stygian Orcus" (*Stygioque . . . Orco*). The phrase might have seemed poetic to a Roman of the Augustan period, but it is artificial out of its Roman context. Roger Ascham and other hard-line English humanists would have fancied it, but one suspects that even in the sixteenth century it would have struck most readers as dead erudition.

Douglas tries to have his classical allusion and gloss it too. He translates Vergil's phrase with "the Stygian hellis fludd." Surrey is more decisive. He has translated *Olympo* as "heauen" in line 3. The word "hell" completes the earlier initiative. "Hell" is more grim than the original, but that is appropriate too. St. Augustine wrote in his *Confessions* (I, 13) that he wept for Dido when he was an adolescent, but that she was, after all, a debauched woman and a suicide and not worth the tears of a Christian convert, while Dante placed her in hell in the *Inferno* (V, 61–62) as an example of lust along with Paolo and Francesca.

Surrey did not invent, but he took full advantage of, the lovely Vergilian transition in the next period away from the anguished queen to the descent of Iris, goddess of the rainbow, who receives Dido's soul and thus ends her torment. The transition is made in a unit of three and one-half lines (ll. 11–14). The Day-Owen punctuation is unhelpful. The phrase "On Didos heade" is part of the sentence that begins on line 11. "Where as she gan alyght" (l. 14) either could be the conclusion of this sentence or could belong to the next. In the Latin it is the conclusion of the preceding sentence: ". . . et supra caput adstitit." Surrey, on the other hand, uses it to begin the next unit, as we will see below.

The subject of the transition sentence ("Iris") is separated from the verb ("flye") by a parenthetical description of the wings of the goddess that occupies all of line 12. The effect of the parenthesis is enhanced by the irregularity of the line:

```
   |       / * /                    /
A thousand hues shewyng agaynst the sunne.
```
[4*2+4]

In line 13 the verb is further delayed by the inversion of the adverbial phrase "Amyd the skyes." Since the parenthesis and the inversion obscure the connection between subject and verb, we are not surprised that Surrey repeats the device of the second subject used previously in line 3: "The dewye Iris . . . then dyd *she* flye adowne."

The fourth unit (the speech of Iris, ll. 14–17) begins with "where as she gan alyght." Surrey's meaning is plain enough. "As" is used in the sense of "when." The sentence means something like, "Where—as she began to alight—she said. . . ." Line 14 has two instructive features. First, regular iambic meter would call for a light stress on "where" and a heavy on "as." This makes the words sound like the logical connective "whereas," and, in fact, Hargrave gives "whereas" as a single word, producing the meaningless comment, "Whereas she began to alight."[24] To make the meaning clear, the line needs a pause after "where." This works well in syllabic scansion, since "where" can be regarded as a measure of one syllable with "terminal" accent. It is more complicated in accentual scansion because of the problem of proper stress on "as." Probably a light stress is best:

   | /   *   /   /
On Didos heade, where as she gan alyght.

$$[4*1+5]$$

Versus:

                    x   /[or?: \]
x   / x   /   *   /   x   x /   x /
On Didos heade, where as she gan alyght.

The second ambiguity is more difficult, but fortunately Vergil's Latin solves the problem. In line 15 the word "consecrate" looks like an imperative. The end-punctuation (i.e., the period) that follows it makes this interpretation mandatory for the reader who does not consult the original. To read the sentence in this way is to make Iris's statement a command to Dido to consecrate her hair to Pluto. Since Dido is all but dead on the pyre at this moment, the interpretation is wrong. The Latin text confirms this. It reads: "Hunc ego Diti / Sacrum iussa fero teque isto corpore soluo." Fairclough translates: "This offering, sacred to Dis [i.e., Pluto], I take as bidden."

Hunc ("this") refers to the offering, which is the lock of Dido's hair clipped by Iris as she releases the soul from the body. Surrey simply calls it "Thys heare." *Sacrum* is an adjective meaning "sacred" in the sense of "sacred to Dis," or Pluto. Surrey (and Douglas before him) translates it as "consecrate" in the sense of "consecrated." The word, in other words, is not an imperative but a participial adjective with the terminal *ed* removed by apocope. Finally, *iussa* is a participle meaning "bidden" or "commanded" and *fero* is the main verb, meaning "I take," or in Surrey's words, "I bereue."

The Day-Owen punctuation of the passage is therefore misleading to the modern reader. Instead of ending with a period, in modern punctuation, line 15 would have no end-punctuation or at most a comma. When read with the proper meaning understood, the fourth unit ceases to be confusing and becomes a rich, highly contrapuntal Latinate period. It is beautifully effective in conveying Vergil's tone, but it is—if only because of its success in imitating the Latin—unlike anything that had appeared in English poetry before Surrey.

Two other features should be noted. First, line 16 ("Commanded I bereue . . .") is, syllabically, an Alexandrine. Second, in line 17 ("From thys body . . ."), "body" looks like a trochee, and thus, syllabically (because the *dy* is necessary to the syllable count of the line), a lyric caesura. Since the *dy* is necessary, *y* cannot be elided with the *a* of "and," and the result is hiatus. Day-Owen makes the hiatus unmistakable by punctuating it with a colon. In terms of accentual meter, the two lines scan in something of the following manner:

```
    x    /  x  /  x /  *x   \       / x   x  /
    Commanded I bereue, and eke thy spiryte unloose
       x   \   / x *x    \   x  /   x   /
    From thys body: and when she had thus sayde.
```

From a syllabic point of view, the first line is regular because of the elision (syncope) of "spiryte":

```
         /          /   *              /         /
    Commanded I bereue, and eke thy spiryte unloose
                                                              [3 + 3*4 + 2]
        /   *                           /
    From thys body: and when she had thus sayde.
      [hiatus]                                                [4*6]
```

This scansion has already brought us to the final unit of the passage under consideration. It is probably the most famous example in the *Aeneid*—other than *sunt lacrimae rerum*—of Vergil's tone of elevated melancholy. It begins with a sentence of one and one-half lines in which the claim of accent vies strongly with the claim of syntax if it is read in terms of accentual meter:

```
     x     /   x  /   \   /
     and when she had thus sayde.
```

Assuming that secondary accents are permissible in English syllabic verse, and the syllabic scansion is straightforward:

     | /
  and when she had thus sayde.

                    [*6]

Again:

    | /
  With her right hand.

                    [4*]

Versus:

  x / \ /
  With her right hand.

In line 19 accentual meter would call for regular iambs and a normal caesura. This is acceptable if the second word in the line is the adverbial compound "therewythal." In fact, Douglas's translation and some modern editions of Surrey's translation give "therewythal" as one word, in the sense, perhaps, of "as this was happening." Again, however, reference to Vergil's Latin provides the correct reading. The Latin reads, "omnis et una / Delapsus calor," translated by the Loeb editor as "and therewyth, all the warmth ebbed away." Surrey's "therewyth" corresponds to Vergil's *una,* which means something like "all at once." As the Loeb translation shows, "therewyth" is an acceptable equivalent.[25] Surrey's "al" is not adverbial. It means "all" in the normal English sense, and it modifies "heate," being the exact equivalent of Vergil's *omnis.* Since it is grammatically linked to "heate" rather than "therewyth," a pause is required after "therewyth." The first half-line in this analysis is, syllabically, a measure of three syllables with terminal accent. The second half-line is a measure of seven syllables if "naturall" is counted as two syllables by syncope:[26]

    / *| | /   /
  And therewyth al the naturall heate gan quenche.

                  [3*5 + 2]

Versus:

  x / \ */ x / x x / x /
  And therewyth al the naturall heate gan quenche.

The final line of the passage (l. 20) is the second clause of a compound sentence. The two clauses are parallel, with the verb ("gan") being understood in the second. The parallelism is emphasized by the repetition of the conjunction "and" at the beginning of each. The second clause is regular whether considered syllabically or accentually.

The larger movement of the final unit is thus from periodic to loose structure and from irregularity to regularity. The effect of this unit is that of a progressive release from tension and expresses nicely, in a sense enacts, the action being described—the release of Dido from her torment.

There is, however, a residue of the earlier Latinate structure. The two final lines of the passage use verb-object inversion so they can end with verbs. Surrey's purpose is clearly to end both lines with thematic words: "quenche" and "resolue." The final line in Vergil, it should be noted, begins with what Surrey translates as "quenche" (*delapsus*) and ends with his "resolue" (*recessit*). In other words, the imitation is, at this point, extraordinarily precise, but it reaches its goal by a different path:

And therewyth al the naturall heate gan quenche,
/   *   /   /
And into wynde the lyfe foorthwyth resolue.

[4*2+4]

Versus:

x \ x /   x / x   /   x /
And into wynde the lyfe foorthwyth resolue.

Surrey and His Editors

Prosodic analysis suggests strongly that the Day-Owen text of Surrey's translation is superior. Conversely, the changes made by the other Tudor editors suggest the inadequacy of their understanding of what Surrey was about. The problem seems to come from the difference between Surrey's Italianate approach to blank verse and the tendency of his editors to read it as French-style regular decasyllabics. Presumably the editors also sensed the regular iambic stress pattern they were introducing into the verse by their revisions and sought regular iambic patterns of word stress, but this concern was probably minor given the syllabic emphasis of midcentury prosody.

At the beginning, Day-Owen avoids punctuation until the thought is completed. Hargrave, conversely, inserts a comma after "Iuno," thereby asserting line integrity but cutting the subject adrift from the rest of the sentence and obscuring its construction. In lines 4 and 16, as we have noted, Tottel and Hargrave substitute "sprite" for "spiryte." This produces an accurate syllable count at the expense of the poetic expressiveness. Tottel and Hargrave compound their mischief in line 4 by rejecting the word "thrallyng." Hargrave substitutes "striving," which is modern but loses the connotation of imprisonment that is present in "thrallyng." There is a loss of poetic expressiveness, since Dido's spirit is clearly described as imprisoned in her body and struggling for release. Tottel substitutes "throwing" for "thrallyng," a reading taken from Douglas's "throwand."

Two lines later, Day-Owen reads, "Nor yet by naturall death she peryshed." The Latin equivalent for "not natural" is *nec merita,* meaning (in the Loeb translation) "not by a death she had earned [i.e., deserved]." Surrey found "natural" in Douglas, who, in turn, derived it from a gloss on this passage by Servius.[27] Dido's fate, Servius observes, was *nec merita* in the sense that it was a suicide rather than death by a natural cause. But unless it is counted by syncope as "nat'ral," "naturall" is three syllables where the verse wants two. Tottel (or his editor) wants pronunciation to follow spelling. He substitutes the two-syllable word "kindly." Since "kindly" can mean "of the same species"—hence, very generally, "natural"—in the sixteenth century, the substitution may have seemed reasonable. However, "kindly" can also have the sense of "friendly" or "merciful," and the change therefore undercuts the pathos so important to the line.

George Wright believes that in Wyatt's poetry "the metrical line and the natural rhythm of the language engage each other in a continuing struggle."[28] Most readers find the result highly expressive, and preferable to the regularity of midcentury English verse. In present terms, Wyatt's "natural rhythm" results from his interst in construction. Surrey's *Aeneid* verse carries Wyatt's innovations decisively forward. It remains one of the curiosities of the history of English poetry that Surrey's achievement was ignored by his successors. Later efforts to create heroic poetry in English in the sixteenth century use almost every form *but* blank verse—fourteeners, poulter's measure, decasyllabic couplets, quantitative dactylic hexameter, ottava rima, and Spenserian stanzas. Christopher Marlowe translated book 1 of Lucan's *Pharsalia* into excellent blank verse, but judging from lack of later references to it, this translation was ignored even more resolutely than Surrey's *Aeneid.*

There is no reason to doubt Milton's sincerity when he writes that *Paradise Lost* is "the first [example] in English" to use blank verse for heroic poetry. It is a pity he did not know Surrey's translation, because in spite of the help he received from the dramatic blank verse of Marlowe and Shakespeare and the *versi sciolti* of Tasso's *Le Sette giornate del mondo creato*, he had to make many of Surrey's discoveries about English heroic verse all over again.

CHAPTER VII

Jasper Heywood's Fourteeners

In 1560, roughly a year before the publication of England's first regular tragedy in blank verse, Jasper Heywood, son of the early Tudor dramatist John Heywood, published a translation of Seneca's *Thyestes*. He had already published a translation of Seneca's *Troas* in 1559, the first English translation of any of Seneca's plays, and would publish a translation of *Hercules furens* in 1561. Although he had dedicated *Troas* to Elizabeth, calling her "defender of the faith" and emphasizing her providential mission, he would leave England in 1562 to enter the Jesuit Order in Rome. Thereafter he would lead a troubled, nomadic life until his death in Naples in 1598.[1]

Heywood was the first of several English translators of the plays of Seneca. All but one of the translations were made between 1559 and 1567. Alexander Nevyle translated *Oedipus* in 1560 (printed 1563). Thomas Nuce's translation of *Octavia* appeared in 1566, John Studley's *Agamemnon* and *Medea* in 1566, and *Hippolytus* in 1566–67. His *Hercules Oetaeus*, presumably written about the same time, was not printed until 1581.[2] The *Thebais*, the last of the series, was translated by Thomas Newton and incorporated into Newton's collection of all of the plays, the *Tenne Tragedies* (1581).[3]

Why the interest in Seneca? The question becomes more puzzling if one contrasts the fate of two other classical dramatists at midcentury. Plautus and Terence were performed in Latin in the schools and were imitated in Latin and English plays.[4] Plautus was mined by Elizabethan dramatists, both indirectly, as in the case of Gascoigne's

Supposes, which draws its Plautus from Ariosto's comedy *I Suppositi*, and directly, as for example in Shakespeare's *Comedy of Errors*. However, there is only one English translation of a play by Plautus in the sixteenth century, the 1595 prose *Menaechmi* by "W. W.," probably William Warner.[5]

Terence fared marginally better. A book titled *Vulgaria Terentii* was published at Oxford in 1483 by T. Rood and T. Hunt. It is a collection of English phrases followed by Latin equivalents, many but by no means all from Terence. It went through six editions by 1526, after which it was supplanted by Nicholas Udall's *Flowers for Latin Speaking Selected and Gathered out of Terence* (1533).[6] Udall's book has special interest because his English comedy *Ralph Roister Doister* imitates Roman comedy and also because the reprint by John Higgins of its 1575 enlargement includes a prefatory poem by none other than Thomas Newton of the *Tenne Tragedies*. However, the *Flowers* is a phrase-book, not a drama.

John Rastell published a verse translation of Terence's *Andria* around 1520. The fact that actors enter as the "Prologue" departs shows the translation was intended for performance. No other translation of a comedy by Terence was published until Maurice Kyffin published a second translation of the *Andria* in 1588. This translation was revised by Richard Bernard for his edition of Terence's *Plays*, which appeared in 1598, with later editions in 1607, 1614, and 1629. The prefaces to Kyffin and Bernard make it clear their editions are for the classroom rather than the stage.[7]

In sum, in the century between 1490 and 1590, only one Roman comedy, Terence's *Andria*, was translated. But between 1559 and 1570 all but one of Seneca's ten tragedies and a tragedy by Euripides were translated. This period also saw the first "regular" English tragedy, Sackville and Norton's *Gorboduc* (1561).

The obvious reason for the interest in Seneca's tragedies is that they were considered culturally essential by English humanists. After epic, tragedy is the noblest of genres. However, by the 1550s, although tragedy was flourishing in Italy, England had produced no drama remotely comparable to the ancient form. The Seneca translators were concerned primarily with literary issues rather than with Seneca's philosophical and political ideas. They knew very little, however, about performance, and they were much more interested in Seneca's elevated rhetoric and lurid imagery than his talents—whatever they may be—as a writer of plays for the stage.

The Seneca Project

The concentration of translations of Seneca in the decade following Elizabeth's accession to the throne suggests a plan of some sort. This suggestion is reinforced by many links among the translations and between the Seneca translations and other translations and imitations of the same period.

An obvious link among the translators is provided by the title pages of the translations. They have a common form. In addition to the title of the play, each gives the number of the play in the Seneca canon. *Troas* is "the Sixt Tragedie of the most Grave and prudent Lucius Anneus, Seneca." *Thyestes* is "the Seconde Tragedie of Seneca." *Hercules* is "the First."

Another common element is the fact that the tragedies are dedicated to individuals at the highest level in court. Heywood dedicated the *Troas*, which is the first of the translations, to "the moste high and vertuous princesse, Elizabeth by grace of God Queene of England." Elizabeth had ascended the throne only a few months before *Troas* was published, so the dedication is at the very least opportune. Heywood seems to know a good deal about the queen's interests. He praises her scholarly attainments and states that being a scholar herself, she is certain to appreciate the work of other scholars. After confessing youth and inexperience, Heywood boasts that he "onely among so many fine wittes and towardly youth . . . enterprised to set forth in englishe this present piece of the flowre of all writers Seneca."[8]

Heywood's *Thyestes* is dedicated to John Mason, a member of the Privy Council and Chancellor of Oxford, and his *Hercules furens* to William Herbert, also a member of the Privy Council. Studley's *Agamemnon* is dedicated to William Cecil and his *Medea* to Francis Russell, both members of the Privy Council. Nevyle's *Oedipus* is dedicated to Henry Wotton and Nuce's *Octavia* to Robert Dudley, both of the Privy Council.

The prefaces to the Seneca translations reveal further links among the translators and among those engaged in related literary activities. In the preface to *Thyestes*, Heywood dreams of being approached by the ghost of Seneca, who asks him to become a translator again.[9] He replies that he is inadequate for the task but that there are many English writers who are well qualified. They are "Minerva's men," and many are lawyers at the Inns of Court.

The list includes many important midcentury literary figures: Thomas North, translator of Guevara's *Dial of Princes* (1557) and later

(1579) of Plutarch's *Lives;* Thomas Sackville, author (with Thomas Norton) of *Gorboduc* (1561) and contributor of the famous "Induction" and "Complaint of Buckingham" to *A Mirror for Magistrates;* Thomas Norton, co-author of *Gorboduc* and translator (1561) of Calvin's *Institutes of the Christian Religion;* Christopher Ylverton, author of the "Epilogue" to Gascoigne's *Jocasta* (1566) and also of the dumb shows of *The Misfortunes of Arthur* (1587–88), a play heavily influenced by Heywood's *Thyestes;* William Baldwin, editor of *A Mirror for Magistrates* (1559 and later); Thomas Blunderville, translator of Plutarch (1561); William Bavand, translator of Montanus (1559); and Barnabe Googe, translator (1561) of Palingenius's *Zodiacus vitae.* Among other Seneca translators, Studley refers in the preface to *Agamemnon* to "*Jasper Heywood* and *Alexander Nevyle,*" as well as to Barnabe Googe and to Thomas Phaer, translator of the *Aeneid.*[10]

Heywood's *Troas* was begun "for myne owne private exercise," but he agreed to publish it "by request, and friendship of those, to whom I could denye nothing." Since the first edition was printed by Tottel and Tottel was closely associated with translations of the classics, he may have figured significantly among the "friends."[11] The friendship cooled after 1559. In the preface to *Thyestes,* Heywood accuses Tottel of having "corrupted all" of *Troas* (ll. 125–32). Interestingly, Heywood has the ghost of Seneca remark of misprints that "sense and latin, verse and all / they violate and breake / And eke what I yet nevre ment / they me enforce to speake." The comment shows a sensitivity to prosody, since it distinguishes between errors that violate "sense" and "verse." Heywood entrusted the next printing of *Troas* to a new printer, Thomas Powell, who also printed *Thyestes.*

Was Tottel the only instigator of the Seneca project? Surely the dedications would not have been made so consistently to members of the Privy Council unless the authors believed they would be welcome. And surely, unless the Council members knew about the project and approved it, they would not have so consistently accepted the honors heaped upon them by the translators. Another point. If the encouragement had come from one or two members of the Privy Council with special interests in literature, would not the plays have been dedicated only to these patrons? Would not authors like Heywood and Studley, who completed several translations, have dedicated more than one play to one Council member? Yet each new translation is dedicated to a different member, and no member is recipient of more than one dedication.

There is another interesting piece to the puzzle. As an enthusiastic humanist, Elizabeth translated several classical works. In the 1550s and 1560s, when, according to Leicester Bradner, much of her translating was done, she was reading regularly with Roger Ascham. Her own interest, warmly supported by Ascham, and the complementary interest of members of the Privy Council who shared her (and Ascham's) commitment to elevating the English language, seem likely to have been factors in the plan to translate all of Seneca's tragedies.

The likelihood is increased by a translation of the second chorus of *Hercules Oetaeus* that was probably done by Elizabeth in the 1550s or early 1560s. Bradner describes it as in "the rough-hewn, vigorous . . . style of the middle of the sixteenth century, the style of Richard Edwards, Nicholas Grimald, and Jasper Heywood."[12] It is apparently independent of John Studley's *Hercules Oetaeus* and is—rather remarkably—in a rough kind of blank verse. About one-third of it is invention rather than translation.

Elizabeth translated other classical works that interested writers of the 1560s. Although no manuscript survives, she is said to have translated bits of Euripides, and we have noticed that the only Greek tragedy Englished in the 1560s was *Jocasta*, adapted from Euripides. She also undertook a translation of Horace's *Ars poetica* in the 1590s.[13] The only other Elizabethan verse translation of Horace was published in 1567 by Thomas Drant.

The Seneca translations of the 1560s were part of a larger effort. The effort was influenced by the ideals of Erasmus and English esoteric humanists. It included many classical works, with the most sustained effort being the plays of Seneca. The Seneca project was given unofficial encouragement by the Privy Council and was probably encouraged by the queen herself, to whom the first of the translations was dedicated. The queen also participated in the exercise of translation, although she published none of her works.

The project was not limited to ancient classics or to translations. Well-regarded renaissance works like the *Eclogues* of Mantuan and the *Zodiacus vitae* of Palingenius were included, and imitation was encouraged as well as translation. *Gorboduc* by Sackville and Norton is the first regular English tragedy. It violates the parliamentary statute, passed with Elizabeth's approval, against literature concerned with politics—most especially with the succession question. Yet instead of punishing its authors, Elizabeth commanded that the play be performed at Whitehall Palace shortly after it was produced at the Inner Temple.

The ghost of Seneca who approaches Heywood in the preface to

Thyestes states that the motive of the translators should be the "glory" of keeping Seneca's art alive, and making him available "in metre of thy mother tongue." Heywood replies that this is all very well, but that good literature is opposed by "the hatefull cursed broode . . . of Zoylus' bloode." Zoilus, he complains, "hath crouched every wheare / In corner close some Ympe of his that sits and lives to see / And heare what each man dothe." Several other Seneca translators also refer to the despicable Zoilus.[14] Are the references strictly conventional—Zoilus being a symbol of philistinism—or does the vehemence of Heywood's comment show that the translation project had aroused the opposition of a faction, presumably extreme Protestant, opposed to the liberal tendencies of Erasmian humanism? And if so, does it expose tensions that contributed to Heywood's decision to become a Catholic exile in spite of his earlier admiration for the Protestant Elizabeth?

Comic and Tragic Verse at Midcentury

According to Heywood, his *Troas* seeks to convey "the true sence" of the original and to convey "the roialty of speach, meete for a tragedie." "True sence" is self-explanatory, although the translation shows that it did not preclude paraphrase or occasional additions. "Roialty of speach" refers to elevation of language. The characters of tragedy are from the highest social class—"kings and princes," to quote a phrase from the *ars metrica*. If the language of tragedy fails to match their status, no matter how impressive or pathetic their actions, the tragedy will fail to convince and its ennobling potential will be lost.

Readers and audiences are trained by their experience of drama to accept certain forms as having the elevation appropriate to "roialty" and others as resembling the conversation of ordinary men and women. This is a way of saying that, at least within the tradition of verse drama as defined by the *ars metrica,* comic and tragic verse are mutually defining. If there is a well-defined convention for comic verse, tragic verse should differ recognizably from it, and vice versa. In the *Ars poetica,* Horace notes that comic dialogue can have moments of elevation and pathos and tragedic dialogue is sometimes prosy, but the norm is to keep the forms clearly differentiated: "Thyestes' banquet should not be related in everyday lines close to the comic level" (l. 90).

To appreciate Heywood's solution to the problem of finding a verse form appropriate to tragic dialogue, we need to place his translations against the background of midcentury conventions for dramatic verse. Fortunately, a good deal is known about this subject.

J. E. Bernard, Jr., has studied the prosody of the Tudor interludes. He concludes that it was "indigenous to England and had no connexion with Continental poetics."[15] By "indigenous" Bernard means that the forms all have precedents in popular literature of the period, including the morality play and the ballad. The authors of interludes were writing for the stage rather than the library. By plan or instinct they adopted forms that were well known to their English audiences.

The interludes sometimes use quatrains and rhyme royal stanzas, but the three most common forms are (1) couplets of two to four stresses, (2) rime coué of six and eight lines, and (3) ballad measures of from four to eight lines. Occasionally the four-stress lines flirt with iambic measure, but the flirtation never becomes serious. Unstressed syllables are regularly ignored, and the lines usually resist regular scansion. Bernard remarks, "Few in fact will submit to the standardization of iambus or anapest. They were not written to be iambic or anapestic."[16] John Heywood, the father of Jasper, popularized what came as close as any form to being the standard dialogue verse for interludes. It is an irregular four-stress line, usually in couplets, called "cantilevered verse" by Bernard and related to "ballad eight" and "common meter." It begins with John Rastell's *Nature of the 4 Elements* (1517–18) and continues with John Heywood's several interludes and Redford's *The Marriage of Wit and Science* (1531–47).[17]

In general, the forms used in the interlude come close to formlessness by later standards. This lack of form became more rather than less prominent in midcentury comic dialogue. Perhaps the lack of form is produced by the prosodic impasse so often invoked to explain Wyatt's irregularities. Perhaps, however, there is another explanation.

The verse of the English interludes seems awkward in the twentieth century. It can be called "formless," but formless verse is simply verse that does not sound like verse—that is, it sounds like prose. Bernard suggests there may be more method in the apparent chaos of interlude verse than modern readers detect. The writers were neither metrical anarchists nor untutored clowns. They were "concerned with varying their verse in accord with what took place in the drama."[18]

Is it possible that the apparent lack of form in interlude verse imitates what the authors understood to be the quality of Latin comic dialogue? John Heywood was a member of the humanistic circle of

Sir Thomas More. He would have understood the nature of Roman comic verse very well. On the other hand, there is absolutely no evidence that he thought of his interludes as imitations of ancient comedies, and Bernard is undoubtedly right to conclude his line is drawn from native English tradition. Without more information, his motives for writing as he did will remain conjectural.

The case is different for two midcentury imitators of Roman comedy, Nicholas Udall, the probable author of *Ralph Roister Doister*, and William Stevenson, the probable author of *Gammer Gurton's Needle*. Udall was an accomplished academic humanist—collector and publisher of *Flowers* from Terence (1533), translator of (among other items) Erasmus's *Paraphrase* of the New Testament and Peter Martyr's *Discourse on the Eucharist*, and headmaster of Eton from 1534 to 1541. Stevenson was also an academic—a fellow of Christ's College, Cambridge. If he was not the author of *Gammer Gurton's Needle*, it is clear the author was an academic like Stevenson and probably associated with Christ's College, since the play was acted there twice, first in 1553/54 and again in 1559/60.

Both plays are free but disciplined imitations. That is, they adopt Roman form, character types, and rhetoric, although their subject matter is Anglicized. It is logical to assume that plays imitating classical comedy in respect to form, character types, and rhetoric will show sensitivity to the form of its dialogue, and that if comic subject matter is adapted to an English setting, its verse will also be adapted.

We will return to this question when we consider comic "speech" in chapter 8. For the present, let us concentrate on tragedy.

Formal tragedy did not exist in English prior to Jasper Heywood's translation of *Troas*. However, drama that can be described as "serious," even by the standards of Aristotle's word *spoudaioteron*, had been written in the first half of the sixteenth century. As we saw in chapter 3, the writers of the French second rhetoric speculated that morality plays are equivalent to ancient tragedy. In England the standards for serious drama prior to Jasper Heywood are evident from three plays: John Skelton's *Magnificence* (ca. 1515), John Bale's *King John* (ca. 1535), and the anonymous *Respublica* of 1553.

All three plays use several different verse forms, but the variety has no obvious dramatic function. Probably it reflects a feeling that variety is ornamental in itself. Much of the dialogue verse of the serious plays is as irregular as the verse of the interludes, but the relaxed four-stress couplet is by no means standard for serious dialogue. As might be anticipated, *Magnificence* is the most various of the serious plays. Its dialogue includes passages in cantilevered verse, ballad eight, three-beat couplets, rhyme royal stanzas using Alexandrines, seven-line stanzas of four-beat lines in monorhyme, and six-line stanzas with two-beat lines. Sometimes the variety seems to be there simply to amuse, even though the play teaches a serious political lesson.

When we turn from the serious drama of the early Tudor period to the Seneca translations that begin with Heywood's *Troas*, the situation changes markedly. The verse is uniformly serious and (by the standards of its creators) elevated. All but one of the Seneca translations make the fourteener the norm for dialogue. Nuce's *Octavia* is the exception. Its dialogue is in decasyllabic quatrains.[19] A first observation is that the translators have turned away from the medieval habit of equating elevation with variety of verse forms. Like classical tragedies, the Seneca translations have a standard verse form for dialogue.

Since the translators were well versed in Latin, we can say that a consensus is evident in their work: the English equivalent of tragic iambic trimeter is the fourteen-syllable line in rising rhythm and rhymed in couplets.

Consensus regarding verse forms is evident from another standard practice. Seneca's choruses are in meters other than iambic trimeter. If the translators had been indifferent to the Latin meters of the original, they would not have bothered to create special meters for their choruses. The reverse is true. They all devise meters—usually decasyllabic—and rhyme schemes for the choruses that are different from the fourteeners used for dialogue. Moreover, many of the translations intentionally vary rhyme scheme from one chorus to the next, just as Seneca varies the Latin meters of his choruses.

Each play has its own variations on the general pattern. In *Troas*, for example, act 1, scene 1, is in fourteeners; scene 2, which is a long choral speech by the Trojan women, is in decasyllabic quatrains (with occasional couplets) and repeated refrains ("We bewaile Hector"). It is followed by dialogue (still in decasyllables) between Hecuba and the chorus of women.

In act 2, scene 1, the ghost of Achilles speaks in rhyme royal, and in the second and third scenes the fourteeners return, with a chorus at the end in rhyme royal. The third act is entirely in fourteeners except for scene 2, which is in decasyllabic quatrains. In the fourth act, the final chorus is in rhyme royal. The fifth act is entirely in fourteeners.

The choice of the fourteener for dialogue seems odd today, but it obviously seemed right to Heywood and the other translators. Iambic trimeter has a norm of twelve syllables, but can exceed this limit by means of substitutions. The fourteener has a roughly equivalent syllable count, making it relatively easy to translate line-for-line and convey what Heywood calls in the preface to *Troas* "the true sence" of the original.

The fourteener also preserves a vital relation to speech through its association with a popular form, the ballad, but it is more formal than the irregular verse of the Tudor interlude and midcentury comedy. It is thus suitable for conveying "roialty of speech." The ballad quality of the fourteener is especially noticeable in the single-play quartos in which the Seneca translations were first published, since the small size of the page requires the verse to be printed "eight and six" like a ballad. When dressed up and printed in fourteen-syllable lines, however, the form can be ceremonial, as is shown by Newton's edition of the *Tenne Tragedies*.

Seneca's tragedies were probably written to be declaimed with musical accompaniment rather than performed.[20] This does not mean that Seneca's verse ignores the speaking voice. Declamation is a verbal art, and Seneca is well aware of the fact. His dialogue abounds in constructions that shape the voice of the individual who is declaiming, in rapid give-and-take exchanges, including stichomythia, and in ironies, dramatic and verbal. Often the way a passage is to be spoken or declaimed is influenced by the deployment and behavior of nonspeaking characters, and this element, too, has to be factored into the construction of the lines. Since characters do not physically interact in declamation, the enactment of a declaimed play is heavily dependent on suggestions in the dialogue itself, including the constructions. Whether or not Seneca's tragedies were intended for the stage, their verse therefore has inherent dramatic qualities. The term I will use for verse adapted to verbal performance is "actorly." Some qualities of this sort of verse will become evident in the following discussion. The topic will be raised again in relation to *Gorboduc* in the next chapter, and in relation to Marlowe and Shakespeare in chapter 10.

Heywood and the other Seneca translators cannot have had direct experience with actorly verse. Nevyle's statement in the preface to *Oedipus* that he wishes to create a "Tragicall and pompous showe upon the Stage" is best understood as a reference to ancient theater rather than to Elizabethan practice.[21] No other translator makes even a perfunctory bow to the idea of performance. On the other hand, the Seneca translators must have assumed that Seneca's tragedies were performable because they were given academic performances in Latin. *Troas* was staged at Trinity College, Cambridge, in 1551, and Trinity supported four other Seneca performances between 1559 and 1561.

THYESTES

Thyestes stands out among the Seneca translations for two reasons. First, it is a mean between the extremes of *Troas*, which is a free translation, and *Hercules furens*, which uses the Loeb Library technique of printing Latin on one page and English on the other. Second, *Thyestes* has more of the actorly element than the other Seneca translations, including the other translations by Heywood. On occasion one hears living voices through the tortured constructions and heavy rhythms of its lines.

As *Thyestes* begins, Tantalus appears, pursued by the Fury Megaera brandishing her serpents. His first speech has four logical units: (1) What power has brought me here? (2) Is some new torture planned for me? (3) Punish me yet more severely! (4) My descendants will perform crimes even greater than mine.

In the edition of Bodius Ascensius (1514), Seneca's introductory lines are:[22]

Quis me furor nunc sede ab infausta abstrahit:
Avido fugaces ore captantem cibos?
Quis male deorum Tantalo vivas domos
Ostendit iterum? peius inventum est siti
Arente in undis aliquid: et peius fame
Hiante semper. Sisyphi numquid lapis
Gustandus umeris lubricus nostris venit?
Aut membra celeri differens cursu rota

Heywood translates these eight lines into exactly eight fourteeners:

What furye fell enforceth mee to fle thunhappie seate,
That gape and gaspe with greedy jawe, the fleeyng foode to eate:

> What god to Tantalus the bowres wher breathyng bodies dwel
> Doth showe agayne? is ought found worse then burning thurst of hell
> In lakes aglowe? or yet worse plague then hunger is there one,
> In vayne that evre gapes for food? Shal Sisyphus his stone,
> That slypper restles rollyng payse upon my backe be borne
> Or shall my lymms with swyfter swynge of whirlyng wheele be torne?

The coincidence of the Latin and English lines is striking evidence of the equivalence of the iambic trimeter and the fourteener. It extends to the enjambments in lines 4 and 6 of the original and the translation. The differences are also notable. The Latin is relatively simple in construction, and its diction is standard. The English is convoluted, and its diction wavers between formal and colloquial. In both versions the caesura is regular, but there are two cases in the English (ll. 4 and 5) of tension between normal caesura and pauses associated with sentence endings.

Let us look more closely.

"What furye" reproduces *Quis furor*, although Seneca's *furor* preserves an ambiguity that is lost in Heywood's "fury." *Furor* can be "rage" as well as the Fury Megaera, and jealous rage is the besetting sin of Tantalus and Thyestes. Seneca's general "furor" emphasizes theme. On the other hand, by referring to a "Fury" Heywood shows sensitivity to the dramatic aspect of the text. There is nothing abstract about Megaera. In both Latin and English, Tantalus is imagined stumbling onto the stage "enforced" (Latin, *abstrahit*; other renaissance editions read *extrahit*) by the whips and serpents she is brandishing. The English and Latin lines are both actorly: they require specific tonalities of voice plus gestures not only by Tantalus but also by Megaera. Megaera should menace; Tantalus must shrink away. In the third speech of Tantalus (l. 96) the brandishing of the serpents is explicit:

> With strypes why dooste thou me affryght? why threatst thou me to fraye
> Those crallyng snakes?

Whether or not Heywood had performance in mind, he catches an important aspect of dramatic speech; namely, that it exists not in itself but in relation to the actions, gestures, and voice tones of a speaker and to those characters with whom the speaker interacts, even though they themselves are silent. Although Heywood could have learned about dramatic speech from Latin school performances, the actorly elements that have been noted are already present in Seneca's text. Heywood could not have ignored them without being false to that text. The question is whether he recognized them for what they are.

During a performance, interaction between Megaera and Tantalus might save the first two lines. However, the English is more heavily "poetic" than the Latin. The singsong of the midcentury English fourteener is often the result of four elements: closed couplets, a strong caesura at the end of the eighth syllable of each line, heavy alliteration, and internal rhyme. The first couplet of Thyestes has all of these elements:

> What furye fell enforceth me to fle thunhappie seate,
> That gape and gaspe with greedy jawe, the fleeyng foode to eate:
> What god. . . .

These lines form a complete unit—a rhetorical question. The closure of the second line is evident from end-punctuation (the colon) as well as from the fact that the third line starts a new rhetorical question by repeating the "What" of line 1. The two lines are grammatically complete as well as being joined by the rhyme. The grammatical pause in the first line follows "me," and this is where the caesura falls. In the second line the caesura is emphasized by the comma after "jawe."

The influence of the alliterative tradition on Heywood is apparently illustrated by line 1. The line can be scanned accentually as having five stresses with the "subletter/chief letter" alliteration found in Old English verse. It divides into three stresses in the first half-line, which ends with "me," and two in the second. If one applies the subletter/chief letter pattern, the subletters are the f's in "furye," "fell," and "enforceth." The chief letter is the f of "fle" in the second half-line. Line 2 is symmetrical with line 1, having three alliterated words (g words) in its first half-line and presumably three stresses. The lines can also be considered metrical fourteeners with a rising (iambic) rhythm. Less obvious but also contributing to the apparent singsong effect are internal and echo rhyme ("me," "fle," "fleeyng") and a and e assonance.

Probably Heywood thought of his line as a "fourteener" in the romance sense of a fourteen-syllable line. If regarded in this way, the first of the two lines would have the form $[4+4*6]$, and the second, the form $[4+4*4+2]$. Syllable count is strict and preserved by synaloepha ("thunhappy"). The problem is that the lines are no better when understood in this way than they are understood as accentual verse. They follow practices long domesticated into English popular verse, and they make little use of the Italianate strategies of Surrey's verse. When the versification rises above its generally modest norm, the inspiration seems to be direct imitation of the Latin original rather than renaissance experiments in vernacular dramatic verse. Imitation explains the remarkably close fit of Heywood's lines to Seneca's. In fact, Heywood's elision ("thunhappy") may be not romance-inspired but an imitation of Seneca's elision in the equivalent Latin phrase (*infaust'abstrahit*).

In both Latin and English, the second line is an adjectival unit modifying "me" in line 1. The construction is satisfactory in the Latin because the accusative ending of *captantem* links it to its antecedent (*me*). However, when carried over into English, the construction radically displaces the modifier from its normal English position following the modified pronoun. The displacement is especially disturbing because it involves an element not necessary to the meaning of the sentence. The second line therefore dangles awkwardly from the first. It is not actorly. That is, it is very difficult to speak in a way that will make it intelligible to a listener.[23]

In spite of the problems they pose, the two English lines have an impressive number of sound effects. They are "artificial" in the sense of being produced by use of figures of construction. The figures, however, move the lines away from speech rather than toward it. Seneca's Latin, while formal and dignified, is less self-consciously poetic.

One final point. Heywood's alliteration has the effect of tying pairs of feet closely together:

/   /
What furye fell. . . .

And:

  /   /
That gape and gaspe. . . .

Heywood used the edition of Seneca by Sebastian Gryphius (1541) for his translation.[24] Gryphius calls Seneca's dialogue meter *iambicum trimetrum* rather than *senarius*. Jakob Schipper suggested many years ago that paired iambics may be English equivalents of classical dipodic feet.[25] Since iambic trimeter consists of pairs of iambic feet, it is just possible that Heywood considered the tendency of alliteration to bind the iambics of the fourteener into pairs an analogue to ancient dramatic meter.

Lines 3 to 6 continue the rhetorical questions. Again it should be noted that they are quite close to the Latin, although Heywood has used padding to fill out his lines (in italics):

> What god to Tantalus the bowres wher breathyng bodies dwel
> Doth showe agayne? is ought found worse then burning thurst *of hell*
> *In lakes aglowe*? or yet worse plague then hunger *is there one*,
> *In vayne* that evre gapes for foode?

The grammatical units are parallel but vary in length, complexity, and sound patterning. Both Latin sentences are enjambed, and this pattern is exactly reproduced in the English. Many variations in their scansion are possible. Let us concentrate here on effects adapted to vocal performance, whether in declamation or on a stage. This approach can be called actorly scansion or intonational scansion.

The first grammatical unit in these lines extends to "agayne." It is periodic in form because of the inversion of verb ("doth showe") and object ("the bowres"). The first line is therefore enjambed, and the syntactical unit is sixteen syllables. Syllabically, the line itself is [6*2+6], with a caesura after "Tantalus" and a pause after "dwel." This contrasts strongly with an accentual reading of the line, which would locate the caesura after "bowres." There is alliteration ("bowres . . . breathyng bodies"), but it is not oppressive and may, in fact, enhance the actorly quality by calling attention to the difference between hell and earth. Alliteration ("dwel/doth") links the first line closely with the second, reinforcing the grammatical enjambment. The second line is even more emphatically a departure from a normal fourteener than the first. It has a syllabic form of [4*4+6], here reinforced by the end of the sentence ("agayne"), that again places the caesura in a position quite different from the one it has in an accentual reading.

Regarded syllabically, the unit is not singsong. It has a complex formality—a "roialty of speach"—that distances it from everyday language, but it is something a human being might be imagined to utter if assumed to have the larger-than-life qualities appropriate to a tragic protagonist.

The next grammatical unit is interesting because it is apparently a perfect fourteen-syllable line, complete with an internal near-rhyme ("worse/thurst") marking the fourth and eighth syllables. The problem is that this apparent line is displaced by the four syllables that precede it: "Doth showe agayne." The device of fourteeners that run four syllables beyond the line where they begin is frequent in Heywood's prosody. It creates a counterpoint to the verse line. In the present instance, the accentual caesura (designated by *) comes after "worse," while the caesura of the displaced line (designated by |) would come, if it were recognized, after "thurst":

> [Doth showe agayne?] is ought found worse then burning thurst of hell
> In lakes aglowe?

The next rhetorical question also ignores line unity:

> . . . or yet worse plague then hunger is there one,
> In vayne that evre gapes for food?

The grammatical unit here is eighteen syllables. However, it is poorly sustained because the structure is loose rather than periodic. The phrase "that evre gapes" modifies "hunger" in the preceding line. As in the first couplet of the speech, the modifier dangles awkwardly.

Having asked if there are worse punishments than his, Tantalus now answers the question by listing the tortures of the three other classical sinners—Sisyphus, Ixion, and Tytius (Prometheus). The ideas are simple. Heywood's language, however, is so involuted that at times one has to refer to the Latin to be sure of his meaning. A long unit is created by apposition ("his stone, / That slypper . . . payse") and by suspension of the verb until the end of the grammatical unit:

> . . . shal Sisyphus his stone,
> That slypper restles rollyng payse upon my backe be borne.

There is a difference between elevation and obscurity, and the passage is obscure. It is further undercut by the colloquial vocabulary and the heavy alliteration: "That slypper restles rollyng payse." This is an extended translation of the Latin adjective *lubricus*. It is apparently intended to fill out the line so that parity can be maintained between the English and Latin texts. The heavy alliteration continues into the description of Ixion's wheel in the next line, which returns us to the fourteener in its elemental form:

> Or shall my lymms with swyfter swynge of whirlyng wheele be torne?

The next four lines must be considered a unit in spite of the question mark after the second:

> Or shall my paynes be Tytius pangs, thencreasyng lyvre styll,
> Whose growyng gutts, the gnawyng grypes and fylthie foules doe fyll?
> That styll by night repayres the panche that was devowrde by daie,
> And wondrows wombe unwasted lythe a new prepared praie.

The subject of the sentence is the liver of Tytius, which grows back even as it is eaten by the vultures. The passage is clumsy and obscure. While attempting to reproduce Seneca's Latin word order, Heywood has lost contact with English "grammatical order." The obscurity would be disturbing in an epic intended for reading; it is disastrous in a drama because it produces lines utterly unsuited for speech.

In the phrase "thencreasing lyvre styll," the word "styll" modifies "thencreasing," meaning that the liver is "continually regenerating." The phrase itself is in apposition to "pangs"—that is, the "pangs" *are*, by synecdoche, "thencreasing lyvre." "Whose" in the next line refers to Tytius. Again Heywood shows his willingness to let an adjectival clause dangle loosely from the line preceding it. "That" in the next line is parallel to "whose" and also refers to Tytius. Here again the line dangles so far from the word modified that the connection is lost. The next line is parallel, with the reservation that "whose" (referring still to Tytius) is omitted (ellipsis).

Heywood's sentence can be summed up in the following paraphrase: "Or shall my pains be like those of Prometheus [Tytius], which are those of a continually increasing liver. His growing guts fill the gnawing vultures and filthy birds. Each night he continually repairs the stomach that was devoured by day and with his wondrous womb undestroyed, he lies a newly prepared prey." Even in paraphrase, the description is hard to follow; in Heywood's version it is unintelligible to any but a determined explicator.

The remainder of this speech has no surprises but a few features worth noting:

> What yll am I appoynted for? O cruell judge of sprights,
> Who so thou be that torments newe among the soules delights
> Styll to dyspose, adde what thou canst to all my deadly woe,
> That kepre even of dungeon darke would sore abhorre to knoe
> Or hell it selfe it quake to see

The apostrophe to the "judge of sprights"—presumably Minos or Rhadamanthus—begins with an impressive period that is sustained to "adde." Here the complex construction almost works. There is no heavy alliteration to emphasize the singsong or create dipodic effects, and the clauses in lines 2 to 3 are elegantly nested: "Who so [that . . . delights / Styll to dyspose] . . ."—an instance of secondary enjambment. Because the "what" clause of line 3 is the direct object of "adde," the rhythm is sustained to "deadly woe." Unfortunately, the period breaks down in the next line as Heywood reverts to the practice of tacking on modifiers ("That kepre . . . would sore abhorre . . . / Or hell . . . quake to see").

Tantalus eventually turns from the torments of hell to the condition of his descendants. They will commit even more horrible crimes than he. Recognition of this fact answers the rhetorical questions that began the speech. No matter how much he has suffered, worse is in store. Tantalus has been driven out of hell to incite his son Atreus to unimaginable crimes. As he ends the speech, Megaera shakes her serpents again and drives him forward: "Goe forthe thou detestable spright."

The first scene of *Thyestes* is intentionally written at the highest possible emotional pitch. It is to the whole play what the ghost scene is to *Hamlet*. Even in this first scene, however, as Tantalus and Megaera converse, the lines become less showy and better adapted to declamation or acting.

Later in the play, rapid give-and-take dialogue and stichomythia are used effectively and in ways that capture Seneca's fondness for adages (*sententiae*). In act 2, after Atreus has vowed horrible revenge on Thyestes, a prudent servant tries to reason with him. The text for this scene begins to look like dialogue. Some of the lines break in the middle, a strategy Heywood has adopted from the Latin and one that encourages enjambment. Devices that call attention to the line as poetry like alliteration, internal rhyme, and assonance are suppressed:

> Atre[us]: He wil destroy or be destroyde, in midst the mischiefe lies,
> Preparde to him that takes it first.
>   Ser.: Dooth fame of people naught
> Adverse thee feare?
>   Atre.: The greatest good of kyngdome may be thought,
> That still the people are constraynde theyr princes deedes as well
> To praise, as them to suffer all.
>   Ser.: Whome feare doth so compell
> To prayse, the same his foes to be, doothe feare enforce agayne:
> But who in deede the glory seekes of favour true tobtayne,
> He rather wolde with hartes of eche be praysde, then tongues of all.
> Atre.: The truer prayse full ofte hathe hapte to meaner men to fall
> The false but unto mightie man what nyll they, let them wyll.
> Ser.: Let first the kyng will honest thyngs, and none the same dare nyll.
> Atre.: Where leefull are to him that rules but honest thyngs alone, There
> raygnes the kyng by others leave.
>   Ser.: And where that shame is none,
> Noe care of right, faythe, pietie, nor holines none staythe,
> That kingdome swarves.
>   Atre.: Suche holines, such pietie and faythe,
> Are private goods: let kyngs run on in that that likes their will.

The lines are instructive. They *look* like actorly dialogue. However, they are not. They are an elegant balancing of opposing aphorisms, more like a verbal duet than true dialogue. The duet analogy is exact, since a duet implies an understanding of procedures that is shared by both parties before anything is sung. Conversely, a dialogue is an exchange in which two individuals begin in ignorance and discover what each is thinking by means of speeches. Heywood is not responsible for the ritual quality of the exchange; it is pure Seneca. However, he carries over into English the figures that give the dialogue its ritual quality in Latin; among them, rhetorical question, aphorism, parallelism, and balance.

The discussion of revenge that follows has a more actorly quality because the speakers begin with different understandings of things. Atreus knows what he will do; the Servant is ignorant until the discovery created by the words "Thyestes selfe." The dialogue is actorly because it takes the characters seriously. It resembles speech in the sense of reproducing patterns of inquiry and informing typical of everyday conversation. The movement of the dialogue is also quickened by the breaking of one of the lines into four segments. Atreus has vowed revenge. The Servant asks whether it will be by the sword:

>   Ser.: What mischefe new dooste thou in rage provide?
> Atre.: Not such a one as may the meane of woonted griefe abide.
>   No guilt will I forbeare, nor none may be enough despight.
> Ser.: What sworde?
>   Atre.: To litel that.
>   Ser.: What fire?
>   Atre.: And that is yet to light.
> Ser.: What weapon then shall sorow suche fynde fit to worke thy wyll?
> Atre.: Thyestes selfe.
>   Ser.: Then yre it self yet thats a greater yll.
> Atre.: I graunte. . . .

Dramatic irony occurs when the audience knows something a character does not know. It may be considered an extension of the "knowledge-ignorance" situation illustrated by the dialogue between Atreus and the Servant. Seneca was fond of this device, and it was also a favorite with Elizabethan dramatists. *Hamlet*, for example, is filled with situations where the audience knows more than one or another of the characters knows. Since irony is a figure of thought, it may seem remote from prosody. However, it is an important part of the strategy that makes straightforward verse into dramatic speech. Verbal irony must be enacted by tone of voice. Dramatic irony is also frequently enacted by a tone of voice strikingly incongruous to the situation the audience knows to obtain, as, for example, when a character enthusiastically welcomes an invitation the audience knows will lead to disaster.

Act 3, scene 2, of *Thyestes* makes extensive use of dramatic irony. Two overt devices convey it—the aside, which is part of the "speech," and visual contrast, which is implicit in speech but expressed by costume and gesture. The aside, it should be noted, clearly implies onstage action from which the speaker turns to deliver the aside, and an audience to hear it. It is thus an intrinsically actorly form of dialogue. At the beginning of the scene, Atreus gloats that Thyestes is in his power: "Entrapt in trayne the beast is caught."

Thyestes must enter about two-thirds of the way through the speech because Atreus abruptly changes the subject by remarking how wretchedly Thyestes is dressed:

> . . . beholde, with uglye heare to syght
> How yrkesomely deformde with fylthe his fowlest face is dyght.

Note that if the scene were acted, the visual event—the appearance of Thyestes in rags—would *precede* Atreus's comment and seem to motivate it. The speech assumes the presence of Thyestes and his children and does not make sense unless they enter while it is being spoken. Note that the children are necessary although they have no lines and are not mentioned in the list of characters at the beginning of the scene. They must be present because about two-thirds of the way through the scene Thyestes presents them to Atreus as "these gyltles babes." Since they are present, we must assume they are used to intensify the irony of the scene. Once their presence is assumed, it implies gestures and vocal inflections. Clearly, Seneca's imagination was engaged by the dramatic situation he was creating, and the engagement produced dialogue written *as though* it were to be enacted on a stage. The joyful tone of voice of Thyestes in this scene also enacts dramatic irony by being grossly incongruous to the horrible fate being prepared for him.

Having acknowledged the entrance of Thyestes, Atreus announces in the classic aside of the stage villain that he will dissemble: "but let us freendship fayne." The dialogue again changes tone as he turns back to Thyestes and addresses him with oily enthusiasm: "To see my brother me delights: give now to me agayne / Embraicyng long desyred for." Thyestes now prostrates himself before Atreus. Atreus lifts him up and embraces the "lyttle infants all." These acts are made necessary by the "speech" of the scene, which obviously requires them if the words are to be intelligible. Yet the acts come first and in performance they appear to be the motives of the words:

> . . . Thy hands yet from my kneese
> remove, and rather me to take in armes, uppon me fall.
> And ye O aydes of elders age, ye lyttle infants all,
> me clyp and colle about the necke.

The scene ends with an apparent reconciliation. Atreus lifts the prostrate Thyestes and embraces him. The children approach their uncle and kiss him. The chorus is completely taken in. Seneca gives it a lyric celebration of the triumph of love over hate that nicely sustains the irony of the preceding dialogue.

Heywood uses decasyllabic verse for speech three times in *Troas*. He uses it only once in *Thyestes,* but the use is effective. Act 5, scene 2, is the most harrowing scene in the play. It is a "song" in the Latin, written in a lyric meter—anapestic dimeter—with free substitutions.[26] Thyestes is alone in the banquet hall. He is somewhat the worse for drink. At the same time that he feels overjoyed at his good fortune, he feels inexplicable sorrow. During the banquet he has a long soliloquy in which tone of voice and situation are again grossly at variance. Seneca's Latin is exceptionally expressive. It has more of lyrical sorrow than rhetorical posturing. The sense of pathos is very strong, and Heywood obviously responded.

His version of the soliloquy is fifty lines of English decasyllables with crossed rhyme. In the course of it Thyestes refers to setting (the banquet hall), costume (including a wreath of roses on his head), props (drinking cup, plate with meats), events (the wreath falls), gestures (tears), and facial expressions (joy, sorrow). As he speaks, the emotions—and thus the intonations—change. The soliloquy allows the full range of these effects to be expressed and must therefore be considered extremely actorly. The irony is overpowering. The audience has already been told in horrible detail of the slaughter of the children. It knows that as Thyestes speaks, he is eating their flesh and drinking their blood. Heywood cannot be given credit for inventing the speech—it is Seneca's—but he recognized the actorly quality and preserved it in his translation.

Because the soliloquy is in quatrains rather than couplets, the rhyme almost disappears when the lines are spoken in an actorly manner. The result is something close to dramatic blank verse and is more expressive than anything in *Gorboduc*—perhaps more expressive than any other tragic speech written before the 1580s. Note in the following excerpt how enjambment blurs the line-endings and rhymes and how grammatical parallelism simplifies understanding the speech when spoken. Thyestes thinks he is alone as he speaks, but it is possible that Atreus is eavesdropping. He is speaking to a personified "Sorrow," who constantly interrupts his efforts to be joyful:

> Awaye with all the myserable markes.
> to joyfull state returne thy chearefull face. . . .
> Why calst thou me abacke, and hyndrest me
> this happie daie to celebrate? wherefore
> Bydst thou me (sorowe) weepe without a cause?
> who doth me let with flowers so freshe and gaye,
> To decke my heares? it letts, and me withdrawes.
> downe from my head the roses fall awaye.[27]

Although it is brief, the excerpt is full of emotional changes that are objectified in exclamations, rhetorical questions, abrupt pauses, and apparent *non sequiturs*. In these respects as well as in its allusions to facial expression (tears) and props (rose wreath) and its suitability to the speaking voice, it has actorly qualities. Clearly, at his best Heywood is quite good.[28] The credit for this is primarily Seneca's, but Heywood can, on occasion, reproduce Seneca's effects quite faithfully.

Heywood uses Latinate constructions—parallelism, inversion, interruption, apposition, and the like—to give the fourteener the syntactic elevation appropriate to tragedy. To some degree these devices do what they are supposed to do. Joost Daalder, Heywood's most recent editor, points out that not all Latinate syntax is bad and that in some ways Heywood anticipates Milton.[29] However, the comparison of a dramatist with an epic poet nicely defines the problem created by Heywood's syntax. It is artificial and unnatural.

At the same time that tragic verse must be elevated, it must be "like speech." The two imperatives are—or seem to be—contradictory. Heywood's fourteeners are formal and serious and distinctly different from the comic verse of his age, but the effort to make them so led to constructions nearly unintelligible to a reader, to say nothing of an audience. At the same time, the imperative to write dialogue that resembles everyday speech led to grotesque colloquialisms and heavy alliterations that undercut the effort of verse to be elevated. However, to dismiss *Thyestes* with a list of defects is to miss its significance.

The play fascinated Elizabethan readers, and it is Heywood's masterpiece. It is only the second formal tragedy—translated or original—to appear in English, and Heywood is England's first tragedian. *Thyestes* is significant in itself and also a very considerable contribution to the development of Elizabethan drama.

CHAPTER VIII

Gorboduc and Dramatic Blank Verse, with a Note on Comedy

IMPERATIVES OF STATE AND OF PERFORMANCE

Gorboduc was first performed at the Inner Temple on Twelfth Night, 1561/62. Its authors were Thomas Sackville, then 25, and Thomas Norton, 29. They were in the same age group as Jasper Heywood, then 26. Norton had already published a few poems, including an "Epitaph of Henry Williams," in Tottel's *Miscellany,* and twenty-eight psalms in Sternhold and Hopkins's collection. In 1561 he also published his translation of Calvin's *Institutes of the Christian Religion,* which contains two short passages from the *Aeneid* in blank verse. Before *Gorboduc,* Sackville's only published verse was a commendatory poem for Thomas Hoby's translation of Castiglione's *Courtier.* He would later (1563) publish the brilliant "Induction" and "Complaint of Buckingham" in *A Mirror for Magistrates.* Thereafter, both men would exchange literary for administrative careers.

Three purposes intersect in *Gorboduc.* In the first place, the play has an overriding political object. Written within two years after Elizabeth's accession to the throne, it is a lesson in the danger of failing to settle the question of succession. This is explained in the "Argument of the Tragedie" in the John Day edition (1570): "For want of an issue of the prince . . . the succession of the crowene became uncertaine, [and] they fell into civill warre, in which both they and many of their issues were slaine, and the land for a long time almost desolate and miserably wasted."[1]

Henry VIII had established the succession in 1544, and Parliament had ratified his decision.[2] In spite of wrenching changes in religious preference, political bias, qualifications, and sex of succeeding claimants, the plan worked. But Elizabeth is the last of Henry's children. *Gorboduc* ends with a proposal (V, ii, 264–71) that Parliament end the civil war disrupting the England of the play by establishing the succession—and with a gloomy prediction that the plan will fail. Only a legitimate monarch can settle such a major question. "Act now to forestall later disaster" is the message *Gorboduc* was intended to convey when it was performed before Elizabeth on January 18, 1561/62.

A second purpose of *Gorboduc* is literary imitation. It was written, as we have seen, during a period in which Seneca's plays were being translated with semi-official encouragement. The effort was complemented during the 1560s by efforts, reviewed in chapter 7, to translate other ancient and renaissance classics. Sackville and Norton were members of the circle responsible for most of the translations, and they were associated with the Inns of Court, from which many of the translators came.

Gorboduc has many obvious classical features. It is divided into five acts. It uses choruses. Its violence occurs offstage. It includes elaborate speeches, formal aphorisms, and, on occasion, laments and lurid imagery of the sort found in Seneca. Seneca's plays had political import, but their major emphasis is on a fatalistic, even despairing philosophy. *Gorboduc* is also didactic, but in this respect its imitation is creative. The emphasis is less on philosophy than politics, and this emphasis relates the play more closely to native historical moralities like Skelton's *Magnificence* and Bale's *King John* than to *Thyestes* or *Hercules furens*.[3] The dumb shows are also innovative. They are suggested by Italian imitations of ancient tragedy, not classical drama.

Indeed, in spite of the classical qualities of *Gorboduc*, its considerable independence of Seneca deserves to be stressed.[4] Seneca's choruses sometimes behave like characters. For example, the chorus in *Thyestes* is as deceived as Thyestes himself by the pretended friendship of Atreus. The choruses of *Gorboduc* are not characters and exist only to offer lyric and moral comments. Again, Seneca normally begins his tragedies with a lurid and extended soliloquy like the opening speech of Tantalus in *Thyestes*. *Gorboduc* begins with dialogue. Seneca delights in vivid descriptions—*enargia*. Sackville and Norton place far greater emphasis, as is understandable in a work by two young lawyers, on formal debate. Seneca emphasizes pathos (a horrible tragic deed like the slaughter of children) and dramatic irony. Sackville and

Norton make only modest use of pathos and generally ignore dramatic irony. Revenge is central in Seneca's tragedies; in *Gorboduc* the emphasis is on political power.

From the present point of view, the most interesting aspect of classical imitation in *Gorboduc* is its use of blank verse. The verse is entirely different in texture from the verse of Surrey's *Aeneid*, not to mention Heywood's fourteeners. Since they are familiar with Italian dumb show technique, Sackville and Norton must have known Italian discussions of the suitability of *versi sciolti* for drama, and the obvious source for their decision to use blank verse rather than fourteeners is Italian drama. They agreed with the Italians that the proper vernacular form for imitating ancient iambic trimeter is a simple, unrhymed form that remains highly flexible and avoids the recurring units of couplet, quatrain, and stanzaic poetry.

This leads to the last of the three major purposes that intersect in *Gorboduc*. The play was written expressly for performance. It was not written by authors who were conversant with professional drama, since there was no established professional English theater in the 1560s. It was, however, written by authors who were used to declamation. Declamation was a staple of the training of lawyers in the sixteenth century. Experience in declamation was complemented at the Inns of Court by annual revels at which dramatic and quasi-dramatic entertainments were offered. Something like a nascent performance tradition had developed from these revels, and the expertise created by that tradition is an element in the success of *Gorboduc*.

The most obvious way in which the traditions of declamation and performance contribute to *Gorboduc* is their influence on the play's dialogue. Yet readers have been all but unanimous about the monotony of the play's blank verse. It seems to go with the regularity of the structure of the play. The verse is at best a faint hint of the instrument that would be perfected in the dramas of Marlowe, Kyd, and Shakespeare, and it is bland even when compared with the most successful passages of *Thyestes*.

But monotony is only part of the story. In one key respect, the verse of *Gorboduc* is a major advance over anything that can be found in earlier attempts at serious drama in England. Unlike the verse of *Thyestes*, it can almost always be spoken easily. It is clear, dignified, free of dissonant colloquialisms and opaque allusions, and capable of both simple and elevated effects, depending on the circumstances giving rise to it. In all these ways it shows that it was written for performance.

Speech as Speaking

The clarity of the blank verse of *Gorboduc* is largely a matter of construction. The sentences are sometimes several lines long, but when they are loose, they tend to follow grammatical order so that they are easy to follow. When they are periodic, as is often the case in the long narrations and set speeches, the thought units are separated by pauses adjusted to the breath pattern of the speaking voice, and key words—adjectives and modified nouns, subjects and verbs—are grouped together, so that their relations never become confused.

The verse adheres closely to a decasyllabic norm. The caesura tends to follow the fourth syllable. Enjambment is used—often to good effect—but it is used sparingly. Line integrity is the norm. Although the verse has features associated with the syllabic tradition, it can also be described as unrhymed iambic pentameter with substitutions. The ambiguity is nicely illustrated by the following line:

O my beloved sonne! O my swete childe!

If this is syllabic verse, it presents no problems. It has ten syllables, ends with an accented syllable, and has a midline break after a strongly stressed sixth syllable. The syllabic formula would be $[1+5*1+3]$. An analysis that assumes the use of foot meter is also possible, but it has to be permissive:

/ x x / x / / x \ /
O my beloved sonne! O my swete childe!

If this scansion is adopted, the first foot is a trochee. This is a common substitution and thus not a problem. The second and third feet are standard iambs. The caesura follows "son." The next foot must be a trochee for the same reason that the first foot is a trochee.

The fifth and last foot either is a spondee, or—accepting the idea that stress is relative and that within a foot one stress must be dominant—consists of a secondary stress followed by a primary stress. In this sense the fifth foot is iambic and the line can be considered acceptable, though irregular, iambic pentameter. On the other hand, the line is exceptional for *Gorboduc,* and most of the lines in the play are regular by accentual as well as syllabic standards.

In addition to being suited to the speaking voice by syntax and meter, *Gorboduc* uses a standard vocabulary. There are no jarring colloquialisms of the kind one encounters in *Thyestes,* nor is the verse clotted with mythological allusions. When classical names are used, they are used sparingly to ornament the verse, and they tend to be commonplace—hence easy to understand—rather than recondite.[5]

In all these respects the verse of *Gorboduc* is like speech. Given the fact that *Gorboduc* is not the work of a professional dramatist writing for an established theater, it is not surprising that the speech is less flexible than the dramatic speech of the 1590s. The verse, in other words, has the potential to be actorly but does not exploit this potential aggressively.

The play begins with a dialogue in which Videna reveals the plan of King Gorboduc to divide the kingdom between his two sons rather than allowing the oldest, Ferrex, to succeed to the throne:[6]

> Videna: The silent night that bringes the quiet pawse
> From painefull travailes of the wearie day
> Prolonges my carefull thoughtes, and makes me blame
> The slowe Aurore, that so for love or shame
> Doth long delay to shewe her blushing face;   5
> And now the day renewes my griefull plaint.
> Ferrex: My gracious lady and my mother deare,
> Pardon my griefe for your so grieved minde
> To aske what cause tormenteth so your hart.
> Videna: So great a wrong, and so unjust despite,   10
> Without all cause, against all course of kinde!
> Ferrex: Such causelesse wrong, and so unjust despite,
> May have redresse, or, at the least, revenge.
>
> (I, i, 1–13)

Videna's initial sentence is long, but it has a simple subject-modifier-verb-object-modifier pattern. It is easy to follow and to make clear in speaking. The words flow smoothly—perhaps a little too smoothly to express the agitation Videna is supposed to feel. The introductory description is concluded by the turn in the last line (6) from night to day and from blushing Aurora to "griefull plaint." Significantly, there is none of the heavy alliteration so frequent in Heywood's fourteeners. Finally, "Aurore" in line 4 is shortened by apocope, making the line a perfectly regular decasyllabic.

The reply of Ferrex is as direct as Videna's opening statement. It has potential for actorly performance and suggests actions to reinforce the intonations. Videna might, for example, falter after her speech, and Ferrex might step forward to support her. If something like this occurred, it would be entirely the actor's doing. The verse allows it but does not require it. Surely, however, Ferrex's words "My gracious lady" are an exclamation, and surely Videna's reply ought to be vehement. However, the actorly quality of these lines is undercut by their artificiality, beginning with "So great a wrong. . . ." The repetition of Videna's line in Ferrex's reply (anaphora) recalls the ritualistic exchanges in Seneca. It is elegant, but it has little to do with speech.

Twice in the scene the verse catches the tone of a human voice registering strong emotion. When Videna reveals to Ferrex that he is about to be betrayed by his father, Ferrex replies:

> My father? Why, I know nothing at all
> Wherein I have misdone unto his Grace.

Here the effect of construction is especially clear. The strong pause after "father" registers shocked surprise. The short pause after "Why" and the heavy stress on "all" suggest confusion followed by a rush of emotion. The verse makes sense syllabically; it makes little sense as accentual meter. The suggestion of human motive—the illocutionary quality of the verse—returns when Videna expresses fear that the injustices being committed will bring ruin to the kingdom. Ferrex attempts to reassure her:

> Ferrex: Mother, content you; you shall see the end.
> Videna: The end? Thy end, I feare! Jove end me first!

Videna's line is segmented into three parts. Each is an illocution that invites actorly performance: question, confession, prayer. The wordplay (paranomasia; diaphora: "The/Thy"; "end/end/end") is also effective and does not trivialize the seriousness of the moment.

Speech as Speeches

Although the verse of act 1, scene 1, of *Gorboduc* has actorly qualities, scene 2 appears to be utterly undramatic. It consists essentially of four long speeches. King Gorboduc asks whether he should divide his kingdom. Arostus (a "speaking name" meaning something like "weak") speaks in favor. Philander ("friend of man") speaks against. And Eubulus ("wise counselor") also speaks against. Classical rhetoric recognizes three types of speech: forensic (or judicial), deliberative, and epideictic. Forensic speeches are concerned with what has been done in the past. Deliberative speeches deal with future action and are typical of political debate. Epideictic speeches deal with the present and tend to praise or blame. The speeches in act 1, scene 2, are textbook examples of deliberative orations.[7] In their use of standard kinds of oratory, they point toward the formal orations of later Elizabethan drama: Portia's great forensic oration in *The Merchant of Venice*, or Antony's funeral oration in the Roman Forum in *Julius Caesar*.

The rhetorical character of the speeches in act 1, scene 2, shows that Sackville and Norton interpreted in a literal way the imperative to make dramatic language like speech. "Speech" in Latin is *oratio*, which means both "speaking" and "oration." Many of the long speeches in *Gorboduc* are straight out of rhetoric texts like the *Ad Herennium* and the *Progymnasmata* of Aphthonius. Sackville and Norton are much more inclined to write formal orations than Seneca, who prefers narration, description, and thought-revealing expression (*sermocinatio*). The orations in act 1, scene 2, occur in an appropriate setting. They are examples of a special type of deliberative oration, the council speech, delivered in a throne room or council chamber.

Arostus's speech illustrates the rhetorical bias of the dialogue of *Gorboduc*. The object of rhetoric is persuasion. The three basic appeals are dianoia (logical argumentation), ethos (the character of the speaker), and pathos (emotional appeal). The emphasis in this and all other deliberative speeches in the play is on logical argument. The point is made explicit when Arostus invokes "rightfull reason." He presents his reasoning in a series of enthymemes: "Since ease is healthy, you will live longer if you resign the throne"; "Since children respect fathers, you can advise your sons."

But Arostus is not indifferent to ethos and pathos. Character is exhibited when Arostus speaks of the desire of courtiers to serve the king: "Whose honours, goods, and lyves are whole avowed / To serve, to ayde and to defende your Grace." Appeal to emotion is evident in the vocabulary Arostus uses: continuing to rule is associated with "crooked age . . . furrowed face . . . enfeebled lymmes . . . creepyng death." Giving up the throne is associated with "ease" and "life in joyfulness."

Finally, the organization (*dispositio*) of the speech follows standard formulas. It begins with an introduction that includes a *narratio*, or summary of the situation, and a *propositio*, or statement of the thesis. It offers three proofs in favor (*demonstratio*): you will live longer; your sons will rule half-kingdoms more easily than a whole kingdom; as a former king you will be able to advise them. There is also a proof against inaction (*refutatio*): if you do not act, your sons may plot against you. The conclusion (*peroratio*) summarizes the arguments and restates the thesis. The speeches of Philander and Eubulus follow the same pattern and add nothing to what has already been observed about the use in the play of rhetorical formulas.

Deliberative oratory accounts for most of act 2 of *Gorboduc*. The debates between Hermon and Dordan at the court of Ferrex (II, i) and between Tyndar and Philander at the court of Porrex (II, ii) are both deliberative.

Acts 3–5 present the tragic result of the decisions made in acts 1 and 2. They have a Senecan quality because of the prominence in them of narration and lament. In general, however, they lack the *enargia*—vivid (including lurid) visual detail—of Seneca's speeches. Seneca's messengers, who describe violence that has occurred off stage, are often especially lurid. By contrast, the *Nuntius* who announces the death of Ferrex at the hand of Porrex is brief and matter-of-fact:

> . . . with his owne most bloudy hand he hath
> His brother slaine, and doth possesse his realm.
>
> (III, i, 161–162)

Act 4 begins with a long speech by Videna. It seems to be modeled on the speeches of Seneca's *Medea*, and it provides splendid actorly opportunities:

> O my beloved sonne! O my swete childe!
> My deare Ferrex, my joye, my lyves delight!
> Is my beloved sonne, is my sweete childe,
> My deare Ferrex, my joye, my lives delight,
> Murdered with cruell death? O hatefull wretch!
> O heynous traitour both to heaven and earth!
> Thou, Porrex, thou this damned dede hast wrought!
> Thou, Porrex, thou shalt dearely bye the same!
> Traitour to kin and kinde. . . .
>
> (IV, i, 23–32)

The lines are end-stopped, but the caesura is variable. In the first line it comes after the sixth syllable. In the second, there are two pauses, after the fourth and the sixth syllable, creating three segments within the line. In the next line the caesura follows the fourth syllable, and in the next, the line is divided again into three units. In the fifth line of the passage the caesura comes after the sixth syllable, as in line 1. It then moves to the common position after the fourth syllable, but the next two lines each have two pauses, the minor after the first, and the major after the third syllable. Further variation is provided by the fact that two of the ten lines (ll. 5, 9) begin with an unambiguously stressed, rather than an unstressed, syllable, and four others (ll. 1, 6, 7, 8) have, at the least, secondary stress on the first syllable. Only three lines (ll. 2, 3, 4) begin with unambiguously unstressed syllables, and in two of these, the word "Ferrex" causes problems because its natural stress is on the first syllable. In other words, the lines are much easier to understand as syllabic than as regular accentual verse.

It may be added that the passage exploits all of the rhetorical devices that would become clichés of the later Elizabethan lament—exclamation, rhetorical question, choppy construction, anaphora, parallelism, and the like. The devices give the lines a strong illocutionary quality and provide both convenient pauses for the speaking voice and moments where facial expression, gesture, and interaction with the silent speaker can reinforce intonation.

In the second scene of act 4 the stabbing of Porrex by his mother Videna is reported by Marcella. Here the description makes a bid in its lurid and pathetic details for Senecan *enargia:*

> The noble prince, pearst with the sodeine wound,
> Out of his wretched slumber hastely start,
> Whose strength now fayling, straight he overthrew,—
> When in the fall his eyes, even new unclosed,
> Behelde the queene, and cryed to her for helpe.   5
> We then, alas! the ladies which that time
> Did there attend, seing that heynous deede,
> And hearing him oft call the wretched name
> Of mother, and to crye to her for aide
> Whose dierefull hand gave him the mortall wound,   10
> Pitying, alas!—for nought else could we do,—
> His ruthefull end, ranne to the woefull bedde,
> Dispoyled straight his brest, and, all we might,
> Wiped in vaine with napkins next at hand
> The sodaine streames of bloud that flushed fast   15
> Out of the gaping wound.
>   (IV, ii, 204–19)

This is effective tragic speech. It has a Latinate quality recalling the constructions in Surrey's *Aeneid* and thus nicely illustrates the tendency of tragic verse to approximate the elevation of epic at moments of intense emotion. Most obvious is the use of periodic structure to create verse units of several lines. The first period extends for three lines from "prince" to "overthrew," with two additional lines that carry an adverbial clause modifying the main verb ("When in the fall . . . for helpe"). With "We" the focus shifts from the prince to the attending ladies. The sentence is a long period with the form "We . . . the ladies . . . seing . . . hearing . . . pitying . . . dispoyled . . . and . . . wiped . . . the . . . streames." Along with the periodic structure comes enjambment. Five lines (ll. 6, 8, 9, 14, 15) have no end-punctuation.

The basic strategy for achieving periodic suspension is interruption of the normally close link between subject and verb by participial phrases in parallel series. Thus, the passage falls into units—the participial phrases—that are easily accommodated to the breathing pattern of speech and that are dependent on grammar rather than the line unit. Apposition (ll. 6–7) and inversion (antistrophe, ll. 2, 7) are also notable, as is the extensive separation of subject (l. 6) from verb (l. 12) in the second sentence. Elements that escape the periodic structure—notably the "When" clause beginning in line 4—do not have the awkward quality of the modifiers that dangle so painfully in Heywood's fourteeners. The narrative comes in a series of short packets, each packet offering a new detail or sensation. The modifiers fit this pattern, and—in that they break up the artifice of the periodic structure—they suggest emotion breaking through rational control. Notably absent from the passage are the clichés of lament that are so prominent in the speech of Videna (IV, i) examined earlier.

Finally, the vocabulary of the passage is dignified and standard. Its seriousness is not undercut by colloquialisms or heavy-handed alliteration. At the same time, it avoids inkhorn terms—polysyllables and ornamental allusions. It is elevated but it preserves a vital relation to living language; that is, "everyday speech."

Marcella's speech is a high point in *Gorboduc* and a prophecy of what would be accomplished with greater assurance by the drama of the 1590s. Act 5 depicts the civil wars that follow from the death of the two legitimate heirs. It does not concentrate on pathos—that is, the terrible suffering caused by civil war. Instead it offers more orations of the sort found in act 2. Eubulus (V, i) counsels immediate preparations to repress the approaching armies, combined with offers of clemency for those who surrender and plans for the destruction of those who do not. In the next scene he describes the failure of the rebellion, only to be informed of another plot. The problem is that no one has clear title to the throne. Arostus delivers an oration proposing that Parliament be convened to name a king. He concludes by stressing the danger that a foreign power may claim the throne if Parliament does not act. Eubulus ends the play with another long oration predicting that Parliament will be unable to resolve the problem of succession. The civil war will continue.

The speeches in act 5 of *Gorboduc* are appropriate to the play. They touch directly on the problems of succession created by the will of Henry VIII and Elizabeth's refusal either to marry or to name a successor.[8] These considerations were doubtless paramount for Sackville and Norton, and they must have registered emphatically with Elizabeth and her courtiers. However, their effect on the play as drama is negative. *Gorboduc* ends with a message rather than the somber emotion appropriate for the conclusion of a tragedy.

In spite of their limitations, Sackville and Norton made two discoveries about dramatic speech that are important for the drama at the end of the century. The first is that blank verse is better adapted to speech than the fourteener, precisely because it is less rigidly patterned. Its flexibility allows it to be broken into short fragments or sustained in long periods. Even long periods can be segmented in grammatical units that can be spoken clearly and with appropriate emotional inflection and that can build their effects cumulatively. In this way dramatic verse can both resemble speech and suggest on occasion the larger-than-life quality appropriate for the climactic moments of tragedy.

Sackville and Norton preferred clarity to other possible virtues in their dramatic speech. The fact that *Gorboduc* was to be performed made them sensitive to the limitations—and, occasionally, the potentialities—of the speaking voice. In addition, they had lessons to teach that they very much wanted their audience to understand. For both reasons they needed verse that is transparent—easy to speak and articulated so as to make its meanings obvious. Wolfgang Clemen remarks, "The language and style of *Gorboduc* are calculated . . . to make [the] 'matter' as easily intelligible as possible."[9] What the verse of *Gorboduc* lacks for the most part (though not entirely) is elevation—the "roialty of speech" to which Heywood so obviously aspired with his Latinate diction, his complex vocabulary, and his long line. The verse of *Gorboduc* is appropriately like speech, but it is too seldom "like epic." The greatest Elizabethan tragedies manage a better balance. One thinks especially of *Othello* and *Antony and Cleopatra*.

The second important discovery made by Sackville and Norton is that "speech" can be interpreted as *oratio*—that is, "speeches" modeled on the formulas of the rhetoric that Sackville and Norton had studied as law students. Such speeches can be "English" in style and "classical" in form.

The discovery could be—and was—used by others. In chapter 5, we noted that Gascoigne provided a rationale for it by arguing in *Certayne Notes of Instruction* for "mother phrase and proper idióma" and against the artificial style illustrated, for example, by Surrey's *Aeneid*. Gascoigne's own poetry combines "English" style with rhetorical formulas for genre and for organization, and this formula is used by many later sixteenth-century poets. It would prove especially congenial to seventeenth-century English rationalists and would, of course, be rejected by Milton. As Sackville and Norton understood, it is directly applicable to tragic speech, which must be relatively easy for audiences to understand and give the impression of elegance at the same time. We can see William Shakespeare applying it with gusto in the set speeches of his early plays.

A Note on Comedy

The problem of comic speech is more complex than the problem of tragic speech. On the one hand, the principles are clear. As we have already noted, the *ars metrica* assumes comic speech will be more irregular than tragic speech. If tragic speech at its most serious can approach epic, comic speech at its most relaxed approaches prose. The comic line is the source of the term "licensed iambic," meaning an iambic line filled with substitutions. The judgment of the *ars metrica* is based on the practice of Plautus and Terence. Complementing their poetic license, both dramatists use colloquial language, and both adapt their dialogue fully to the conditions of performance, which is to say they write actorly speeches assuming that elements expressed visually during performance are (or seem to be) causes of the speeches.

In Italy formal comedy began being written in the vernacular early in the sixteenth century. Ariosto is one of the pioneers. He wrote two comedies in prose around 1508—*La Cassaria* and *I Suppositi*. Some twenty years later he rewrote both in *sdruccioli*—unrhymed lines ending with two unaccented syllables. After Ariosto, Italian comedy alternated between prose and verse. Cardinal Bibbiena's *La Calandria* (1513) is in prose, as are Machiavelli's comedies *Clizia* and *La Mandragola,* written around 1515, and the five comedies of Pietro Aretino.

Comedies in verse, however, are at least as popular as comedies in prose.[10]

Marvin Herrick sums up the renaissance position regarding comic language: "If comedy is the mirror of daily life, and the Renaissance certainly thought it should be such a mirror, then the speech of the Terentian characters must be accepted as a standard of familiar discourse."[11] The reason for the uncertainty illustrated by Ariosto's alternation between prose and verse is the *ars metrica*. If comedy is a mirror of daily life and if comic verse is so free as to be unscannable, why not write comedies in prose to begin with? That verse is a matter of tradition rather than logic is illustrated by Giraldi Cintio's rather lame summary of the case for verse in his *Discorsi . . . intorno al comporre de i Romanzi, delle Commedie, e delle Tragedie* (1554): "Since domestic and popular matters are dealt with [in comedy], it is desirable that the mode of speech should be familiar. Since prose is not proper to comedy, that sort of verse is appropriate which, though having number, is most like prose, and such is blank verse that lacks rhyme."[12] John Palsgrave's translation of *Acolastus* (1540), reviewed in chapter 5, shows that English humanists of the age of Henry VIII thoroughly understood Roman comic verse. Henry Medwall, John Rastell, John Heywood, and John Redford were well-educated humanists, and presumably they understood ancient prosody as well as Palsgrave. Their preferred form for dialogue is an irregular four-accent line rhymed in couplets. It is racy and colloquial in vocabulary, idiomatic, and straightforward in syntax.

As observed in chapter 7, J. E. Bernard, Jr., calls the form "cantilevered verse." R. W. Bond calls it "doggerel verse" and suggests that it arises from "a dramatic verse whose native principle was anapestic, undergoing about 1550–60 an iambic influence due to the nondramatic work of Wyatt, Surrey, Grimald, and others collected in Tottel."[13] Bond is convinced that the form is the result of careful thought about comic versification. His statement is so clear that it merits full quotation:

> When we remember that ['doggerel verse'] is used not merely by skilless scribblers who could do no better, but by scholars and schoolmasters like Udall and Preston, Edwards and Fulwell, Jeffre and Bayons, some of whom were writing at the same time or even in the same play verse of smooth correctness . . . we cannot dismiss the doggerel of 1560 onwards as mere sloth, ignorance, or incompetence. It persisted . . . because the dramatists believed it better adapted for average comic uses,—for dialogue

as opposed to set speech, and for farcical matters—than more regular measures. . . . Had *Supposes* been an original work, had the Latin use of verse for comedy been less authoritative, a successful and consistent comic prose would doubtless have arrived earlier. In default of such the doggerel survived the introduction of regular measures by a quarter of a century; and did so largely as a matter of reasoned choice, as a compromise, parallel in fact to Ariosto's choice of *sdruccioli*, and to Italian critical preference for a verse which, while not prose, might be as near to prose as possible.[14]

Bond is suggesting that authors like Udall understood their so-called "doggerel" as an English equivalent of the "verse close to prose" advocated both by the authors of the *ars metrica* and Italian renaissance authors like Trissino and Cintio.

Here a distinction must be made. The interlude line is obviously not a failed attempt at regular accentual meter. It is probably indigenous as Bernard argues, but it must also owe a debt to French rhymed octosyllabic verse as used, especially, in *débat* and farce. The evidence for this comes from the interludes themselves. Heywood's *The Foure P. P.* is based on French *débat*, and *Johan Johan* is based on the French *Farce du Paste*.

The dialogue line of *The Foure P. P.* (ca. 1520) nicely illustrates the difference between "poetry" and actorly verse. It is in a form that is dismissed by scholars as "cantilevered" or "doggerel," but it is nicely adjusted to performance and well adapted to the speaking voice. The opening speech is an example of ethopoeia, a speech revealing the character of the speaker. It would be called a soliloquy if it appeared in an Elizabethan play. The speaker is a Palmer who sells religious relics:[15]

> Nowe Gode be here! Who kepeth this place?
> Now, by my fayth, I crye you mercy!
> Of reason I must sew for grace,
> My rewdness sheweth me no[w] so homely.
> Whereof, your pardon axt, and wonne,
> I sew you, as curtsey doth me bynde,
> To tell thys which shalbe bigonne
> In order as may come beste in mynde. . . .
> To Iosophat and Olyvete
> On fote, God wote, I wente ryght bare,—
> Many a salt tere dyde I swete
> Before thys carkes coulde come there. . . .
> At Saynt Toncomber; and Saynt Tronion;
> At Saynt Bothulph; and Saynt Anne of Buckston;

> On the hylles of Armony, where I see Noes arke;
> With holy Iob; and Saynt George in Suthwarke. . . .
>
> (ll. 1–34)

The form is an irregular four-beat line with a norm of eight syllables that begins with cross rhyme (initially alternating masculine and feminine rhyme) and then settles into couplets, the standard for the rest of the play. If one seeks ancestors of this line, the romance octosyllabic couplet would seem at least possible. The construction is natural and flows easily. Enjambment occurs but without Latinate syntax. The vocabulary is standard, with the place names being introduced as a kind of verbal game to show off the author's ability to stuff even the most unlikely word into his couplets. The passage is relaxed, and its performance has been "visualized" so that it creates numerous opportunities for expressive gesture, facial expression, and intonation. Heywood's Palmer enters and faces the audience. At first he is confused. The result is an oath followed by a question: "Who kepeth this place?" Then the Palmer sees the audience. He expresses surprise and asks pardon for not being more forthcoming: "My rewdness sheweth me no[w] so homely." Then he begins to explain who he is. He is proud of his travels and obviously enjoys listing the countries—and later the towns—he has visited.

There is no obvious classical influence here; but Heywood is clearly more at home with stage performance than either the Seneca translators or Sackville and Norton. He writes easily in the actorly style because he thinks of his text as a script, not as the translation of an ancient masterpiece intended for reading or as a collection of orations tied together by a plot.

Heywood is as accomplished in rapid give-and-take dialogue as in comic soliloquy. The following exchange is pure slapstick. It is *not* rapid dialogue of the type found in Seneca's tragedies. It is entirely free of aphorisms, and its appeal comes from its extensive use of wordplay complemented by interaction between the speakers:

> Pedler: Devyse what pastyme ye thinke beste,
>   And make ye sure to fynde me prest.
> Potycary: Why, be ye so universall
>   That you can do what-ever-so ye shall?
> Pedler: Syr yf ye liste to appose me,
>   What I can do then shall ye see.
> Potycary: Than tell me thys: be ye perfyt in drynkynge?
> Pedler: Perfyt in drynkyng as may be wished by thynkyng!

> Potycary: Then after your drynkyng, how? fall ye to wynkyng?
> Pedler: Syr, after drynkynge, whyle the shot is tynkynge,
> Some hedes be swynking, but myne wyl be synkynge,
> And upon drynkynge myne eyse wyll be pynkynge,
> For wynkynge to drynkynge is alway lynkynge.

What is one to make of the prosody of this passage? There tend to be four beats to the line. Beyond that, the verse goes where it wants. An intriguing feature of the passage is that it plays language games with itself. The Pedler and the Potycary fall into an absurd rhyming contest, the only point of which is the absurdity. The comedy is there for its own sake. Shakespeare's clowns indulge in wordplay that is generically related to Heywood's, but their absurdities tend to be parts of the larger design of the play. Perhaps that is a measure of the difference between the interlude as it grows out of the medieval *débat*—a form intent on showing itself off—and drama.

The Tudor interlude thus seems independent of Roman comedy, although, as the presence of Jupiter in Heywood's *Play of the Wether* shows, a touch of classical influence is sometimes apparent in it. In that play, interestingly, there is also evidence of a concern for decorum. Although it includes word games (e.g., ll. 200-211) of the sort found in *The Foure P. P.*, its dialogue is more serious and so are its speakers. It consists essentially of a series of interviews with individuals about ideal weather conditions. It thus has the qualities of a rhetorical debate. Jupiter regularly speaks in rhyme royal stanzas in irregular twelve-syllable lines. The human characters tend to alternate between twelve- and ten-syllable couplets. Merry-report tends to use irregular decasyllabic couplets. Some of the lines seem on the way to becoming proper Alexandrines and decasyllables, but nothing suggests that Heywood was experimenting with French or classical comic verse forms. Why should he? He was writing in a well-established tradition, and to experiment would only risk confusing his audience.

CLASSICAL TRENDS

Ralph Roister Doister by Nicholas Udall, Headmaster of Eton, was probably written around 1540 at about the same time as Palsgrave's translation of *Acolastus*. It was printed around 1566. *Gammer Gurton's Needle* is probably by William Stevenson, fellow of Christ's College, Cambridge. It was printed in 1575.

Both plays are introduced by prologues and are neatly divided into acts and scenes. Both show a lively sense of the plot structure and character types of Roman comedy. Both observe unity of plot, place, and time. The prologue of *Roister Doister* specifically cites Plautus and Terence as writers of comedy and as moralists presenting "very vertuous lore." During the play, a few Latin tags are used: *exeant ambae* and *cantent*, among others.

Roister Doister is the more sedate and morally serious play. The obvious direct influence is Plautus's *Miles gloriosus*. *Gammer Gurton's Needle* is more boisterous and more absurd. It has affinities with Plautus, but it has obviously learned as much or more from the farce tradition. Each comedy has a character (Merrygreek, Diccon of Bedlam) who resembles the conniving slave of Roman comedy but whose deeper affinities are with the Vice figure of the morality play. Merrygreek, however, is a sober Puritan if contrasted to the madcap Diccon.

Gammer Gurton alternates generally between twelve- and fourteen-syllable couplets with masculine rhyme. At times the alternation of shorter and longer lines suggests poulter's measure; more frequently the variations are so arbitrary that no pattern is evident.[16]

Roister Doister tends to twelve-syllable couplets. Most of the rhymes are masculine, giving the lines an iambic form. In other words, they look like something a classically trained dramatist might consider equivalent to iambic trimeter or *senarii*.

The play begins with a sixty-six-line soliloquy by Merrygreek. Thirty-two of the lines have twelve syllables. Two more can be counted as having twelve syllables on the basis of counted (though not necessarily pronounced) *es* or *ed*. If this possibility is ignored, twenty-six lines have eleven syllables. Several of the eleven-syllable lines might be read as "headless" (acephalic)—that is, missing an initial unstressed syllable. The remaining eight lines have ten syllables. Most of these seem to omit syllables in two places—at the beginning of the line and immediately after the caesura.

Although the lines have many iambic feet, one of the striking features of their prosody is the lack of coordination between the stress positions in a regular iambic pattern and the natural accents of the words.

The following ten-line excerpt is representative:

	Syllables
But now of Roister Doister somewhat to expresse,	12
That ye may esteeme him after hys worthinesse:	12

In these twentie townes, and seke them throughout,	10 or 11
Is not the like stocke whereon to graffe a loute.	11
All the day long is he facing and craking	11
Of his great actes in fighting and fraymaking;	11 or 12
But, when Roister Doister is put to his proofe,	11
To keep the Queenes peace is more for his behoofe.	11 or 12
If any woman smyle, or cast on hym an eye,	12
Up is he to the harde eares in love by-and-by!	12 or 13
	(I, i, 31–40)

The first line of this quotation might be considered either an Alexandrine with a lyric caesura or a regular accentual iambic hexameter. There are twelve syllables and the caesura comes after the seventh. The first half-line ends with a weak rather than a heavy stress, the second with a heavy. An accentual iambic interpretation also works. The natural stresses of the words occur in the places that call for stress in an iambic line.

There is a third possible interpretation. The lyric caesura seems awkward in the accentual iambic reading, but it provides an argument for reading the line as an imitation of a Roman *senarius*. Being a lyric caesura, it comes in the middle of the foot in the preferred classical way rather than at the end of the foot. Associated with this device is the interlacing of the feet. In four of the feet (2, 3, 4, 5) the words extend across the foot boundaries, avoiding what ancient prosody called diaeresis.

The regularity of the first line, however, changes to irregularity as we proceed. Often words are placed in positions where their natural accent violates the iambic pattern ("esteeme," "after," "facing," etc.), making the accentual iambic interpretation difficult. Syllable count is also irregular, making a syllabic interpretation difficult.

Is Udall's irregular verse a by-product of (1) a native tradition of metrical irregularity ("cantilevered verse") or (2) a syllabic understanding of verse; or (3) are the irregularities there because they are allowable—and even appropriate—in the *senarius*? The first suggestion is unsatisfactory because the verse seems more regular than interlude verse. The second is unsatisfactory because the lines vary in syllable count. On the face of things, the third possibility also looks remote, but let us recall a primary fact about the *senarius* of Roman comedy: it was so licensed that an uninformed reader approaching Terence might think his plays written in no meter at all. This irregularity was not accidental but intentional. It was part of the "art" of writing comedies, and it made their dialogue resemble speech. This understanding would explain the variable number of syllables in Udall's lines. Ancient comedy uses lines of six, seven, and eight feet. Although Plautus writes scenes all in one line form, Terence mixes the forms. Truncation and substitution of trisyllabic for disyllabic feet in Latin comic verse produce additional variations in line length. The same understanding would also help explain the strong, though not unvarying, preference of Udall for masculine (i.e., iambic) line terminations to feminine ones. In the Latin comic *senarius*, the only hard-and-fast rule is that the final foot be iambic.

Before returning to Udall's prosody, let us complete our survey of the line types and possible scansions of the passage quoted. The eleven-syllable line is illustrated by "Is not the like stocke whereon to graffe a loute." The line could be a headless (acephalic) accentual *senarius*, although the accent on "the" would be awkward. "In these twentie townes, and seke them throughout" is a ten-syllable line, although if the *es* in "townes" could be counted, whether pronounced or not, the syllable tally would rise to eleven.

Having made these observations, we can offer four different scansions of a four-line sample, recognizing in each case that alternative scansions are possible. The first assumes regular accentual iambics (with substitutions) ignoring natural word stress. A bar (|) is used for syllables that should theoretically not have stress but do:

```
     x  /  x  /  x   /  x * /    x  / x   /
     But now of Roister Doister somewhat to expresse,
       x  /  x  | x     / *x |  x   /   x /
       That ye may esteeme him after hys worthinesse:
     /  x   /  x  /  [x] *x   /    /    x   /
     [x] In these twentie townes, and seke them throughout,
      /  x  / x   /    *     /  /   x  x /
     [x] Is not the like stocke whereon to graffe a loute.
```

In the second scansion, the lines are treated as rough and ready Alexandrines (secondary accents shown with a bar [|]):

```
         /              /    *            /
         But now of Roister Doister somewhat to expresse,
                                                              [2+5*5]
              |           / *           /
              That ye may esteeme him after hys worthinesse:
                                                              [6*6]
```

<pre>
        | /   * | /
In these twentie townes, and seke them throughout,
</pre>
                                                    [5*5]

<pre>
            /   *   /   /
Is not the like stocke whereon to graffe a loute.
</pre>
                                                    [5*4+2]

In the third scansion, it is assumed that Udall wrote a singsong four-stress line resembling "cantilevered verse":

<pre>
 x x x / x   / x */   x x x   /
But now of Roister Doister somewhat to expresse,
 x / x x /   x */ x x   x   x /
That ye may esteeme him after hys worthinesse:
 x   x   / x /   *x   /   x   x   /
In these twentie townes, and seke them throughout,
 / x x x   / * x x x /   x /
Is not the like stocke whereon to graffe a loute.
</pre>

The fourth scansion assumes that Heywood recognized the natural stress of the words and felt free to use substitutions on the basis of similar license exercised by Roman dramatists. This does not mean that he literally copied the *senarius* in English in the manner of the reformed versifying of Harvey, Spenser, and Sidney. It means only that he imitated it by creating an English equivalent. The equivalent had the same tendency to vary in syllable count and the same tendency to vary its feet, but the variations are English rather than modifications created by using Latin feet like the tribrach or cretic:

<pre>
 x   / x / x   / x */   x \ x   /
But now of Roister Doister somewhat to expresse,
 x   / x   /   x */ x x   /   x \
That ye may esteeme him after hys worthinesse:
 /   x   / x /   *x   /   \   x   /
In these twentie townes, and seke them throughout,
 \ x x \   / * x / x /   x /
Is not the like stocke whereon to graffe a loute.
</pre>

Before proceeding, one might ask whether or not Udall knew how to write regular verse. The following songs, from act 1, scene 4, and act 3, scene 3, show that when he wanted to, he could write effective regular (or only slightly irregular) verse:

Who-so to marry a minion wife
Hath hadde good chaunce and happe,
Must love hir and cherish hir all his life,
And dandle hir in his lappe.

And:

> Christian Custance have I founde,
> Christian Custance have I founde,
> A widowe worthe a thousande pounde.
> I mun be married a Sunday.[18]

Evidently Udall's dialogue takes the form it does by intention.

The third (singsong) scansion can be ruled out. It is at variance with the dramatic function of the verse. It might conceivably be acceptable for the long soliloquy with which Merrygreek begins the play, though at the cost of overriding the actorly elements that Udall has introduced. It would vary, however, from awkward to impossible in the rapid one- and two-line exchanges later in the play, and would be utterly impossible in the many cases when single lines are divided among two or three speakers—of which more below.

The second (syllabic) scansion also leaves a great deal to be desired. The lines are quite different from French syllabic verse of the second rhetoric. Nothing seems to be gained and a good deal to be lost by interpreting the verse in relation to French versification, which, in fact, develops entirely different strategies for objectifying speech.

This leaves the first (regular iambic) and the fourth (classical) interpretation. The first interpretation is weak because of the frequent clash between natural word stress and position. Given Udall's classical background, the classical quality of the play, and the similarities already noted between Udall's line and the comic *senarius,* the classical reading seems better than its rivals.

Consider the following passage in which Ralph forgets the name of his beloved:

> Merrygreek: And what, or who, is she with whome ye are in love?
> Ralph: A woman, whome I knowe not by what meanes to move.
> Merrygreek: Who is it?
>   Ralph: A woman, yond! [*Points to her house*]
>   Merrygreek: What is hir name?
> Ralph: Hir, yonder. [*Points again*]
>   Merrygreek: Whom?
>   Ralph: Mistress—ah—
>   Merrygreek: Fy, fy, for shame!
> Love ye, and know not whome, but "hir, yonde," "a woman"?
> We shall then get you a wyfe I can not tell whan!
> Ralph: The faire woman that supped wyth us yesternight;
>   And I hearde hir name twice or thrice, and had it right. . . .
>   (I, ii, 67–74)

In spite of the fragmentation of the lines in this dialogue, they continue to reveal the tendency to a 12-syllable norm observed in the play's initial soliloquy. The counts by line are 12, 12, 11, 11, 12, 12, 12, and 12. Regularity is increased if it is assumed that the missing syllables of the third and fourth lines are intended to signify speech pauses. The singsong interpretation of this verse can be ruled out on the basis of the impossibility of maintaining the singsong in lines split into three parts by two speakers. The lines also resist interpretation as regular accentual iambic verse or rough Alexandrines. In other words, if the initial soliloquy consists of something like English *senarii*, these lines do also.

Beyond their prosodic form, the lines are skillfully composed dramatic speech. They catch the teasing of Merrygreek and the fatuity of Ralph in love. They rhyme, but the rhyme is almost irrelevant when the lines are given an actorly performance. This is obvious in the case of the segmented lines. To write them required visualizing the set and providing for gestures like pointing, for character traits like absentmindedness (a trait that invites gestures like shrugging shoulders, a foolish intonation of "ah"), and for the mocking illocutions implicit in the quoting. Evidently, the verse has an intention directly opposite to the intention of the comically rhyming verses at the beginning of *The Foure P. P.* In the former case the language is the source of the humor and intended to call attention to itself; in the present case it is the vehicle of humor that stems from action, timing, and character.

A final example of actorly dialogue in *Ralph Roister Doister* is the comic battle of the sexes in act 4 which is, as the stage directions tell us, enlivened by "Two drummes, with their ensignes." The beat of the *senarii* picks up, but they still irregular:

	Syllables
Merrygreek: God send us a faire day.	
Ralph: See, they marche on hither.	12
Tib: Talk-a-pace: But, mistresse!	
Custance: What sayest thou?	
Tib: Shall I go fet our goose?	12
Custance: What to do?	
Tib: To yonder captain I wil turne hir loose:	13
And she gape and hisse at him, as she doth at me,	12
I durst ieoparde my hande she wyll make him flee.	12
Custance: On! Forward!	
Ralph: They com!	
Merrygreek: Stand!	

>   Ralph: Hold!
> Merrygreek: Kepe!
>   Ralph: There!
>   Merrygreek: Strike!
>   Ralph: Take heede.   12
> Custance: Well sayde, Trupenny!
>   Trupeny: Ah, whooresons!
>   Custance: Wel don, in-deede.   12
> Merrygreek: Hold thine owne, Harpax! Downe with them Dobinet! 11
> Custance: Now, Madge! There, Annot! Now, sticke them, Tibet!   10
>   (IV, viii, 13–21)

These lines speak eloquently for themselves. They are actorly because they assume an entire *mise en scène*. They are not the cause of anything; they are, rather, the result of causes that must be created on the stage to make them intelligible. They are unquestionably in verse, and couplet rhymes can be found by readers who look for them. But the verse has become secondary. It is swallowed up, along with the rhymes, by the action. In sum, the passage is dramatic verse of a high order, and it is dramatic precisely because it imitates speech rather than imposing an arbitrary shape on the dialogue. Udall did not leave an explanation of what he was doing, but the explanation can be reconstructed from the comments of Italian critics like Trissino and Giraldi Cintio whom we examined in chapter 4.

Gascoigne and Comic Dialogue in Prose

It is appropriate to conclude this survey of dramatic speech at mid-century with a brief notice of the work of George Gascoigne. In addition to being the first author to attempt a treatise on English prosody, around 1565 Gascoigne translated two plays from the Italian.[19] The first is the tragedy *Jocasta*, drawn from Lodovico Dolce's version, in *versi sciolti*, of Euripides' *Phoenissae*. Dolce's *versi sciolti* are indebted directly to the efforts of Giangiorgio Trissino to discover Italian equivalents of ancient epic and dramatic verse and his demonstration in *Sophonisba* (1524) that *versi sciolti* approximate the effects of Latin iambic trimeter. Gascoigne agreed. He used blank verse for his English version.

The second play is a comedy, *Supposes*, from *I Suppositi* by Lodovico Ariosto. Ariosto initially composed the comedy in prose. After several critics had pointed out that, prosy or not, Latin comedy is most emphatically in verse, he rewrote *I Suppositi* in *sdruccioli*. Gascoigne relied on the prose version of the comedy but he also consulted the versified revision. His English translation uses prose. Clearly, the decision was made deliberately. He had, after all, chosen blank verse for *Jocasta*.

Neither of Gascoigne's translations need detain us long. The fact that *Jocasta* is in blank verse is interesting but not astonishing. Gascoigne was probably following his Italian source (Lodovico Dolce) rather than the precedent of *Gorboduc*, but the fact remains that in *Jocasta* as in *Gorboduc* blank verse is associated with a self-consciously classical tragedy. The verse itself is no better than the blank verse of *Gorboduc* and in some ways more stiff. Gascoigne follows Dolce's Italian without, one feels, having a strong response to the play.

Supposes is more interesting. Gascoigne's comic prose is lively, germane, and flexible. It varies from comic soliloquy, as in the long complaint of Pasiphilio the parasite after Cleander neglects to invite him to dinner (II, iii), to rapid give-and-take dialogue. The following passage, in which the true identity of Dulipo, the servant-lover of the heroine, is revealed, is a good sample:[20]

> Philogano: . . . amongst other things that [the pirates] had was . . . my servaunt, a boy at that time, I thinke not past five yeeres olde.
> Cleander: Alas, I loste one of that same age there.
> Philogano: And I beying there, and liking the childes favour well, proffered them foure and twentie ducates for him, and had him.
> Cleander: What! was the childe a Turke? or had the Turkes brought him from Otranto?
> Philogano: They saide he was a childe of Otranto. But what is that to the matter? Once xxiiii Ducates he cost me—that I wot well.
> Cleander: Alas, I speake it not for that, sir. I would it were he whome I meane.
> Philogano: Why, whom meane you, sir?
> Litio: Beware sir; be not to lavish!
> Cleanthes: Was his name Dulipo then? or had he not another name?
> Litio: Beware what you say, sir!
> Philogano: What the devill hast thou to doe!—Dulipo? No, sir; his name was Carino.
> Litio: Yea, well said! Tell all, and more to. Doe!
> Cleander: O Lord, if this be as I thinke how happy were I!
>
> (V, v, 114–41)

This is clear, easy to speak, and often pointed. It nicely reproduces the gradual recognition that is intrinsic to the scene. An effective and actorly counterpoint to the main conversation is provided by Litio's asides. In one instance—Philogano's last speech—the line is divided between a snarled insult to Litio and a friendly comment to Cleander. Although there are many parts of *Supposes* that seem wooden, the fault is not Gascoigne's prose but the naive classicism that placed more emphasis on imitating the creaking plot structures of Plautus and Terence than on representing the real world. The habit originates with Latin school comedy. Ariosto imported it into vernacular comedy, and Italian comedy of the Cinquecento would never quite solve it. English popular drama would, of course, solve it by rejecting direct classical imitation.

A secondary problem is that Gascoigne regarded himself as a "man of letters" rather than a dramatist. *Supposes* was written for presentation at Gray's Inn in 1566 and doubtless benefits from this fact, but Gascoigne was not, like Thomas Kyd or Christopher Marlowe, or even John Lyly, continuously involved with theatrical productions. Consequently, his dialogue lacks the deeper actorly qualities these later and more significant dramatists introduce simply because they know more about dramatic speech through their association with a living theater.

The concept of a meter so licensed that it might as well be prose is translated quite literally in the sixteenth century into prose comedy. This happened first in Italy and later in England as a result of Italian influence. Lyly followed the lead of Gascoigne when he used prose for his comedy *Campaspe* (1583), and thereafter plays entirely or chiefly in prose are fairly common. *The Famous Victories of Henry V* (ca. 1586) and Lyly's *Endymion* (1588) are in prose. Peele's *Old Wive's Tale* (1591) is chiefly in prose, and Ben Jonson used prose for *Epicoene* in 1609.

The use of prose for comedy and for low-life scenes in drama of all types foreshadows a larger shift in English dramatic form that was not completed until the twentieth century—namely, the abandonment of the idea that verse is needed for drama, whether comic or tragic. This appears to be the direction in which Shakespeare was moving in his later blank verse, but it is a direction from which English drama drew back in the later seventeenth century. In the nineteenth century, prose triumphed. Was anything lost? Does verse really have a constitutive function as the *ars metrica* maintained? For the present, the jury is out. The efforts of T. S. Eliot, Maxwell Anderson, and Christopher Fry to reassert the place of verse in drama have only made the passing of the tradition the more obvious.

CHAPTER IX

Heroic Experiments

The success of Surrey's *Aeneid* appears to have had very little effect on later poets. Although Sackville and Norton used blank verse for *Gorboduc* and their choice was ratified by George Gascoigne in *Jocasta*, as we have seen, dramatic verse has a pedigree quite different from that of narrative verse. Among narrative poets, Nicholas Grimald used blank verse to translate two short narrative works in hexameter, both of which appeared in Tottel's *Miscellany* (1557). The first is *Marcus Tullius Cicero's Death*, translated from Theodore Beza's poem *Mors Ciceronis*, and the second is *The Death of Zoroas*, translated from the *Alexandreis* of Phillip Gualtherius. George Turberville used blank verse for roughly one-third of *The Heroical Epistles of Ovid* (1667).

The poems translated by Grimald and Turberville are elevated compositions in Latin hexameter, but they do not pretend to be epics.[1] George Gascoigne's satire *The Steele Glas* (1576) uses blank verse for satire. Like much of Gascoigne's other work, the poem shows a sophisticated interpretation of the options available to an English author adopting a Roman literary form. For that very reason, however, the blank verse is intentionally different—more medieval, more colloquial in vocabulary and syntax, more choppy—than heroic blank verse.[2]

The first bid for heroic elevation after Surrey is Thomas Phaer's translation of the *Aeneid*. Phaer may have begun without knowing of Surrey's work. He translated book 1 in 1555, only a year after the Day-Owen edition of book 4 and well before Tottel's 1557 edition of books 2 and 4. His translation of the first seven books was published in 1558 and of the first nine in 1562, a year after his death.

The second important bid for heroic elevation is also an *Aeneid* translation. Richard Stanyhurst's rendering of the first four books into English quantitative hexameters was published in Leyden in 1582 and in London in 1583. If Phaer turned from the classicizing tendency of blank verse to a native English verse form, Stanyhurst moved in the opposite direction and flatly rejected native English prosody.

Two other translations are significant in the history of the search for an appropriate English heroic verse form: George Chapman's translation of the *Iliad* into fourteeners (1598 and later) and of the *Odyssey* into decasyllabic couplets (1614). The translation of Du-Bartas's *Holy Weeks* by Joshua Sylvester is significant because of its influence on Milton,[3] but the poem is not especially innovative, and DuBartas will not be treated here.

Achieving heroic elevation in original poems was at least as great a concern for English renaissance poets as translating classical epics. Two poems are sufficiently distinctive to require treatment: Edmund Spenser's *Faerie Queene* (1590 and later) and William Davenant's *Gondibert* (1651). The first is important for its achievement and influence as well as for the critical theories that underlie its verse form. The second is insignificant as poetry but important because its verse form embodies radical new ideas about the nature of heroic poetry.

Thomas Phaer and Moderate Classicism

Thomas Phaer was a member of the same circle that included Thomas Sackville and William Baldwin. He was a lawyer and an early contributor ("Owen Glendower") to *A Mirror for Magistrates*. Like Jasper Heywood, Phaer complains, in a postscript to the *Seven Books* of 1558, that he is not up to his task of translating the *Aeneid*. He has undertaken it in spite of his inadequacy in order to provide an example for younger writers of the potentialities of English: "They may finde in this language both large and aboundant Campes of varietie, wherein they maie gather innumerable sortes of most beautifull floures, figures, and phrases, not onely to supplie the imperfection of me: but also to garnishe al kindes of their owne verses with a more cleane and compendious order of meter than heretofore comonly hath ben accustomed."[4] Phaer's translation is paraphrastic. He observes that Vergil has "many mystical secrets . . . which, uttered in English, would shew little pleasure. . . . I have, therefore, followed the counsel of Horace, teaching the duty of a good interpreter: *Qui quae desperat nitescere posse, relinquit.* By which occasion, somewhat I have in places omitted, somewhat have alt'red, and some thing I have expounded, and all to the ease of inferior readers."[5]

The most interesting point here is Phaer's claim that he is providing an example of "a more cleane and compendious order of meter than heretofore comonly hath ben accustomed." We are reminded of John Day's announcement on the title page of his edition of Surrey's *Aeneid* that the work has been drawn into "a straunge metre."

In what sense is the fourteener a "more . . . compendious order of meter than heretofore comonly hath ben" used? The fourteener can hardly be said to have been unfamiliar in 1558. Quite the contrary, it was a standard form used regularly by the authors included in Tottel's *Miscellany* and used for many different types of poem. Phaer must be referring not to meter in general but to heroic meter. It is true that the fourteener is "more compendious," in the sense of being longer, than other meters used for heroic poetry. If this is Phaer's meaning, he can have only two poems in mind, the *Aeneid* of Gavin Douglas and the *Aeneid* of Surrey. Both of these poems use a decasyllabic line.

Although Phaer may not have known of Surrey's translation in 1555 when he began his own work, he must have been aware of it in 1558 when he commented on his choice of meter. Probably, then, he is claiming that the fourteener is superior to blank verse for translating dactylic hexameter. A line of dactylic hexameter has a theoretical maximum of seventeen syllables (the last foot is always two rather than three syllables), but the norm is lower because of substitution of spondees for dactyls. A fourteener has, on the average, about the same number of syllables. It is the longest standard English line, assuming one considers it a line rather than a combination of a four-stress and a three-stress line. It can therefore be considered an English equivalent to classical hexameter.

The prosody of the fourteeners in Phaer's translation reveals something else about his motives. In contrast to Surrey—and in even sharper contrast to Richard Stanyhurst—he is a moderate.

The fourteener can be used in two ways. On the one hand it is a traditional English form contrasting in this respect with the Italian-inspired blank verse chosen by Surrey. On the other, as *Thyestes* shows, it can be "classicized" by inversion and other strategies of construction. Phaer's syntax is more English than Latinate, and, especially in the earlier books, it often falls into the characteristic fourteener singsong. The word order is normally standard. Perhaps that is the meaning of Phaer's claim that the fourteener is a "clene" as well as a "compendious order of meter." Although minor inversions for the sake of rhyme are common in his lines, they seldom give rise to units of more than two lines or create effects that convey either the general tone of epic (elevation) or emotions specific to the situation being described. If the first line of a couplet ends with punctuation, the second usually ends with a stronger punctuation. A comma, for example, is normally followed by a semicolon or a period. There is some evidence that Phaer learned as the translation progressed. In consequence, the singsong occasionally gives way to larger, more varied sound patterns.

As a classicist, Phaer avoids the heavy alliteration that disfigures much poetry using the fourteener. His vocabulary tends to be standard, dignified, and not obtrusively ornamental. Jarring lapses into colloquial language are infrequent, and Latin-derived words and polysyllables are used sparingly. The proper names, place names, and mythological allusions of the original are accommodated easily. In other words, the translation achieves a respectable English equivalent of *Latinitas*.

Vergil's music is beyond Phaer. Like Gavin Douglas, he was satisfied to get the meaning more or less line by line and did not usually try to reproduce the poetic effects that challenged Surrey. The beginning of the *Aeneid* is given below in Vergil's Latin and in Phaer's English (I omit the four-line introduction found in renaissance Latin editions and faithfully translated by Phaer). The passage is representative. There are better passages in the translation, but there are also worse:

> Arma virumque cano Troiae qui primus ab oris
> Italiam fato profugus Laviniaque venit
> litora—multum ille et terris iactatus et alto
> vi superum, saevae memorem Iunonis ob iram,
> multa quoque et bello passus, dum conderet urbem
> inferretque deos Latio; genus unde Latinum
> Albanique patres atque altae moenia Romae.

For which Phaer offers:

> Of arms and of the man of Troy that first by fatal flight
> Did thence arrive at Lavine land, that now Italia hight,

> But shaken sore with many a storm, by seas and lands ytoss'd,
> And all for Juno's endless wrath, that wrought to have had him lost,
> And sorrows great in wars he bode ere he the walls could frame
> Of mighty Rome and bring the gods to avance the Romain name.⁶

Phaer manages seven lines of Latin hexameter in six fourteeners. Alliteration is used lightly, and the vocabulary is clear, dignified, and restrained. Only one word ("Italia") has more than two syllables. One word ("hight") is archaic but not obtrusively so. Metaplasms are frequent, suggesting a strong syllabic orientation. "Lavinian" becomes "Lavine" by apocope, and "Italia" becomes "Italya" by synizesis. "Many a," "to have had," and "to avance" become "man'ya," "to'v'ad," and "t'avance" by synaloepha. And "tossed" becomes "ytoss'd," first by prosthesis (the *y*) and second by syncope (the dropped *e* in *ed*. The caesura regularly follows the eighth syllable. The pause is consistently reinforced by grammatical construction ("that first/that now/by seas/that wrought/ere he/to advance"), a strategy that emphasizes the singsong typical of the fourteener. Couplet integrity is respected, but there is weak enjambment between the next-to-last and last lines. Alliteration can be heard in several lines but is not obtrusive.

The first line is a direct translation of Vergil's first line, a feat made possible by attaching the Latin possessive (*Troiae*) to "man": "Of arms and of the man of Troy." This is technically incorrect because it leaves "coast" (*oris*) dangling, but it is possible here because Phaer has simply omitted "coast." Although the singer (*cano*) disappears in the translation, the most important rhetorical figure in the line—"arms and the man" (hendiadys)—is preserved.

Line 2 is evidently an example of Phaer's desire to consider "the ease of inferior readers." Vergil has Aeneas coming "to Italy and the Lavinian shores"—another instance of hendiadys. "Lavinian" may be opaque to the untutored, so Phaer abandons the hendiadys and makes the second half of the line a gloss: "Lavine land, that now Italia hight." Vergil's line has one example of metaplasm (*Laviniaque*, scanned as –⏑⏑). Phaer shortens this word and also *Italiam*, which Vergil treats as four syllables (–⏑⏑–). Vergil strongly enjambs the line (*Laviniaque venit/litora*), but Phaer ends it with a completed construction and begins the next line with a conjunction ("hight,/But")—an excellent example of his preference for natural constructions and observance of line integrity in the romance manner.

The next line seems to translate Vergil's third line twice. The first half gives us a "storm" that is implied but not expressed in Vergil, and that has "shaken sore" the hero. It is a reasonable paraphrase, but its effect is blunted by the fact that it is translated again with considerably more fidelity in the next grammatical unit: "by seas and lands ytoss'd." The reference to "lands" (*terris*) has been anticipated by the word "land" in the preceding line. Except for the omission of *multum*—"much" vexed—the English is equivalent to the Latin. The merging of the *y* of "many" with the following *a* is of special interest because it echoes the Latin *mult'ille* (ecthlipsis). There is no equivalent for the merging in the Latin of *ille* with *et*. However, metaplasm is used twice in one English word—"ytoss'd." Line integrity is again emphasized by an initial conjunction ("ytoss'd,/And"). *S* alliteration becomes prominent in this line and extends across the caesura ("shaken sore/storm/seas").

Line 4 picks up the tenacious (*memorem*, "endless") wrath of Juno, but omits the idea that Aeneas suffers because of "the power of the gods" (*vi superum*). Since Christianity rejects the idea of gods who perversely seek to harm virtuous mortals, the omission may be related to the "mystical secrets" from which Phaer vows to protect English readers. This may also be why, although she remains wrathful, Juno is no longer "cruel" (*saeva*). At any rate, the translating is finished by the eighth syllable of the line, which has to be filled out with padding: "that wrought to have him lost." The meaning is hazy, and to the degree that it can be followed, it repeats what has already been said in the first part of the line. Of interest from a prosodic point of view is the fact that the three words "to have had" must be merged ("to'v'ad") to conserve syllable count.

Line 5 closely follows its Latin counterpart. It is also the only line of the passage that is enjambed, even though Vergil's is not. Vergil can work the reference to Rome (*urbem*) into his fifth line; Phaer has to carry the English sentence into the sixth line in order to include the reference: "frame / Of mighty Rome." The strategy makes the English more rather than less compact than the Latin, compressing three lines into one. At the same time that "Rome" equals Vergil's *urbem*, the line translates the phrase *altae moenia Romae* from Vergil's line 7. The sense of the original is preserved, although the rhetorical effect is lost.

The bringing of the household gods (*inferretque deos Latio*) is handled adroitly by "bring the gods." The next passage is translated by Fairclough (in the Loeb Vergil) as "whence came the Latin race, the lords of Alba, and the walls of lofty Rome." These lines are surely blunted by Phaer's "to advance the Romain name."

Judged by its opening lines, Phaer's translation is a competent paraphrase but not a work that conveys the elevation of the original to an English reader or—more important—provides lessons in how to obtain epic elevation in English. The point is obvious from Phaer's treatment of the fourteener. There is no attempt to mold the construction in nonstandard ways so that it shapes complex intonations, nor is there any effort to imitate Vergil's enjambments or his skillful segmentations of the hexameter line and complexly deployed phrases and clauses. Vergil's line is supple, constantly changing, and musical. Phaer's is closed by its construction and its rhymes, and its music is all too predictable.

Yet the lessons of the opening lines are not the whole story of Phaer's translation. There are moments of genuine elevation that suggest Phaer had a touch of the poet as well as competence in Latin.

Eduard Brenner points out that Phaer is especially responsive to romantic natural descriptions. The following translation of the description of the bay in which the ships of Aeneas anchor in book 1 (ll. 159–66) is genuine poetry:

> Far in the shore there lieth an yle and there besides a baie,
> Where from the chanel depe the ocean goeth in and out alwaye.
> On either side the rockes hie, to heaven up clyme do growe,
> And under them the sea still lieth, for there no breth can blowe.
> But grene wood like a gerland growes and hides them all with shade.
> And in the middes a pleasaunt cave there stands of nature made,
> Where sit the Nymphes among the springes in seates of mosse and stone.
> When ships are in no cables nede nor ankers nede thei none.

Phaer has, however, missed the flowing effect of Vergil's description. His verses fall into couplets, and the caesuras follow the eighth syllable with dreary regularity. He is also incapable of the lovely sound effects of the most famous lines in the original:

> Fronte sub adversa scopulis pendentibus antrum,
> intus aquae dulces vivoque sedilia saxo,
> Nympharum domus. . . .

Occasionally, Phaer transcends himself. The description of the death of Hecuba is charged with poetic feeling. Prominent characteristics are synaloepha, displacement of the caesura from the end of the eighth syllable, enjambment, even across couplet divisions, and construction that approximates the syntactical freedom of the Latin. The last three characteristics are atypical of the translation as a whole. The effects they create anticipate, if only faintly, effects that Chapman achieves regularly in his translation of the *Iliad*. Also significant is the avoidance of strong alliteration:

> There Hecuba and her doughters all (poor soules) at the altars side
> In heapes together affrayed them drew, like doues when doth betide
> Some storme them headlong driue, and clipping fast their gods did hold,
> But when syre *Priam* thus beclad in armes of youth so bold
> Espied; what made alas (quoth she) O wofull husband you
> In harnass dight: and whither away with weapons run ye now?
> No such defence, no not if Hector mine now present were.
> Stand here by me, this alter us from slaughter all shal shelde.
> Or die together at ones we shall.[7]

This is not the work of a poetic incompetent. Although Phaer's translation has not been reprinted since the seventeenth century, it was reprinted (with Twyne's additions) in 1573, 1584, 1596, 1600, 1607, and 1620, and it provided a model to be followed by such later translators of Latin hexameters as William Golding and Thomas Drant. Bishop Hall cites Phaer with respect in the dedication of his *Homer* (1581), and the dedication to Fulwood's *Enemie of Idlenesse* (1597) states that those who wish to climb Parnassus should "the worthy worke survie / Of *Phare* the famous wight." A perhaps more impressive testimonial is John Brinsley's respectful citation in the *Ludus literarius* (1612).

RICHARD STANYHURST AND THE CLASSICAL ABSURD

Between 1575 and 1580, several English poets took up the challenge issued by Roger Ascham to create English quantitative verse. A special interest in heroic poetry is evident in the work of these writers. "Three Proper and wittie, familiar Letters . . . touching . . . our English refourmed Versifying," by Spenser and Harvey, begins with heroic meter. Spenser praises Harvey for "your late Englishe Hexameters" and admits, "I also enure my Penne sometime in that kinde, whych I fynde indeede, as I have heard you often defende in worde, neither so harde, nor so harshe, that it will easily and freely, yeelde it selfe to our Mother tongue."[8]

In spite of the initial emphasis of the "Three . . . Letters" on hexameters, the later examples written by Spenser and Harvey are not heroic. However, in another set of letters, published in 1592, Harvey makes the surprising claim that he invented quantitative hexameters: "If I never deserve anye better remembraunce, let mee rather be epitaphed. The Inventour of the English Hexameter: whom learned M. *Stanihurst* imitatyed in his *Virgill*, and excellent Sir *Philip Sidney* disdained not to follow in his *Arcadia*, and elsewhere."⁹

Richard Stanyhurst is all but forgotten today. During the Renaissance, he was occasionally praised and frequently pilloried for his translation of the first four books of the *Aeneid* into quantitative hexameters based on a method explained in detail in the introduction to the work. The translation is one of the oddest productions of the period. It uses an eccentric orthography reflecting the consensus of the period that reformed spelling is necessary if the reform of versifying is to be successful. But its spelling is a minor curiosity in comparison to its vocabulary, which is a surrealistic blend of inkhorn terms, English colloquialisms and slang words, neologisms, and standard expressions.

Stanyhurst's *Aeneid* began collecting bad notices as soon as it appeared. In the preface to Greene's *Menaphon* Thomas Nashe speaks of its "hissed barbarisme . . . as no hodge plowman in a countrie, but would have held as the extremetie of clownerie; a patterne whereof . . . is this: 'Then did he make, heavens vault to rebounde, with rounce robble hobble / Of ruffe raffe roaring, with thwick thwack thurlery bouncing.'"¹⁰ Nashe adds tartly in *Strange News* (1592) that Stanyhurst "had never been praisd by *Gabriel* [Harvey] for his labour, if therein hee had not bin so famously absurd."¹¹ Thomas Warton quotes the definitive comment on Stanyhurst: "As Chaucer has been called the well of English undefiled, so might Stanyhurst be denominated the common sewer of the language."¹²

In spite of his failure, Stanyhurst's motives are lofty and familiar. In his introduction he invokes Roger Ascham, "who, in his goulden pamphlet, intitled *thee Scholemaster*, dooth wish thee Universitie students to applie theyre wittes in bewtifying oure English language with heroical verses."¹³ According to Stanyhurst, Phaer's translation made his work harder rather than easier because it forced him to seek words other than those used by Phaer. The argument is an odd one, but perhaps it helps to explain the bizarre vocabulary of the translation. It makes explicit the fact that Stanyhurst has consciously rejected Phaer's standard English vocabulary along with his fourteeners.

The charge that the verse form is too easy is answered by an explanation of the intricacies of quantitative meter. The form is hard, but it can be learned with practice so that it becomes "as easye a veyne in thee English, as in thee Latin verses, yee and much more easye than in the *English rythmes*."[14] There follows a detailed presentation "Too thee Learned Reader" of the rules of English quantity.[15] Stanyhurst sides with Harvey on native idiom versus rules based on Greek or Latin usage: "As every countrie hath his peculiar law, so they permit everye language too use his particular loare."

Two short quotations represent Stanyhurst's work in contrast to Surrey and Phaer. The first passage translates the opening lines of book 4 of the *Aeneid*:

Now manhod and garbroyls I chaunt, and martial horror.
I blaze thee captayne first from Troy cittye repairing,
Lyke wandring pilgrim too famoused Italie trudging,
And coast of Lavyn: soust wyth tempestuus hurlwynd,
On land and sayling, bi Gods predestinate order:
But chiefe through Iunoes long fostred deadlye revengement.[16]

All the faults of Stanyhurst are apparent in this passage. The lines in some sense scan as dactylic hexameters with frequent spondaic substitution if one accepts the conventions outlined in the introductory essay on versification. On the other hand, the effort to reform the versifying has been fatal to Vergil. "Manhod" is a possible translation for *virum*, but "garbroyls" ("garbroyl"—disturbance, tumult) is simply unintelligible as an equivalent for *arma*.[17] Aeneas has become as medievalized here as in Gavin Douglas. He is a "captayne" and a "wandring pilgrim." A "whirlwind" has become a "hurlwynd," presumably to avoid the s/w slur that would otherwise be present. And the power of the gods, *vi superum*, has taken on a novel Protestant coloration: "bi Gods predestinate order." Finally, the elevation of the passage is hopelessly undercut by colloquialisms like "soust" and "trudging." This point, in fact, is noticed by George Puttenham in *The Arte of English Poesie* (1589): "In speaking or writing of a Princes affaires and fortunes there is a certaine *Decorum*, that we may not use the same termes in their busines, as we might very wel doe in a meaner persons. . . . As one, who translating certaine bookes of *Virgils Aeneidos* into English meetre, said that *Aeneas* was fayne to trudge out of Troye: which terme became better to be spoken of a beggar, or of a rogue, or of a lackye: for so we used to say to such maner of people, be trudging hence."[18]

A second passage illustrating Stanyhurst's translation—that describing Dido's death—is more successful. It reminds us that there are moments when the quantitative strategy begins to work. Although they are easy to overlook, they show the translation is more than the "clownerie" ridiculed by Greene. Stanyhurst deserves at least a modicum of charity from a generation of readers brought up on *Four in America* and "Le Monocle de Mon Oncle":

> Than loa the fayre Raynebow saffronlyke feathered, hoov'ring
> With thowsand gay colours, by the soon contrarye reshyning,
> From the skye downe flickring, on her head moste joyfulye standing,
> Thus sayde: I doo Gods heast, from corps thy spirit I sunder.
> Streight, with al, her fayre locks with right hand speedelye snipped:
> Foorth with her heat fading, her liefe too windpuf avoyded.

CHAPMAN AND HOMER

George Chapman's choice of fourteeners for the *Iliad* in 1598 has puzzled critics. It looks regressive until one realizes that Chapman was taking what seemed to be the standard option of sixteenth-century translators of ancient heroic poetry. Surrey was all but forgotten. Marlowe's blank verse translation of book 1 of Lucan's *Pharsalia* has much to recommend it, but it was not printed until 1600, long after Chapman had committed himself to an *Iliad* in English septenaries.

The translation is an astonishing demonstration of the power of genius to overcome almost every obstacle. Keats was right. There is nothing quite like Chapman's *Iliad* in the rest of English literature. There is, however, a good deal that is in the same tradition, including work by Phaer, Golding, and the Seneca translators. The translation should thus be understood as the last and most successful experiment in Latinate construction coming from the effort of English esoteric humanism to translate the classics into living vernacular forms.

Chapman had thought more deeply than his predecessors about the psychology of poetic form. He expresses his ideas in terms of a Neoplatonic theory of poetry as a "true manner of communication and combination of soules."[19] The theory is both more personal and more sophisticated than the concept of poetry as the shaper of language and agent of civilization found in writers like Coxe, Tottel, and Ascham. True translation requires a thorough understanding of the construction of the original and then discovery of equivalent constructions in the language of the translation. Chapman explains in the preface to the reader of *Seaven Bookes of the Iliades* (1598), "The worth of a skilfull and worthy translator is to observe the sentence, figures and formes of speech proposed in his author, his true sence and height, and to adorne them with figures and formes of oration fitted to the originall in the same tongue to which they are translated."[20]

In the *Seaven Bookes* of 1598, Chapman chooses fourteeners as the "formes of oration fitted to the originall" in English. Yet he was clearly uncertain about the choice. His translation of *Achilles' Shield*, which appeared the same year (1598) as the *Seaven Bookes*, is in decasyllabic couplets. There is less emphasis in this translation on finding native equivalents of the original and more on introducing elements of the original into English. In the preface "To the Understander" of *Achilles' Shield*, he speaks of "my farre-fetcht and, as it were, beyond-sea manner of writing" and contrasts this style with writing that follows natural order—"that fals naked . . . and hath nothing but what mixeth it selfe with ordenarie table talk." In keeping with the "beyond-sea manner," he claims a free right to use foreign words and neologisms.[21] It would seem that Chapman considered decasyllabic couplets less "native" and more "artificial" than fourteeners. The "beyond-sea manner" is the style recommended by Italian critics for elevated vernacular poems.

One principle, however, is common to both translations. It is a conviction that couplets are the proper medium for narrative. Chapman ridicules those Italians and their English followers who would translate Homer into ottava rima and other stanzaic forms: "Let the length of the verse never discourage your endeavours, for, talke our quidditicall Italianistes of what proportion soever their strooting [i.e., swelling] lips affect, unlesse it be in these coopplets into which I have hastely translated this Shield they shall never doe Homere so much right in any octaves, canzons, canzonets or with whatever fustian Epigraphes they shall entitle their measures."[22]

Chapman revised the *Iliad* translation between 1597 and 1611. In the process, the translation changed significantly. It became less sympathetic to Achilles and more sympathetic to Odysseus and Hector, which is to say more sober and more Stoic. Its verse form remained the same—fourteeners. However, Chapman was criticized for using them.

He defends himself in a long poem "To the Reader" included in the twenty-four-book edition of 1611 and reprinted in *The Whole Works of Homer, Prince of Poets* (1616). He argues—rather surprisingly, given the fact that he is writing around 1610—that the fourteener is the most honored of English verse forms and that a "long Poeme" demands a "long verse." The reference must be to the length of the fourteener in contrast to the decasyllabic line:

> ... yet hath detraction got
> My blinde side in the forme my verse puts on. ...
> The long verse hath by proofe receiv'd applause
> Beyond each other number, and the foile
> That squint-ey'd Envie takes is censur'd plaine:
> For this long Poeme askes this length of verse,
> Which I myselfe ingenuously maintaine
> Too long our shorter Authors to reherse.[23]

When one turns from theory to practice, what is immediately striking is that one of the main objects of Chapman's revisions is syntax. He is determined to suppress the singsong of the fourteener as used in earlier versions. Alliteration is reduced, and the caesura becomes extremely varied, reflecting new and more varied phrasal patterning. The new approach suppresses the fourteener's tendency to pause at the end of the eighth syllable and thus to break up into ballad meter. The strategies are familiar from Surrey and Jasper Heywood. They are the devices of construction—inversion, interruption, parenthesis, balance, and the like, and the enjambment encouraged by these devices.

Apparently, Chapman decided that the strategy recommended in the *Achilles' Shield* translation—importing techniques from the original into English—was proper for his *Iliad* in spite of the "native English" quality of the fourteener. It was the right decision. Because of the complex syntax, the rhymes—and the lines they so powerfully define in the singsong fourteener—seem to vanish. What is left is a sustained narrative form having the qualities of seriousness and elevation. It is also a controlled form, if only because constant vigilance is needed to keep it from surrendering to the natural tendencies of the fourteener. The sense of control subtly distances the poet from the actions and passions being described. The reader can sympathize—can react with pity and fear—but is held in the position of an observer rather than a participant. The movement from singsong to heroic verse is nicely illustrated by the first four lines of the poem in the versions of 1598 and 1611.[24] In each, significant pauses are marked with an asterisk:

1598

Achilles' banefull wrath resound, great Goddesse of my verse,

That through th'afflicted host of Greece did worlds of woes disperse

And timelesse sent by troopes to hell the glorie-thirsting soules

Of great Heroes, but their lims left foode for beasts and foules.

1611

Achilles' banefull wrath resound, O Goddesse, that imposd

Infinite sorrowes on the Greekes and many brave soules losd

From breasts Heroique— sent them farre, to that invisible cave

That no light comforts; and their lims to dogs and vultures gave.

The first version is notable for its respect of line integrity. Lines 1 and 2 form a couplet with the emphatic rhyme. The couplet effect is enhanced by the use of a conjunction ("And") to separate lines 2 and 3. The rhythm is strong and tends to shape response even where it is awkward (e.g., "great," "through," "Heroes"). Alliteration occurs in "wrath/resound," "great/Goddesse," "through/th'," "worlds/woes," "timelesse/troopes," "lims/left," and "foode/foules." The last line departs somewhat from the clichés of the first three. The pause tries to come after "Heroes" rather than "lims," and the couplet pattern is softened by eye-rhyme ("soules/foules"). However, the reader is tempted to ignore the pause after "Heroes" and to pause after "lims" to match the strong pattern of the first three lines.

In the revised version, all lines are enjambed. The unit tends to be a free-floating syntactical one that varies between three and five stresses. The *wr/r* alliteration in line 1 remains, but other alliteration has been reduced. The strong rhyme of the first couplet has been softened ("imposd/losd"), and the strong enjambment between lines 2 and 3 further reduces the feeling of couplet verse. Both versions begin with an inverted main clause—object, verb, subject—and follow it with a string of modifiers. The revised version tightens the structure, however, by making the participial phrases after "Heroique" appositives to "imposd" instead of stringing them out as in the 1598 version. The verse form is complemented by, and complements, the tendency of the second version to present its material in striking chunks of imagery ("Infinite sorrowes," "brave soules losd / From breasts Heroique," "invisible cave / That no light comforts") and to substitute specific for the general images of the 1598 version ("their lims to dogs and vultures gave")—*enargia*.

The preceding discussion ignores the relation between Chapman's verses and the Greek edition with Latin translation of Spondanus (1583), which Chapman used.[25] However, it is sufficient for the point to be made here. Chapman's *Iliad* in its final (1611/16) form combines two traditions that began with Surrey on the one hand and Phaer on the other. Chapman solved the problem of creating an English heroic line with the fourteener through strategies of construction that suppress the fourteener's internal imperatives, making it more like Latin verse and less like a native form. Complementing these strategies are strong and regular enjambment, de-emphasis of rhyme, elimination of the eighth-syllable caesura, and avoidance of heavy alliteration. Other strategies are less easy to define but important: "roughness" of sound, enrichment of vocabulary, and a preference for the specific over the generalized image.

A final note is needed on what might have been a significant development in English heroic prosody but was not. Chapman moved to decasyllabic couplets in his *Odyssey* (1616). Chapman's editor Allardyce Nicoll suggests he may have felt that decorum required the shift, the *Odyssey* being less warlike than the *Iliad*. Whether or not this is true, the decasyllabic couplet is a precursor of the heroic couplet. Chapman's decision is therefore of considerable interest.

Except for the comment about the "beyond-sea manner of writing" in the preface to *Achilles' Shield*, Chapman does not seem to have discussed the form. A review of the couplets themselves suggests at least one reason why discussion was unnecessary. They use the same strategies found in the mature fourteeners. In the opinion of Allardyce Nicoll, the strategies are used more aggressively in the *Odyssey* than in the *Iliad*—so aggressively, in fact, that they often lead to obscurity:

> For some reason, after having declared emphatically that the fourteener was the ideal measure for dealing with the Homeric Greek, he has turned the text of the *Odyssey* into rhymed decasyllabic couplets. Perhaps he wished to emphasize the difference between the wrath which forms the theme of the *Iliad* and the patient suffering celebrated in the story of Ulysses. Whatever the cause, the result is that his involved sentence structure tends to be even more involved. Frequently we stumble on passages so obscure that we become utterly lost.... There can be no doubt that as he

advanced in age and in his task, Chapman permitted stylistic mannerisms to grow upon him.[26]

Chapman's decasyllabic couplets seem to Nicoll to be an aberration. They are, however, much more successful than his comment suggests. Their chief problem is that they waver between two poles. Frequently they are closed and the internal rhetoric of the line is adjusted to take advantage of that fact in the manner, for example, of the couplets of Christopher Marlowe's *Hero and Leander*, for which Chapman wrote a conclusion after Marlowe's death. In this form they anticipate the heroic couplet and seem quite English in their construction. At other times, however, Chapman suppresses the couplet pattern. When this happens, the lines take on the "beyond-sea manner." This style often occurs in the *Odyssey* when a character is speaking, and we recall that Chapman wrote excellent dramatic blank verse.

The two passages that follow are offered as exhibits of the two modes of Chapman's decasyllabic couplet rather than for extended discussion. Both are effective and neither is seriously marred by Nicoll's "mannerisms." The first is Homer's description of Demodicus (VIII, 77–84). The order is natural. The couplets are end-stopped and provide one example (ll. 3–4) of a type of witty internal balance that looks forward to the later seventeenth-century couplet:

> To whose accomplisht state the Herald then
> The lovely Singer led, who past all men
> The Muse affected, gave him good and ill—
> His eies put out, but put in soule at will.
> His place was given him in a chaire all grac't
> With silver studs and gainst a Pillar plac't,
> Where as the Center to the State he rests,
> And round about the circle of the Guests.

In the following passage Ulysses describes to Alcinous how the Cyclops closed his cave with a stone (IX, 462–78). It illustrates the enjambed, "classical" mode of Chapman's couplet:

> Then came the Even; and he came from the feast
> Of his fat cattell, drave in all, nor kept
> One male abroad: if, or his memory slept
> By God's direct will, or of purpose was
> His driving in of all then, doth surpasse
> My comprehension. But he closde againe
> The mightie barre, milk't, and did still maintaine

All other observation as before.
His worke all done, two of my soldiers more
At once he snatcht up, and to supper went.
Then dar'd I words to him, and did present
A boll of wine with these words: "Cyclop! take
A boll of wine from my hand, that may make
Way for the man's flesh thou hast eate, and show
What drinke our ship held—which in sacred vow
I offer to thee, to take ruth on me
In my dismission home."

Both of the preceding passages show that Chapman was able to write heroic verse effectively in decasyllabic couplets. The first passage has strong rhymes, mildly witty syntax, and effective imagery, but it could hardly be called a masterpiece in spite of the fact that the Demodicus passage is a high point of book 8 of the *Odyssey*.

The Cyclops passage, conversely, is comparable in quality to the best passages of the *Iliad* translation. The verse moves strongly and with a complex, sometimes difficult, but never impenetrable construction. The vocabulary is standard and dignified rather than ornamental. There is no striving for exotic sound effects through alliteration or onomatopoeia, and the enjambment suppresses the rhyme sounds. In these respects the verse is understated. It is reported dialogue rather than inspired bardic vision. The speech is itself restrained, in contrast to the horrors being described. Perhaps the understatement is intended to be expressive—Chapman's Odysseus is something of a Stoic. If so, we have a nice correlation between classically oriented prosody and characterization that draws on classical philosophy.

SPENSER AND THE RETURN TO ROMANCE

Edmund Spenser's contribution to the discussion of reformed versifying places him in the line of hard-edge classicism that extends from Roger Ascham to Thomas Campion. His comments on the subject appear first in the "Three Proper, and wittie, familiar Letters" of 1580. Yet it was already clear before 1580 that Spenser was committed as an artist to rhyme and to the romance tradition rhyme implies.

The Shepheardes Calender appeared in 1579 and made Spenser a celebrity. He mentions it—and the gloss by "E. K."—with obvious pride in the "Postscripte" to the first letter in the series. The letter proper also shows that he has sent Harvey a draft of part of *The Faerie Queene*.

Linking *The Shepheardes Calender* with *The Faerie Queene* was inevitable. Vergil showed that any poet who planned an epic should begin by writing a pastoral. In case anyone has forgotten, "E. K." repeats the story in the "Epistle" prefacing *The Shepheardes Calender*. The *Calender* not only introduces a new poet, it introduces a future epic poet, and it makes a statement about the kind of verse the new poet will write.

In rejecting quantitative meter, Spenser was following an alternative that had already been fully explored in Italy and France. He obviously agreed with DuBellay's argument in the *Deffence et illustration de la langue francoyse* that the poet should ennoble his native language, but he disagreed with DuBellay's argument that "rondeaux, ballades, virelays, chants royal, chansons, and other such groceries . . . corrupt the taste of our language and only serve to bear testimony to our ignorance."[27] Because it enacts his rejection of this position—and with it a considerable amount of the theory of the Pléiade—*The Shepheardes Calender* is a more radical manifesto than it may at first seem to be. Spenser's contemporaries understood his position clearly. William Webbe, for example, mines *The Shepherdes Calender* for poems to illustrate romance (in contrast to classical) poetic forms in his *Discourse of English Poetrie* of 1586.

Pastoral is a well-defined classical genre, frequently imitated in the Renaissance. The best imitations are classical in form—for example, the eclogues of Mantuan and Sannazaro and the eclogues in Sidney's *Arcadia*. There was, however, an alternative. It can be called the "popular" or "realistic" pastoral. It is represented by the *Zodiacus vitae* (1531) of Palingenius (Pier Angelo Manzolli) in Italy and the *Kalendrier des bergers* in France. The realistic pastoral has two significant features. First, it is intentionally crude. The poems create the fiction that they have been written by real-life rustics. Second, to support the fiction, realistic pastoral uses forms its readers will recognize as crude—namely, forms that are archaic or associated with folk literature or both. In renaissance France and England, this meant forms associated with the Middle Ages.

The title of *The Shepheardes Calender* is an allusion to the *Kalendrier des bergers,* and it pretends to be the creation of genuine rustics. Another gauge of Spenser's intent is his use of Marot. He drew the name "Colin" from Marot with some help also from John Skelton. He was aware of DuBellay's scornful rejection of Marot. "E. K." explains apologetically in the gloss of the January eclogue that, ". . . indeede the word Colin is Frenche, and used of the French Poete Marot (*if he be worthy of the name of Poete*) in a certein Aeglogue." Yet both the January and the November eclogue draw heavily on Marot. The motto for November—"La mort ny mord"—was Marot's, and he included it in the prefaces of several of his works.[28] In affirming Marot, Spenser is simultaneously rejecting the attack of the Pléiade on second rhetoric.

Spenser's pastoral also includes English medieval elements. His shepherds are English, as are the religious and political issues that run through his allegory. The presiding genius of the eclogues is "Tityrus," who is both Vergil and Chaucer, and whose presence announces that Chaucer is to English poetry what Vergil is to Roman poetry.

Most important for a study of prosody, the tradition of the *Calender* is that of medieval, not classical, prosody. Native English traditions are invoked by the heavy alliteration of the six-line stanzas of January, the irregular four-stress couplets of February, and the ballad-like fourteeners of the song contest in July. Curiously absent is rhyme royal, used elsewhere by Spenser in *The Ruines of Time* and *Fowre Hymnes*. Some of the poems are imitations of what Elizabethan readers heard when they read fourteenth-century English poetry. They recall the intentionally archaic verse of Gascoigne's *Steele Glas*. Others draw on romance tradition. In general, these poems are highly polished. Among them are the "Lay of Fair Eliza" in April, the "roundelay" and sestina to Rosalind in August, and the elegy for Dido in November (translated from Marot), in which each stanza begins with an Alexandrine.

These considerations point toward the concerns underlying the prosody of *The Faerie Queene*.

In Italy the debate over language broadened into a debate over genre. Was Dante to be accepted in spite of his "Gothicism," his allegory, and his terza rima? Was Ariosto to be accepted in spite of his sprawling story, his indifference to verisimilitude, and his ottava rima? As the debate enlarged, stylistic questions were linked to aesthetic and historical ones. Is ancient poetry superior to modern (i.e., vernacular) poetry? Are all products of the Middle Ages brutish and crude, or does the medieval—which is to say the vernacular—tradition have values equal, perhaps, to those expressed by ancient art? Even as these questions were being asked, the medieval tradition was being undercut by a rationalistic analysis that expressed itself in satire, a point illustrated by Erasmus's *Praise of Folly*, Luigi Pulci's *Morgante maggiore* and Cervantes's *Don Quixote*.

The sixteenth-century defense of the medieval tradition culminated in Italy with the poetry and critical theorizing of Torquato Tasso. *Gerusalemme liberata* abounds in fantasy. It also delights in the tapestry-like descriptions, the mazy digressions, and the idealized characters of medieval romance, and it rejects the absurdist undercutting found in *Don Quixote*, which is to say that it takes its chivalric values seriously.

Tasso's ottava rima complements the romance quality of the narrative. In Pulci (and often in Ariosto) the form satirizes itself like the ottava rima of Byron's *Don Juan*. Tasso, however, insists in his *Discorsi del poema eroico* (1594)[29] that romance poetry is capable of true elevation and that its noblest quality is *magnificenza*. All aspects of the poem contribute to this—its mixing of human and divine characters, its use of the marvelous, its immensity, its variety, and its style.

Tasso's argument is philosophical and derived ultimately from Neoplatonic theories of art.[30] The object of the highest art is the imitation of absolute beauty. This is why poets invoke heavenly powers. The epic, being the highest form of poetry, should express the highest vision. The world of the poem should be as various and as intricate as the larger world made by God. By the same token, the poem's versification should be larger than life. The first and third strategies cited by Tasso as contributing to *magnificenza* of style are periodic structure and enjambment—both related to construction. These are illustrated by verses in which the rhyme divisions play intricately against the syntactical units.[31] Later Tasso argues that ottava rima has been recognized by almost all important poets since Boccaccio as the best epic form because it can be divided into many different "proportions," and it allows a thought or conceit to be extended when necessary from one stanza into the next.[32]

Length is as important as syntax: "The length of the members and the periods, or of the clauses as we generally call them, makes the language great and magnificent."[33] Having said this Tasso illustrates with quotations from a canzone and two sonnets of Petrarch—all examples of complex rhyme enriching sustained syntactical rhythms. "Roughness" (*asprezza*) also contributes to magnificence, as do enjambment ("versi spezzati, i quali entrano l'uno ne l'altro"), and rhymes with double consonants (e.g., *arsi / sparsi*). Among the figures of diction contributing magnificence are climax, hyperbole, polysyndeton, asyndeton, antipallage (non-normal word order with the effect enhanced by increasing displacement), repetition, allegory, prosopopoeia, metaphor, exclamation, inversion, synecdoche, hendiadys, zeugma, transposition, hyperbaton, and apposition.[34]

Spenser was well advanced in writing *The Faerie Queene* before the first version of Tasso's theories, the *Discorsi del'arte poetica*, was published in 1587. That he was, however, sympathetic to Tasso's point of view is shown by the many borrowings and reminiscences of *Gerusalemme* in *The Faerie Queene*.[35] He also must have been aware of the arguments for romance advanced by Italians like Pigna (1554), Giraldi Cintio (1554), and Minturno (*L'Arte poetica*, 1563).[36] A specific debt to Tasso is suggested by the fact that Spenser defines the supreme epic quality as "magnificence" in the *Letter to Raleigh* written in January 1589 to explain the allegory of *The Faerie Queene*.[37]

In both the letter and the poem Spenser aligns himself with the defenders of the romance. Ariosto and Tasso wrote poems that were given allegorical interpretations after the fact. Spenser's poem was allegorical from the beginning. It is set in a quasi-historical never-never land associated closely with the English nation and the ruling family. It abounds in the marvelous, the improbable, and the fantastic. It offers kaleidoscopic variety that the reader is expected to understand in relation to a larger unity.[38] It is filled with heroic characters, noble and despicable deeds, emblematic and ornamental episodes, and brilliant descriptions. The allegory of the first book is explicitly religious—the story of St. George, patron saint of England.

In keeping with the emphasis of his poetics on native tradition, Spenser probably derived the *Faerie Queene* stanza from native English sources. A good possibility is the eight-line decasyllabic stanza used by Chaucer for the Monk's Tale, modified by the addition of a final Alexandrine to provide a closure not unlike that of rhyme royal. Whether or not this genealogy is correct, Spenser chose his stanza form for the same reason that Tasso chose ottava rima. It has obvious links with traditional romance verse, and it is capable of all of the effects associated with *magnificenza*.[39]

Actually, it is more ornate than ottava rima. Having nine lines, it has a natural "proportion" of three. However, the rhymes cut across this proportion, creating proportions of four and five, five and four, seven and two (the final couplet), and eight and one (the concluding hexameter). As these proportions suggest, if ottava rima delights because of its Pythagorean elegance, the Spenserian stanza delights, puzzles, and continuously stimulates because of its *discordia concors*. The uniformity is there but the surface of the verse is constantly changing.

Whatever one may think of the Spenserian stanza today as a vehicle for heroic narrative, it was ideal for a heroic poem in the form of a romance with Platonic and, on occasion, prophetic aspirations.

The Spenserian stanza is not, however, without liabilities. In the first place it shares a certain lack of flexibility with ottava rima. This lack of flexibility in the narrative stanza was noted early in the sixteenth century by Trissino in the preface to *Italia liberata* and in England by Chapman in his defense of couplets for *Achilles' Shield*. The problem is real. The Spenserian stanza is even more stanzaic than ottava rima because the Alexandrine acts as terminal punctuation every nine lines. The stanzas tend to segment the narrative into arbitrary chunks. Spenser normally overcomes the problem, but even Homer nods, and so does he.

A second problem is that the stanza lacks force. It is *too* elegant. Consequently, it has difficulty achieving sustained elevation of the sort illustrated by Surrey's *Aeneid* at its best and by Chapman's *Iliad* and Milton's *Paradise Lost*. Fairyland stubbornly refuses to assume the tragic grandeur of the plains of Troy or the burning lake of Milton's hell. Because the stanza has a lyric quality, it can achieve moments of great emotional intensity, as in the Redcross Knight's vision of the Heavenly Jerusalem (I, x, 53–68). But a lyric is the objectification of a momentary emotion, and the vision fades. The stanza is also an effective vehicle for ornamental description—the monster Error (I, i, 25), the pageant of the Seven Deadly Sins (I, iv, 16–37), the Bower of Bliss (II, xii, 42–87). On the other hand, when it descends to everyday narration, it can become perfunctory. Too often the blood spilled in such profusion seems to be colored water, and the monsters, figures of string and papier-mâché.

One way of defining Spenser's poetic techniques is to contrast them with the techniques of other poets dealing with the same material. In renaissance editions, the *Aeneid* begins with several lines in which Vergil comments on the shift from pastoral to Georgic to epic style.[40] Phaer and Stanyhurst included these lines as a matter of course in their translations. Spenser also translated them. They begin *The Faerie Queene*. The three versions are given below:

Phaer:
I that my slender oaten pipe in verse was wont to sound
Of woods, and next to that, I taught for husbandman the ground,
How fruit unto their greedy lust they might constrain to bring,
A work of thanks, lo, now of Mars and dreadful wars I sing.

Stanyhurst:
I that in this old season wyth reeds oten harmonye whistled
My rural sonnet; from forrest flitted (I) forced
Thee sulcking swincker thee soyle, thoghe craggie, to sunder.
A labor and a travaile too plowswayns hertelye welcoom.
Now manhod and garbroyls I chaunt.

Spenser:
Lo I the man, whose Muse whilome did maske,
As time her taught, in lowly Shepheards weeds,
Am now enforst a far unfitter taske,
For trumpets sterne to chaunge mine Oaten reeds,
And sing of Knights and Ladies gentle deeds.

Stanyhurst is not in the running here. He has been thoroughly defeated by his system. But the difference between Phaer and Spenser is more complex than a contrast between competence and genius. Phaer seeks a verse form that can be larger than the normal English line. He uses a periodic sentence sustained over four fourteen-syllable lines, beginning with the subject ("I") and ending with the verb ("sing"). Inversion and extended subordinate clauses are used, and there is some enjambment and syntactical patterning. In two lines (ll. 2, 4), the caesura is shifted away from its normal position after the eighth syllable. The result is difficult, even grotesque, but the strategy seeks to honor the tonality of the work being translated.

Spenser's lines are doubtless better in every respect than Phaer's, but that is not the point. The point is that Spenser is seeking effects different from those of Phaer. The reference to "lowly Shepheards weeds" alludes not to elegant pastorals but to the realistic pastoral, with its archaisms and native and romance forms. The word "weeds" is itself slightly archaic; "whilome" is definitely so. "Oaten" is used by Phaer and Stanyhurst as well as Spenser, but Phaer makes the instrument a "pipe." Vergil's *avena* means literally "oats," but by metonymy, a flute made from oat straw. Spenser sides here with Stanyhurst. Calling it a "reed" is more literal and therefore presumably more rustic than calling it a "pipe." The word "Knights" definitively banishes classical Vergil in favor of medieval Vergil and the Arthurian legends on which Spenser will base his plot. The romance flavor of Spenser's stanza is thus nicely complemented by his vocabulary.

Like Phaer, Spenser translates the passage in a single sentence, but the syntax is loose. Its larger movement follows natural word order from subject ("I") to passive verb ("am . . . enforst") to verbal complement ("to chaunge" and "sing"). In fact, the sentence continues three lines beyond the four quoted by adding a long adjectival clause ("Ladies . . . / Whose prayses . . . the sacred Muse areeds / [Me] To blazon. . . ."). The loose structure is complemented by lines that terminate with phrase- or clause-endings emphasized by commas. The verse gives the feeling of being neatly packaged. Although the lines themselves can be understood as being in accentual meter, the syllabic interpretation is preferable. It fits the romance background of the stanza—including the French flavor of the terminal Alexandrine—and it allows for easy variation in the number of primary stresses per line. Underneath the surface, one can also hear an alliterative music: "*m*an . . . *M*use * . . . *m*aske"; "*t*ime . . . *t*aught" *; " en*f*orst . . * *f*ar . . . un*f*itter."

Spenser's verse flows more smoothly than Phaer's, in large part because of the natural word order. It is melodic and pleasing, but it is not epic. Spenser wants it that way. He wants it to evoke the imaginative world of Chaucer's *Knight's Tale* rather than the world of the *Iliad*. He deliberately rejected the hard classicism that led to quantitative experiments and also the moderate classicism embodied in Phaer's *Aeneid*. The rejection was motivated by nationalism and complements the medieval subject matter of *The Faerie Queene*, and thus its fantasy and its use of allegory. The opening lines of *The Faerie Queene* are not intended to be showy. They illustrate a style that might be called "expository." The poem is rich in later passages that strive for—and achieve—magnificence. Magnificence is splendid even if it is not quite the same thing as heroic.

DAVENANT AND THE RATIONAL QUATRAIN

William Davenant wrote his epic *Gondibert* with a clear sense that it represented a break with the past. He had experimented with metaphysical poetry in *Madagascar* (1638, 1648), but the old style somehow failed to satisfy.

The new style recognizes a fundamental cultural change. It is the poetic aspect of the movement away from imagination and toward the norm of reason, and it is associated in England with Francis Bacon. For Bacon, imagination is the enemy of truth, and poets are little more than the masters of lying Plato claimed they were. In "The Wisdom of the Ancients" (1609), Bacon turned his attention to the claim that mythology is veiled revelation. He admits that some of the myths may have originated as allegories, but he adds with dry irony that "if any one be determined to believe that the allegorical meaning of the fable was in no case original and genuine, but that always the fable was first and the allegory put in after, I will not press the point."[41]

For Bacon, man's prime duty is to understand nature. Since poetry offers images of things that are not rather than of things that are, it is at best trivial and at worst pernicious. Poetry, says Bacon in *The Advancement of Learning*, "was ever thought to have some participation of divinesse, because it doth raise and erect the Minde, by submitting the shewes of things to the desires of the Mind, whereas reason doth buckle and bowe the Mind unto the Nature of things."[42] At the end of the discussion of poetry, Bacon condescendingly rejects it: "But it is not good to stay too long in the Theater: let us now passe on to the judicial Place or Pallace of the Mind, which we are to approach and view, with more reverence and attention."[43]

Ben Jonson's *Timber, or Discoveries* is an exemplary mix of Baconian rationalism with the critical doctrines of Horace and J. C. Scaliger. The emphasis is on thinking things through; far be it from Jonson to include inspiration as a factor in successful art: the poet "must first thinke and excogitate his matter, then choose his words, and examine the weight of either. Then take care, in placing and ranking both matter and words, that the composition be comely."[44] These requirements repeat ancient prescriptions for the successful orator: natural wit, exercise, and imitation.[45] The poet should write clearly and in the standard idiom, and Jonson disapproves of allegory, complex conceits, and wordplay. Drummond recalls in his *Conversations* that Jonson thought couplets "the bravest sort of verses" and that "Spensers stanzaes pleased him not, nor his matter."[46]

Henry Reynolds's *Mythomystes* (1632) defended the old theory of poetry against the onslaught of Baconians and neoclassicists. To Reynolds, the much-vaunted clarity of the moderns is a confession of poverty. The obscurity of the ancients conceals deep truths, "which doth no lesse commend their wisdome then conclude, by their contrary course, our Modernes empty and barren of any thing rare and pretious in them; who in all probability would not prostitute all they know to the rape and spoile of every illiterate reader, were they not conscious to themselves their treasor deserves not many locks to guard it under."[47]

Gondibert was conceived under the influence of Baconian rationalism and written between 1646 and 1650, when Davenant was an exile in Paris because of his support of the royalists in the Civil War. During composition, it was influenced by the greatest of the second-generation English rationalists. Davenant writes that Thomas Hobbes, also a Parisian exile, did him "the honour to allow this Poem a daily examination as it was writing."[48] In other words, *Gondibert* was written by a partisan of the new rationalism and was scrutinized by one of the new rationalism's most impressive thinkers. Whatever its merits—and they are few—it is significant in the history of English heroic prosody. The import of its prosody is made clear in not one but two documents: Davenant's preface to the 1650 edition of the poem, and "The Answer of Mr. Hobbs to Sr. Will. Davenant's Preface," also 1650.[49]

Davenant's position is evident from the first section of his preface. Homer, Vergil, Lucan, Statius, Tasso, and Spenser are deficient because they are more concerned with things divine (read "superstition") than "the Worlds true image." Spenser is also guilty of "obsolete Language" and for "his allegoricall Story . . . resembling, methinks, a continuance of extraordinary Dreams, such as excellent Poets and Painters . . . may have in the beginning of Feavers." If his story is a kind of delirium, his stanza is no better because it forces him to use archaisms: "The unlucky choice of his *Stanza* hath by repetition of Rime brought him to the necessity of many exploded words."[50] This is a lame comment. It is, however, understandable in view of the emphasis of rationalists on standard and current English and on simple verse forms. As for Davenant's characters, they will be Christians and patterns of virtue and vice appropriate for both "the camp and the court," and the story will be in five acts like a drama.

Davenant will tell the story in decasyllabic quatrains. The choice results from the confluence of several factors. One is the desire to avoid Spenserian complexity. Another is to avoid the opposite error of too simple a verse form:

> I shall say a little why I have chosen my interwoven *Stanza* of four. . . . I may declare that I beleev'd it would be more pleasant to the Reader, in a Work of length, to give this respite, or pause between every *Stanza*, having endeavour'd that each should contain a period, then to run him out of breath with continu'd *Couplets*. Nor doth alternate Rime by any lowliness of Cadence make the sound less Heroick, but rather adapt it to a plain and stately composing of Musick; and the brevity of the *Stanza* renders it less subtle to the Composer and more easie to the Singer, which, in *stilo recitativo*, when the Story is long, is chiefly requisite.[51]

The most obvious feature of this comment is its abandonment of the idea of epic elevation that is intrinsic to all discussions of epic prosody from the treatises of the *ars metrica* to Tasso's *Discorsi* and Chapman's various prefaces. The emphasis will be not on elevation or magnificence but on accommodating the reader. This is perfectly consistent with the prosy quality of Davenant's poetry in *Gondibert* and to the relation between Davenant's numbingly regular composition and his stanzas. Although he retains a fondness for metaphysical conceits, Davenant's sentences are usually simple to the point of simple-mindedness when compared with Chapman's. The word order tends to be standard and the structure loose. Although enjambment sometimes occurs within the stanza, normally a pause comes at the end of each line, and the sentence is regularly completed (as Davenant says it will be) at the end of the fourth line. In sum, the order is natural and the "Cadence" is anything but "Heroick."

Since the decasyllabic quatrain is not a common medieval English form, it cannot claim, like the forms of *The Shepheardes Calender*, to honor a native tradition. Nor does Davenant argue—as Dryden would for the couplet—that the quatrain forces the poet to stop and think and thus cools his overheated fancy. Davenant's main positive claim is that the form has musical potential—not that the form is "musical" in the manner of the Spenserian stanza, but that it is singable.

Spenser's shepherds compose ditties, and many Elizabethan lyrics are for singing, but until Davenant, no English writer of epic took the conventional command of the poet to the Muse—"Sing!"—in a literal sense. The reason for Davenant's innovation is that he has picked up an interest in opera while in Paris. *Gondibert* is written in the hope that some composer will use it as a libretto; hence the quatrains which are "easie to the Singer, which, in *stilo recitativo*, . . . is chiefly requisite." Interestingly, when he returned to England during the Commonwealth, Davenant staged musical interludes—proto-operas. Failing operatic performance, says Davenant, with a glance back at Homer and also at Sir Philip Sidney's comment on the rustic nobility of "The Ballad of Chevy Chase," there is reason to hope that the quatrains will be suited to singing as ballads "at Village-feasts."[52] He apparently thinks his quatrains are a superior kind of ballad meter.

Many passages of the poem could be quoted to illustrate Davenant's successful achievement of anti-epic blandness, but Davenant himself makes the selection. In his preface he quotes with special pride the passage on religious devotion in *Gondibert*, book 2, canto 6:

> *Praise* is Devotion fit for mighty Mindes,
>   The diff'ring Worlds agreeing Sacrifice,

> Where Heaven divided, Faiths united findes;
> But *Pray'r* in various discord upward flyes.
> For *Pray'r* the Ocean is, where diversely
> Men steer their course, each to a sev'ral Coast,
> Where all our Int'rests so discordant be,
> That half beg windes by which the rest are lost.
> By *Penitence* when We our selves forsake,
> 'Tis but in wise design on piteous Heaven;
> In *Praise* We nobly give what God may take,
> And are without a Beggars blush forgiven.[53]

This is not, in fact, an impossible passage. The metaphor of prayer as a universally understood sacrifice in a world torn by religious strife recalls the wording of the English Communion service and doubtless reflects bitter experiences of Davenant with the religious divisions of his age. The development of the metaphor into the image of an ocean sailed by lost pilgrims is clever—a metaphysical conceit that contradicts Davenant's rationalist principles—but it is obviously not so obscure as to be unacceptable.

The problem is that the verse has nothing to do with what was usually considered "heroic" in the Renaissance. If Davenant's rational quatrains are related to any common type of verse, they anticipate the meditative vein of Gray's "Elegy in a Country Churchyard." In addition to being bland, they go on interminably. The stanzas quoted are 89 to 91 of what is only the sixth canto of book 2, and there are (or will be) five books.

Hobbes approved highly of Davenant's effort. He would translate Homer into rhymed verse at 80 and conclude that the virtues of the heroic poem "are comprehended all in this one word, *Discretion*."[54] In responding to Davenant in 1650 he rebukes poets for fictions that "not onely exceed the *work* but the *possibility* of nature," because "beyond the actual works of nature a Poet may now go; but beyond the conceived possibility of nature, never."[55] Invocations are superfluous for the modern poet because by them "a man, enabled to speak wisely from the principles of nature and his own meditation, loves rather to be thought to speak by inspiration, like a Bagpipe."[56] He also rejects conceits, obscure language, and violation of decorum of character. Fortunately, Davenant's poem commits none of these errors. It is therefore excellent: "I never yet saw a poem that had so much of Art, health of Morality, and vigour and beauty of Expresion."[57]

It follows that the verse form of *Gondibert* is also appropriate.

Hobbes either is unfamiliar with Chapman's *Iliad* or (more probably) disapproves of it, for he remarks that in place of ancient hexameter, English poets "use the line of ten Syllables, recompensing the neglect of their quantity with the diligence of Rime. And this measure is so proper for an Heroique Poem as without some losse of gravity and dignity it was never changed. A longer is not far from ill Prose." He also glances at rhyme schemes, contrasting Davenant's choice with the choice of unnamed poetasters, among whom Hobbes undoubtedly includes Spenser: "To chuse a needlesse and difficult correspondence of Rime is but a difficult toy, and forces a man sometimes for the stopping of a chink to say somewhat he did never think; I cannot therefore but very much approve your *Stanza,* wherein the syllables in every Verse are ten, and the Rime Alternate."[58]

Surrey was familiar with Italian experiments in *versi sciolti,* and he was also aware of the syntactical, rhetorical, and musical sophistication of Latin dactylic hexameter. The second generation of poets seeking to ennoble the English language was more moderate. They knew each other or at least of each other, and they shared many theories about translation and imitation. George Gascoigne, author of two important contributions to this movement, was also the author of the first English treatise on prosody.

With the third generation and Spenser, there is a reaction against rhetorical classicism. *The Faerie Queene* is part of a medieval revival that began in Italy. Its medievalism is exotically mixed with Neoplatonic theories of poetry as truth hidden under an allegorical veil and of epic as the exhibition of a magnificence comparable to divine creation itself. Both influences led Spenser to the *Faerie Queene* stanza. The stanza was probably suggested by Ariosto's ottava rima, but just as Ariosto looked to Boccaccio, Spenser looked to native sources for inspiration. Chapman, conversely, continued the attempt to reshape English to make it capable of the elevation of ancient verse.

Neither Spenser nor Chapman was interested in poetry that bowed its neck to the yoke of reason. Spenser makes this clear through his fantastic inventions and complex musicality; Chapman makes it clear through his praise of Homer's divine wisdom and his citation of ancient and renaissance Neoplatonic philosophers in his prefaces. It remained for Davenant to devise a form of heroic verse suited to rationalism. Decasyllabic quatrains, natural construction, and matching of syntax to line and stanza are carefully worked out. The resulting form is neat, controlled, and can, on occasion, elaborate images in the old metaphysical way. It rejects the irregularities, the great sweeps of vision, and the turbulent ebb and flow of passion in Surrey and Chapman, but it does so by choice. It seems to Hobbes ideally suited to the needs of an Age of Reason.

CHAPTER X

Speech and Verse in Later Elizabethan Drama

The cult of Shakespeare the poet began early and continued late. As recently as 1954, F. E. Halliday observed, "The plays must be read as we read the works of Milton or any other non-dramatic poet. To hear in a theatre a Shakespearean play that we do not know almost by heart is to miss half its beauty."[1]

Today few students of theater would accept this assessment. Without denying the beauty of Shakespeare's poetry when read, they would place much greater emphasis on the idea that dramatic speech must be understood as a text for performance. Keir Elam puts the position as follows in *The Semiotics of Theatre and Drama:*

> Since, chronologically, the writing of the play precedes any given performance, it might appear quite legitimate to suppose the simple priority of the one over the other. But it is equally legitimate to claim that it is the performance, or at least a possible or 'model' performance, that constrains the dramatic text in its very articulation. The 'incompleteness' factor—that is, the constant pointing within a dialogue to a non-described context—suggests that the dramatic text is radically conditioned by its performability. The written text, in other words, is determined by its very need for stage contextualization, and indicates throughout its allegiance to the physical conditions of performance.[2]

Actorly Speech

It is difficult to discuss dramatic dialogue without terms that identify the performance aspect of dialogue—the qualities that are present in it because it is "conditioned by performability." The term "actorly" has been used in connection with the dialogue of Heywood's Seneca translations and *Gorboduc* and will continue to be used below.

An actorly text is written for performance rather than reading. It is "conditioned by its performability." It is a potential. Part of the potential may be evident from the words themselves. In chapter 14 of the *Poetics* (1456b9–18), Aristotle notes that the figures of diction include "what a command is, what a prayer is, what a statement is, what a threat and question and answer [are] and any other such matters."[3] An interrogative sentence, for example, is actorly in itself because it implies a specific voice intonation and is associated with complementary gestures—raised eyebrows, a shrug of the shoulders, and the like.[4] The illocutionary aspect of language is controlled, at least in part, by construction. In terms of construction an actorly text must have two features. It must be speakable—and comprehensible when spoken; and it must invite the actor's voice to explore and express the causes it implies.

An important part of the potential of dramatic speech is invisible on the page. It arises not from language but from context—from such elements as the relation of speaker to stage props, the eye contacts and gestures of the character to whom the speech is directed, the deployment of nonspeaking characters around the speaker. Actorly speech is a score for performance. It is only realized—it only "means what it says"—when it is integrated with everything else happening on the stage. Moreover, actorly speeches can always be vocally enacted in several ways. Whether or not a given enactment is valid depends on the specific production in which it occurs as well as the words in the text.

A good verse dramatist writes actorly speeches, not poems. Their meanings are intended to be discovered during rehearsal and cannot ever be fully present on the page. This is why it is difficult for writers of narrative, who create texts for readers, to write effective drama, and why dramatic scripts that are richly complex when performed can seem thin when read.

A theater is from one point of view a repository of conventions. The conventions include those forced on it by the design of its stage, those established by audience expectations, and those established by performance traditions. Actorly speech is written in accord with the conventions of its theater, which are certain to be different from the conventions of a theater in a different country or a different century. To a much greater degree than the language of a poem or narrative, it is a code. The break that occurred in 1642 with the closing of the English theaters was a deep fracture. After it, the world of Shakespeare's dramas could be evoked as a memory but never fully recovered.

How does a dramatist learn to write actorly speeches if there is no established theater for which to write them? This was the dilemma of the dramatists who wrote in England before the later 1580s. They were creating conventions rather than absorbing and modifying them. They had to rely on what was available. One body of theory that related directly to the problem of writing actorly speeches was the *ars metrica*. Two other useful sources of information were the dramas of Seneca and the ancient rhetorical formulas for making orations.

Opsis and Illocution

As early as Plato's *Republic* the requirement that dialogue be "like speech" is related to a larger concept of genre. In book 3 of the *Republic* (392C) Socrates defines two genres of poetry. They are genres based on the place of the author in the work. One is narrative (diegetic), the other dramatic or imitative (mimetic). After quoting a passage from Homer that has both description and direct quotation, Socrates observes that in the descriptive part, "the poet speaks in his own person and does not in any way attempt to make us suppose that anyone else than himself is talking." Conversely, in the direct quotation, "the poet attempts to make it seem to us as though it were not Homer who is speaking but the priest, who is an old man."

For Aristotle, all poetry is imitation because poetry is the making of plots, and plots are imitations of actions. The other five parts of a tragedy help objectify the imitation. Diction objectifies it by making character and thought manifest in words. Horace is recalling this idea when he observes in the *Ars poetica* that iambic meter is "born for action" (*natum rebus agendis*, l. 82). Complementing diction in the *Poetics* are "song" and "spectacle" (*opsis*).

"Song" may be self-explanatory, but "spectacle" has always given commentators difficulty. Does it refer to the play as seen—that is, scenery and costume and the physical motions of actors on a stage? Evidence can be offered in favor of this interpretation, but it appears to be contradicted by two points that Aristotle makes very emphatic. First, the parts of a tragedy are inherent in the tragedy—none of them is "added" by performance. And second, all of the parts of a tragedy can be appreciated when read as well as when the work is acted.

In *Aristotle's Poetics: The Argument* Gerald Else proposes a solution. Commenting on Aristotle's first reference to *opsis* (49b33), he concludes, "The characters must be thought of . . . as being in certain places, being on or off stage at certain times, etc. These are necessities that a dramatist cannot dodge, a condition which he has laid upon himself by the act of writing a play, and which necessarily must affect the way he writes it and the way a reader—independently of any actual performance—will visualize it."[5] The interpretation is brilliantly developed in a comment on chapter 17 (55a22–32), where the poet is advised to "visualize the action" and "work it out with the figures."[6] Aristotle's word for "figures" is *schemata*, and Else argues persuasively that it is a reference to the *schemata lexeos* discussed in chapter 19 of the *Poetics*, that is, the illocutionary forms of language—questioning, commanding, threatening, pleading, declaiming, praying, and the like.

This interpretation makes "spectacle" the adjustment of the language to the fact that it will be performed. The fact that such an adjustment is made is obvious from the physical difference between a narrative and a play script. The narrative is continuous, while the play script is divided into speeches. But the difference goes much deeper than that. The play script is to be spoken by agents represented physically on stage. The speeches all have motives, and the motives *precede* the speeches, being their causes.

The illocutionary quality of dialogue implies a speaking voice, not the chant of the professional rhapsodist. Hence iambic meter, hence the avoidance of epic similes, hence the simplicity of the vocabulary of drama as compared with the vocabulary of epic. Hence, too, the emphasis on a syntax that expresses intention and motive through the *schemata*.

But this is not the end of the story. In advising the dramatist to "visualize" the action, Aristotle is recognizing that the speeches must reflect awareness of where the agents are at all times. Certain arrangements will be physically impossible. Others may be possible but risk being ludicrous if performed. In other cases—the presence of Megaera and her serpents at the beginning of *Thyestes* is an example—a character may be silent but may shape the speech of another character. When writing the speech, the dramatist must keep the silent character vividly present in imagination and write the speech in terms of what the silent character is understood to be doing while the speech proceeds. For example, even though it is not verbalized, a lunge by Megaera must be complemented by a verbal equivalent of flinching in the speech composed for Tantalus.

If a performance of *Thyestes* includes such a lunge, it seems to the audience to be a cause, and the "flinch" in the speech seems to be its effect. This is a curious situation. In real life, cause precedes effect and leads to it. In a dramatic script the situation is reversed. The script, which is the effect, comes first, and the cause must be deduced from it and then inserted into the play in order to create the illusion of real life. Yet the causes are the life of the play. They arise from the action that the play is imitating and thus from what Aristotle calls its "soul."

We will return to this point. For the present we note that it is the equivalent in ancient critical theory of the concept of actorly dialogue. The ability of ancient dramatists to write actorly speeches is especially clear in the comic dialogue of Plautus and Terence, but it is discernible, as we have seen, in the tragedies of Seneca, even though they were probably written for declamation. A memory of what constitutes actorly dialogue is preserved in these dramas.

A memory of the actorly nature of dialogue is also preserved in the common late classical distinction among manners of imitation. Diomedes, for example, observes that certain kinds of verse are "biotic" because they are like speech. He begins his chapter "On Poems" with a comment on the kinds of literature as determined by manner of imitation: "There are three kinds of poem—a poem is either 'active' or 'imitative,' which the Greeks call *dramatikon* or *mimetikon;* or it is narrative or 'presentational,' which the Greeks call *exegetikon* or *apangeltikon;* or it is common or 'mixed,' which the Greeks call *koinon* or *mikton.*"[7] The influential renaissance commentary of Badius Ascensius on Horace's *Ars poetica* begins with the same distinctions.

In a print-oriented culture it is almost impossible not to read dramatic speeches as words on a page. However, whether we take Keir Elam's semiotics or Aristotle's *opsis* or Diomedes' concept of biotic verse or his three genres as our basis, the words on the page must be considered as potential rather than adequate symbols of their own meaning.

To regard dramatic speech as words on a page is inappropriate because it ignores the basic realities of drama. No dramatist working closely with a group of actors, as the Elizabethan playwrights did, can have failed to understand the fact. When Ben Jonson attacks those who write "furious vociferation to warrant them to the ignorant gapers" and praises the dramatist who "knowes it is his onely Art so to carry it, as none but Artificers perceive it," he is making this point in renaissance terms.

The Mirror of Custom

Hamlet explains that the purpose of drama is "to hold, as 't were, the mirror up to nature." The metaphor should be taken seriously. It opposes life, which we do not see because we are in it, to an image of life, which we can see because it is separate from us. This is precisely the interpretation of the mirror image used in the following exchange between Brutus and Cassius in *Julius Caesar*:

> Cassius: Tell me, good Brutus, can you see your face?
> Brutus: No, Cassius; for the eye sees not itself
>   But by reflection, by some other things. . . .
> Cassius: Therefore, good Brutus, be prepar'd to hear;
>   And since you know you cannot see yourself
>   So well, as by reflection, I, your glass,
>   Will modestly discover to yourself
>   That of yourself which you yet know not of.
>   (I, ii, 51–70)

In other words, by being a mirror, art shows us what we cannot see otherwise; that is, what we are. The metaphor is especially interesting because an image in a mirror is an illusion. It seems to be like life, but in it, everything is reversed.

In life we are always involved in situations that cause responses. I enter a dining room and notice that the table is set. My response is a question: "What are we having for dinner?" The table set for dinner is the cause of my question. In a play script the sequence is reversed. If it is a renaissance script and lacks detailed stage directions, it will contain a laconic statement followed by dialogue; for example:

Enter Trencher

Trench.: What are we having for dinner?

The director must infer from Trencher's question the table and the place-mats and glasses and silverware that are needed to explain why he asks the question. Once inferred, they are put on the stage, and when the play is performed, an illusion is created. The table with its place settings seems to cause the question, as it would do in real life. In fact, however, the question came first and caused the table setting. Without the question there would be no table setting. The play is thus an artifice. It is not an image of life but the illusion of an image, an image in a mirror.

A dramatic speech always arises from a situation, which may be defined as an array of causes. The causes are corollaries of the action being imitated. Some of them are obvious from the speech, which can act as an indirect stage direction. In such cases the task of inferring the causes is simple. Othello says, "Keep up your bright swords." The speech indicates that the characters he is addressing are brandishing swords. Without them the speech would be absurd—an effect without a cause. Once the swords are brandished, the speech seems perfectly reasonable, like a speech in real life.

Are not the speeches in a drama normally caused by other speeches? If character A in a drama asks, "What day is today?" and character B answers, "Wednesday," the question seems to be the cause of the answer. Questions and answers are *schemata*. Is not the "What day is today" sequence a perfect example of dialogue with illocutionary qualities?

Yes and no. The illocutionary element is only the beginning of the actorly significance of the exchange. Any question is obviously one cause of its answer, but it may not be the only cause or the most important one.

Why did the dramatist write A's question? Suppose the question is there to make a point: B is a liar. In this case the audience will have learned previously that today is not Wednesday but Friday. The true cause of B's answer will then be dishonesty, which is a character trait and has nothing to do with the calendar. The question is a strategy to allow the dishonesty to be exhibited. If the dishonesty is not sufficiently obvious from what has already happened, B may wink at the audience while speaking the line (gesture).

Suppose B says "*Wednesday*" in an agitated whisper. This is because Wednesday is the day A and B plan to escape from prison. The escape is the cause of B's agitation. The microphone hanging from the ceiling of the cell is the cause of the whisper. The microphone is part of the set.

If B shouts "WEDNESDAY!" perhaps this is because A is hard of hearing. Perhaps A has been given a hearing aid by the prop department so the cause cannot be missed. If B says "Wednesday" in an angry tone of voice, this may be because A has been pestering him. If B pauses after A's question and looks at a wall calendar, this is because B is absent-minded or distracted. The wall calendar has been tacked to the wall of the set specifically so that B can look at it before replying.

"Wednesday" is neutral. It has only the general meaning assigned it in the dictionary. It does not take on a precise dramatic meaning until its causes have been discovered and incorporated into set, blocking, costume, gesture, expression, and voice inflection at the moment it is spoken. When all of these elements are present, the word expresses motive as well as meaning. It is part of the play's action as well as its script.

An actorly speech must be constructed so as to be speakable and comprehensible by an audience. Beyond these basic requirements, it must be written in such a way as to invite the exploration of its causes.

The creation of an actorly sequence for a brief speech is nicely illustrated by the three-line speech in which Hamlet notices the presence of Ophelia. Usually these lines are spoken continuously, with brief pauses to separate the three sentences:

> Soft you now!
> The fair Ophelia! Nymph, in thy orisons
> Be all my sins rememb'red.
>
> (III, i, 88–90)

The most obvious cause of this speech is the presence of Ophelia, who does not, at this point, have a line. The cause is visual rather than verbal. Ophelia appears, and her presence causes Hamlet's words. Many performances of *Hamlet* stop there.

In Sir Laurence Olivier's film version of *Hamlet* the lines are given additional causes. Hamlet is shown walking in a corridor. We know he is convinced Claudius is spying on him. He hears a noise but cannot see who has made it. His line "Soft you now!" means something like "Something unexpected is happening. I must be careful." Note that the presence of Ophelia is not the cause of the speech in Olivier's version, because when Hamlet speaks, he has not yet seen her. After speaking, he walks to the end of the corridor and sees Ophelia. She does not "enter" in this version but is "discovered." Hamlet is relieved and pleased. He exclaims, "The fair Ophelia!" He then walks to her and takes her arm. He notices she is holding a book. It is the book Polonius gave her before concealing himself behind the arras. It is probably a book of religious devotions because when Polonius gave it to her, he remarked,

> 'Tis too much prov'd, that with devotion's visage
> And pious action we do sugar o'er
> The devil himself.
>
> (III, i, 47–49)

Olivier's decision to make Ophelia's book a devotional manual is justified by the speech, but it is not inevitable. The reason for Olivier's decision is that seeing the devotional manual becomes the cause for Hamlet's next words to Ophelia: "Nymph, in thy orisons / Be all my sins rememb'red."

Instead of being spoken continuously, the speech in Olivier's version is broken by three extended pauses during which Hamlet (1) discovers Ophelia, (2) walks to her, and (3) notices her book. What is normally a rather bland transition becomes, in this performance, a powerfully charged expression of causes that are at the center of the play. The speech seems perfectly, even transparently, natural, but the naturalness is an illusion created by a cluster of causes put there by the director and actor on the basis of their analysis of the speech in relation to everything happening when it is spoken. It is poetry of the highest order not because it is in verse but because it is perfectly expressive.

Is Olivier's performance "what Shakespeare intended"? On one level the answer is a flat no. Elizabethan stages did not permit characters to wander down corridors and "discover" other characters at their ends. On another level the answer is both yes and no. Yes for two reasons. The enactment could easily be adjusted to Elizabethan stage conditions. In Shakespeare's play Hamlet is ending his soliloquy as Ophelia "enters." There is no reason why he has to be facing her. His "Soft you now!" could be an aside to the audience caused by a noise she makes while walking and made before he sees her. Yes also because the enactment brilliantly exploits the actorly potential of the lines. And no because there is no way of proving or disproving Shakespeare's "intention" for the lines. His general intention when writing the lines was to create a speech that had actorly potential. Quite possibly he was often as surprised and delighted as his audiences by the enactments that Burbage worked out for the first performances of his scripts. Quite possibly he would have been equally pleased by other enactments.

Desdemona tells a lie about her handkerchief in *Othello*. It occurs in the following exchange:

> Oth.: Is't lost? Is't gone? Speak, is't out o'the way?
> Des.: Heaven bless us!
> Oth.: Say you?
> Des.: It is not lost; but what an if it were?
> Oth.: How?
> Des.: I say, it is not lost.

On paper, this seems to be a mild little exchange. Desdemona knows her handkerchief is lost. Why doesn't she admit it? Readers of the play often feel that her equivocation contributes, in a small way, to her downfall.

In a performance several things qualify the words spoken. There is a difference between the physical presence of Othello and Desdemona. He is large, powerful, probably dressed in full uniform. She is slight and weak, probably wearing a white gown. When he asks the questions, there is suppressed violence in his voice. She is not only cautious, she is physically intimidated. Her fear can be made obvious if the actor playing Othello makes a menacing gesture or—even more frightening—begins to make one and then represses it. Her lie thus seems to arise from her fear that Othello may do her physical harm.

On the stage the exchange becomes perfectly clear and brilliantly expressive. It is actorly in the best sense. The fact that it is apparently barren of all ornament illustrates the complete humility of actorly writing. It is committed to its function rather than to making an impression on potential readers. For that very reason, it may be confusing—even disappointing—to anyone who considers *Othello* poetry to be read.

In certain modern plays—Sam Shepherd's *The Buried Child*, for example—lack of causality is one point of the play. Shakespeare's universe is often strange, but his speeches tend to be richly suggestive of possible causes, and the problem of the Shakespearean actor is to select the causes relevant to a particular dramatic production. Olivier's enactment of Hamlet's "Soft you now" speech about Ophelia shows how rich the opportunities are. It also shows that the problem of inferring causes is usually far more difficult—and the options far more numerous—than setting a table so that an actor can say, "What are we having for dinner?"

Properly understood the prosodic analysis of dialogue must begin with its rhythms, which are the rhythms of illocutions shaped by causes. Drinking cups should certainly be used in the tavern scenes in Shakespeare's *1 Henry IV* because the speeches mention drinking. But how should the drinking cups relate to the speeches? Should they be banged on the table as punctuation? Should Falstaff drink only at the end of a speech to create a significant pause, or should he freely interrupt the speech with drinks of sack? If so, how often? When?

Pauses in speech are elements of the prosody of the speech. They are usually created by construction, as are illocutions and many other actorly speech elements. We have seen in earlier chapters that the traditions of romance prosody are sensitive to the rhythms of construction—that, in fact, they were probably shaped by these rhythms during the formative age of romance prosody. We have also seen that renaissance schoolmasters explicitly taught the priority of the rhythms of construction over the metrical rhythms of classical verse. Both points of view fit nicely with one's empirical experience of the dialogue of renaissance verse drama of the 1590s.

Renaissance Comments on Dramatic Verse and on Acting

It is also useful to consider renaissance testimony on the subject. Shakespeare and his contemporaries wrote plays in a blank verse that looks very much like poetry and sounds exactly like it when recited. Did they intend their dramatic speech to be melodic or actorly? After the speeches were written, they were spoken by actors. Did the actors emphasize the melody of the verse or de-emphasize it? And did the audience respond to the melody or ignore it?

In *The Poetics of Jacobean Drama* Coburn Freer argues that verse drama was valued both as poetry and as dramatic speech by Elizabethan actors and audiences. Later, when the plays were read more often than seen in the theater, the poetry began to be considered more important than the speech. The playwrights began to consider themselves "men of letters" and to write for the reading public. For Freer, poetry in the sense of melodic language is essential to the effect of English renaissance drama. Its justification is that it is functional as well as poetic.[8]

However, many of the renaissance authors Freer cites to prove his case attack drama that is self-consciously poetic. Thomas Nashe, for example, condemns "ideot Art-masters . . . who (mounted on a stage of arrogance) thinke to out-brave better pennes with the swelling bumbast of bragging blanke verse . . . and the spacious volubilitie of a drumming decasyllabon."[9]

The word "bombast" occurs frequently in Elizabethan comments on dramatic verse. It is normally used, as here by Nashe, to criticize verse that calls attention to itself and panders to the groundlings. One of Greene's charges against Shakespeare is that he "supposes he is as well able to bombast out a blank verse as the best of you."[10] The prime exemplar of writing bombast that pleased the rabble was also the prime teacher of the art of blank verse to the later Elizabethans—Christopher Marlowe. Joseph Hall cites *Tamburlaine* as a notorious example of inflated verse and goes on to ridicule all attempts by dramatists to be "poetic." Their "*Iambick*"—i.e., dramatic—poetry delights the crowd because of its sonorous constructions ("Big-sounding sentences") and its exotic vocabulary, but it does not mean very much:

> [If the author] can with termes Italianate,
> Big-sounding sentences, and words of state,
> Faire patch me up his pure *Iambick* verse,
> He ravishes the gazing Scaffolders.[11]

As Freer observes, Hall "rejects [verse drama] altogether, emphasizing in particular the link between its emptiness of content and its sloppiness of technique."[12] One cannot say that Ben Jonson rejected verse drama. He did, however, condemn Marlovian bombast in highly specific terms:

> The true Artificer will not run away from nature, as hee were afraid of her, or depart from life and the likenesse of Truth, but speake to the capacity of his hearers. And though his language differ from the vulgar somewhat, it shall not fly from all humanity, with the *Tamerlanes* and *Tamer-Chams* of the late Age, which had nothing in them but the *scenicall* strutting and furious vociferation to warrant them to the ignorant gapers.[13]

Charges of bombast and sloppy technique do not show special appreciation of the verse element in drama. Instead they show that the dramatists were scornful of inflated rhetoric. The groundlings loved this sort of thing. As Hamlet says, "O, it offends me to the soul to see a robustious periwig-pated fellow tear a passion to tatters, to very rags, to split the ears of the groundlings, who for the most part are capable of nothing but inexplicable dumb-shows and noise" (III, ii, 9–14). The dramatists regarded such "noise" as sham. The proper test of dramatic speech is its ability to express motive—its actorly quality.

For this reason, complaints about bombast are complemented by arguments that plays are essentially action. These arguments appear first in England in Sir Philip Sidney's assertion in the *Apology for Poetry* that verse is "but an ornament and no cause to Poetry."[14] Nine years after the publication of the *Apology,* John Marston emphatically contrasts the effect of a play on the stage, where the lines have their proper meaning, with the disappointing quality of a play in printed form. The comment is in the preface to *The Malcontent:* "I would fain leave the paper; only one thing affects me to think that scenes invented merely [i.e., only] to be spoken, should be enforcively published to be read . . . but I shall entreat . . . that the unhandsome shape which this trifle in reading presents may be pardoned for the pleasure it afforded you when it was presented with the soul of lively action."[15] The word "soul" suggests that Marston is thinking of Aristotle's statement that the soul of drama is plot. A similar position is taken by Sir Richard Baker in *Theatrum triumphans* (1670) in a comment on the sources of dramatic pleasure: "A play *read,* hath not half the pleasure of a Play *Acted*...and we may well acknowledge that *Gracefulness of Action* is the greatest pleasure of a Play."[16]

The word "action" as used by Marston and Baker may refer either to the action imitated by the plot or to the activity that occurs on stage when the play is performed. Marston seems closer to, and Baker more distant from, Aristotle. We are on solidly Aristotelian ground with the preface by John Dennis to *The Comicall Gallant* (1702):

> As in the mixture of the Human frame,
> 'Tis not the Flesh, 'tis the soul makes the Man,
> So of Dramatic Poems we may say,
> 'Tis not the lines, 'tis the Plot makes the Play.
> The Soul of every Poem's the design,
> And words but serve to make that move and shine.[17]

The tradition behind this comment is different from the *ars metrica* idea that poetry is language in meter, but it nicely complements the *ars metrica* theory that dramatic verse should be "biotic." In his essay *The Genius and Writings of Shakespeare* (1712), Dennis differentiates explicitly between the formal prosody of "Heroik Harmony" and the tone of "common Conversation" appropriate for comedy. The latter tone is suggested (in Dennis's opinion) by feminine line-endings. The reference to "Trisyllabic Terminations" seems to be an allusion to the *sdruccioli* of classicizing Italian comedy:

> [Shakespeare] seems to have been the very Original of our *English* Tragical Harmony; that is the Harmony of Blank Verse, diversified often by Disyllabic and Trisyllabic Terminations. For that Diversity distinguishes it from Heroick Harmony, and bringing it nearer to common Use, makes it more proper to gain Attention, and more fit for Action and Dialogue. Such Verse we make when we are writing prose; we make such Verse in common Conversation.[18]

The second aspect of the effort to understand renaissance attitudes toward the style of dramatic verse is the way the verse was spoken by actors. Were lines delivered in an artificial manner emphasizing their difference from ordinary language—that is, as recitation—or was the delivery closer to what would be called naturalism today?

We have already noticed John Brinsley's statement in *Ludus literarius* about the right way to read Latin poetry: "So in all Poetry, for the pronuntiation, it is to be uttered as prose; observing distinctions and the nature of the matter; not to be tuned foolishly or childishly after the manner of scanning a Verse, as the use of some is."[19] As if to relate what he is saying to drama, Brinsley adds that students should memorize Vergil's eclogues so they can recite them as dialogue, with proper emphasis on motive and emotion, rather than as verse. In suggesting that verse should be read as prose "observing distinctions and the nature of the matter," he is urging that the verse be spoken in an actorly way.

The advice accords nicely with Hamlet's advice to the players (III, ii, 1–45) to speak the lines "trippingly on the tongue" and to refrain from tearing a passion "to tatters, to very rags"—that is, ranting. Action should be suited to the word and the word to the action. "Action" apparently means stage gesture to Hamlet, so that the advice can be paraphrased: "Suit gesture to statement and statement to gesture."

Thomas Heywood amplifies Hamlet's advice in his *Apology for Actors* (1612). Rhetoric, he says, should teach the actor "to fit his phrases to his action and his action to his phrases, and his pronunciation to them both."[20] In this comment "phrases" means something like "the words in the script." The phrases imply certain gestures, and, as in Hamlet's advice, the two should be complementary. "Pronunciation" means "delivery" (*pronunciatio*). It carries with it the idea of making clear by voice inflections—that is, vocal enactment—the motives and emotions that are the causes of the words.

Currently, the standard review of the evidence about English renaissance acting is that undertaken by Bertram Joseph in *Elizabethan Acting*. Joseph concludes in the 1951 edition of his book that Elizabethan acting followed formulas given in classical rhetoric for delivery of orations. The stylization extended to language. Joseph suggests that the speaking style of the actors may have been like the *stile recitativo* of Italian opera. It follows that "the naturalistic conception of drama" has no relevance to the Elizabethan stage.[21]

However, in the second edition of *Elizabethan Acting* (1964), Joseph had second thoughts. The references to *stile recitativo* and opera have been dropped. The thrust of the second edition is summed up in a word that was explicitly banished from the first edition—"naturalness":

> As the Elizabethan actor responded to variations in the style of his lines, so the style of the performance varied. Rhythm, tempo of speech and movement, and melody of speech would have been affected by stylistic variations, but there would still have remained untouched the essential naturalness of behavior, which was that of such a person communicating what was within him in the circumstances of acting.[22]

The description is all the more persuasive because it requires a reversal of Joseph's earlier position.

The dominant Elizabethan acting style, then, was probably natural. Some actors were doubtless flamboyant, inclined, perhaps, to *stile recitativo*. Most were natural. Shakespeare and Ben Jonson stress words like "modesty" and "nature" when discussing acting. We can conclude with Richard Flecknoe's famous description of Richard Burbage. The description shows that Burbage aimed at "naturalness" and that his method was to identify closely with the character being portrayed:

> *Burbidge*, of whom we may say that he was a delightful *Proteus,* so wholly transforming himself into his Part, and putting himself off with his Cloathes, as he never (not so much as in the Tyring-house) assum'd himself again until the Play was done; there being as much difference betwixt him and one of our common Actors, as between a Ballad-singer who onely mouths it, and an excellent singer, who knows all his Graces, and can artfully vary and modulate his Voice, even to know how much breath he is to give to every syllable. He had all the parts of an excellent Orator, animating his words with speaking, and Speech with Action; his Auditors being never more delighted then when he spake, nor more sorry then when he held his peace; yet even then he was an excellent Actor still, never falling in his Part when he had done speaking, but with his looks and gesture maintaining it still unto the heighth, he imagining *Age quod agis* onely spoke to him: so as those who call him a Player do him wrong, no man being less idle then he whose whole life is nothing else but action;

with only this difference from other mens, that what is but a Play to them is his Business, so their business is but a play to him.²³

MARLOWE'S MIGHTY LINE

Christopher Marlowe burst onto the London theater scene with the force of an explosion around 1587. *Tamburlaine* was the sort of success that transforms the theater. Prominent among Marlowe's achievements is what Ben Jonson rightly called his "mighty line." The mighty line is driving in rhythm, loose in syntactical structure, and divided into well-defined phrase and clause units. These are often emphasized by end-stopped lines, but Marlowe is also capable of enjambment and units that approximate verse paragraphs.²⁴ It is ornamented with exotic terms and polysyllables, and its sound is often at least as important as its sense. It encourages speeches that are there simply because they sound grand. Led by Edward Alleyn, who made the role of Tamburlaine famous, the actors took full advantage of the mighty line. It was new, sensational, and above all, popular. The preface to *Tamburlaine* shows that Marlowe was aware of its power:

> From jygging vaines of riming mother wits,
> And such conceits as clownage keepes in pay,
> Weele leade you to the stately tent of War,
> Where you shall heare the Scythian *Tamburlaine*,
> Threatning the world with high astounding tearms.²⁵

Marlowe's terms "stately" and "high astounding" show he thought of his verse as heroic. As Eugene Waith observes in *The Herculean Hero*, Tamburlaine has qualities that relate him to the Hercules of Seneca's *Hercules Oetaeus* and other well-known titanic and heroic figures.²⁶ On the other hand, current criticism of Marlowe has demonstrated that he had a lively sense of stage action. In spite of its flamboyance, the mighty line is often impressively well suited to performance.²⁷

The fact is that the verse of *Tamburlaine* illustrates nicely two points regularly made about tragic verse in the *ars metrica*. It has heroic qualities, and its verse often sounds like epic verse when recited. At the same time, it is written for performance, and whatever its deviations, its norm is speech.

In book 4 of the *Aeneid*, Aeneas must choose between remaining in Carthage with Dido and following his destiny to Italy. He is torn between the alternatives but finally decides to leave. When Dido hears of his decision she rebukes him. She is a familiar literary figure—a woman scorned. In composing her speech Vergil moved away from the epic norm and toward the colloquial. Surrey's translation reproduces this tone:

> To Italy passe on by helpe of wyndes,
> And through the flouds go searche thy kingdome newe,
> If ruthfull Gods have any power, I trust
> Amyd the rockes thy hyre thou shalt fynde
> When thou shall cleape ful oft on Didoes name,
> Wyth buryal brandes I absent shall thee chase
> And when cold death from lyf these lymbes divydes,
> My gost shall styll upon thee wayte,
> Thou shalt abye and I shall here thereof.
> Among the soules below this brute shall come.[28]

The passage has a moderately illocutionary quality. It is divided into three units: a hortatory sentence (ll. 1–2), a conditional sentence (ll. 3–5), and four threats (ll. 6, 7–8, 9, 10). The flow of the verse is continuous within the units. The second unit (ll. 3–5) is enjambed. Otherwise, a regular rhythm is created by pauses at the end of the lines, with stronger pauses at the line ends that mark transitions from one unit to the next. The construction produces natural rather than artificial order, and generally short sense units. The vocabulary is standard and consists mostly of monosyllables. Line 8 is defective. Since the lack of two syllables does not seem to be expressive, perhaps the defect is the result of a printer's error. This problem aside, the passage is considerably smoother than the translation by Surrey of Vergil's description of Dido's death. The moment is less critical and calls for less in the way of poetic artifice. The result is effective as narrative but lacks actorly potential. This is hardly surprising; the lines are written for reading.

Marlowe's version of the episode in *Dido, Queene of Carthage* (V, i, 169–78) is as follows:

> Goe goe and spare not, seeke out *Italy*,
> I hope that that which love forbids me doe,
> The Rockes and Sea-gulfes will performe at large,
> And thou shalt perish in the billowes waies,
> To whome poor *Dido* doth bequeath revenge.
> I traitor, and the waves shall cast thee up,
> Where thou and false *Achates* first set foot:
> Which, if it chaunce, Ile give ye buriall,

And weepe upon your liveles carcases,
Though thou nor he will pitie me a white.²⁹

This passage is quite different in quality from Surrey's. Its actorly quality is announced by two features of the first line. It begins with a strongly illocutionary form—an imperative. The repetition of "goe" encourages the actor's voice to fill the two words with intense emotion. But what emotion? The question requires an investigation into the causes of the words. Perhaps the first "goe" is said softly, suggesting the inclination of the lover to wish the beloved well. The second "goe" is then said loudly and bitterly, indicating Dido's rising anger over Aeneas's treachery. Since the line is actorly, this is only one possible objectification of it.

The second actorly element in the first line is the heavy pause after "spare not." The pause invites speculation about what Dido is doing while she speaks. Does she raise her hand at the pause to point in the direction of Italy? Does she shrug hopelessly? Does she pause and then almost scream "SEEK OUT ITALY"? What is Aeneas doing? Is he embarrassed? Does he turn away? Look at the ground? Attempt to console her by touching her? There are no definitive answers to these questions. The point is that the line invites the questions. It is written with a sense of spectacle—of *opsis;* that is, of characters physically confronting each other and interacting, even though one of the characters is for the moment silent.

Marlowe has "visualized" the action. He has also utilized strong illocutionary forms. The line consists of three commands: "goe," "spare not," and "seeke out." Finally, the strong pause after "spare not" is nicely adjusted to the actor's breathing rhythm. Pauses for breathing are an aspect of Marlowe's verse seldom noted explicitly. Although there are passages in *Dido* that can leave an actor breathless, most of the speeches have regular pauses that allow easy breathing. In this respect Marlowe's verse recalls the verse of *Gorboduc* and may demand less of the actor, generally, than the verse of the early Shakespeare.

The next four lines are both Marlovian and closer to Surrey than the first line. They must be recited in pairs separated by the conjunction ("and") at the beginning of the second pair. They are not quite like Surrey, however, because their word order is simpler and thus easier to make clear when spoken.

A strong actorly quality returns in the next-to-last line. Dido pauses, draws herself up, and emphasizes the scornful curse that is to follow with "I" ("aye") followed by a pause, followed, in turn, by "traitor," a word expressing hatred and outrage. Perhaps she is weeping as she uses the word. Perhaps she says it softly rather than harshly. Again, the line invites the actor to explore its possible causes. And, of course, like the first line in the quotation, it implies interaction between Dido and the unspeaking Aeneas. Perhaps as she says "traitor," she points accusingly and looks directly into his eyes. Perhaps he flinches. The specifics are not as important as the invitation to explore them.

Lucan's *Pharsalia* is an epic about the Roman civil wars written in the first century A.D. Marlowe probably translated it while a student at Cambridge, but there is no way of knowing. The work was published in 1600, seven years after his death. He may have been working on it in the early 1590s. It is, at any rate, explicitly heroic. Marlowe decided to translate it in blank verse, making him only the second poet of the English Renaissance to use that form for a sustained heroic narrative. Since there is no reason to believe he was aware of Surrey's *Aeneid*, it is interesting to observe how many of the strategies that appear for the first time in Surrey reappear in Marlowe's Lucan. The two authors are not only translating from Latin, they are also imitating in the sense of reaching for the effects of their originals. Evidently they arrive independently at similar conclusions.

The *Pharsalia* begins with an expository passage, followed by the lines that begin the action:[30]

> *Caesars* and *Pompeys* jarring love soone ended,
> T'was peace against their wils; betwixt them both
> Stept *Crassus* in: even as the slender *Isthmos*
> Betwixt the *Agean* and the *Ionian* sea,
> Keepes each from other, but being worne away
> They both burst out, and each incounter other:
> So when as *Crassus* wretched death who stayd them,
> Had fild *Assirian Carras* wals with bloud,
> His losse made way for Roman outrages.
>
> (ll. 98–106)

This verse is less musical than the verse of Surrey's *Aeneid*. The harsh effect is probably intentional. Lucan is less musical than Vergil. He is describing the ugly death throes of a culture, not its noble beginnings. Given this fact, Marlowe's translation is nicely expressive of its source. It is filled with heroic *enargia*, complex constructions, "rough" sound, and ornamental words, and it is larger than life.

The passage begins with two short units that would have actorly potential if used in a passage of dramatic exposition. However, even these passages are Latinate rather than English and are therefore distanced from speech. The first line is an English version of a Latin ablative absolute, with the verb ("ended") used as a participle. Idiomatic English either would treat the line as a complete sentence and the verb as finite or would use a subordinating conjunction and a finite verb, as, for example, "*Since* Caesar's and Pompey's love soon ended. . . ." The second unit uses inversion and ends with a preposition. The normal English order would be subject, verb, and adverbial modifier, as, for example, "Crassus stepped in between them both." The inversion here is well within the bounds of what can be spoken and used to good effect by the voice, but it distances the sentence from speech. The dependence of the ablative absolute (l. 1) on the main clause (l. 2) and the enjambment between the second and third lines hurries the verse along in spite of the pause at the sentence boundary. The units are short, but the form announces its capacity to create large, sustained units.

Just such a unit follows. The unit begins with "betwixt" and continues to the end of the passage quoted. It is an epic simile comparing a natural phenomenon—the separation of the Aegean and Ionian seas by the isthmus of Corinth—with the separation of two great antagonists by Crassus. The need to complete the comparison begun with the phrase "even as" sustains the verse for seven lines. The effect is reinforced by syntax. The first half of the simile is not completed until the final, climactic line: "They . . . burst out, and each incounter[s] [the] other." The second half of the simile is likewise withheld until the final line: "[When as Crassus . . . fild . . . *Carras* wals] . . . His losse made way. . . ."

The simile is impressive, and it is obviously heroic. Although the first three lines of the passage could be made into dramatic exposition, the seven lines of the simile are clearly intended for reading. They would be as difficult as Jasper Heywood's Latinate fourteeners to speak effectively on stage. This is proper. Marlowe understands the nature of heroic verse and quite effectively objectifies it in his lines.

Two additional effects may be mentioned. Ellipsis accounts for the omission of "the" in "each incounter other." The use of ornamental words is also apparent. Here they are place names, italicized to make them stand out: *Agean, Ionian, Assirian Carras*. These devices complement the effect of the syntax in distancing the verse from speech.[31]

Tamburlaine is the most sonorous of Marlowe's plays and also the one that comes closest to epic. In fact, it seems more epic than most other serious plays in blank verse because its intensity is sustained. The result is often grand but becomes, after a time, predictable. This is the play's greatest fault if compared with another play that makes an explicit bid for epic elevation—Shakespeare's *Henry V.* In Shakespeare's play the moments of epic intensity are brilliantly alternated with scenes devoted to the practical affairs of state and comic horseplay. Henry is given to ringing speeches, but he also has a long passage in prose when he walks disguised among his troops on the night before Agincourt.

In spite of the one-dimensional quality of *Tamburlaine*, the groundlings were transported by its verse, and well they might have been. Nothing quite like the mighty line had been heard before on the English stage. At times—and these times are easy to identify—the mighty line is more sound than content. In the very first scene of *Tamburlaine*, for example, Marlowe pulls out the stops in a speech by Ortygius:

> And in assurance of desir'd successe,
> We here doo crowne thee Monarch of the East,
> Emperour of *Asia,* and of *Persea,*
> Great Lord of *Medea* and *Armenia:*
> Duke of *Assiria* and *Albania,*
> *Mesopotamia* and of *Parthia,*
> East *India* and the late discovered Isles,
> Chiefe Lord of all the wide vast *Euxine* sea. . . . [32]

These lines can hardly be considered speech. They amount to a list of ornamental words. They ask to be recited, like lines from an epic, and recitation is undoubtedly the proper way to deliver them. In addition to exotic vocabulary and strong assonance, five of the eight lines use elisions at the caesuras that contrast with nonelided double vowels with stress on the second vowel at the ends of four of the lines. Presumably, the elisions are invoked for syllable count but not pronounced. Clearly, Marlowe is enjoying language-play here, and just as clearly, because the language is making its own music, the actorly quality is diminished. As John Russell Brown, otherwise a defender of Marlowe's dramatic sense, remarks, "The most obvious demand that Marlowe makes upon his actors is to speak grandiloquent poetry."[33]

There is another side to the coin. Even the Ortygius speech is divided into a series of short grammatical units that make it easy to recite, and to that extent it is adapted to stage performance.

Often Marlowe's line has strong actorly qualities. Here, for example, is a famous moment in the play—Tamburlaine's grandiloquent self-justification in act 1. He has just captured a convoy transporting Zenocrate, daughter of the sultan of Egypt, to the prince of Araby. Smitten with love for her, he asks whether she is betrothed. She replies, and he answers:

> Zen.: I am (my Lord) for so you do import.
> Tam.: I am a Lord, for so my deeds shall proove,
>   And yet a shepheard by my Parentage:
>   But Lady, this fair face and heavenly hew,
>   Must grace the bed that conquers *Asia:*
>   And meanes to be a terrour to the world,
>   Measuring the limits of his Emperie
>   By East and west, as *Phoebus* doth his course:
>   Lie here ye weedes, that I disdaine to weare,
>   This compleat armor, and this curtle-axe
>   Are adjuncts more beseeming *Tamburlaine*.[34]

The lines are typical of the elevated verse of the play as a whole. They seem to be epic. The rhythm is pronounced and powerful. The vocabulary is ornamented with polysyllables and strange words ("Parentage," "Emperie," "*Phoebus*").

However, if this passage is contrasted with the passage from *Pharsalia*—or even with the speech just quoted from scene 1—significant differences emerge. In the first place, in spite of the sprinkling of ornamental words, the vocabulary is pretty much standard, and there are no obtrusive language games going on in the versification. The word order in *Pharsalia* is generally artificial; here it is natural and the sentence structure is loose. Like normal English conversation, Tamburlaine's announcement moves forward by addition of later elements to earlier ones (parataxis): "I am a Lord . . . *and* yet a shepheard"; "the bed that conquers . . . *and* meanes." The natural syntax is complemented by a prosody that is simple in comparison with the prosody of the *Tamburlaine* passage quoted earlier.

If understood as accentual meter, Tamburlaine's speech seems to begin with an inversion. The word "I" seems to ask for stress in the first line. If this intonation is accepted, it has the effect of making "I" especially prominent and thus suggesting that the cause of the speech is the egotism of the speaker. This is appropriate and actorly. However, for other reasons—also actorly—to be discussed shortly, the stress is probably on "am."

In general the key words in these lines have what Halle and Keyser call stress maximum,[35] for example, "Lord", "shep-[heard]," "La-[dy]," "grace," "con-[quers]," "Mea-[suring]," and "Em-[perie]." Syllable count is observed; syncope is used twice ("heavenly," "measuring"). "Compleat" (l. 10) creates problems in an accentual scansion but none if one understands the lines as syllabic verse. Coordination of prosody with syntax is evident in the coincidence of caesuras with phrase boundaries and the tendency of the lines to be stopped by punctuation. These strategies aid the speaking voice as it attempts to delimit segments of meaning for auditors. Other syllabic qualities are evident in the recurrence of lyric caesura (ll. 3, 4, 7, 10, 11), in the irregularity of many lines if judged in terms of accentual meter (ll. 4, 7, 10), and in the tendency of a syntactical rhythm of from two to four heavy accents per line to predominate. Of special interest is the alternation of trisyllabic end-words with a promoted last syllable (ll. 3, 5, 7, 11) with monosyllables (ll. 2, 4, 6, 8, 9, 10), a strategy recalling the French fondness for alternation of terminal rhyme forms.

Coincidence of pauses with phrase boundaries and lack of complex periodic structure make the lines easy to speak in a way that is clear to an audience. However, the regularity works against the actorly quality of the lines by encouraging the actor to recite rather than speak. When recited (rather than spoken), the verse sounds like heroic verse, even though it is different in structure and technique from Marlowe's heroic verse. Undoubtedly actors recited it and audiences responded to the recitation with enthusiasm. It is simplification of speech, a first effort rather than a fully developed dramatic medium. This is how Marlowe himself must have understood it, because after the second part of *Tamburlaine*—and in spite of the popularity of the mighty line—his dialogue became more like speech.

Even in the passage quoted, however, there are striking actorly effects. In writing it, Marlowe practiced visualization. It assumes a stage filled with Tamburlaine's henchmen in exotic dress and flushed with their victory over Zenocrate's convoy. The spoils of the convoy are displayed on the stage. The two dominant figures are Tamburlaine and Zenocrate. The henchmen crowd around as their leader speaks. They certainly gesture; probably they also murmur approval from time to time. The speech is astonishingly bold. It is an invitation to Zenocrate to become Tamburlaine's empress. Zenocrate is dressed in the finery of an Oriental princess. Tamburlaine is dressed meanly. When Zenocrate first sees him, she exclaims, "Ah Shepheard, pity my distressed plight, / (If as thou seem'st, thou art so meane a man)."

When he asks whether she is betrothed, she replies, "I am (my Lord)." He repeats the words: "I am a Lord." The repetition depends for its effect on interaction between the two speakers. It also suggests how the words "I am" should be stressed. The stress should fall on "am" because the statement is affirmative. This intonation assumes (and projects) a specific set of causes for the exchange. Zenocrate has used the term "my Lord" in spite of the fact that her captor is not much more than an outlaw and his lowly status is evident from his dress. She is trying to ingratiate herself. Tamburlaine interprets her reply literally. The stress on "am" conveys a meaning something like "Yes, you are right. I am, indeed, a Lord, even though I may not look like one." The next clause completes the idea: "I will soon prove so by my deeds."

Tamburlaine's first two lines are spoken in a defiant manner. But he wishes to marry Zenocrate. The next two lines are therefore gentler. Perhaps he stops, gazes at her admiringly, and touches her dress. Whatever he does, a change of some sort is announced by his use of a disjunction ("But") followed by direct address: "But Lady. . . ." Now he outlines his plans. His lines are ornamented by hyperbole, but they are not complex. Because the sentence structure is loose, they move ahead in simple units with regular pauses for breathing.

The speech turns again when Tamburlaine comments on his costume. Perhaps while he speaks, he continues to touch Zenocrate's splendid gown. At any rate, he suddenly says, "Lie here ye weedes" and throws his shepherd's robe to the ground. In the next line he evidently displays "this compleat armor, and this curtle-axe." Where do they come from? Either he has been wearing them under the shepherd's robe or he has picked them from the booty of the convoy. If the latter, he begins to put them on as he speaks. Probably when he says his name again, he is fully dressed in a warrior's costume.

The dialogue is actorly in the fullest sense of the word. However it is worked out, it requires the creation of several causes to be intelligible.[36] The causes include prior speech (Zenocrate's "I am [my Lord]"), costume (the shepherd's robe; the base appearance of the entire band), character (egotism, love), gestures (pointing), participation of nonspeaking characters (the henchmen), stage props (the booty), and activity (changing costume). Note that the causes arise from the level of *praxis*—the interplay of event and motive. They must be deduced from the script, but in performance, the speeches seem to be their effects, not their source. At least in this passage, the text is truly oriented toward its performance.

Additional actorly features can easily be imagined. Zenocrate cannot stand woodenly by while Tamburlaine makes the amazing announcement that she is to "grace [his] bed." How should she react? Does Tamburlaine wait until the words "Lie here . . ." to take off the shepherd's robe, or does he begin to disrobe early in the speech, using the removal of his robes as a cause of interruptions in the speech? The questions need not be answered here. The speech suggests all of them and requires that several be answered by anyone who plans to stage the scene.

Perhaps the most striking feature of Marlowe's meteoric dramatic career is the rapidity with which he moved away from the quasi-heroic speech of *Tamburlaine*.[37] "Marlovian" passages can be found in all of his plays, but they become less frequent. Emphasis changes from grandiloquent language to complex action in *Edward II* (1591), *The Jew of Malta*, and *The Massacre at Paris* (both 1591–92?). As the action becomes more complex, the dialogue becomes less ornamental. If current theories of dating are correct, Marlowe had already moved decisively toward dramatic speech by the writing of *Doctor Faustus* (1588–89). In fact, the final soliloquy in *Faustus* is probably Marlowe's supreme dramatic achievement. It is, by the same token, his least "Marlovian" and most actorly extended speech. It goes in and out of blank verse. When it is spoken in an actorly manner, the verse rhythms all but disappear.

The speech requires intensive study by the actor of physical gesture and blocking. A few props would be useful: a painting of the Crucifixion, an astrolabe, several heavy books, a glass of water. The words should be spoken slowly—how slowly?—with frequent gestures. The speech is brilliantly punctuated by the striking of the clock. At the end there is thunder, and devils appear. Do they come from a hell-mouth? Although they have no stage directions, they are active. The "Schollers" who enter Faustus's study after his death find his limbs "torne assunder" and "mangled." Although his speech does not reveal this fact, the scene must end with a horrible visual effect: dismemberment. Does it occur onstage? The "Schollers" also speak of hearing shrieks. Presumably while the dismemberment is happening Faustus is screaming in agony. Do the screams begin with Faustus's speech, "My God, my God . . ."? Or are they symbolized by the single innocent-looking "ah" in the last line? Or are they to be improvised? The text allows any of these enactments.

One is tempted to discuss the actorly qualities of the speech in detail. If the preceding analysis has been effective, however, they will be evident without further discussion:[38]

> The Stars move still, Time runs, the Clocke will strike,
> The devill will come, and *Faustus* must be damn'd.
> O, I'le leape up to my God: who puls me downe?
> See see where Christs bloud streames in the firmament,
> One drop would save my soule, halfe a drop, ah my Christ.
> Rend not my heart, for naming of my Christ,
> Yet will I call on him: O spare me *Lucifer*.
> Where is it now? 'tis gone. And see where God
> Stretcheth out his Arme, and bends his irefull Browes. . . .
>   [*The Watch strikes*]
> Ah, halfe the houre is past: 'twill all be past anone:
> O God. . . .
> Ah *Pythagoras Metemsycosis;* were that true,
> This soule should flie from me, and I be chang'd
> Unto some brutish beast. . . .
>   [*The clocke striketh twelve.*]
> It strikes, it strikes; now, body, turne to aire,
> Or *Lucifer* will beare thee quicke to hell.
> O soule be chang'd into little water drops,
> And fall into the Ocean, ne're be found.
>   [*Thunder and enter the devils*]
> My God, my God, looke not so fierce on me;
> Adders and serpents, let me breathe a while:
> Ugly hell gape not; come not, *Lucifer,*
> I'le burne my bookes; ah *Mephistophilis.*   [*Exeunt with him*]

KYD AND SHAKESPEARE

The blank verse of *The Spanish Tragedy* (1586?) has been overshadowed by the mighty line of *Tamburlaine*. It is different in kind, and the difference is instructive. The ghost of Andrea, who opens the play, has stepped directly out of Seneca, and the language used in the ghost's soliloquy is reminiscent of the soliloquy of Tantalus on the horrors of hell that begins Seneca's *Thyestes:*

> The left hand path, declining fearefully,
> Was ready dounfall to the deepest hell,
> Where bloudie furies shake their whips of steele,
> And poore *Ixion* turnes an endles wheele;

> Where usurers are choakt with melting golde,
> And wantons are imbraste with ouglie Snakes,
> And murderers grone with never killing wounds. [39]

Seneca (and Jasper Heywood) provide a modicum of actorly tension for the first speech of Tantalus in *Thyestes* by having the Fury Megaera drive him on stage and then menace him with her whips and serpents while he speaks. Kyd's stage directions call for "Revenge" to accompany Andrea's ghost, but no use is made of the character, and its presence is irrelevant. Andrea's opening soliloquy is exposition pure and simple. The syntax is also simple. Kyd will have none of Heywood's Latinate strategies. Probably this reflects the fact that Kyd wrote for the stage. His verse is direct, easily spoken, and easily understood. Its spectacular effects come from imagery and allusion. Rhythmically, it is a somewhat improved version of the verse of *Gorboduc*.

Kyd also makes frequent use of rapid give-and-take dialogue with ritualistic qualities underscored by repetition, parallelism, and related figures. The following exchange is typical. It is formal, but an actorly quality is introduced by the fact that Balthazar and Lorenzo are eavesdropping and make brutal comments that are inaudible to Horatio and Bel-Imperia:

> Bel-Imperia: Why stands *Horatio* speecheles all this while?
> Horatio: The lesse I speak, the more I meditate.
> Bel.: But whereon doost thou chiefly meditate?
> Hor.: On dangers past, and pleasures to ensue.
> Balthazar: On pleasures past, and dangers to ensue.
> Bel.: What dangers and what pleasures doost thou mean?
> Hor.: Dangers of warre, and pleasures of our love.
> Lorenzo: Dangers of death, but pleasures none at all.
> Bel: Let dangers goe, thy warre shall be with me. . . . [40]

The exchange obviously does not imitate Seneca's use of aphorisms, but its rhetoric makes it into a verbal ballet much like Seneca's give-and-take dialogue, heavily dependent on parallelism, antithesis, and word repetition at the beginning of clauses (anaphora). One can imagine an actorly performance of the lines, but it would be working against their style. The chief actorly element is the powerful dramatic irony, quite Senecan in flavor, created by the comments of Balthazar and Lorenzo. The lovers are doomed even as they confess their love. The passage recalls Thyestes attempting to enjoy his banquet even while the audience (or auditors) understands that his children have been murdered and he is eating their flesh.

When Kyd moves from dialogue to formal lament, the regularity of the rhythm, the end-stopping of the lines, and the use of exclamation, repetition, and parallelism recall *Gorboduc:*

> O eis, no eis but fountains fraught with teares;
> O life, no life but lively fourme of death;
> O world, no world, but masse of publique wrongs,
> Confusde and filde with murder and misdeeds.
> O sacred heavens if this unhallowed deed,
> If this inhumane and barberous attempt,
> If this incomparable murder thus
> Of mine, but now no more my sonne,
> Shall unreveald and unrevenged passe,
> How should we tearme your dealings to be just,
> If you unjustly deale with those, that in your justice trust.[41]

Even this passage is not, however, without interest. Its multiple figures of diction and its syntax are neatly coordinated to the line unit (all but one line end with punctuation). The whole is topped off with a fourteen-syllable line linked to its decasyllabic predecessor by rhyme.

In one important respect, Kyd rejects the lesson provided by Sackville and Norton. The longer speeches in *Gorboduc* are formal orations. Kyd has many soliloquies, laments, descriptions, and the like, but his verse is not "speech" in the sense of being oratory. Its virtue is that it is a means rather than an end.

The norms of dramatic speech are determined by the ability of an audience to understand it when it is spoken by actors. This ability is extremely variable. Drama is a code, and as long as the code is shared by actors and audience, almost any stylistic norm, from kabuki to Stanislavski, will work. Opera and musical comedy show how liberal the code can be for the modern theater.

In the 1560s the code included fourteeners. They were accepted as an adequate representation of natural speech. By 1590 the code had changed. Blank verse had become standard, and Kyd and Marlowe define the two paths blank verse could take. Presumably Kyd employs it because it is closer to speech than the fourteener. His verse is often ornamental, but its thrust is toward becoming a medium for dialogue. In *Tamburlaine* Marlowe defines an alternative—a verse that creates excitement because it is verse. Quite often, the verse of *Tamburlaine* is as actorly as the verse of *The Spanish Tragedy*. It is, however, oriented in a direction that points away from drama rather than toward it, and Marlowe himself adopted a different style after the second part of *Tamburlaine*.

The distinction between the two styles is significant for Shakespeare. It used to be assumed that *Edward II* preceded the Henry VI plays and that Marlowe popularized the history play. Today there is agreement that the Henry VI plays were probably written before *Edward II* and that Shakespeare may have been the prime influence in popularizing historical drama. As F. P. Wilson remarked in a review of the subject in 1953, "My conclusion is, though I am frightened at my own temerity in saying so, that for all we know there were no popular plays on English history before the Armada and that Shakespeare may have been the first to write one."[42] This does not mean Shakespeare learned nothing from Marlowe—he obviously learned a great deal. It merely means lines of influence are more complicated than they once appeared to be.

The early Shakespeare is fully as mesmerized by the delights of language as the Marlowe of *Tamburlaine*. If Wilson is correct, he was more fascinated than Marlowe with rhetorical figures and word games.[43] Moreover, the early plays abound in rhymed verse (e.g., *A Midsummer Night's Dream, Romeo and Juliet*), in set speeches using formal rhetorical patterns (*Richard III*), in lurid Ovidian and Senecan descriptions (*Titus Andronicus*), in laments (*Richard III, Richard II*), and in passages where the poetry is as noticeable as the action being presented (*Richard II*).

Shakespeare gradually lost interest in showy poetry. In the mature plays the norm is closer to natural speech. It is because this norm is so clearly established that the moments when the norm is transcended are so impressive. In *Hamlet* Shakespeare calls attention to the dialogue norm by writing passages that contrast strikingly with it. The "play within the play" is shown by its dumb show to be archaic. Accordingly, it is written in stiff decasyllabic couplets, which are probably as close as Shakespeare dared come to the fourteeners of the older drama except in overtly comic episodes like the performance of *Pyramus and Thisby* in *A Midsummer Night's Dream*. The player's speech about the death of Priam and Hecuba is another matter. It is old-fashioned but not archaic. It is written in a regular, end-stopped blank verse with artificial constructions a little reminiscent of Surrey's *Aeneid*. Both the "play within the play" and the player's speech stand out because they are so noticeably different from the *Hamlet* norm.[44]

The language of Shakespeare's mature drama is neither poetic nor prosy. It is written with a deep sense of the way it will be used by the actors who perform it. That is to say, it is written with an understanding, sharpened by years of involvement in the theater, of the causes that give rise to it. It reveals an awareness that it will not be recited but will be modulated by specific voice patterns of stress, pitch, duration, rhythm, gradation, and silence, and will be given causes by gesture, body orientation, character interaction, stage props, costume, and the like. It is wonderfully plastic. It invites explorations of its causes without imposing a solution on the actor.

No one would deny that Shakespeare wrote supremely beautiful and melodic passages. Obviously he did. In the mature plays these passages coincide with significant dramatic moments, often of great emotional intensity, like the moment when Perdita is named queen of the sheep-shearing festival in *The Winter's Tale* or the moment when Prospero abandons his magic in *The Tempest*. Even normally prosy characters like Enobarbus and Caliban can rise to exquisite poetry when deeply moved. The melody, in other words, is, in this case, an objectification of elements inherent in the action of the play and not ornamental. A fine example is provided by what G. Wilson Knight first called "the Othello music." The musicality of Othello's speech at the beginning of the play is correlative to the harmonies of his soul; the disintegration of the melody in the later acts is correlative to the "chaos" that descends on him when he begins to suspect Desdemona.

Sometimes the Shakespearean actor has the option of stressing or suppressing verbal melody according to his or her interpretation of the character. For example, Macbeth's "Tomorrow and tomorrow and tomorrow" can be richly and darkly musical, or it can be fragmented and devoid of melody—an objectification of the emptiness of despair. Sometimes Shakespeare's speeches seem intentionally lacking in melody. "To be or not to be" asks the audience to share in a reasoning process. The meaning constitutes the poetry, and the verse is almost transparent. And sometimes, of course, the verse is swallowed by tumultuous events. Antony's "Friends, Romans, countrymen, lend me your ears" is not spoken as a continuous line. The first word is shouted to a noisy and disrespectful crowd. It is answered by more noise, so after a pause Antony tries again. Perhaps things settle down a little, but another pause and another appeal is necessary. Then, after another pause, the final appeal is made. Probably by this time, the crowd is mostly silent, although one can imagine a few jeers and catcalls even when Antony has begun the oration proper.

Whether melody is emphasized or suppressed, the primary emphasis of Shakespeare's mature dialogue is on actorly qualities that become evident only when it is considered in relation to performance. In this sense it is "like speech" and also "like prose." Its success depends on its construction. A Shakespearean prosody must recognize this fact. If it seeks a basis in tradition, the phrase orientation of romance prosody is a good beginning, but it is only a beginning. Shakespeare and his contemporaries had learned far more about dramatic verse from writing it than is dreamed of in the treatises of second rhetoric and the theories of dramatic verse of the Italian Cinquecento.

Verse and Memory

A final question. If renaissance dramatists valued blank verse because of its conversational quality, why were they reluctant to use prose? Dramatic dialogue begins in England with the chanted dialogue of Latin liturgical drama. It changes into complex rhyming stanzas in the Corpus Christi plays, and into cantilevered verse and fourteeners in the mid-sixteenth century. Cantilevered verse gives way to prose for comedy beginning with George Gascoigne's *Supposes* (1567) and fourteeners to blank verse for tragedy beginning with *Gorboduc* (1561). By the 1590s prose is being used for history plays along with blank verse, and it alternates with blank verse in Shakespeare's histories.

There, however, the movement toward simplification of the medium of dramatic speech stops. In the seventeenth century, in fact, the movement is reversed. Seventeenth-century playwrights begin writing for readers as much as for performance. When they do so, they write verse that reads well, whether or not it has actorly qualities. During the Restoration, a new set of conditions resulted in the use of heroic couplets for serious drama. Heroic plays died a merciful death before the end of the seventeenth century. Nathaniel Lee's *Rival Queens*, in blank verse, appeared in March 1677, and Dryden's *All for Love* a few months later, but the first English tragedy in prose—George Lillo's *London Merchant*—was not written until 1731. Not until the later nineteenth century did prose become the preferred vehicle for serious drama.

The shift from chanted dialogue to prose is part of a larger movement. It is a movement from ritual to naturalistic expression. Verse and stylized acting are signs that the English theatre continued to be influenced, at least until the 1590s, by the ritual traditions of medieval drama. Between *Tamburlaine* and the first decade of the seventeenth century there seems to have been a move toward naturalism. The naturalistic tendency was encouraged by the Aristotelian definition of poetry as the imitation of an action, rather than as language shaped into verse. Some of the naturalistic bias comes out in the criticism that we have already reviewed of "bombast" in dramatic dialogue. On the other hand, the naturalistic bias remained tentative. The continuing use of verse for upper-class characters and prose for lower-class characters, and the continued presence of explicitly lyrical passages in Shakespeare and the Jacobean dramatists show that the older tradition continued to be influential long after the conditions that created it had ceased to be operative.

Renaissance dramatists, however, probably had a practical as well as an aesthetic reason for retaining blank verse. A recurrent explanation of the value of verse from the Greeks to Wordsworth's "Preface" to *Lyrical Ballads* is that it is easy to memorize.[45] The explanation is correct. Verse *is* easier to memorize than prose. The point has relevance for drama. Renaissance actors had to commit a staggering number of lines to memory. Not only did they frequently play double or triple roles in a single play, they had to perform in more than one play in the course of a single week.

The actors must have needed all the aids to memory they could get. If, by 1600, the norm for acting was speech rather than recitation, one significant motive for retaining verse must have been that it is easier to memorize than prose. It follows that actors share responsibility with the dramatic tradition, the bombast-loving groundlings, and readers of play quartos for the retention of blank verse in serious drama until the closing of the theatres in 1642. Blank verse survived at least partly because it is easy to memorize and provides a ready basis for faking when memory falters.

CHAPTER XI

True Musical Delight

MUSIC AND MUSE

To T. S. Eliot the style of *Paradise Lost* was its chief liability. In his essay on Christopher Marlowe he complains about the "Chinese Wall of Milton," that crosses the English poetic landscape.[1] He means that Milton's verse is as remote as possible from ordinary speech and therefore a source of corruption of poetic taste. After Milton, "blank verse suffered not only arrest but retrogression."

Eliot's criticism derives from Ezra Pound's emphasis on "phanopoeia"—the visual element of poetry—which is, in turn, shaped by Ernest Fenollosa's theory of Chinese poetry as the visual concretion of emotion through ideographs.[2] Since Milton was blind, try as he might (so the theory goes) he could not produce the precise visual images that poetry requires. Therefore he turned from phanopoeia to melopoeia—from image to sound, and from objectivity to music. To create that music he used a vocabulary remote from normal speech, rich in polysyllables and exotic names.[3] The words are set like jewels in sentences that are only barely English because of their richly Latinate construction.

As Eliot knew, one of the basic sources of Milton's style is Vergil, but Vergil is not the most immediate influence. Native English poetry—especially the poetry of Spenser—is also a factor. The native influence was encouraged by Alexander Gil, who taught Milton in grammar school and who devoted an important section of his *Logonomia Anglica* to the prosody of English renaissance poets. The most direct influence on Milton's style, however, is probably Italian. Milton learned about the freedom of unrhymed verse and its musical qualities and ability to project *enargia* from Italian discussions of *versi sciolti*, and Italian experiments in the form helped him relate theory to practice. Torquato Tasso's *Discorsi del poema eroico* was an important source of theory, and the *versi sciolti* of Annibale Caro's translation of the *Aeneid* and Torquato Tasso's *Le Sette giornate del mondo creato* were especially instructive examples.[4] Milton's syllabism—especially his handling of metaplasm—and his construction follow leads provided by Italian models.

Whatever the immediate sources of Milton's style, Eliot is right about its emphasis on musical effects. The problem is to set his insight in the proper context. In the first place, contrary to Eliot, Milton's poetry is filled with visual images. As Roland Frye has demonstrated, many of them are identical with images made into paintings by renaissance artists,[5] while others, perhaps the more interesting group, attempt through the technique of accommodation to suggest truths impossible to present literally because they transcend human understanding. In the second place, Eliot's concern with the tonalities of everyday speech causes him to ignore the tradition associating poetry and music. As noted at the beginning of the present study, the tradition is older than the earliest treatises on the *ars metrica*, and it runs through the history of thought about prosody. It was still influential in the seventeenth century, although interest was divided between practical musical concerns and Neoplatonic symbolism of the sort that is the basis of Sir John Davies's *Orchestra* (1596).[6]

We thus return to an idea that is central to the *ars metrica*—namely, that poetry is constitutive rather than imitative. The music of each meter allows the poet to "body forth" images of the real that would otherwise be inexpressible. This idea is perhaps more significant for Milton than for any earlier English poet, and it recurs in ever-changing ways throughout *Paradise Lost* precisely because Milton seeks to express "Things unattempted yet in Prose or Rhyme." Milton's phrase does not refer to ideas and themes. The ideas and themes of *Paradise Lost* were anything but "unattempted" in the seventeenth century. What earlier authors had *not* achieved, in Milton's opinion—and what he dared attempt—was a bodying forth of ideas and themes inexpressible through the music of his heroic verse.

Milton recognized that he could not himself make them live. As a radical Protestant dependent on the guidance of the Holy Spirit and as a poet familiar with the doctrine of inspiration, he knew that he could only succeed if assisted by a heavenly Muse. His Muse is an aspect of the Holy Spirit and a symbol of the constitutive aspect of poetry, the fact that poetry in some sense makes itself. The Muse takes Milton to the pit of hell, where he finds "darkness visible," and to the pinnacle of heaven, where he encounters an unimaginable brightness—"bright effluence of bright essence increate." She visits him in nightly dreams, filling his mind with her music, so that his "numbers" seem "voluntary" and flow "unpremeditated" while he sleeps. The music is "natural" in the sense intended by Eustache Deschamps in *L'Art de dictier.*

Whatever Milton's references to the Muse might mean to a psychoanalyst or to a theologian, they have a very specific meaning in relation to the history of poetry. Milton has heard the music of epic. He commands the Muse to sing, and *Paradise Lost* is the song that follows. Its facade of images is sustained by—in a way, it crystallizes out of—the music, which is instinctive, coming from beyond him like the song of a bird. In his blindness, he is like a nightingale that "Sings darkling, and in shadiest Covert hid / Tunes her nocturnal note." Like Orpheus, the archetypal musician-poet, he is "Taught by the heav'nly Muse to venture down / The dark descent, and up to reascend." Also like Orpheus, he has "fall'n on evil dayes." The threat appears in the poem as a threat to its music, and he prays the Muse to "drive far off the barbarous dissonance" of those unsympathetic to his art.

Eliot was not primarily interested in the relations between music and poetry or, for that matter, in Milton. He was distressed by the banalities that passed for poetry in the early twentieth century, and he traced them to imitations of Milton by poets who understood only Milton's surface techniques.[7] He believed that if poetry was once again to have a living relation to culture, Milton's influence had to be opposed, and other poets—especially Donne and the Jacobean dramatists, who aimed in their poetry at the tonalities of everyday speech—had to be set up in Milton's place. The distinction is the old one between heroic and dramatic verse. Although Eliot chose to emphasize "mimetic" and "biotic" poetry and "speech," he was as committed as Milton to the prosodic options first defined by the *ars metrica.*

Prosody and the Irrational

By the mid-seventeenth century, in addition to the standard sources of prosodic theory, there was a philosophical discussion of prosody arising from tensions between humanism and rationalism. Milton had studied ancient prosody and was an accomplished neo-Latin poet. He was familiar with Horace's *Ars poetica* and with later classical treatments of poetry. He had also read Aristotle's *Poetics* and (at least) the sixteenth-century treatises of Minturno and Castelvetro, which he mentions in "Of Education." He touches on the moral purification theory of catharsis in his comments on poetry in *The Reason of Church Government*, and he outlines the purgation theory in some detail in the preface to *Samson Agonistes*.[8]

Chapter 24 of the *Poetics* discusses heroic prosody.[9] It links this comment to the fact that epic is more hospitable than tragedy to "the irrational" (*to alogon*). The reason for this is that epic is partly narrated. Because in narration, events are described—thus distanced from the reader—rather than visibly enacted, narrative has greater freedom than epic to present divine agents and natural impossibilities, all of which are "irrational" in the sense of being outside the bounds of reason and nature. There is, however, always a danger that the reader will find the irrational materials absurd (*atopos*) rather than imposing. Here, the style of epic complements the effect of its narrative form. Chapter 24 ends with an example of how style can make the irrational acceptable: "If the poet takes [an irrational] plot . . . the situation is also absurd. It is clear that the improbable elements (*aloga*) in the *Odyssey* concerning the casting away of Odysseus would not have been bearable if a poor poet had written them. Here the poet conceals the absurdity by making it pleasing through his other skillful techniques."[10]

Spenser's *The Faerie Queene* and Shakespeare's *The Tempest* show that at least two major renaissance artists, one of them a dramatist, felt quite at home with the irrational and not inclined to apologize for it. However, by the mid-seventeenth century, the irrational was beginning to seem not only irrational but unscientific and unnatural as well. In short, it was beginning to seem absurd. Heroic poetry was especially vulnerable to the rationalist critique because it is committed by its nature to impossibilities and irrationalities and must present them with high seriousness. The age responded more readily to comic deconstructions of the heroic like *Hudibras* and *Mac Flecknoe* and *Absalom and Achitophel*, and to operatic fantasies like Purcell's *Dido and Aeneas*, which make no claim whatever on belief.

Aristotle's observation that style can make the irrational acceptable suggests a way of reconciling the opposition between the subject matter demanded by epic and the adherence to nature demanded by rationalism. The style of *Paradise Lost* did, in fact, make the poem palatable for many readers of the seventeenth and eighteenth centuries and can still do this for many normally skeptical twentieth-century readers. Milton's style should not, however, be considered a clever trick to divert attention from what would otherwise be considered absurdities. In *Paradise Lost* "the irrational" is not accidental but essential. The impossibilities of the poem are also its fundamental truths. To omit them would be to lie. In the context of Milton's poetics, the device that makes the irrational acceptable is thus the device that allows truth to be bodied forth in ways that can be accepted as truthful rather than absurd. Milton admits in the invocation to book 9 that he will succeed only "If answerable style I can obtain / Of my Celestial patroness, who . . . inspires / Easy my unpremeditated Verse."

Milton's search for "answerable style" began with his decision to use blank verse. Even this decision required, however, that he go against the dominant sentiment of his age.

As we have seen, in the sixteenth century, classical purists had followed Ascham in arguing that only quantitative verse could reproduce the elevated music of epic. They had been defeated, and by the beginning of the seventeenth century, the real debate was between advocates of complex vernacular forms derived from French or Italian romance tradition—the Spenserians—and advocates of simple rhymed forms including the heroic couplet and Horatian lyrics of the sort favored by the tribe of Ben Jonson. In spite of Davenant's efforts on behalf of the quatrain, the age chose couplets. Not only did couplets become standard for serious narrative and verse satire, they would also become standard for the heroic play.

Samuel Daniel argues that although linguistic change may have caused the loss of one musical element in the vernacular languages—precise control of time—rhyme is a compensating gain and creates its own kind of music. He adds that poetry is a matter of convention in any age. Like Varro explaining the basis of *Latinitas,* he remarks that custom takes precedence over theory: "All verse is but a frame of wordes confined within certaine measure. . . . Which frame of words consisting of *Rithmus* and *Metrum,* Number or measure, are disposed in divers fashions, according to the humour of the Composer and the set of the time." [11]

Powerful support for Daniel's position came from rationalism itself. The rationalists approved of simple rather than complicated rhyme schemes, and they tended to downplay the value of verbal music. They also advocated natural order, simple images, and standard vocabulary. As noted in chapter 9, William Davenant's preface to *Gon-*

dibert provides a clear statement of the rationalist position. Davenant believes Spenser's choice of stanza was "unhappy" because that stanza seeks "the Musick of words." This sort of music interferes with sense. The parallel to T. S. Eliot's criticism of Milton is striking. Because a complex vocabulary also interferes with sense, Davenant also rejects speech "above the vulgar dialect" and highly figured language—"what are commonly called *Conceits*."[12]

The emphasis on simplicity is correlative to suspicion of the irrational. Davenant's object is not to body forth realities that would otherwise be inexpressible but to present what is already known: "To bring Truth, too often absent, home to mens bosoms . . . by representing Nature, though not in an affected, yet in an unusuall dress."[13] We are close, here, to the idea that the best poetry is "what oft was thought but ne'er so well express'd."

It is a valid question whether the poets anticipated the critics or vice versa. Critical approval of the norm of nature is evident as early as the concluding section of Sidney's *Apology for Poetry*, in which Sidney attacks the "Curtizan-like painted affectation" and "farre fette words" and absurd "similitudes" and "conceits" of English poets and calls for a more restrained poetic diction.[14] Ben Jonson sympathized with this trend, and in his criticism, he consistently sides with reason and nature. It is indicative of his rationalist mind-set that he told William Drummond "that he wrote all of his [verse] first in prose" and "that verses stood by sense without either colours or accent."[15]

Bacon is not merely suspicious of conceits; he despises poetry because in it, reason gives way to fantasy and nature to wish-fulfillment. The culprit is imagination, which, says Bacon, creates absurdities by combining in poetic images things never combined in nature: "Beeing not tyed to the Lawes of Matter, [poetry] may at pleasure joyne that which Nature hath severed, & sever that which Nature hath joyned, and so make unlawfull Matches & divorses of things."[16] The same attitude is evident in Thomas Sprat's *History of the Royal Society*, which lauds the efforts of disciples of reason "to reject all amplifications, digressions, and swellings of style; to return back to the primitive purity and shortness, when men deliver'd so many *things* almost in an equal number of *words*."[17]

One way to solve the problem of imaginative literature is to relegate it to the status of trivial but harmless entertainment having no relation to truth. In canto 3 of *L'Art poétique*, Boileau takes this position. To prevent the confusion of literature with truth, the poet should avoid Christian subject matter. If the supernatural is essential, it should be presented through classical or romantic myths that nobody takes seriously. Such Christian mysteries as the Virgin Birth, the Resurrection, and the miracles of the saints are mysteries precisely because they are true, or, at least, are so regarded. They should never be used in poetic fictions. The same position is expressed in rococo art in imagery that reduces classical myths to the level of decorative and colorful (and often erotic) illustrations in picture-books. This is, however, farther than most rationalists were willing to go. The common position was that of Horace's *Ars poetica*. If properly disciplined, poetry can be an instrument of instruction as well as delight.

In the rationalist view, the doctrine of inspiration is an especially fertile source of poetic error. It is one thing to invoke a Muse, but it is another entirely to take the idea seriously. Treating the invocation as a pretty convention accords with Boileau's advice to keep fiction and truth separate. In seventeenth-century England, however, even as the idea of inspiration was being attacked, it was being powerfully asserted by Protestants who sought guidance from the Holy Spirit in both their preaching and their personal lives. In other words, among the Puritans, inspiration had ceased to be a pleasant Neoplatonic conceit and was widely considered a literal truth about human experience.

Inspiration claims to come from a source higher than reason, beside which reason seems like folly or insanity. The wisdom of man, after all, is the foolishness of God, and the wisdom of God is the foolishness of man. Inspiration asserts the existence of a vital and continuous link between human experience and the invisible world. The inspired poet not only ignores the norm of nature and the rule of reason but claims to do so in the name of truth. To rationalists, such a poet is at best ridiculous and at worst a madman. Such thoughts led Thomas Hobbes to castigate the poet who "enabled to speak wisely . . . loves rather to be thought to speak by inspiration like a Bagpipe."[18]

The common term for inspiration in its religious context was "enthusiasm." In *Enthusiasmus triumphatus* (1656) Henry More argues that the inspiration claimed by Puritan ministers is not divine vision but a kind of insanity brought about by sexual excitement. It is the besetting weakness of the sort of Protestantism that makes the guidance of an Inner Light the bedrock of theology. Because this theology encourages radical individualism, it is not only irrational but also a source of political subversion. Royalists found a common ground with rationalists in their scorn for enthusiasm. The savagery of their attacks is illustrated by Jonathan Swift's satire of enthusiastic preaching in *A Tale of a Tub*.[19]

We are interested here in prosodic theory. A review of the idea of inspiration is appropriate because distrust of inspiration is an important motive for the seventeenth-century rejection of blank verse. From the rationalist point of view, rhyme has a wonderful virtue over and above its pleasing sound: it forces the poet to stop and think. In other words, it asserts the rule of reason over inspiration. Dryden concludes the *Essay of Dramatic Poesy* (1668) with the observation that rhyme is "an help to the poet's judgment, by putting bounds to a wild overflowing fancy . . . [and] a rule and line by which he keeps his building compact and even, which otherwise lawless imagination would raise either irregularly or loosely."[20] In the "Epistle Dedicatory" to *The Rival Ladies* (rev. 1694), he repeats the argument, relating it directly to the question of whether or not blank verse is a suitable poetic form: "Imagination in a poet is a faculty so wild and lawless that, like an high-ranging spaniel, it must have clogs tied to it lest it outrun the judgment. The great easiness of blank verse renders the poet too luxuriant . . . but when the difficulty of artful rhyming is interposed . . . the fancy then gives leisure to the judgment to come in."[21] Dryden's comments are an explanation in little of why the heroic couplet became the dominant poetic form of the Age of Reason.

In sustained narrative, the couplet tends to be most effective when its tendencies to closure and to neatly balanced logical patterns are suppressed by complex syntax and enjambment—a point illustrated by Chapman's couplet translation of the *Odyssey*. As Samuel Daniel recognized, a narrative in closed couplets can quickly become tedious. Conversely, when the inherent rhetoric of the closed couplet is exploited, the result tends to be witty rather than heroic. Gilbert Murray's verdict about Dryden's translation of the *Aeneid*, which aims at high seriousness, is harsh but just. The couplets of Dryden's translation, he says, exchange "for a deep and sonorous music, a thin, impetuous rattle of sound."[22] On the other hand, the versification of *Mac Flecknoe* and *Absalom and Achitophel* is brilliantly successful. In Restoration drama, the comedies, which are in prose, continue to sparkle with life, while the heroic plays, which are in couplets, often seem more than faintly ridiculous.

For all the above reasons, Restoration artists who attempted high seriousness risked being only grandiose or, to use Aristotle's term, absurd. The age invented a term for the effect of high seriousness that fails to convince—bathos, popularized by Alexander Pope in PERI BATHOS or *The Art of Sinking in Poetry*.

In sum, everything essential to the renaissance concept of epic as a divine music or Neoplatonic vision of Truth or of a divine gift was at odds with everything that seemed essential for poetry at the time *Paradise Lost* appeared. The dominant culture celebrated nature; Milton sought "things invisible to mortal sight." The culture was uncomfortable with the heroic; Milton was committed to writing of actions "not less but more heroic than the wrath of stern Achilles." The culture disapproved of poetry that mingled Christian truth with overt fiction and ridiculed the "monsters" of the poetry of an earlier age.[23] The basis of *Paradise Lost* is Christian history, and the centerpiece of book 2 is the tableau of the monsters Sin and Death. The culture celebrated the necessary and the probable; Milton made impossibilities the context within which possibilities are imagined. The culture thought imagination a source of error and inspiration a rationalization for hallucination. Milton insisted—and believed deeply—that his poem was a gift from the heavenly Muse.

Finally, the culture rejected magnificence and considered the proper object of style to be objectification of the truths of inanimate and human nature. In poetry, the best style should use a standard vocabulary, should be sparing and restrained in its figurative language, and should use rhyme to discipline the unruly tendencies of poetic imagination. Poetry that ignores these stylistic norms is not elevated but absurd or banal. This explains the otherwise odd remark by Neander in Dryden's *Essay of Dramatic Poesy* that "blank verse is . . . too low for a poem, nay more, for a paper of verses."[24]

Milton not only rejected rhyme, but he created a form that is unrivaled, even today, for the rich complexity of its syntax, its epic similes and its metaphors based on the *via negativa*, and the polysyllabic and ornamental nature of its vocabulary. To do this he turned away from the purposes associated with the couplet in the seventeenth century. In their place, he embraced the purposes associated with the heroic by Tasso and Spenser, but he did so with a vivid sense of the burden of proof that the age placed on him. It was a burden that had to be sustained more by prosody than by themes or ideas.

Aristotle's theory about the relation between style and "the irrational" suggests that if Milton's readers are caught up in the music of his poem, they may surrender their skepticism and accept, if only provisionally, the idea that a heroic vision of life is possible. This is one of the implications of the idea that poetry bodies forth otherwise inexpressible realities. However, to attempt heroic style was to risk ridicule—to be accused of enthusiasm and bathos. Milton took the risk and succeeded. Given the moment in history when he did so, his success comes close to being a miracle. As Anne Ferry remarks in *Milton's Epic Voice*, "The style itself is a miracle like the heavenly inspiration breathed into the poet. It is 'unpremeditated' not because it is unconscious, but because it is mysterious, more than human, a gift of grace. We are meant to be aware of it, to feel its intensity, its importance, its mystery, because these qualities express the poem's meanings."[25]

THE NOTE ON THE VERSE OF *PARADISE LOST*

Let us now turn from the historical tensions that helped to shape Milton's thinking about style to his own comments on his verse form. These comments are concentrated in the brief note on "The Verse" that he added to the fourth (1667 or 1668) issue of the first edition of *Paradise Lost*. Milton's publisher Samuel Simmons had requested the note because so many readers asked (as he says) "a reason of that which stumbled many . . . why the Poem Rimes not." One recalls the title page of the Day-Owen edition of Surrey's *Aeneid*, describing the poem as in "a straunge metre." Surrey's *Aeneid* was published more than a century before *Paradise Lost*. Far from being familiar to Milton's readers, however, narrative blank verse was still strange—so strange, in fact, as to be incomprehensible without explanation.

The note is brief enough to quote in full:

> The measure is *English* Heroic Verse without Rime, as that of *Homer* in *Greek*, and of *Virgil* in *Latin*; Rime being no necessary Adjunct or true Ornament of Poem or good Verse, in longer Works especially, but the Invention of a barbarous Age, to set off wretched matter and lame Metre; grac't indeed since by the use of some famous modern Poets, carried away by Custom, but much to their own vexation, hindrance, and constraint to express many things otherwise, and for the most part worse than else they would have exprest them. Not without cause therefore some both *Italian* and *Spanish* Poets of prime note have rejected Rime both in longer and shorter Works, as have also long since our best *English* Tragedies, as a thing of itself, to all judicious ears, trivial and of no true musical delight; which consists only in apt Numbers, fit quantity of Syllables, and the sense variously drawn out from one Verse into another, not in the jingling sound of like endings, a fault avoided by the learned Ancients both in Poetry and all good Oratory. This neglect then of Rime so little is to be taken for a defect, though it may seem so perhaps to vulgar Readers, that it rather is to be esteem'd an example set, the first in *English,* of ancient liberty recover'd to Heroic Poem from the troublesome and modern bondage of Riming.[26]

Milton begins with a definition that is also a manifesto: blank verse is "*English* Heroic Verse without Rime." At the end of the note he adds that it is "an example set, the first in *English*." Even if he was aware of Surrey's *Aeneid,* he might have felt he could still claim to be "first in *English*" because he is the first English poet to give formal consideration to the problem of English heroic verse in the light of ancient and modern theory. Certainly he was the first English poet to announce that the equivalence of blank verse with ancient dactylic hexameter is an established fact.

In Milton's note the dominant emphasis is on rejection of rhyme. Like Ascham, both Dryden and Milton associate rhyme with the Middle Ages. Dryden says (in the person of Neander), "When, by the inundation of the Goths and Vandals into Italy, new languages were introduced, and barbarously mingled with the Latin, of which the Italian, Spanish, French, and ours (made out of them and the Teutonic) are dialects, a new way of poesy was practiced. . . . This new way consisted in measure or number of feet and rhyme."[27] Dryden, of course, agreed with Samuel Daniel in approving of the change. And Milton, of course, agreed with Roger Ascham in disapproving the change. Like Ascham, he was contemptuous of both the religion and the learning of the Middle Ages. To him rhyme is "the Invention of a barbarous Age, to set off wretched matter and lame Metre." The point is exactly parallel to Ascham's argument in *The Scholemaster* that the corruption of language and the corruption of learning are complementary—they cannot be separated any more than thought can occur apart from words.

To reject rhyme implies more, however, than eliminating "like endings." As is evident in the case of Surrey's *Aeneid,* it is to adopt principles different from those of traditional English versification. The problem of describing exactly what principles Milton adopted has engaged a number of able critics. If one begins at the most basic level of prosody—the level of meter—his verse has both accentual and syllabic elements. The latter were first described by Robert Bridges, and although modifications have been proposed in the Bridges analysis, in the opinion of Edward Weismiller, Bridges's conclusions "have not . . . been superseded."[28] Bridges argued that Milton's line is always decasyllabic, but there are rules that allow the reduction or increase of syllable count. Bridges did not justify these rules by the ancient rules of the *ars metrica* governing metaplasm, but that work was done by George Kellog in a supplement to Bridges's analysis.[29]

Bridges also suggested, in a striking intuition that is supported by renaissance prosodic theory, that "Milton came to scan his lines in one way, and to read them in another." In this he differs from Dryden and later English poets, who took elisions as evidence for pronunciation. Here, Milton is following Italian precedent, while Dryden and his successors are following French precedent. Moreover, Milton always allows accent to fall where word stress makes it appropriate, even if this violates some abstract criterion of meter: "The intended accent in *Paradise Lost* is always given by the unmitigated accentuation of the words as Milton pronounced them."[30] The position taken here by Bridges is also supported by renaissance theory. As observed in chapter 5, John Brinsley distinguishes between a classroom reading to bring out the meter of a verse and a correct reading that brings out the rhythms inherent in the poem's construction.

Milton's verse is thus a mixture of romance and classical elements. He is as scornful as Ascham of the Gothic ignorance that allowed rhyme to prosper, and he praises the "liberty" that ancient poets achieved by resisting rhyme. In spite of this classical bias, his prosody is essentially syllabic and thus linked to the prosody of Tasso and also to that of Spenser and Chaucer. He has either forgotten the intimate historical linkage between "rhyme" and "rhythm," or he has come to regard blank verse in the Italian way, as a form that breaks decisively with medieval tradition even though it preserves some syllabic conventions.

Milton's handling of syllable count is only one part of his strategy. Several additional aspects of this strategy will be examined as we proceed. For the present, we may note that in syllabic poetry the line tends to be the fundamental unit. As F. T. Prince remarks, in syllabic poetry, "the metrical unit is . . . the decasyllabic line itself, with all its possible variations, not the five 'disyllabic feet' which are said to compose it."[31] This is true for medieval Latin verse as described by John of Garland in the *Parisiana poetria* and, in general, for French verse, but it must be qualified for classical quantitative verse and for the heavily enjambed and artfully "constructed" blank verse of Surrey's *Aeneid* and Milton's *Paradise Lost*. Milton would have learned to write in units other than the line when composing Latin verse, but he must have learned the technique of doing this in the vernacular from the Italians. Whatever the source of the technique, phrase and clause play freely against line throughout *Paradise Lost*. The devices that make this effective are familiar. They are the devices of construction. As Christopher Ricks observes in *Milton's Grand Style*, "It is his ability to harness the thrust of his syntax which sustains Milton's great argument." Both Ricks and Prince identify the devices and provide examples, so the task is unnecessary here.[32]

Milton grudgingly admits that "some famous modern Poets, carried away by Custom," have used rhyme. The word "Custom" recalls Daniel's *Defence of Ryme*. If so, Milton alludes to that work only to reject it. In his note, custom is pernicious—a habit that interferes with the perception of truth, and hence a form of "tyranny" rather than the adjustment of expression to the nature of the language. The observation that "some . . . modern Poets" use rhyme probably refers to Spenser's *Faerie Queene* and Tasso's *Gerusalemme liberata*, and perhaps to Cowley's *Davideis*, which is in couplets. It may also refer to Milton's own youthful English poetry, which is rhymed.

The comment recognizes the existence of a romance and a classical literary tradition, each incompatible with the other. Milton admired *Gerusalemme liberata* and *The Faerie Queene*, and the influence of both can be felt in many passages in *Paradise Lost*. Yet in deciding to write a regular epic in blank verse he had to reject the aesthetic that shaped these poems—to opt, as it were, for heroic elevation rather than magnificence. Dryden rejected the aesthetic of Elizabethan drama in favor of neoclassicism, and the result is a tension, almost a schizophrenia, between his critical principles and his instinctive admiration of Shakespeare. If Milton had conflicting feelings about the rejection of rhyme, there is no evidence for it in his note.

The objection to rhyme involves more than scorn for medieval poetry and scholastic philosophy. It involves Milton's deepest feelings about the purpose of *Paradise Lost*. Rhyme, he complains, is a "vexation, hindrance, and constraint to express many things otherwise, and for the most part worse than else they would have exprest them." The comment acknowledges that rhyme does what Dryden says it does: it forces the poet to think twice. To Milton, being forced to think twice impairs the poem's ability to present the communications of the heavenly Muse.

If there is one fact that is clear about his invocations, it is the sincerity of his belief that he is being guided in the process of composition by some higher power. This is what Anne Ferry calls "a gift of grace." Whether the gift is from the Holy Spirit or Urania or some subtly different power is beside the point. It is a gift Milton considers available to all those who seek it devoutly, but it is bestowed with special generosity on prophets and poets who ready themselves for it by a lifetime of self-discipline. He believes he has had direct experience of it in his own life.[33] Through this power he has had visions of "things invisible to mortal sight" and through this same power, he feels he can discover truth in Scripture, which is "not but by the Spirit understood."[34]

If the power exists, it is the source of the poem. It is beyond reason—hence "irrational" (*alogos*). If rhyme forces the poet to stop, think, and revise, it interposes a lower faculty—reason or "judgment"—between the Muse and the poem. In doing this it also forces the poet "to express many things otherwise, and for the most part worse than else [he] would have exprest them."

Milton's point had been made many times, both in Italy and in England, by poets frustrated with the arbitrary requirements imposed by rhyme and by stanza forms. Ben Jonson's "Fit of Rime against Rime" sums up their complaints, adding a wry comment on the free use of metaplasm in syllabic verse:

> Rime the rack of finest wits,
> That expresseth but by fits,
> > True Conceipt.
> Spoyling Senses of their Treasure,
> Cosening Judgement with a measure,
> > But false weight.
> Wresting words from their true calling;
> Propping Verse, for feare of falling
> > To the ground.
> Joyning Syllabes, drowning Letters,
> Fastning Vowells, as with fetters
> > They were bound![35]

A more direct expression of this idea is found in Alexander Gil's *Logonomia Anglica*, which points out that the requirements of "number" and rhyme often lead to "synchesis"—distorted word order related to hyperbaton.[36] Since Gil was Milton's teacher, his comments on prosody are of more than casual interest. The position, however, is common. In the *Observations*, Campion observes that rhyme "inforceth a man oftentimes to abjure his matter and extend a short conceit beyond all bounds of art; for in Quatorzens [i.e., sonnets], methinks, the poet handles his subject as tyranically as *Procrustes*."[37] To this it was always possible to answer with Samuel Daniel, "In an eminent spirit, whome Nature hath fitted for that mysterie, Ryme is no impediment to his conceit, but rather gives him wings to mount, but as it were beyond his power to a farre happier flight."[38] However, Milton, who hoped to soar "with no middle flight," obviously sides with Gil and Campion.

Gil carries the argument further. Rhyme may diminish rather than elevate the gravity of the work.[39] Gil observes that English tragedians have abandoned rhyme except at the end of long speeches. In their plays, number is kept but rhyme ignored: "manente numero neglectus est rythmus." He is obviously thinking of the blank verse of Shakespeare, Jonson, and their contemporaries. Milton agrees. Rhyme, he says, has been rejected in the "best *English* Tragedies." Even Samuel Daniel admits that rhyme has its limits. After arguing with commendable passion in favor of rhyme, he adds, "I must confesse that to mine owne eare those continuall cadences of couplets used in long and continued Poemes are verie tyresome and unpleasing, by reason that still, me thinks, they run on with a sound of one nature, and a kinde of certaintie which stuffs the delight rather than intertaines it."[40] Daniel prefers blank verse to couplets for sustained narrative, and, like Milton, he approves of enjambment, which is "rather gracefull then otherwise" when the subject has a violence about it that seeks to "breake thorow" the end of the line.

Rhyme distorts meaning and makes a long poem monotonous. Both effects touch the center of Milton's understanding of heroic poetry. Changes forced on the poem by the need to preserve rhyme falsify the words breathed into the poet by the Muse. In other words, they make truth into a lie.

Consideration of style leads to Milton's next topic, the music of English poetry. Rhyme was frequently said to add to the beauty of poetry by making it more musical. Following a long line of advocates of quantitative poetry, Milton takes the opposite position. Rhyme is a mechanical device created by "the jingling sound of like endings," and it is "trivial and of no true musical delight." Whether this should be taken as a general condemnation of rhyme or a rejection of rhyme only for heroic poetry is a valid question. The passage is not clear, but it seems likely that Milton is rejecting rhyme only for heroic poetry. There is no evidence that he ever repudiated his own youthful poems, which were rhymed, and he apparently enjoyed songs in rhyming stanzas throughout his life.

Milton had a grander music in mind for the heroic poem. As precedents he cites the ancients in general, certain modern Italian and

Spanish poets, and English tragedies. The allusion to Italian and Spanish poets is probably not to advocates of classical quantity like Claudio Tolomei but to advocates of blank verse or its equivalent: Giangiorgio Trissino and Torquato Tasso among the Italians, and—in all probability—Gonzalo Perez, who translated Homer into Spanish *versos sueltos* in 1550, and Juan de Jauregui, who used the same form for a Spanish translation of Tasso's *Aminta* printed in Rome in 1607.[41] Milton's English tragedians are undoubtedly Marlowe, whom he occasionally echoes, and Shakespeare, whom he praised in the sonnet he wrote for the Second Folio of 1632.

This raises the question of what, exactly, Milton means by "true musical delight." Here explanations differ. In comments on poetic theory in places other than the note on "The Verse," Milton frequently refers to music. In *Reason of Church Government,* for example, he suggests that poetry should "allay the perturbations of the mind and set the affections in right tune."[42] The reference unquestionably recalls Greek theories of the relation between harmony and the well-tempered soul. Given the political context of Milton's remark, the reference to musical catharsis in Aristotle's *Politics* (1341b37–42a17) is a likely precedent:

> We maintain further that music should be studied . . . with a view to . . . purgation [catharsis] (the word "purgation" we use at present without explanation, but when hereafter we speak of poetry we will treat the subject with more precision). . . . In listening to the performances of others we may admit the modes of action and passion also. For feelings such as pity and fear, or, again, enthusiasm, exist very strongly in some souls, and have more or less influence over all. Some persons fall into a religious frenzy, whom we have seen as a result of the sacred melodies . . . restored as though they have found healing and purgation. Those who are influenced by pity and fear, and every emotional nature, must have a like experience . . . and all are in a manner purged and their souls lightened and delighted.[43]

In addition to recognizing the power of music to allay perturbations of the mind, Milton refers in his early verse and throughout *Paradise Lost* to heavenly music—of the spheres, of angelic hymns, of the process of creation, of the heavenly Muse obeying the command to sing—and to earthly music—of the human voices of Adam and Eve in songs of thanksgiving, of choirs of angels celebrating God, of birds and the sounds of wind in the trees of Eden and water flowing. Milton's verse accompanies all of these kinds of music with the music of words measured by harmonious numbers and ornamented with figures of sound and syntax. The "true musical delight" of the poem is part of its meaning. It is a stately and elevated music created by "apt Numbers" and "fit quantity of Syllables" and would be destroyed by the "jingling sound of like endings," which are strictly man-made. T. S. Eliot was correct about Milton: whatever else he may or may not be, he is a supremely musical poet.

The phrases "apt Numbers," "fit quantity of Syllables," and "sense variously drawn out from one Verse into another" require further comment. "Apt Numbers" is clear enough. It is a syllabic concept. The degree to which Milton observed the "Numbers" of his verse is the principal subject of Robert Bridges's *Milton's Prosody*.

"Fit quantity of Syllables" is less easy to explain. Milton was steeped in classical prosody. He composed skillful Latin poems, and one of his most interesting lyrics is his translation of Horace's "Fifth Ode," "Rend'red almost word for word without Rhyme according to the Latin Measure, as near as the Language will permit." Consequently, it is impossible not to associate "fit quantity of Syllables" with Latin quantity and the effort to create English quantitative forms. Again, the musicality of verse enters the equation. Rhyme is "trivial and of no true musical delight," but quantitative verse is by nature musical. Campion begins his *Observations on the Art of English Poesy* with the remark, "The world is made of Simmetry and proportion, and is in that respect compared to Musick, and Musick to Poetry.... What musick can there be when there is no proportion served?"[44]

On the other hand, if *Paradise Lost* is basically syllabic, "fit quantity of Syllables" may not be an allusion to syllabic quantity. It could simply mean "correct number of syllables." Probably not. Probably Milton is suggesting that quantitative effects are important even in syllabic-accentual poetry. The alternative spellings of the personal pronouns ("she/shee," "he/hee," "me/mee") have sometimes been understood to indicate different vowel quantities. Alternatively, they may indicate different degrees of stress, in which case Milton's term "quantity" may reflect the general equation of English renaissance prosodists of quantity with stress.

Milton's requirement that the sense be "variously drawn out from one Verse into another" has generally been considered a reference to enjambment.[45] Milton did not discover the importance of enjambment and the verse paragraph to heroic effects. Surrey's *Aeneid* and Chapman's *Iliad* anticipate Milton in this respect. Drawing out sense is related to the rejection of rhyme. Although Chapman writes in couplets, his fourteeners and decasyllabics succeed by constantly refusing closure. By the Restoration most poets had given up the battle with rhyme. Instead of resisting it, they worked with it. Milton's Muse, however, needed a verse form that could be completed in a single word or drawn out to the length of a paragraph.

Such a form has two virtues. From the point of view of the poetic craftsman, it permits a flexibility close to that of free verse. This is the virtue stressed in Italian discussions of *versi sciolti*. It allows the poet to adjust his music to the specific subject being treated. In practice, Milton's verse has a sustained underlying quality like a musical key but makes constant adjustments to subject and context. The tonal variation is established by constructions as well as vocabulary. The blank verse of *Paradise Lost* is far more complex in its constructions than the blank verse of Marlowe's *Tamburlaine*, though not necessarily a great deal more so than the blank verse of his *Pharsalia*; and it is much more finely controlled than the Miltonizing blank verse of the nineteenth century.

From the point of view of the inspired poet, which is Milton's point of view, extending the sense variously from one verse to another has a still more important virtue. It guarantees the freedom of the heavenly Muse to express things "as they ought to be expressed and not otherwise." One does not need to be a reader of Marsilio Ficino or a familiar of the heavenly Muse to realize that this sort of freedom is essential to visionary poetry.

Since Milton believed, probably wrongly, that classical antiquity afforded the poet the liberty of his imagination, he proudly claimed that his program was to be deemed "an example . . . of ancient liberty recover'd." This is vintage Milton and recalls his boast in the *Second Defense* that he had devoted his life to the defense of liberty in the areas of religion, politics, and the family.[46] From the perspective of the twentieth century, Milton's claim does not seem as revolutionary as he imagined it. Dante achieved a similar liberty in spite of living in an age of "wretched matter and lame Metre," and he managed to convey an inspired vision in spite of the "bondage" of terza rima. But it is certainly true that Milton stood practically alone in the England of 1668 when he wrote his note on the verse of *Paradise Lost*. If the note is the cry of a poetic Gulliver among the poetic Lilliputians who sprang up in the shadow of Bacon, it is even more poignantly a statement about the conditions under which the poetic imagination can survive in a rationalistic—which is to say a modern—culture.

TAGGING THE VERSE

The seventeenth-century debate about blank verse was a minor skirmish in a long and bitter war between imagination and reason that is not over yet. There can be no better way to put this skirmish into perspective—and to conclude the present volume—than to recall that Dryden admired *Paradise Lost* in spite of the fact that it violated every one of his carefully fabricated critical principles. He admired it so much that he decided to make it over into an acceptable modern poem.

He therefore visited its aged and blind author to ask permission to turn it into a drama to be called *The State of Innocence*.[47] To do this, Dryden explained, he would have to convert it into couplets. Was Milton outraged by this brash suggestion? Quite the contrary. According to Aubrey, "Mr. Milton received him civilly, and told him he would give him leave to tag his verses." Milton did not feel threatened. Probably he was amused.

Andrew Marvell was obviously amused. In the dedicatory poem he wrote for the 1674 edition of *Paradise Lost*, he contrasts Dryden, nicknamed *Town-Bayes* from the satirical image of him in the duke of Buckingham's *Rehearsal*, with the grand old master of blank verse:

> Well mightst thou scorn thy Readers to allure
> With tinkling Rime, of thy own sense secure;
> While the *Town-Bayes* writes all the while and spells,
> And like a Pack-horse tires without his Bells. . . .
> Thy Verse, created like thy Theme sublime,
> In Number, Weight, and Measure, needs not Rime.[48]

Notes

CHAPTER I: PROSODY AND PURPOSE

1. Clive Scott, *French Verse-Art: A Study* (Cambridge, 1980), p. 39.
2. Aldo Scaglione, *The Classical Theory of Composition from Its Origin to the Present* (Chapel Hill, N.C., 1972), esp. pp. 126–44, and Jean-Claude Chevalier, *Histoire de la syntaxe: Naissance de la notion de complément dans la grammaire française (1530–1750)* (Geneva, 1968), esp. ch. 2, "La Grammaire au début du XVI siècle." For prose rhythms in the later sixteenth century, Morris Croll, *Style, Rhetoric, and Rhythm: Essays by Morris Croll,* ed. J. Max Patrick et al. (Princeton, 1966). For Carlino and "rhetorical accent," Seth Weiner, "Spenser's Study of English Syllables and Its Completion by Thomas Campion," *Spenser Studies,* 3(1982), 3–7.
3. *Donat et la tradition de l'enseignement grammatical,* intr. and ed. Louis Holtz (Paris, 1981), *Ars major,* I, 5 (pp. 609–10).
4. Thus Jean Suberville, *Histoire et théorie de la versification française* (rev. ed., rpt. Paris, 1968), refers (p. 21) to "l'accent tonique ou élévation de la voix sur une des syllabes du mot, qui est appelée, de ce fait, syllabe tonique. Les autres syllabes sont dites atones."
5. Jürgen Klausenburger, *French Prosodics and Phonotactics* (Tübingen, 1970); Michel Burger, *Recherches sur la structure et l'origine des vers romans* (Paris, 1957); Roger Dragonetti, *La Technique poétique des trouvères* (Bruges, 1960). In "Spenser's Study of English Syllables," p. 6, Seth Weiner notes that in spite of efforts to distinguish between "stress" and "accent" the terms are entangled: "The reason it so often makes sense to substitute our word *stress* for the Elizabethan *accent* follows naturally from the fact that stress is the most notable feature of English phonology. But every time we make this substitution, we miss the connotations associated by the Renaissance with *accent.*"

6. Scott, *French Verse-Art*, p. 25. Cf. also L. E. Kastner, *A History of French Versification* (Oxford, 1903).

7. A well-known advocate of the theory is Northrop Frye, *The Anatomy of Criticism* (Princeton, 1957), pp. 251–62.

8. The history is reviewed by Paul Fussell, Jr., *The Theory of Prosody in Eighteenth-Century England* (rpt. Hamden, Conn., 1966). Fussell believes that in the sixteenth century poetry moved strongly toward the norm of accentual foot verse under the influence of classical prosodic theory. With the ascendancy of French influence in England during the Restoration, syllabic theory became supreme. It was challenged in the 1740s by Samuel Say, but the accentual position did not become dominant until after 1770 (cf. ch. 5, "1770 and After: The Ascendancy of Accentualism"). For a famous quarrel between advocates of syllabic and "classical" theory, A.D. Culler, "Edward Bysshe and the Poet's Handbook," *PMLA*, 63(1948), 858–85.

9. Rpt. New York, 1971. See Culler, "Edward Bysshe."

10. The different lines are listed in Suberville, *Histoire et théorie*, pp. 128–41.

11. Suberville, *Histoire et théorie*, p. 37.

12. Jakob Schipper, *A History of English Versification* (Oxford, 1910; rpt. New York, 1971), p. 131.

13. Scott, *French Verse-Art*, p. 48. The normal maximum is four (p. 17).

14. Scott, *French Verse-Art*, p. 24.

15. See Edward Weismiller, "The Metrical Treatment of Syllables," in *The Princeton Handbook of Poetry and Poetics*, ed. Alex Preminger et al. (Princeton, 1986), pp. 144–46.

16. *Cinna*, in *Théâtre complet de Corneille*, ed. Georges Couton (Paris, 1971), I, 916.

17. Suberville, *Histoire et théorie*, p. 23.

18. Scott, *French Verse-Art*, p. 17.

19. The standard types are (1) pauvre (vowel sounds only are shared; equivalent to assonance: *arles/ages/asse/ables*); (2) suffisante (a vowel plus a consonant: *subit/habit, cité/beauté*); (4) riche (a vowel and two consonants: *sport/port, tordu/perdu*); (5) Léonine (two-syllable rhyme: *abonder/inonder*); (6) équivoque (punning rhyme: *Dante en/d'antan*). There are, however, variations in classification and terminology. Cf. ibid., pp. 104–10; Suberville, *Histoire et théorie*, pp. 83–92.

20. George Puttenham, *The Arte of English Poesie*, in *Elizabethan Critical Essays*, ed. G. Gregory Smith (Oxford, 1904; rpt. 1950), II, 83–84 (bk. 2, chs. 8, 9). Hereafter cited as *ECE*.

21. Ibid., I, 204–5.

22. Sidney, as quoted by William Ringler, "Master Drant's Rules," *PQ*, 29(1950), 72.

23. Gabriel Harvey, *ECE*, I, 125–26.

24. Schipper, *History of English Versification*, outlines the romance background of the English decasyllabic couplet (pp. 208–18) and the Italian-inspired provenance, via Trissino, of blank verse (pp. 219–41). He calls the fourteener the "septenary" and notes its relation to medieval Latin trochaic tetrameter poems like "Mihi est propositum / in taberna mori / Vinum sit oppositum / morientis ori" (pp. 192–98). He considers poulter's measure a combination of a fourteener with an Alexandrine (pp. 201–3).

25. Cf. Weismiller, "Metrical Treatment of Syllables," p. 146.

26. David Crystal, "Intonation and Metrical Theory," *Transactions of the Philological Society* (1971), pp. 1–33. Quotation: D. W. Harding, *Words into Rhythm: English Speech Rhythm in Verse and Prose* (Cambridge, 1976), p. 37. H. A. Mason refers to Harding's work to explain Wyatt's "phrasal poetry" (*Editing Wyatt* [Cambridge, England, 1972], p. 97).

27. Cf. Edward Weismiller's two articles on verse form in *A Variorum Commentary on the Poems of John Milton*, ed. A. S. P. Woodhouse and Douglas Bush, vol. IV (New York, 1975), pp. 254–57. Weismiller considers both Chaucer's octosyllabic and his decasyllabic line to be French-derived (p. 254), but also stresses (p. 255) the influence of "much sharper patterns of accent . . . in the Italian line." Still useful as a survey of Chaucer's debt to romance prosody is Theodore Maynard, *The Connection Between the Ballade, Chaucer's Modification of It, Rime Royal and the Spenserian Stanza* (Washington, D. C., 1934). Maynard considers the French contribution decisive but believes Italian influence helped Chaucer achieve greater prosodic flexibility. Many scholars deny that Chaucer's versification was influenced significantly by Continental practice. See, e.g., note 28. Their position is criticized by John H. Fisher, "Chaucer and French Influence," in *New Perspectives in Chaucer Criticism*, ed. Donald M. Rose (Norman, Okla., 1981), pp. 177–92. Fisher calls (pp. 187–88) for a syllabic approach to Chaucer's verse. For a still stronger statement, Rossell Hope Robins, "Geoffroi Chaucier, Poete François, Father of English Poetry," *Chaucer Review*, 13(1978), 93–115. Susanne Woods, *Natural Emphasis: English Versification from Chaucer to Dryden* (San Marino, Ca., 1985), pp. 21–48, also favors the syllabic position.

28. A potentially significant line of inquiry was introduced and then abandoned by James G. Southworth in *The Prosody of Chaucer and His Followers* (Oxford, 1962). Southworth suggested in his initial chapter (pp. 1–24) that there is a relation between the rhythmical, nonmetrical forms of the medieval *cursus* and Chaucer's verse forms. It is a pity he did not follow up the line of inquiry he opened. He seems not to have known Eduard Norden's analysis of the relation between prose rhythm and rhyme, *Die Antike Kunstprosa* (5th ed., 2 vols, Berlin, 1958). As ch. 3 shows, the relation between medieval Latin syntax, prose rhythm, and versification is close, and it carries over into romance prosody. Like Robinson, in *Verses of Cadence* (Oxford, 1954) Southworth called the idea of French or Italian influence on Chaucer a "myth."

29. Weismiller, in *Variorum Commentary*, IV, 256, agrees with Bridges but later (p. 268) points out that Prince accused Bridges of being obsessed with disyllabic feet and hence with the "traditional view that English prosody must be interpreted in terms of classical prosody." Cf. F. T. Prince, *The Italian Element in Milton's Verse* (Oxford, 1954), p. 137. Prince denies (p. 144) that there are any feet in English poetry: "The metrical unit is . . . in the decasyllable, the line itself, with all its possible variations, not the five 'disyllabic feet' which are said to compose it." Yet Weismiller remarks [*Variorum Commentary*, vol. 2, pt. 2 (1972), p. 1017], "Bridges' studies have not . . . been superseded."

30. For a review of current progress, which concludes that, if anything, there has been regression, see Alan T. Gaylord, "Scanning the Prosodists: An Essay in Metacriticism," *Chaucer Review*, 11(1976), 27–82. Includes illustrative scansions. Gaylord remarks (p. 74): "To establish Chaucer's conception of meter, we need a much richer contribution from continental and insular literary history. . . . We must try to characterize the prosodic universes of French and Italian poetry." Weismiller concludes (*Variorum Commentary*, IV, 253, "The laws that govern the writing of English accentual-syllabic verse in general are not agreed on."

31. Jack Conner, *English Prosody from Chaucer to Wyatt* (Hawthorne, N. Y., 1974), p. 91. The same point is made by Paull Baum, *Chaucer's Verse* (Durham, N. C., 1961), p. 9.

32. Campion's use of Augustinian music symbolism is thoroughly explored by Seth Weiner in "Spenser's Study of English Syllables."

Chapter II: Ars Metrica

1. *Poetics*, ch. 4 (49a15–28). English translation from Leon Golden and O. B. Hardison, *Aristotle's 'Poetics': A Translation and Commentary for Students of Literature* (Gainesville, Fla., 1981). For comment, Gerald Else, *Aristotle's Poetics: The Argument* (Cambridge, Mass., 1957), pp. 164–82.

2. For scholarship, see below, notes 7–10.

3. *Poetics*, ch. 18 (56a25–32). In Euripides, the same piece, for example, comes at the end of *Helen, The Bacchae, Andromache,* and (with minor variations) *Medea*.

4. Ibid., ch. 1 (47b13–17).

5. Ibid., ch. 9 (51b2). The comments about Empedocles and Herodotus led in the sixteenth century to two lively chapters of rebuttal in Francesco Patrizi's *Della Poetica: La deca disputata* (Ferrara, 1586). Patrizi takes the position of the *ars metrica* that verse is the defining characteristic of poetry rather than "imitation" in Aristotle's sense.

6. W. S. Allen, *Accent and Rhythm: Prosodic Features of Greek and Latin* (Cambridge, 1973), pp. 3–6, discusses the history of the word *prosodia*. In

classical grammar it refers to phonetics, especially natural word accent. The grammarian Diomedes provides a definition of "prosody" as it was understood in the fourth century: "Accentus est dictus ab accinendo, quod sit quasi quidam cuiusque syllabae cantus. Apud Graecos quoque ideo *prosodia* dicitur, quia *prosadetai tais syllabais.*" Artis grammaticae libri III, ed. Heinrich Keil, *Grammatici Latini* (7 vols., Leipzig, 1857–80), I, 431.

7. C. M. Bowra, *Primitive Song* (New York, 1963), p. 254: "Primitive song is the basic form of poetry, and though other forms which have grown from it bear little resemblance to it, it sets the start for them and provides the elements of their technique."

8. *Poetics,* ch. 4 (48b21–22). Cf. Hugo Gleditsch, *Metrik nebst einem Abhang über die Musik der Grieschen,* in *Rhetorik und Metrik der Grieschen und Römer* (Munich, 1901). A summary of the history of Greek and Roman metrical theory is given on pp. 67–75.

9. Cf. Mario Pazzaglia, *Il Verso e l'arte della canzone nel 'De vulgari eloquentia'* (Florence, 1967), "La 'Musica' di Boezio e di S. Agostino," pp. 19–46.

10. The major Latin treatises are collected in Keil, *Grammatici Latini.* For music and poetry, see esp. *Frag. Censorini de musica et de metris,* VI, 607–17. For the idea that music and poetry arose from the same instinct, Victorinus, VI, 158–60.

11. *Poetics,* ch. 24 (59b31–37).

12. Ibid. (59b37–60a5).

13. Antonio Garcia Barrio, *La Formación de la teoría literia moderna: La topica horaciana en Europa* (Madrid, 1977), p. 85. Cf. Paul Zumthor, *Langue et techniques poétiques a l'époque romaine* (Paris, 1963), p. 60: "On peut dire que le vers n'est identifiable, par la mémoire individuelle, qu'au sein d'une tradition et par rapport à elle. Ce fait apparaîtra, par la suite, d'une grande conséquence. Faire du langage—d'un fragment de discours pourvu initialment d'un sens à lui—un rythme, selon l'un de ces schémas valorisés par la tradition, c'est provoquer un cumul de significations et, à la limite, modifier de façon essentielle la portée et la valeur des signes. La production d'un vers est ainsi une opération complexe de mise-en-sens-et-en-rythme, dont les facteurs répugnant à la dissociation analytique."

14. W. R. Hardie, *Res Metrica: An Introduction to the Study of Greek and Roman Versification* (Oxford, 1920; rpt. New York, 1979), p. 85. Cf. p. 133: "The hexameter of Satire (or Epistle) is a different thing from the Epic hexameter, and should be treated separately, as a stream flowing in a channel of its own."

15. Barrio, *Formación,* p. 90.

16. Ibid., p. 82.

17. *Spenser: Poetical Works,* ed. J. C. Smith and E. de Selincourt (Oxford, 1966), p. 458.

18. For the history of ancient grammar, R. H. Robins, *Ancient and Medieval Grammatical Theory in Europe* (London, 1951). Robins notes (p. 12) that

grammatike is first used technically in Plato's *Sophist* (253A) and that the parts of speech are distinguished in the *Cratylus* (431B–32A). Also Aldo D. Scaglione, "The Historical Study of the Ars Grammatica," *Ars grammatica* (Hawthorne, N.Y., 1970), pp. 11–43. Scaglione explains (p. 44) that an ancient "comprehensive grammar" includes "all or most of the following: phonetics (*voces*), the alphabet (*litterae*), spelling (*orthographia*), analysis of and precepts on the eight parts of speech, accents, writing marks (*notae*), punctuation, prosody (quantity), metrics, stylistics or, rather, study of 'grammatical' figures of speech (metaplasms, schemata, and tropi), the whole topped off by an essential discussion of the value of poetry and history." For the influence of Donatus, Louis Holtz, ed., *Donat et la tradition de l'enseignement grammatical* (Paris, 1981), pp. 219–23.

19. *Latinitas* is defined by Quintilian (I, 6, 1) as consisting of "ratione, vetustate, auctoritate, consuetudine." *Consuetudine* is translated "custom" or "use." Diomedes (Keil, I, 439) quotes Varro: "Constat autem, ut adserit Varro, his quattuor, natura analogia consuetudine auctoritate." *Analogia* is equated with artificial (*technichos*) rules, meaning rules of grammar and diction. *Consuetudo* involves word choice and such problems as the correct and incorrect use of archaisms and foreign words. *Auctoritas* is usage found in the great writers. For *Latinitas* and *explanatio* see also *Rhetorica ad Herennium*, IV, 12, 17.

20. Dionysius of Halicarnassus uses the term *synthesis* in *Peri syntheseos*, ed. W. Rhys Roberts, *On Literary Composition* (Cambridge, 1910). The *Rhetorica ad Herennium* calls it both *conpositio* and *constructio* (IV, 12, 18ff.), defining it as "verborum constructio quae facit omnes partes orationis aequabiliter perpolitas." Cicero calls it *collocatio* in the *Orator* (149–34). He equates it with *componere . . . verba* and discusses it at length in the *De oratore* (III, 42, 171ff.). He is especially interested in the theory of metrical terminations of clauses (*clausulae*). Quintilian uses *constructio* and *structura* (*Inst.*, IX, 4, 10ff.). Diomedes uses *conpositio*. He explains the figures of diction in relation to word order varied for metrical effect or emphasis (Keil, VI, 443): "Schema lexeos est *ordo verborum aliter quam debet figuratus* metri aut decoris aut emphaseos gratia" (italics added). Priscian (Keil, III, 108 [bk. XVII, i]) uses *constructio* in the basic sense of the correct grammatical joining of words. Detailed historical discussion of construction is in Aldo Scaglione, *The Classical Theory from Its Origin to the Present* (Chapel Hill, N.C., 1972). The introductory chapter, pp. 8–96, treats the placing of composition in grammar, loose and periodic sentence structure, and word order. For *constructio* in the Middle Ages, see pp. 97–125, and for Dante, see Pazzaglia, *Il verso e l'arte della canzone*, pp. 77–82, 92–97, 134–39. For the *clausulae*, Eduard Norden, *Die Antike Kunstprosa* (5th ed., 2 vols., Berlin, 1958), II, 909–52, "Uber die Geschichte des rhythmischen Satzschluss."

21. Scaglione, *The Classical Theory*, p. 21–33, discusses the figures and their rationale. Zeugma, hypozeuxis, anaphora, epanalepsis, polysyndeton,

asyndeton, paronomasia, and homoeoteleuton are already defined in the text. Among other figures mentioned by Donatus, syllepsis is one verb for subjects that differ in number, so it involves lack of verb-subject agreement. Epizeuxis is repetition of words. Hyperbaton is a general term for artificial word order but often has the specific meaning of the separation of words normally close together. Anastrophe is unnatural word order, especially, inversion; tmesis is "cutting," words introduced between parts of a compound word; hysteron proteron is inversion of normal time or causal sequence; hypallage is wrong use of the word; parenthesis is interrupting material; and epergesis is apposition. Not mentioned by Donatus but important are isocolon, clauses of the same length and structure; antithesis, contrasting clauses; gradatio, climax; parison, clauses of similar sound; hirmus, periodic sentence structure; metabasis, transitional statement; hendiadys, two nouns or adjectives for one; and paroemi, alliteration. There are other figures of diction, including illocutionary schemata such as question (interrogatio), address (apostrophe), command, prayer, and the like. Different grammars define and classify the terms differently. The *Rhetorica ad Herennium*, IV, 18–46, has a comprehensive list. For comparative lists, see Holtz, *Donat*, pp. 189–99. The reader for whom the Greek terms are opaque can consult the definitions, illustrated by quotations from Shakespeare, by Sister Miriam Joseph, *Shakespeare's Use of the Arts of Language* (New York, 1947), pp. 54–64. For a more recent review of the terms and their definitions, Lee A. Sonnino, *A Handbook to Sixteenth-Century Rhetoric* (London, 1968).

22. Stockwood, *Progymnasma scholasticum* (London, 1597).

23. Tr. in Roberts, *On Literary Composition*. The Greek terms are *austera*, *glaphyra*, and *eukrata*. For comment on Dionysus, see Scaglione, *The Classical Theory*, pp. 53–60; for ad Herennium, pp. 42–46.

24. Holtz, *Donat*, p. 660: "Metaplasmus est transformatio quaedam recti solutique sermonis in alteram speciem metri ornatusve causa." Charisius (Keil, I, 277): "Metaplasmus est dictio aliter quam debuit figurata metri aut decoris causa."

25. Holtz, *Donat*, pp. 660–63. In addition to the figures listed in the text, there are prosthesis (adding at the beginning of a word), epenthesis (adding in the middle), paragoge (adding at the end), aphaeresis (omitting at the beginning), ectasis (lengthening vowels), diastole (lengthening a short syllable), systole (shortening a long syllable), episynaloepha (reducing two vowels to a diphthong), antithesis (substitution of one letter for another), and metathesis (changing the order of letters). For *synizesis*, a general term for blending vowels, see J. M. van Ophuijsen, *Hephaestion on Metre: A Translation and Commentary* (Leiden, 1987), p. 14.

26. E.g., Bede (*De arte metrica*, ed. C. B. Kendall, in *Corpus Christianorum, Series Latina*, vol. 123A [Turnholt, 1975], pp. 81–141); Charisius, Keil, I, 277–79; Diomedes, Keil, I, 440–43; Victorinus, Keil, VI, 66.

27. Most of these authors are in Keil's vol. 6: Terentianus, 313–413;

Aphthonius—taken over wholesale by Victorinus—occupies pp. 31–173 of the latter's treatise in Keil, VI, 1–184. Servius on Horace is in Keil, IV, 468–72; and Priscian on Terence is in Keil, III, 418–29.

28. Keil, VI, 94.

29. Cf. van Ophuijsen, *Hephaestion on Metre*. This work includes selections from the *Musical Encyclopedia* of Aristides Quintilianus. For a summary history of Greek prosodic theory, Gleditsch, *Metrik*, pp. 67–75; for Aristides Quintilianus, pp. 70–72; van Ophuijsen, *Hephaestion on Metre*, pp. 8–9.

30. The prototype meters are dactylic (−⏑⏑), iambic (⏑−), trochaic (−⏑)anapestic (⏑⏑−), antispastic (⏑−−⏑), choriambic (−⏑⏑−), ionic major (−−⏑⏑), and ionic minor (⏑⏑−−). Lists of nine prototype meters include the proceleusmatic (⏑⏑⏑⏑). Cf. Diomedes, Keil, I, 501; Victorinus, Keil, VI, 69. Also Servius, *De centum metris*, Keil, IV, 457. All Latin authors known to me recognize at least nine prototype feet. Victorinus (Keil, IV, 98–99) raises the question (from Philoxenos) of whether there is not a tenth prototype foot, the obverse of the proceleusmatic (i.e., a dispondee: −−−−). Given the number of variations on the prototypes, the number of possible lines is astronomical. Victorinus calculates (Keil, VI, 107) that there are 4,114 possibilities. Considering the Varronian theory that the prototypes are themselves derived from two archetypes, the heroic and iambic trimeter, he adds (VI, 146), "Et mehercules siquis excutere penitus velet, inveniet, ut supra diximus, omnia genera ab hexametro heroo et trimetro iambico derivata. . . . unde, ut diximus, haec duo metra ut elementa ceterorum ac semina habenda merito ac dicenda sunt."

31. Varro's extant works are edited by R. G. Kent in the Loeb Classical Library (2 vols., Cambridge, Mass., 1938).

32. Cf. Robins, *Ancient and Medieval Grammatical Theory*, pp. 50–57; Gleditsch, *Metrik*, pp. 71–73. Diomedes (Keil, I, 501) notes (from Varro) that there are two archetypal meters, dactylic and iambic, and then follows "others" (*aliorum . . . auctoritas*) in recognizing nine basic meters. Victorinus also draws on Varro (Keil, VI, 69).

33. For classical prosody, Hardie, *Res Metrica*; M. L. West, *Greek Metre* (Oxford, 1982) (with an appendix on Latin meter, pp. 186–90); D. S. Raven, *Latin Metre* (London, 1965). Useful definitions of ictus, arsis, thesis, and many other technical terms used here are given, with supplementary bibliography, in *The Princeton Handbook of Poetry and Poetics*, ed. Alex Preminger et al. (Princeton, 1986). See also in this edition the longer entries on "Classical Prosody" and "Classical Meters in Modern Languages."

34. Holtz, *Donat*, p. 607: "Pes est syllabarum et temporum certa dinumeratio. Accidunt uni cuique pedi arsis et thesis, numerus syllabarum, tempus, resolutio, figura, metrum. Pedes disyllabi sunt quattuor, trisyllabi octo, duplices sedecim." Holtz suggests (p. 63) that Donatus was not interested in poetry and includes the definition only because of its application to the theory of prose rhythm.

35. The four-syllable feet are proceleusmatic (⏑⏑⏑⏑), dispondee (----), diiambus (⏑-⏑-), ditrochee (-⏑-⏑), antispastus (⏑--⏑), choriambus (-⏑⏑-), ionic minor (⏑⏑--), ionic major (--⏑⏑), first to fourth paeon (-⏑⏑⏑; ⏑-⏑⏑; ⏑⏑-⏑; ⏑⏑⏑-), and first to fourth epitritic (⏑---; -⏑--; --⏑-; ---⏑). Donatus also recognizes the composites (*syzygiae*). "Simple" feet are those with three syllables or less. Double (dipodic) feet cannot have more than six syllables. *Syzygiae* are double feet in which each unit is different. Cf. *Hephaestion on Metre*, pp. 14–16.

36. For rhythm, Allen, *Accent and Rhythm*, esp. pp. 97ff. For an aesthetic approach, informed with a knowledge of linguistics, see L. P. Wilkinson, *Golden Latin Artistry* (Cambridge, 1963), pp. 89–134. Wilkinson acknowledges (p. 90) that rhythm is "one of the thorniest questions in classical scholarship."

37. The space from ictus to ictus is the space occupied by arsis and thesis and hence also the time (i.e., duration) of the foot: "Tempus enim solum metitur, ut a sublatione [arsis] ad positione [thesis] idem spatii sit." Rhythm distinguishes time intervals but not meters (*Inst.*, IX, 4, 48), so that from the point of view of rhythm a dactyl (-⏑⏑) is equivalent to a spondee (--). In dipodic meters an entire unit acts as arsis or thesis. The term *modulatio* appears frequently in the *ars metrica*. It refers to the regularization of discourse by any system of measurement and can apply to rhythmic prose (cf. e.g. Diomedes, Keil, I, 439): "Modulatio est continuati sermonis in iocundiorem dicendi rationem artificialis flexus in delectabilem auditus formam conversus asperitatis atque inperitiae vitandae grata."

38. Dionysius, *On Composition*, 15, notes that the first syllables of *odos*, *rodos*, *tropos*, and *strophos* are all short but they all have different values.

39. Cicero, *De oratore*, III, 186, uses the metaphor of dripping water to illustrate the need for some sort of marking of divisions if rhythm is to be sensed: "Numerus autem in continuatione nullus est; distinctio et aequalium et saepe variorum intervallorum percussio numerum conficit, quem in cadentibus guttis, quod intervallis distinguntur, notare possumus, in amni praecipitante non possumus." A more philosophical explanation, using the classical metaphor of measuring rhythm by hammer blows, is given by Hans Drexler in *Einführung in die Römische Metrik* (Darmstadt, 1967), p. 9: "Metrum unterscheidet sich vom Rhythmus, für die Metra nämlich sind das materia (*hyle*) die Silben, und ohne Silben gibt es kein Metrum, Rhythmus dagegen gibt es in Silben, gibt es aber auch ohne Silben, nämlich beim Geräusch von Schlagen, z. B. dem Hammerschlag des Schmeids. Rhythmus und Metrum verhalten sich dennoch wie genus und species."

40. *Inst.*, IX, 4, 51, 55, also (foot-tapping image) I, 12, 3. "Number" is related to the number of "times" in the line. "Numeri spatio temporum constant" (IX, 4, 46; see also next note). Since the Renaissance, the terms *numerus* and "number" have become ambivalent. They can refer to "number of syl-

lables" in syllabic verse, "number of times" or "of feet" in quantitative or accentual meters, and "numeric proportions" (including harmonic numbers) in numerological poetry.

41. Allen, *Accent and Rhythm*, p. 98. Cf. West, *Greek Metre*, p. 18: "The scansion of a particular series of words forming a verse must be distinguished from the abstract metrical scheme of the verse. The particular verse is made up of syllables: the metrical scheme is made up of *positions* in which syllables of suitable length are accommodated. Positions, like syllables, are long or short, or *anceps* [ambivalent] . . . where the quantity of the syllable is unregulated or regulated only at the poet's discretion." Cf. *Hephaestion on Metre*, p. 17. Mere equivalency of "times" is not sufficient for substitution. The location of the ictus at the end or beginning of the foot defines a rhythm that is rising (e.g., iambic, anapestic) or falling (trochaic, dactylic). Feet that can be either falling or rising (e.g., pyrrhic [⌣⌣], spondee [--], tribrach [⌣⌣⌣]) can be used in either type of verse.

42. Cf. Diomedes, Keil, I, 496. Cf. *Ars Palaemonis*, Keil, VI, 211–12; *Fragmentum de heroo hexametro*, VI, 634–37. The number thirty-two is reached by a mechanical consideration of the different arrangements possible in an epic line with no spondees, one spondee, and so on, to a line of five spondees. The last foot of the heroic line can be either a spondee or a trochee. Vergil is said to have used only seventeen of the possible "figures." The discussion can be compared with discussions of the thirty-six possible types of the French Alexandrine. These types are, however, defined by "measure" rather than foot-pattern.

43. There are four different licenses possible in regard to line length—catalectic, acatalectic, hypercatalectic, brachicatalectic. The *qualitates metri* are "finite" (defined by a specific normative foot and a specific number of syllables) and "nonfinite" (a mixture of feet and different line lengths, as in the Sapphic stanza).

44. Holtz, *Donat*, p. 82.

45. Keil, I, 473: "Poetica est fictae veraeve narrationis congruenti rythmo ac pede conposita metrica structura ad utilitatem voluptatemque accommodata." He continues with a curious distinction also found in Victorinus (Keil, VI, 56): "Distat autem poetica a poemate et poesi, quod poetica ars ipsa intellegitur, poema autem pars operis, ut tragoedia, poesis contextus et corpus totius operis effecti, ut Ilias Odyssia Aeneis." E. R. Curtius remarks, *European Literature and the Latin Middle Ages*, tr. W. Trask (London, 1953), p. 439: "This we cannot understand—because the author himself did not understand what he was copying from." For the emphasis on meter, compare Victorinus's definition of a poet, Keil, VI, 56: "Qui versus facit *para to poiein* dictus est *poietes*, latina lingua vates, quod verba modulatione conectat."

46. Keil, I, 473–74. Later (pp. 501–2, "De modis metrorum") he lists six "modes"—*definitivus vel principalis, compositus, incompositus, confusus, coniunc-*

tus, derivatus. The first mode is a line entirely in feet identical with the meter (e.g., all iambic). The second is "artful," being composed of a variety of feet according to accepted substitution formulas. The third uses nonstandard substitutions (*peregrinis pedibus*), and the fourth uses any and all sorts of feet. The fifth joins two different types of meter like heroic and iambic and appears to be a variant of the type called "asynartete" by Hephaestion (*Hephaestion on Metre*, pp. 137–60). The sixth is presumably "derived" from the other five. "Mode" thus refers to the way feet are related to the meter in its idealized sense.

47. Ibid., p. 473: "Rythmus est pedum temporumque iunctura cum levitate sine modo. Alii sic, rythmus est versus imago modulata servans numerum syllabarum positionem saepe sublationemque continens."

48. Ibid., p. 474: "Metrum est pedum iunctura numero modoque finita. Vel sic, metrum est conpositio pedum ordine statuto decurrens modum positionis sublationisque conservans. Clarius sic, metrum est quod certis pedum quantitatibus qualitatibusque rythmo discriminatur. Distat enim metrum a rythmo quod metrum certa qualitate ac numero syllabarum temporumque finitur certisque pedibus constat ac clauditur, rythmus autem temporum ac syllabarum pedumque congruentia infinitum multiplicatur ac profluit." Compare Victorinus, Keil, VI, 41–42: "Rhythmus . . . Latine numerus dicitur . . . differt autem rhythmus a metro, quod metrum in verbis, rhythmus in modulatione ac motu corporis sit; et quod metrum pedum sit quaedam compositio, rhythmus autem temporum inter se ordo quidam; et quod metrum certo numero syllabarum vel pedum finitum sit, rhythmus autem numquam numero circumscribatur."

49. Keil, I, 474. For comedy, Cicero, *Orator*, 184: "Comicorum senarii propter similitudinem sermonis sic saepe sunt abiecti, ut nonnumquam vix in eius numerus et versus intelligi possit." Horace, *Ars poetica*, ll. 80–83; Priscian, "De metris fabularum Terentii," Keil, III, 420: "Comici poetae laxius etiamnum versibus suis quam tragici. . . . Spatium dederunt et illa quoque loca, quae proprie debentur iambo, dactylis occupant pedibus . . . cotidianum sermonem imitari volunt et a versificationis observatione spectatorem ad actum rei convertere, ut non fictis sed veris affectionibus inesse videatur." Victorinus, Keil, VI, 81: "Ita dum cotidianum sermonem imitari nituntur, metra vitiant studio, non imperitia, quod frequentius apud nos quam apud Graecos invenies." On p. 113 Victorinus cites Aristotle to the effect that we speak iambs naturally in everyday conversation. This is one of the few citations of Aristotle in antiquity that might be an echo of the *Poetics*, but it is probably an echo of Aristotle's *Rhetoric*, III, 8, 1408b30–35. Mallius Theodorus, *De metris*, Keil, VI, 594, calls the comic iambic "aptissime ad contidianum loquendi morem." The frequent substitutions of comic writers are a form of *licentia*—license—hence Elizabethan references to the "licenciate iambic."

50. Keil, I, 482: "Poematos genera sunt tria. Aut enim activum est vel

imitativum, quod Graeci dramaticon vel mimeticon, aut ennarativum vel enuntiativum, quod Graeci exegeticon vel apangelticon dicunt, aut commune vel mixtum, quod Graeci *koinon* vel *mikton* appellant."

51. "Natum rebus agendis." "Action" refers most obviously to the activity of actors on the stage and hence to verse that is composed to be spoken rather than read. It has two other connotations. First, "action" recalls the Aristotelian concept of tragedy as an "imitation of an action" (*praxis*); and second, "action" invokes the tradition, found in Aristotle (*Poetics* 49a20–25; 50a1), Horace, Donatus, and Euanthius that drama evolved out of communal celebrations involving dance (dithyrambic chorus; satyr play) and using trochaic meter because trochaic is especially well suited to action in the sense of dance. In the *De metris* . . . *Terentii* Priscian relates the informality of comic verse directly to its effectiveness. Its freedom (Keil, III, 420) leads spectators to think they are seeing real actions: "cotidianum sermonem imitari volunt et a versificationis observatione spectatorem ad *actum* rei convertere, ut non observatione fictis sed veris affectionibus inesse videatur" (italics added). For restatement of these ideas in comments on vernacular dramatic verse during the Cinquecento, see ch. 4.

52. The types are discussed in Horace and explained at length in the *Ars poetica*, in the commentaries on the *Ars poetica* by Acron and Porphyrion, and in Euanthius and Aelius Donatus, ed. Paul Wessner, *Commentum Terentii* (2 vols., Leipzig, 1902–5), I, 13–31.

53. Keil, I, 495: "Versus heroicus is dignitate primus est et plenae rationis perfectione firmatus ac totius gravitatis honore sublimis multoque pulchritudinis venustate praeclarus." Cf. I, 483–84: "Epos dicitur Graece carmine hexametro divinarum rerum et heroicarum humanarumque conprehensio." Mallius Theodorus (Keil, VI, 589) notes of the heroic hexameter: "Ceteris omnibus longe pulchrius celsiusque est." Also Isidore of Seville, *Etymologiarum sive Originum Libri XX* ed. W. M. Lindsay (2 vols., Oxford, 1911), I, 39, 9, and Bede, *De arte metrica*, ed. Kendall, p. 108. An impressive exhibition of the detail possible in the analysis of heroic verse is provided by an essay attributed to Priscian and reprinted in Keil's third volume (pp. 459–516) titled *Partitiones duodecim versuum Aeneidos principalium*. The work is in the question and answer style of a textbook. It is almost entirely prosodic. Grammatical forms, verse type, meter, composition and arrangement of feet, caesura, and special effects are considered. The analysis of the first line ("Arma virumque cano. . .") extends for ten printed pages in Keil's edition. It is (p. 459) "uniform by verse type, dactyl in species, simple but not regular in feet, ending in a disyllabic foot, divided by clause into nine syllables [and six], and by verse caesura into two units of semiquinary and semiseptenary, and by feet into five [dactylic] units [and one disyllabic unit]."

54. Keil, I, 485: The word "satire" comes from "satyr," "quod . . . in hoc carmine ridiculae res pudendaeque dicuntur quae velut Satyris proferentur." However, Diomedes also gives (p. 486) Varro's explanation: the name comes

from *satura* (mixture) because the early Roman satirists Pacuvius and Ennius wrote in mixed meters.

55. Drama is treated, ibid., pp. 487–92, with further comments on iambic verse in drama, pp. 503–4.

56. Ibid., p. 498.

57. Ibid., pp. 518–29. For other essays on the meters of Horace, Victorinus, VI, 160–84, Bassius, VI, 266–72, Fortunatianus, VI, 294–304.

58. *De metris,* Keil, VI, 589, 593. For the rhetorical doctrine of decorum (Greek, *to prepon*) see George Fiske and Mary Grant, *Cicero's* De oratore *and Horace's* Ars poetica (Madison, Wisc., 1929), pp. 43–69. C. O. Brink remarks in *Horace on Poetry,* I (*Prolegomena*) (Cambridge, 1963), p. 228, "Among the basic axioms of the *Ars,* decorum ranks second in importance only to the basic distinction between style (and arrangement) and content, to which in fact it provides an essential complement. Horace refers to it so persistently that one can sympathize with scholars who take *decorum* to be the chief subject and the connecting link of the manifold topics of the *Ars.*" As noted above in the text, this concept of decorum is intimately related to the idea of *constructio.*

59. *Rhetorica ad Herennium,* IV, 8, 11–14. Demetrius identifies four styles in *On Style,* 36 (in G. M. A. Grube, *A Greek Critic: Demetrius on Style* [Toronto, 1961]). They are high (*megaloprepes*), elegant or polished (*glaphyros*), plain (*ischnos*), and forceful (*deinos*). The poor styles corresponding to the excellent ones in the *Ad Herennium* are windy (*sufflata*), lax (*dissoluta*), and bloodless (*exsanguis*) (IV, 9, 15–16). Again, *constructio* and the concept of standard "styles" are interrelated.

60. In Latin: *rota Virgiliana.* See Edmond Faral, *Les Arts poétiques du XIIe et du XIIIe siècle* (Paris, 1924), p. 87. The specific source may be the commentary of Claudius Tiberius Donatus on Vergil. Cf. Curtius, *European Literature,* p. 201n. A picture of the *rota* forms part of the *Parisiana poetria* of John of Garland. See the edition by Traugott Lawler (New Haven, Conn., 1974), pp. 39–43.

61. Bede, *De arte metrica,* ed. Kendall, p. x. The series editor, C. W. Jones, notes, however, that the date may be much later (pp. x–xi).

62. Ibid., p. 108: "Metrum dactylicum exametrum quod et heroicum vocatur, eo quod hoc maxime heroum, hoc est, virorum fortium, facta canerentur, ceteris omnibus pulchrius celsiusque est. Unde opusculis tam prolixis quam succinctis, tam vilibus quam nobilibus aptum esse consuevit." The reference to the adaptability of hexameter to base as well as noble subjects is required by the need to fit Vergil's *Eclogues* into the system. According to the system of genres, they are "base" because they deal with shepherds. Yet they are in dactylic hexameters.

63. Ibid., pp. 110, 139–40. Job is in epic hexameters: "Namque librum beati Iob simplici exametro scriptum esse asseverant" (p. 110). In ch. 25 Bede says that Job is partly in prose (*retorico*) and partly in verse (*metrico vel rythmico sermone*). Contrast the *Ars metrica* of Bonefatius, ed. B. Löfstedt, *Corpus Chris-*

tianorum: Series Latina, 133b (1980), p. 111, which finds Deuteronomy in hexameters and the Psalms in iambic trimeter and tetrameter.

64. *De arte metrica,* ed. Kendall, p. 111: "In exametro carmine concatenatio versuum plurimorum solet esse gratissima, quod in Aratore et Sedulio frequenter invenies . . . nonnumquam sex vel septem vel etiam pluribus [versibus] ad invicem connexis." Bede notes (p. 113) that hymns are end-stopped: "Quos choris anternantibus canere oprotet, necesse est singularis versibus ad purum esse distinctos, ut sunt omnes Ambrosiani."

65. Ibid., p. 110: "Huius modulatio carminis miserorum querimoniae congruit, ubi prior versus exameter, sequens est pentameter."

66. The equation of *fabula* and "drama" is found in the *De fabula* of Euanthius, ed. Wessner. For Diomedes, Keil, VI, 490.

67. In *De arte metrica,* ed. Kendall, p. x.

68. Ibid., p. 138: "Videatur autem rithmus metris esse consimilis, quae est verborum modulata compositio, non metrica ratione, sed numero syllabarum ad iudicium aurium examinata, ut sunt carmina vulgarium poetarum." Following earlier tradition he points out that rhythm can be without meter, but meter cannot be without rhythm: "Metrum est ratio cum modulatione, rithmus modulatio sine ratione." Meter tends to develop without conscious intention in "rhythms" through the influence of music. Vulgar poets have crude meters, learned poets are more polished: "Plerumque tamen casu quodam invenies etiam rationem in rithmo, non artifici moderatione servata, sed sono et ipsa modulatione ducente, quem vulgares poetae necesse est rustice, docti faciunt docte." The gloss for these reads in part that certain material is without a metrical basis (*non metrica ratione*) (ed. Kendall, p. 138): "quia non ibi consideratur productio vel correptio." The gloss later remarks concerning modulation, "Modulata: id est ordinata." The new verse form is illustrated by the "Rex aeterne Domine" of Ambrose (presumably the learned variety of "rhythm") and by an anonymous poem on the Last Judgment, "Apparebit repentina / dies magna Domini."

69. Dag Norberg, *Introduction à l'étude de la versification latine médiévale* (Stockholm, 1958), p. 87.

Chapter III: Rude and Beggerly Ryming

1. Analysis of the accentual aspect of the Ambrosian hymns was initiated by Wilhelm Meyer, *Gesammelte Abhandlungen zum Mittellateinisches Rythmik* (2 vols., Berlin, 1905). Meyer's conclusion (II, 119) that they are in regular accentual meters is accepted by two important recent scholars, Georges Lote, *Histoire du vers français* (3 vols., Paris, 1949–56), and Dag Norberg, *Introduction à l'étude de la versification latine médiévale* (Stockholm, 1958). However, in *Recherches sur la structure et l'origine des vers romans* (Paris, 1957), pp. 85–87, Michel Burger contends that only about one-fourth of the lines of the extant

Ambrosian hymns (124 out of 427 lines) are pure iambic and thus have regular match of accent with mandatory long syllables. If one allows a final stress on a proparoxytonic word (e.g., *conditor*), 38 lines have four standard accentual iambic feet and 98 have three.

2. For text, F. J. E. Raby, *A History of Christian-Latin Poetry from the Beginnings to the Close of the Middle Ages* (2nd ed., Oxford, 1953), p. 34. The Ambrosian hymns show a fondness for using proparoxytonic words at line terminations. In this respect they anticipate much later Latin poetry that is unambiguously accentual. The scansion is from Burger, *Recherches*, p. 84. In line 3, however, I have "promoted" the final syllables of each trisyllabic word so that they have secondary accent.

3. Ed. Kendall, pp. 138–39. Quoted in full in ch. 2, n. 68.

4. Thus the final (accented) unit in a line can sometimes be scanned as a heavy followed by two lights (/ x x) and sometimes as a heavy followed by a light followed by a secondary (/ x \ ). This is the case if the word is proparoxytonic (polysyllabic and accented on the third syllable from the end, including case endings; e.g., *numerus*). Cf. Norberg, *Introduction*, p. 90: "Dans un mot latin proparoxytone, un accent secondaire peut frapper la dernière syllabe, mais . . . ce n'est pas là une règle obligatoire. Un mot comme *temere* peut être accentué *témerè* ou *témere*. Il est donc faux de dire que la cadence finale d'un vers rythmique est toujours / ᴗ ou ᴗ / ; elle peut aussi être / ᴗ ᴗ ."

5. Raby, *History*, p. 36.

6. Lote, *Histoire*, I, 12–13.

7. Meyer, *Rythmik*, II, 6–35. Because Commodian's accents do not produce a regular meter, Meyer thinks they were to be read as prose.

8. Burger, *Recherches*, p. 106. Burger illustrates the effect of failure to "hear" quantity with the following accentual scansion of the first line of the *Aeneid*:

Árma virúmque cáno Tróiae qui prímus ab óris.

Among changes in the pronunciation of liturgical Latin, Lote (*Histoire*, I, 10) notes that when a disyllabic word takes an enclytic, the accent shifts to the antepenultimate (*sìgna, signáque; vòbis, vobísque; òra, oráque*). The rule for polysyllables is similar: e.g., *dolóres, dolorésque*.

9. Burger, *Recherches*, pp. 9, 107–59.

10. Eduard Norden, *Die Antike Kunstprosa* (5th ed., 2 vols., Berlin, 1958), II, "Ueber die Geschichte des Reims" (pp. 811–908) and "Ueber die Geschichte des rhythmischen Satzschluss" (pp. 909–52). Mario Pazzaglia, *Il Verso e l'arte della canzone nel 'De vulgari eloquentia'* (Florence, 1967), pp. 71–85, emphasizes the importance of the *cursus* and thus provides grounds for reconsideration of Norden's ideas about the importance of the *cursus*.

11. Norberg, *Introduction*, pp. 164–174. W. B. Sedgwick, "The Origin of Rhyme," *Revue Bénédictin*, 36(1924), 330–46, traces rhyme to loss of inflec-

tion, which permits more words with accent on the final syllable or monosyllables. See also William Harmon, "Rhyme in English Verse: History, Structures, Function," *SP,* 84(1987), 395–93.

12. Pazzaglia, *Il Verso e l'arte della canzone,* pp. 68–75, esp. 71–72.

13. The story of Notker's discovery of the sequence is retold in Raby, *History,* pp. 210–17.

14. For current views on the sequence, Peter Dronke, "Beginnings of the Latin Sequence," *Beiträge zur Geschichte der deutschen Sprache und Literatur,* 87(1965), 43–73. Notker's sequences are examined in detail by W. von der Steinen, *Notker der Dichter und seine Geistige Welt* (2 vols., Bern, Switzerland, 1948). Meyer, *Rythmik,* I, 47, states (in fact probably overstates) the case for the importance of the sequence in European vernacular poetry: "Wenn meine obigen Darlegungen richtig sind, so hat das Sequenzendichten die Volksdichtung aus der klassizistischen Zwangsjacke und aus dem dürftigen rythmischen Gewande der Karolingerzeit befreit, zu dem Urquell aller dichterischen Schönheit, zur Musik, zurückgefurt, und so eine frie, naturgemässe Entwicklung der mittelalterlichen Dichtung ab ovo ermöglicht, und das gilt nicht nur für die Dichtung in lateinischer, sondern ebenso für die in fransösicher und in deutscher Sprache."

15. The term *clausulae* is shared by music and rhetoric. As noted in ch. 2, it refers in rhetoric to the basic thought unit of the sentence and also to the rhythms for its termination—hence to the *cursus,* which developed out of the ancient treatment of *clausulae.* It also refers in medieval usage (1) to the phrases that comprise the sequence (hence to the theory that rhyme develops from the terminal rhythms of the *clausulae*) and (2) to the musical measures that shape the verbal *clausulae.* A new meaning develops with the emergence of *musica mensurabilis* in the early twelfth century. In the new sense, *clausula* is a bit of Gregorian text that is the ground for a composition for two or three voices singing over it in "measured" rhythm—the ancestor of the motet. Willi Apel, *The Harvard Dictionary of Music* (Cambridge, Mass., 1969), s.v "clausula."

16. Raby, *History,* p. 350.

17. Ibid., p. 212.

18. Ibid., p. 217.

19. The central feature of the "new musical art," as far as scholarship is concerned, is its concept of rhythms as regular units, like poetic meters. This concept was derived from St. Augustine's *De musica.* It resulted in six "modes" of music, of which three, the trochaic, iambic, and dactylic, were commonly used. See William Waite, *The Rhythm of Twelfth-Century Polyphony: Its Theory and Practice* (Westport, Conn., 1973), pp. 13–55; Gustave Reese, *Music in the Middle Ages* (New York, 1940), pp. 272–93. Several theorists have suggested that the result of the new music was to create a heightened sense of accentual meter. The chief early advocate of this position was

Pierre Aubry, *Trouvères and Troubadours* (1910; rpt. New York, 1969). Aubry lists the "laws" of the new form on pp. 158–60. Aubry extended the theory from Latin to vernacular poetry. Close study of the musical settings in relation to the texts of early lyrics has suggested, however, (1) that the music was less important to the poets than the words, and (2) that the surviving musical scores do not support the theory that they are closely correlated to the supposed meters of the texts. See Hendrik van der Werf, *The Chansons of the Troubadours and Trouvères: A Study of the Melodies and Their Relation to the Poems* (Utrecht, 1972), pp. 35–44.

20. Cf. Lote, *Histoire*, I, 53–82. See also van der Werf, *Chansons*.

21. Raby, *History*, p. 214.

22. Norberg, *Introduction*, p. 186.

23. Raby, *History*, pp. 217–18.

24. Ibid., p. 354. This sequence uses elaborate typological rhyme. Eugene R. Cunnar, "Typological Rhyme in a Sequence of Adam of St. Victor," *SP*, 84(1987), 394–417.

25. Meyer, *Rythmik*, I, esp. 32–47. Meyer's argument that Latin rhythmic forms originated with the Psalms as transmitted in Syriac and Byzantine hymns has generally been rejected (cf. Norberg, *Introduction*, pp. 90–91). Cf. also Lote, *Histoire*, "La Cantilène de sainte Eulalie," I, 117–25.

26. Roger Dragonetti, *La Technique poétique des trouvères dans la chanson courtoise* (Bruges, 1960), pp. 461–80.

27. Lote, *Histoire*, II, 140–45.

28. The standard collection is Giovanni Mari, *I Tratatti medievali di rithmica Latina* (Milan, 1899).

29. *Parisiana poetria*, ed. Traugott Lawler (New Haven, Conn., 1974), p. xv.

30. Ibid., p. xvi.

31. Ibid., p. 5.

32. Ibid., p. xix.

33. Texts in Edmond Faral, *Les Arts poétiques du XIIe et du XIIIe siècle* (Paris, 1924).

34. *Parisiana poetria*, ed. Lawler, p. 116. The association of disyllabic rhyme with leonine rhyme (having the proper sense of internal rhyme) links caesura with terminal rhyme in a way recalling the rhymed *clausulae* of the sequence. In ancient usage, *similiter cadens* (homoeoptoton) refers to similar case endings (on nouns and adjectival words). *Similiter desinens* (homoeoteleuton) refers to similar sounds of adverbs, verbs, etc. that do not have case endings (*Rhetorica ad Herennium*, IV, 3, 4–5; 20, 28; 23, 32). These meanings are not those used by John of Garland.

35. Cf. *Parisiana poetria*, ed. Lawler, pp. 159–61. For the musical terminology see Richard Crocker, "*Musica Rhythmica* and *Musica Metrica* in Antique and Medieval Theory," *Journal of Music Theory*, 2(1958), 2–23.

36. *Parisiana Poetria,* ed. Lawler, p. 160. "Sub certo numero sine metricis pedibus ordinata."

37. John makes it clear that a dactylic rhyme is permissible in Latin. In French, such a rhyme is not permissible. Italian verse, on the other hand, permits it (*sdrucciolo*).

38. *Parisiana poetria,* ed. Lawler, p. 268; cf. Puttenham, in *ECE*, ed. Smith (cited ch. 1, no. 20), ii, 67–68: "Our proportion Poeticall resteth in five points: Staff, Measure, Concord, Situation, and Figure."

39. The complete title is *L'Art de dictier et de fere chançons, balades, virelais et rondeaulx.* . . . (1392). It is in vol. 7 of the *Oeuvres complètes de Eustache Deschamps,* ed. Gaston Raynaud (Paris, 1891), pp. 266–92. For comment, Lote, *Histoire*, III, 242–46; W. F. Patterson, *Three Centuries of French Poetic Theory* (Ann Arbor, Mich., 1935), I, 84–96. For medieval French versification, Lote, *Histoire*, II, 53–145 (meters and rhymes), and III, 253–314 (stanza forms). Troubadour prosodic theory develops over a century before northern French theory. Ramon Vidal's *Razos de trobar* and Uc de Faidit's *Donatz proensals* are thirteenth century. The major treatise is *Las Lays d'amors* (ca. 1340), ed., with Fr. trans., M. Gatien-Arnoult, *Monuments de la littérature romane* (4 vols., Paris, 1841–49).

40. *L'Art de dictier,* ed. Raynaud, VII, 270–71.

41. Patterson, *Three Centuries,* I, 3.

42. Sebillet, *L'Art poétique françoys,* ed. Félix Gaiffe (Paris, 1910).

43. Peletier's *L'Art poétique d'Horace* was published in 1544, but the first edition to survive is that of 1545. The *Art* is an imitation of Horace using Horatian ideas rather than a close translation. In the preface, Peletier touches on many subjects that would later become prominent: the dignity of the French language, the need to improve it by imitation of the ancients, the excellent example of the Italians. Peletier rejects the notion of abandoning native traditions for ancient ones. Horace is a useful guide, but Peletier does not counsel contempt for the French past. Cf. André Boulanger, ed., *L'Art poétique de Jacques Peletier du Mans* (1555) (Paris, 1930). The preface is on pp. 228–30. Boulanger summarizes its theme (p. 42): "Le but suprême est de donner à la France une littérature digne du genie national."

44. *L'Art poétique françoyse,* ed. Gaiffe, pp. 186–87.

45. Ibid., II, xxv (p. 194): "[Vers] sans ryme demeurent autant froys, comme un corps sans sang et sans ame." The chief proponent of *vers blancs* was Blaise de Vigénère (1523–96), who wrote Psalm paraphrases in octosyllabic blank verse; Ronsard gave only lukewarm approval to experiments in blank verse. Perhaps Sebillet knew of the experiments in *versi sciolti* by Luigi Alamanni, whose *Rime Toscane* were published in Lyons in 1533, followed in 1546 by *La Coltivazione,* perhaps the most famous of all experiments in *versi sciolti*. Cf. Henri Hauvette, *Luigi Alamanni: Sa vie et son oeuvre* (Paris, 1930), pp. 215–20 ("Le vers blanc") and 264–90 (on *La Coltivazione*).

46. *L'Art poétique françoyse*, ed. Gaiffe, II, viii (pp. 161–2).

47. Ibid.

48. Text of DuBellay, *Deffence et illustration de la langue francoyse*, ed. Louis Terreaux (Paris, 1972). There are several treatments of the poetic theory of the Pléiade. Robert J. Clements, *Critical Theory and Practice of the Pléiade* (Cambridge, Mass., 1942), is primarily concerned with Neoplatonism. Graham Castor, *Pléiade Poetics: A Study in Sixteenth-Century Thought and Terminology* (Cambridge, 1964), is primarily concerned with inspiration. Isidore Silver, *Ronsard's General Theory of Poetry* (St. Louis, Mo., 1973), comments on the problem of language (pp. 26–62), on vocabulary, including neologisms, archaisms, technical terms, and foreign words (pp. 63–72), and on translation and imitation.

49. For the debt of the *Deffence* to Speroni's *Dialogo delle liugue*, Pierre Villey-Desmeserets, *Les sources italiennes de la 'Deffence et illustration de la langue françoise' de Joaquim du Bellay* (Paris, 1908). Select passages are quoted in the edition of Terreaux, pp. 23, 27, 44, 52–53. For the debt to Alamanni, Hauvette, *Luigi Alamanni*, pp. 443–51. The background of these ideas is considered in "L'Ideal di una lingua suprema ai tempi di Giraldi," in Camillo Guerieri Crocetti, *G. B. Giraldi ed il pensiero critico del sec. XVI* (Milan, 1932), pp. 121–66. For a minority view on Italian influence, Franco Simone, "Italianismo e anti-Italianismo nei poeti della Pléiade," *La Pléiade e il rinascimento Italiano* (Rome, 1977), pp. 7–38. Simone argues that DuBellay is declaring French independence of Italy. Rome is dead (pp. 37–38). The truly Italianate Frenchmen were in the generation before the Pléiade.

50. *Deffence*, ed. Terreaux, p. 74. Contrast the comment in the *Quintil Horatian*: "Tu ne faitz autre chose par tout l'oeuvre, mesme au second livre, que nous induire à Greciser et Latiniser en Françoys, vituperant tousjours nostre forme de poësie, comme vile, et populaire, attribuant a iceux toutes les vertus et louanges de bien dire, et bien escrire et par comparison d'icieux monstres la pauverté de nostre langue" (p. 31).

51. II, iv (ibid., p. 76): "Pour le sonnette donques tu as Petrarque et quelques modernes Italiens."

52. Ibid., p. 90: "Autrement, qui ne voudroit reigler sa Rythme comme j'ay dit, il vaudroit beaucoup mieux ne rymer point, mais faire des vers libres, comme a fait Petrarque en quelque endroit, et de notre tens le Seigneur Loys Aleman, en sa non moins docte, que plaisante Agriculture." DuBellay associates rhyme with classical homoeoteleuton and knows that it became popular in the early Middle Ages, but his understanding is weaker than that of the medieval writers on the subject. Alamanni's *Rime Toscane* were published in Lyons (1533) with a dedication to Francis I which traces the conventions of rhymed verse to the Provençal poets and defends the innovation of verse without rhyme. His *La Coltivazione* (called *Agriculture* by DuBellay), an imitation of Vergil's *Georgics* in *versi sciolti*, was printed in Paris in 1546, three

years before the *Deffence*. This work attracted considerable attention. His *Flora* (Florence, 1549) is an experiment in the Italian equivalent of the loose iambic verse of ancient comedy. Hauvette, *Luigi Alamanni*, pp. 335–48.

53. Text in *L'Art poétique de Jacques Peletier*, ed. Boulanger, pp. 105–215.

54. Ronsard, *Abbregé de l'art poetique françois*, in vol. 2 of the *Oeuvres complètes*, ed. Gustave Cohen (Paris, 1950), pp. 995–1009.

55. Ibid., p. 1004.

56. Ibid., p. 997. Ronsard makes the rule about alternation of rhymes more emphatic in the 1567 edition of the *Abbregé* by adding a paragraph calling it "une reigle infallible."

57. Ibid., p. 1015. Ronsard's *magnifique* parallels Tasso's *magnificenza* and Spenser's "magnificence." This preface is longer and more polished than the *Abbregé*. It considers vocabulary, description, knowledge of arts and sciences, presentation of the gods, need for self-criticism, license to create neologisms, and many more topics.

58. A combined edition of the *Quintil* with Sebillet's *Art poétique* appeared in 1551, 1555, and 1556. In the preface to his translation of Euripides' *Iphigeneia* (1549), Sebillet replies with restraint to DuBellay's attacks on Marot, on translation, and (implicitly) on Sebillet himself. DuBellay and Sebillet were eventually reconciled, although the battle between classical imitators and supporters of medieval tradition continued.

59. Patterson, *Three Centuries*, I, 370.

60. See L. Clark Keating, *Etienne Pasquier* (New York, 1972), esp. pp. 82–104, which review Pasquier's literary criticism and theory of language. Pasquier admired Marot but he also praised "vers mesurés." Like many others, he also advocated spelling reform.

61. Patterson, *Three Centuries*, I, 614–38.

62. August Buck, intr., *Julius Caesar Scaliger: 'Poetices libri septem' (Lyons, 1561) Mit einer Einleitung* (Stuttgart, 1964), p. 3 (I, iii): "Poetae igitur nomen non a fingendo, ut putarunt, quia fictis uterentur: sed initio a faciendo versu ductum est."

63. In *Jacques de la Taille's 'La Maniere': A Critical Edition*, ed. Pierre Han (Chapel Hill, N.C., 1970), p. 48. The French quantitative movement is paralleled to the English by A. W. Satterthwaite, *Spenser, Ronsard, and DuBellay* (Princeton, 1960), pp. 37–65.

64. *La Maniere*, ed. Han, p. 69.

65. Ibid., p. 51.

66. Donald Grout, *A Short History of Opera* (rev. ed., New York, 1965), pp. 34–39. Grout notes that one of the objectives of the Camerata theorists was that "the words must be sung with the correct and natural declamation, as they would be spoken" (p. 36). The prosodic aspect of this effort is explored by Jacopo Perli in the preface to *Euridice*, which explains that dialogue in classical drama (and in proper music drama) should be halfway between melody and speech. Iambic verse is ideal for this because it is less formal than

heroic verse but more formal than unadorned speech. Cf. William O. Strunk, *Source Readings in Music History* (New York, 1950), p. 378.

Chapter IV: A Question of Language

1. Franco Simone, "Italianismo e anti-Italianismo nei poeti della Pléiade," in *La Pléiade e il rinascimento Italiano* (Rome, 1977), pp. 1–38, esp. 9–11. Corbinelli, the publisher, had the protection of Catherine de'Medici, and the volume has introductory poems by Dorat praising "Rome reborn" and Baïf praising Dante's love for the Italian language with the clear implication that French writers should have a comparable love for the French language. Simone regards the edition as support for the anti-Protestant—hence anti-German and pro-Italian—faction. Innocent Gentillet's attack on Machiavelli, the notorious *Contre-Machiavel* (1576), is associated in this reading with the opposite (pro-German) faction (Simone, p. 28).

2. The facts are summarized by Aristide Marigo, ed., *De vulgari eloquentia* (3rd ed., Florence, 1968), pp. xliv-xlv. This is the standard modern edition. It has a supplement by Giorgio Ricci. I have used it as my basic text of the *De vulgari* here and below. For a modern English translation of the *De vulgari* with commentary, Robert S. Haller, *Literary Criticism of Dante Alighieri* (Lincoln, Neb., 1973). A facsimile of Trissino's 1529 Italian translation has been published by the Scolar Press (Menston, England, 1970).

3. *De vulgari*, ed. Marigo, p. 1.

4. For Dante's sources, ibid., pp. xxxii-xxxviii. Marigo believes that Dante drew his version of the theory of the three styles from the *Parisiana poetria* (p. xxxvii). However, Dante's concepts of the highest art and of *utilitas* are drawn from *Ad Herennium* (p. cxxiv), which he believed was written by Cicero. He probably knew (pp. xxxii-xxxiii) the *Donatz proensals* of Uc de Faidit (ca. 1250), a treatise on Provençal versification. In book 3 of the *Tesor* Brunetto Latini treats rhetoric. He, too, uses the Tower of Babel story to explain the diversification of languages (pp. xxxv-xxxvi).

5. Mario Pazzaglia, *Il Verso e l'arte della canzone nel 'De vulgari eloquentia'* (Florence, 1967), examines the debt of Dante to Boethius and St. Augustine. Ricci's supplement to Marigo (pp. 373–75) summarizes contributions since Marigo.

6. Texts in Edmond Faral, *Les Arts poétiques du XIIe et du XIIIe siècle* (Paris, 1924). The most obvious contrast with the *De vulgari* is the *Summa artis rithmici vulgaris dictaminis* by Antonio da Tempo in 1332, ed. Richard Andrews (Bologna, 1977). The work consists of seventy-seven chapters devoted chiefly to poetic forms, including sonnet, ballata, canzone, madrigal, and others. It also discusses scansion and rhyme. Between 1340 and 1525 it was considered the standard treatment of the subject. Trissino refers to it frequently in *La Poetica* (1529). It was published in Venice in 1509. Bembo may not have

known it, and Lodovico Dolce and Sebastian Minturno allude to it only to contradict it (*Summa,* ed. Andrews, preface, p. viii).

7. Roger Dragonetti, *La Technique poétique des trouvères dans la chanson courtoise* (Bruges, 1960), p. 432.

8. Pazzaglia, *Il Verso e l'arte della canzone,* p. 208.

9. For early Italian prosody see, in Renzo Cremante and Mario Pazzaglia, eds., *La Metrica* (Milan, 1972), D'Arco Silvio Avalle, "Preistoria della endecasillabo," pp. 243–46, and Francesco D'Ovidio, "Sull'origini dei versi Italiani," pp. 237–46. D'Ovidio agrees with Michel Burger that the hendecasyllabic and the *sdrucciolo* are both derived from quantitative prototypes. Avalle is inclined to Dante's view that the hendecasyllable is derived from the French decasyllable via the Troubadours, who began using lyric caesura. Cf. also the excellent bibliography of Italian versification, pp. 481–506.

10. The quotations used by Dante show that he has the distinction between *ordo naturalis* and *ordo artificialis* in mind. These distinctions were used first in relation to rhetorical organization (*dispositio*). Only in the early twelfth century, apparently, were they applied to grammatical constructions, as in the following comment by Konrad von Maure (fl. 1250): "Naturalis hic est ordo, quando nominativus precedit et verbum cum suis determinationibus . . . subsequitur. Et iste ordo rem, prout gesta est, ordine recto, plano modo . . . exponit. Artificialis ordo est, partibus materie artificialiter transpositis, rei gestae . . . narratio per verba polita . . . quasi dieeretur." Cf. Franz Quadlbauer, "Zur Theorie der Komposition in der mittelalterlichen Rhetorik und Poetik," *Rhetoric Revalued,* ed. Brian Vickers (New York, 1982), pp. 115–31 (quotation from von Maure, p. 123; other authors in *De vulgari,* ed. Marigo, pp. 205–6).

11. Cf. Pazzaglia, *Il Verso e l'arte della canzone,* pp. 147–48.

12. Concetta Greenfield, *Humanist and Scholastic Poetics, 1250–1500* (Lewisburg, Penna., 1981).

13. For an overview of the *questione della lingua,* Francisco Flora, *Storia della letteratura Italiana* (Mondadori, 1952), II, 126–62. Flora notes that the concept of *Latinitas* was applied both to vernacular syntax and to vernacular vocabulary: "La *latinitas* sintattica e lessicale . . . fu già in Dante nel Petrarca e nel Boccaccio . . . l'ideal modello linguistico."

14. Maruzio Vitale, *La Questione della lingua* (Palermo, 1967), pp. 22–63.

15. Pietro Bembo, *Prose della volgar lingua,* ed. Dionisotti-Casalone (Turin, 1931). For a comparison of Bembo with those theorists discussed below, Giancarlo Mazzacurati, *Misure del classicismo rinascimentale* (Naples, 1967). Ch. 1, Castiglione; ch. 2, Pietro Bembo; ch. 3, Trissino.

16. Cf. for Trissino's contribution, Mazzacurati, *Misure,* pp. 263–94, "La Mediazione Trissiniana."

17. The translation is by Sir Thomas Hoby (1561), *The Book of the Courtier,* ed. Walter Raleigh (London, 1900; rpt. 1967), pp. 19–21.

18. Sperone Speroni, *Dialogo delle lingue*, ed. Helene Harth (Munich, 1975).

19. Ibid., pp. 26–32 (on Bembo's vernacular humanism), pp. 40–48 (influence on DuBellay), and pp. 35–39 (Pomponazzi and the *res* and *verba* controversy). The dialogue itself is reprinted from the 1575 edition in facsimile with facing German translation, pp. 62–133.

20. *La Poetica*, rpt. in *Poetiken des Cinquecento*, ed. Bernhard Fabian (Munich, 1967–69), vols. 24 (1529) and 25 (1562). For biography, Barnardo Morsolin, *Giangiorgio Trissino . . . un letterato nel secolo XVI* (Vicenza, 1878). Trissino was associated with most of the important classicizing poets of the age, including Bembo, Giovanni Rucellai (author of *Rosmunda*), Claudio Tolomei, and Luigi Alamanni. His dialogue *Il Castellano* advocates a purified Tuscan in contrast to a Florentine literary language. He was regarded by Giraldi Cintio as the father of Italian *versi sciolti*. Cf. Morsolin, *Giangiorgio Trissino*, pp. 71–92.

21. *La Poetica* (1529), fol. IIv. Dante and Antonio da Tempo "quasi in una medesima età . . . scrisseno."

22. Ibid., fol. XIv: "La rima è questo, che i Greci dimandano rithmo, et i Latini numero, la unde si può dire, che rima, rithmo, e numero siano quasi il medesimo." Trissino appeals to Dante and Antonio da Tempo, who "sempre la rima nominorono rithmus."

23. Ibid., fol. XIVr.

24. *La Poetica* (1562), fol. 29v. Cf. John H. Steadman, "Verse without Rhyme: Sixteenth Century Italian Defences of *Versi Sciolti*," *Italica*, 61(1964), 384–402.

25. *La Italia liberata da Gotthi* (1547), iii v: "come dice Demetrio Phalerio, la enargia, che è la éfficace rapprentazione." *Enargia* is *evidentia* in Latin rhetoric; cf. Quint., *Inst.*, VIII, 3, 61; Erasmus, *De duplici copia verborum ac rerum*, tr. D. B. King and H. D. Rix (Milwaukee, Wisc., 1963), p. 47; and *ECE*, ed. Smith (cited ch. 1, n. 20), I, 400, II, 148, 167.

26. *Italia liberata*, I, iii v: "Si fà col dire diligentemente ogni particolarità de le azioni, e non vi lasciare nulla e non troncare, ne diminuire i periodi, che si dicono."

27. Girolamo Muzio, *Rime diverse del Mutio Iustinopolitano* (Venice, 1551), fol. 86r-v:

> Piu sono atti à la lira che à la tromba
> I ternarii, et le stanze: In quelli, e in queste
> Chiuder conviemmi in numerati versi
> La mia sentenza, et chiuderla conviemmi
> Nel fin del verso, o perdo ogni vaghezza. . . .
> . . . à voler che senza alcuno intoppo
> Corra lo stil continuo, in quella vece
> Che già gli antichi usar le sei misure,

> Porrem le rime senza rime: queste
> Sono oltra l'altre chiare, pure, & alte.

My translation attempts to suggest Muzio's prosodic effects through English blank verse.

28. Ricchi, *I Tre tiranni* (Venice, 1533): "Ha cercato l'authore [Agostino Ricchi] . . . che quanto manco è possibile de la prosa si allontani. Il che ha fatto con un proceder naturale senza transposition di parole, et poi aiutato col continouar de le sentenze de l'un verso ne l'altro, et le fini de le risposte non mai in fine del verso, perche altrimente saria difficile che il suono di esso non impedisse il natural pronuntiare, il che principalmente in questo stile si debbe avertire."

29. *Italia liberata*, p. iv.

30. *Sophonisba* (Rome, 1524), fol. iii r-v: "Non credo gia, che si possa giustamente attribuire a vitio, l'esser scritta in lingua Italiana, et il non havere anchora secondo l'uso commune accordate le rime, ma lasciatele libere in molti luoghi. Perciò che la cagione, la quale m'ha indotto a farla in questa lingua, si è . . . è megliore, e più nobile, e forse men facile ad asseguire, di quello, che per avventura è reputato: E lo vedrà non solamente ne le narrationi, et le oratione utilissimo, ma nel muovere compassione necessario; Perciò che quel sermone, il quale suol muovere questa, nasce dal dolore, et il dolore manda fuori non pensate parole, onde la rima, che pensamento dimonstra, è veramente ala compassione contraria."

31. *Discorso intorno al comporre de i romanzi*, in *Discorsi di M. Giovambattista Giraldi Cinthio* (Venice, 1554), p. 132: "Bembo alquale, come deve molto questa lingua, per essere ella come rinata per lui, e venuta in pregio, deve anco molto, per haverla egli con molta loda arrichita." Other references to Bembo, pp. 4, 87, 91, 110. Cf. Camillo Guerrieri Crocetti, *G. B. Giraldi ed il pensiero critico del sec. XVI* (Milan, 1932), esp. 301-33, "Questione metriche."

32. *Le Tragedie di M. Gio. Battista Giraldi Cinzio* (Venice, 1583). Each play was printed separately and is so paginated. For the quotation, I, 134-35:

> . . . il divin Bembo,
> Bembo divino, che volgar lingua
> Tolt'hà dal career tenebroso, e cieco
> Regno di Dite con più lieto plettro,
> Ch'Orpheo non fè la sua bramata moglie.
> E il Trissino gentil, che col suo canto.
> Prima d'ognun, dal Tebro, e da Illiso
> Già trasse la tragedia a l'onde d'Arno.
> E il gran Molza. . . .
> Et il buon Tolomei, ch'i volgar versi
> Con novo modo a i numeri Latini
> Ha già condotto, e a la Romana forma.
> E . . . Alamanni. . . .

33. In Christina Roaf, ed., *Sperone Speroni: 'Canace' e scritti in sua difesa* . . . [con] *Giambattista Giraldi Cinthio: Scritti contra la 'Canace'* (Bologna, 1982), p. lvii. The various texts in this impassioned controversy are reprinted on pp. 195–304. See also Bernard Weinberg, *A History of Literary Criticism in the Italian Renaissance* (Chicago, 1961), II, 912–54, "The Quarrel over Speroni's *Canace*." Castelvetro was an influential advocate of prose in tragedy.

34. *Le Tragedie di . . . Cinzio (Didone)*, pp. 134: "Compose la sua Sophonisba, in quella maniera di versi, ch'egli prima di ogni uno diede . . . in luogo, del Iambo. . . . [perche] fossero simigliantissimi al parlare familigiare de'nostri tempi, & cadessero come i Iambi, dalla bocca de'favellatori ne'communi ragionamenti. Alla opinione di questo Eccelente Tragico si accostò il Rucellai, nella sua Rosmonda, che uscì con molta loda, e poco dopo la Sophonisba."

35. Giraldi Cintio, *Discorso intorno al comporre . . . delle commedie et delle tragedie*, in *Discorsi*, p. 229.

36. Ibid., p. 234.

37. Ibid.

38. Ibid., *Discorso . . . de i romanzi*, pp. 90–91: "Porti con esso lei la dolcezza del suono, et la gravità accompagnata col numero, et con le altre parti, che alla altezza convengono. Le quali cose non sono, ne possono essere in questa spetie di versi [versi sciolti], che il loro inventore, che fu il Trissino, a nostri tempi, chiamò sciolti perche erano liberi dalla obligazione delle rime."

39. Ibid., p. 90: "Perche se lo [verso] sciolto conviene alla scena, perche egli è simigliarissimo al parlar di ogni dì, vi deve sommamente sconvenire lo sdrucciolo, come numero, che non ha punto di somiglianza con i ragionamenti, che nascono di dì in dì tra gli huomini." Cf. *Discorso . . . delle tragedie*, pp. 227, 229, 234.

40. Ibid., *Discorso . . . delle tragedie*, p. 235.

41. Henri Hauvette, *Un Exilé Florentin a la cour de France au XVIe siècle: Luigi Alamanni* (Paris, 1903), pp. 335–48. Hauvette considers the possible influence of Italian fashions on the French—especially the influence of Alamanni (pp. 443–51). He concludes that DuBellay cannot be understood except against the Italian background. More recent scholarship qualifies this conclusion; e.g., Simone, "Italianismo."

42. *I sei primi libri del Eneide di Vergilio* (Venice, 1540). Book 1 is dedicated to "M. Aurelia Tolomei de Borghesi," which relates it to Claudio Tolomei. It was apparently instigated by "Niccolo d'Aristotile detto Zoppino." Book 1 was translated by Alessandro Sansedoni, 2 by Cardinal Ippolito de'Medici, 3 by Bernardino Borghesi, 4 by Bartolomeo Piccolomini, 5 by Aldobrando Cerretanti Borghesi, and 6 by Alessandro Piccolomini. The complete *Aeneid* was republished frequently, with some changes in translators: e.g., 1556, 1559, 1562, 1586, 1593, 1606, 1613. The edition is noted by Vladimiro Zabughin, *Vergilio nel rinascimento Italiano da Dante a Torquato Tasso* (2 vols., Bologna, 1921), II, 359–61. Zabughin calls it (p. 359) "una bizarra versione." This, however, is patently unfair.

43. *Versi, et regole de la nuova poesia Toscana* (Rome, 1539). The rules have recently been reprinted by Pierre Han in an appendix to *Jacques de la Taille's 'La Maniere': A Critical Edition* (Chapel Hill, N.C., 1970), pp. 83–102. Tolomei's Accademia della Nuova Poesia is the obvious forerunner of Baïf's Academie de Poésie et de Musique and a possible precedent for the Areopagus mentioned, perhaps facetiously, in the correspondence between Edmund Spenser and Gabriel Harvey. Cf. Luigi Sbargli, *Claudio Tolomei: Umanista Senese del cinquecento* (Siena, 1939), pp. 56–69. Like Trissino, Tolomei was interested in reformed spelling and published his theories in *Il Polito di Adriano Franci* (1525) (Sbargli, pp. 18–27); for *Versi, et regole*, Sbargli, pp. 56–69.

44. *Versi, et regole*, fol. Iv: "Si sono messi à caminar per le belle antiche strade."

45. The rules begin fol. XIr.

46. Sbargli, *Claudio Tolomei*, pp. 18–27.

47. Han, *Jacques de la Taille*, p. 31.

48. *Defence of Ryme*, ECE, II, 368.

49. Flora, *Storia della letteratura Italiana*, II, 385.

Chapter V: Notes of Instruction

1. For *syntaxis* as an element of the humanistic program of the reform of language, see Jean-Claude Chevalier, *Histoire de la syntaxe: Naissance de la notion de complément dans la grammaire française (1530–1750)* (Geneva, 1968), ch. 2, "La Grammaire au début du XVI siècle," and Aldo Scaglione, *The Classical Theory of Composition from Its Origin to the Present* (Chapel Hill, N.C., 1972), pp. 126–58. For educational reform, W. H. Woodward, *Vittorino da Feltre and Other Humanist Educators* (New York, 1921).

2. Cf. Craig R. Thompson, "Erasmus as Internationalist and Cosmopolitan," *Archiv für Reformationsgeschichte*, 46(1955), 167–95.

3. The English movement is traced by Richard Foster Jones, *The Triumph of the English Language* (Stanford, Calif., 1953), but Jones underplays the larger European perspective within which the English movement took place.

4. *Toxophilus*, in *The English Works of Roger Ascham*, ed. W. A. Wright (Cambridge, 1904), p. xiv.

5. *The Scholemaster*, ed. Edward Arber (London, 1920; rpt. 1977), pp. 19–20. I have used this edition because G. Gregory Smith prints only excerpts in *Elizabethan Critical Essays*. The modern-spelling edition of *The Schoolmaster (1570)*, ed. Lawrence V. Ryan (Ithaca, N. Y., 1967), should be consulted for its excellent introduction (pp. xx-xxiii).

6. *The Scholemaster*, ed. Arber, p. 117.

7. Ibid., pp. 117–18.

8. Ibid., pp. 144–45.

9. Sir Thomas Hoby, *The Book of the Courtier*, ed. Walter Raleigh (London, 1900; rpt. 1967), p. 9.

10. Webbe, in *ECE*, ed. Smith (cited ch. 1, n. 20), I, 227, 229.

11. Ibid., p. 234. For an expression of the same idea in relation to rhetoric, Thomas Wilson's *Arte of Rhetorique* (1650), ed. G. H. Mair Bowers (Oxford, 1909), preface (unpaginated), "Eloquence First Given by God, After Lost by Man, and Last Repaired by God Again." In Wilson, the emblem of Hercules drawing men by chains attached to their tongues is recalled. Wilson's general source for the preface is Cicero, *De inventione*, I, 2; he also draws on Horace, *Ars poetica*, ll. 391–408. The earliest full-scale Tudor defense of poetry is the *Oratio in laudem artis poeticae*, ed. William Ringler (Princeton, 1940). The commonplaces regarding Orpheus and Amphion are on p. 45. The *Oratio* is attributed by Ringler to John Rainolds. It is more convincingly attributed to Henry Dethick, an Oxford scholar and undisputed author of an *Oratio in laudem poëseos* (ca. 1572), by James Binns, "Henry Dethick in Praise of Poetry," *The Library*, 30(1975), 200–215.

12. William Lily, *A Shorte Introduction of Grammar* and *Brevissima institutio seu ratio grammatices cognoscendae* (1567), ed. V. J. Flynn (New York, 1945). The prosody section extends from fol. G4v to H3v. The history of renaissance grammar is reviewed by G. A. Padley, *Grammatical Theory in Western Europe, 1500–1700* (Cambridge, 1976). See also T. W. Baldwin, *William Shakespere's Small Latine and Lesse Greeke* (Champaign, Ill., 1944), II, 690–701. For discussion of the *prosodia* section, Derek Attridge, *Well-Weighed Syllables* (Cambridge, 1974), pp. 30–68. The seventeenth-century commentaries are Anon., *Animadversions upon Lilies Grammar* (1625), John Danes, *A Light to Lilie* (1637), Wm. Haine, *Lillies Rules Construed* (1638), and R. R., *An English Grammar: Or a Plain Explanation of Lillies Grammar* (1641).

13. The list in Brinsley's *Ludus literarius, Or the Grammar Schoole* (rpt. Menston, England, 1968) is longer than Lily's. It includes isocolon, parenthesis, asyndeton, polysyndeton, hysteron proteron, hendiadys, catachresis, etc.—all of which come into play in departures from what Brinsley calls "grammatical order." Thomas Linacre wrote a treatise on *syntaxis* in six books: *De emendata structura Latina . . . libri sex* (1524) (rpt. Menston, England, 1968). He treats ecthlipsis, aposiopesis, zeugma, syllepsis, prolepsis, anapodoton, pleonasm, parecolon, epanalepsis, hyperbaton, anastrophe, synchysis, enallage, anacoluthon, and various subcategories of these figures. For discussion see Padley, *Grammatical Theory*, pp. 51–54. Linacre calls natural and artificial types of construction *iusta* and *figurata*.

14. Attridge, *Well-Weighed Syllables*, pp. 30–40; Jane Fenyo, "Grammar and Music in Thomas Campion's *Observations in the Art of English Poesie*," *Studies in the Renaissance*, 17(1970), 46–72, provides a rule-by-rule comparison of Lily and Campion.

15. *An English Grammar: Or a Plain Explanation of Lillies Grammar in English*

... By R. R. *Master in Arts* (1641) (rpt. Menston, England, 1972), "Of Parsing," pp. 155–82. Alexander Gil, Milton's tutor, signed an endorsement printed on the end page.

16. *Ludus literarius*, pp. 190–97.

17. The *Flores poetarum* was published under three different titles: *Flores illustrium poetarum, Illustrium poetarum flores,* and *Viridarium poetarum*. It was compiled early in the sixteenth century by Octavianus Mirandula. From the beginning, it included an introduction by Philippus Beroaldus. Reprints were made throughout Europe until the eighteenth century. The London edition of 1611 printed by Arthur Johnson is 814 pages.

18. Ibid., pp. 211–13. John Stockwood's edition of *Progymnasma scholasticum* appeared in London in 1597 and often thereafter. There were many editions of Smetius, e.g., *Prosodia promptissima* (London, 1615). The London edition of 1635 is listed as the fourteenth edition, an indication of the popularity of the work.

19. *Ludus literarius*, p. 213. The eminently intelligent Alexander Gil wrote an English grammar, *Logonomia Anglica* (1619), ed. Bror Danielsson and Arvid Gabrielson (Stockholm, 1972), in which he differentiates between what he calls "grammatical accent" and "rhetorical accent." The latter expresses the sense of a passage: "Accentus est duplex Grammaticus aut Rhetoricus. Grammaticus est qua vocalis una, aut dipthongus, in omni dictione affecta est. Rhetoricus, qui ad sensum animo altius infigendum, emfasin in una voce habet potius quam alia" (p. 124).

20. *Acolastus*, ed. P. L. Carver (London, 1937), pp. 40–44. See also W. E. D. Atkinson, *Acolastus . . . Latin Text with a Critical Introduction and an English Translation* (London, Ontario, 1964).

21. *Acolastus*, ed. Carver, p. 3.

22. Ibid., p. 1.

23. Ibid., p. 6.

24. Ibid., p. 9.

25. Ibid., p. 15.

26. Ibid., p. 41.

27. Joannes Despauterius (Jean Despautère) is the author of a brief grammar, *Rudimenta* (Paris, 1514), a scholarly grammar of ca. 700 pages, *Commentarii grammatici* (Paris, 1527), and a popular *Ars versificatoria* (1512 and many later editions). He also wrote a textbook on *syntaxis* together with a manual on letter writing based on Erasmus (*Syntaxis. . . . Item Epistolae Componendae Ratio ex Erasmo Roterdamo* [1515]). For Despauterius, see Scaglione, *The Classical Theory*, pp. 130–32.

28. *Acolastus*, ed. Carver, p. 44.

29. *The Scholemaster*, ed. Arber, pp. 139–40. Cf. Campion, *ECE*, II, 335.

30. *The Scholemaster*, ed. Arber, p. 144.

31. Ibid., p. 73. Webbe gives the following scansion in *A Discourse of English Poesie, ECE*, I, 283:

All trāvĕllĕrs̄ dō gl̄ădlȳ rēpŏrt grēat prāysĕ tō Ūlȳssĕs̄,

Fōr thăt hē knēw mănȳ mēns mănĕrs̄, ănd sāw mănȳ Cītĭēs̄.

32. *The Scholemaster*, ed. Arber, p. 146. Ascham's pupil Elizabeth wrote at least one quantitative English line: "Persius was a crab-staff, bawdy Martial, Ovid a fine wag" (Leicester Bradner, *The Poems of Queen Elizabeth I* [Providence, R. I., 1964], p. 7).

33. *The Scholemaster*, ed. Arber, p. 147.

34. Ibid., p. 148.

35. In *Toxophilus*, ed. Wright, p. 12.

36. Ed. G. H. Mair (London, 1910), preface (unpaginated).

37. *ECE*, I, 53. George Pettie, on the other hand, commends the use of neologisms in his preface to Guazzo's *Civil Conversations* (1582) because they enlarge the vocabulary of the language.

38. Ibid., p. 49.

39. Ibid., p. 50.

40. Ibid., p. 49. Cf. Susanne Woods, *Natural Emphasis: English Versification from Chaucer to Dryden* (San Marino, Calif., 1985), p. 112. Woods concludes quite reasonably that the reference is not intended in a quantitative sense.

41. *ECE*, I, 49. The best discussion of Gascoigne's theory of prosody is by Edward Weismiller, "Studies of Style and Verse Form in *Paradise Regained*," in *A Variorum Commentary on the Poems of John Milton*, ed. A. S. P. Woodhouse and Douglas Bush, vol. 4 (New York, 1975), pp. 259–63. See also Woods, *Natural Emphasis*, pp. 110–16.

42. *ECE*, I, 54–55. Gascoigne is apparently the first critic to use the term "rhyme royal." For Chaucer's derivation of the form from the French ballade and for the derivation of the name from *chant royal* and *ballad royal*, see Theodore Maynard, *The Connection between the Ballade, Chaucer's Modification of It, Rime Royal, and the Spenserian Stanza* (Washington, D. C., 1934), esp. pp. 83–92.

43. Ibid., 54, 50.

44. Ibid.

45. Gil, *Logonomia Anglica*, p. 126, seems to equate circumflex with what would today be called relative stress. He quotes "I am afráid of him" to illustrate an emphatic statement in contrast to "I am afrâid of him," meaning "I am not immediately frightened, but I am apprehensive about the future."

46. *ECE*, I, 50.

47. John Thompson, *The Founding of English Metre* (London, 1961), pp. 69, 73–74.

48. "Treasure" accented on the second syllable is a romance form also found in Middle English.

49. *ECE*, I, 53.

50. Ibid., pp. 53–54.

51. Woods, *Natural Emphasis*, p. 131.

52. *ECE*, I, 49.

53. Ibid., p. 56. Cf. Woods, *Natural Emphasis*, p. 142, for the suggestion that the rough four-beat lines of the February eclogue of Spenser's *Shepheardes Calender* are intended to reproduce what Elizabethans heard when they read what they called "riding rhyme."

54. *ECE*, II, 79.

55. Ibid., I, 57. A complement to Gascoigne's association of poulter's measure with psalms and hymns is provided by Thomas Lodge's *Defence of Poetry* (1579), written in reply to Stephen Gosson's *Schoole of Abuse* and dedicated to Sir Philip Sidney. (Cf. Lodge, in *ECE*, I, 71.) The argument that the Old Testament poets write in meter goes back to St. Jerome and is repeated by Bede in *De arte metrica*. Attributing the idea to Beroaldus, an Italian humanist, Lodge announces that David wrote in Horatian meters, sometimes in iambics and sometimes in Sapphics, and Isaiah, Job, and Solomon wrote in hexameters.

56. *ECE*, I, 52.

57. Ibid., p. 53. Cf. Webbe, *ECE*, I, 286, and Puttenham ("Of Cesure"), *ECE*, II, 77–80, for the concept of "natural emphasis" and the related concept of natural construction.

58. Cf. Nancy Williams, "The Eight Parts of a Theme in 'Gascoigne's Memories: III,'" *SP*, 83(1986), 117–37. Part of the difference between Wyatt and Gascoigne is the movement from syntactical complexity to rhetorical formulas for organizing works. A similar difference is observable between the verse of Jasper Heywood's Seneca translations and that of *Gorboduc*.

59. Attridge, *Well-Weighed Syllables*. Also G. L. Hendrickson, "Elizabethan Quantitative Hexameters," *PQ*, 28(1949), 237–60. William Ringler, "Master Drant's Rules," *PQ*, 29(1950), 70–74, attempts a reconstruction of the lost rules and quotes a significant note on quantitative meter by Sir Philip Sidney from a Jesus College, Oxford, manuscript. An outstanding addition to this literature, with thorough analysis of the musical symbolism inherent in quantitative poetry, is Seth Weiner, "Spenser's Study of English Syllables and Its Completion by Thomas Campion," *Spenser Studies*, 3(1982), 3–56.

60. *ECE*, I, 89.

61. Ibid., p. 95.

62. Ibid., p. 99.

63. Ibid., p. 102.

64. Ibid., p. 116.

65. Ibid., pp. 125–26. "My lorde Buckhurste" is Thomas Sackville, co-author of *Gorboduc*.

66. Ibid., p. 229.

67. Ibid., p. 266.

68. Ibid., p. 268.

69. Ibid., p. 273.

70. Ibid., II, 329. R. W. Short, "The Metrical Theory and Practice of Thomas Campion," *PMLA*, 51(1944), 1003–18, argues that Campion's song lyrics, usually considered syllabic-accentual, are, by Campion's own rules, quantitative-accentual, a little in the manner of the Ambrosian hymns. He provides examples showing that the quantitative scansion is consistent with the accentual scansion, and he argues that the "equivalence" does not appear in the pentameter couplets Campion used for the dramatic parts of his masques. In "Spenser's Study of English Syllables," Seth Weiner brilliantly analyzes the musical symbolism of Campion's prosody, with special emphasis on the ode "Rose-cheekt Lawra."

71. Fenyo, "Grammar and Music in Thomas Campion's *Observations*," pp. 54–72. See, however, Seth Weiner, "Spenser's Study of English Syllables," for the argument that Campion is essentially a "completing" of the analysis begun in the Spenser-Harvey correspondence.

72. *ECE*, II, 335. Elegy consists (p. 344) of "a meere licenciate *Iambick* [and] . . . two united *Dimeters*."

73. Ibid., p. 338.

74. Ibid.

75. Sidney, *Apology*, in *ECE*, I, 182.

76. Ibid., p. 204.

77. Ibid., II, 63.

78. Ibid., pp. 77–80.

79. Ibid., 76.

80. Ibid., 76.

81. Ibid., 72.

82. Ibid., 83–84.

83. Ibid., 117–22. Scansions, pp. 127–38. A striking illustration of the complexity of differentiating between quantitative and accentual systems in Puttenham is provided (p. 130) by the scansion of a line from Surrey's elegy on Wyatt: "What holy grave? alas, what sepulcher?" Puttenham calls this a "Pentameter . . . of ten sillables." If Puttenham understood accentual prosody as the equivalent in accentual feet of quantitative feet, then he should regard the line as a perfect "iambic pentameter." However, this is not the case. In spite of the fact that the line scans regularly as accentual iambic pentameter, and with no violation of natural word accent, he complains that it "seems odde and defective, for not well observing the natural accent of every word." The first problem is that he considers *u* in "sepulchre" long by position (before the consonant cluster), and therefore (presumably) he places the natural accent of "sepulchre" on the second syllable. The second is that he is not interested in an English "iambic pentameter"—the idea does not seem to have occurred to him. To make the line perfect, he suggests adding a monosyllable ("fit") and scanning the line as a dactyl followed by four trochees. The line, with his scansion, is:

What hōlĭe grāve? ă lās, whăt fĭt sēpŭlchĕr?

Cf. Thomas Campion's discussion of iambic and trochaic meter, *ECE*, II, 330–31.

84. Ibid., p. 134.

85. Ibid., 359. Although it is the most influential and best known, Daniel's essay is not necessarily the most sophisticated answer to Campion. In *Logonomia Anglica* (ed. Danielsson, p. 124) Alexander Gil appears to recognize the nature of English stress accent. Significantly, he uses the same example ("carpenter") that was used in the debates between Spenser and Harvey in 1579: "Animadvertendum autem nos tanto impetu in nonullis vocibus accentum retrahere, ut nulla syllabarum longitudo, natura aut positione facta contravenat. Ex: fóorester or cárpenter; not foréster or carpénter." The work includes a lengthy discussion of *prosodia* as it applies to English (pp. 128ff). Ch. 27 discusses "carmen rythmicum," meaning rhymed poetry. When Gil reviews the arguments of "eruditus Campianus," he finds them wanting. Gil quotes a quantitative poem from Campion's *Observations* in which he has changed the last words of alternate lines to create rhymes and concludes, "Si fiunt homoeoteleuta ["rhymes"], nihil a vulgatissimis cuius vis poetae differe videbantur." Gil admits that long passages are tedious if rhymed and observes that poets have abandoned rhyme in tragedy for blank verse. Gil then praises the elegant verses of Spenser's *Shepheardes Calender* and the *Faerie Queene* stanza, and Ben Jonson's lyrics. With considerable irony, he then cites Campion's "lovely poem" ("illo perbello cantico"), "What If a Day," showing by inclusion of the musical notes of the melody to which the poem is set that the work is harmonious, although it is not quantitative. The entire chapter is as suggestive for its application of classical terminology to accentual-syllabic verse as for its gentle deflation of Campion. It is followed by another on quantitative meters and genres, "De Carminibus ad numeros Latinorum poetarum compositis" (p. 145). Stanyhurst is cited because his effort to domesticate Latin heroic verse is so ludicrous. Sidney and Sir John Davies did better. Quantitative lyric forms are illustrated by examples from Campion's *Observations*.

86. *ECE*, II, 377.

87. Ibid., p. 382.

88. Ibid., p. 368.

89. For the later development of rationalist theories of construction in England, see Scaglione, *The Classical Theory*, pp. 316–36.

CHAPTER VI: A STRAUNGE METRE WORTHY
TO BE EMBRACED

1. Recent discussions of Surrey's translation: Emrys Jones, *Henry Howard Earl of Surrey: Poems* (Oxford, 1964); Priscilla Bowcutt, "Douglas and Surrey: Translators of Vergil," *E&S*, 27(1974), 52–67; David Richardson, "Humanistic Intent in Surrey's *Aeneid*," *ELR*, 6(1976), 204–19; Alan Hagar, "British Virgil: Four Renaissance Disguises of the Laokoon Passage of Book II of the *Aeneid*," *SEL*, 22(1982), 21–38. The early use of blank verse in epic and drama is reviewed by Howard Baker, "The Formation of the Heroic Medium," rept. in *Elizabethan Poetry: Modern Essays in Criticism*, ed. Paul Alpers (New York, 1967), and O. B. Hardison, "Blank Verse before Milton," *SP*, 81(1984), 253–74.

2. *An Apology for Poetry*, in *ECE*, ed. Smith (cited ch. 1, n. 20), I, 179.

3. Henry B. Lathrop, *Translations from the Classics into English from Caxton to Chapman, 1477–1620* (Madison, Wisc., 1933), p. 100.

4. Florence Ridley, *The Aeneid of Henry Howard, Earl of Surrey* (Berkeley and Los Angeles, 1963), pp. 13–45. Alan Hagar, "British Virgil," p. 28, suggests that Surrey's borrowings from Douglas "call to mind Virgil's odd borrowings from Ennius." He believes that Douglas sought to translate Vergil's "fixt sentens or mater"—i.e., his content—while Surrey was interested in Vergil's style.

5. Priscilla Bowcutt, *Gavin Douglas: A Critical Study* (Edinburgh, 1976), p. 198.

6. George T. Wright, "Wyatt's Decasyllabic Line," *SP*, 82(1985), 129–56.

7. Cf. Patricia Thompson, *Sir Thomas Wyatt and His Background* (Stanford, Calif., 1964), pp. 149–272.

8. George Saintsbury, *A History of English Prosody* (London, 1906–10), I, 315; F. M. Padelford, *The Poems of Henry Howard, Earl of Surrey* (rev. ed., Seattle, 1928), p. 233; Edwin Cassidy, *Henry Howard, Earl of Surrey* (New York, 1938), p. 235 (argument for Alamanni's influence). Herbert Hartman, ed., *The Fourth Boke of Virgill* (Purchase, N. Y., 1933), p. xxvi, is alone in arguing that Surrey's inspiration is "strictly English humanism." Hartman notes (p. xxvi) that book 4 is intrinsically much superior to book 2 and that, in addition, the text of book 2 is so corrupt in Tottel's edition that "wanting other texts, II has little value for any study of Surrey's prosody."

9. Sixteenth-century references to Surrey's translation are found in the work of Ascham, Webbe, Meres, and Harvey. See *ECE*, I, 32, 126, 283; and II, 315.

10. Cf. *Surrey*, ed. Padelford, p. 233.

11. The Day-Owen text survives today in a single copy that is preserved at the Carl Pforzheimer Library in New York. It was reprinted by Herbert Hartman in a limited edition in 1933 (see above, n. 8) and it is to this reprint that I refer in subsequent comments.

12. Badius Ascensius, ed., *De arte poetica* (Paris, 1503), fol. VIIv.

13. Derek Attridge, *Well-Weighed Syllables* (Cambridge, 1974), pp. 94, 108–11.

14. Compare Italian *straniero* and French *étranger*, both meaning "foreigner"; *OED*, s.v. "strange." When referring to the highly artificial style that he uses for his Homer translations, Chapman calls it the "beyond-sea manner of writing." *Chapman's Homer*, ed. Allardyce Nicoll (New York, 1956), I, 548.

15. *Fourth Boke*, ed. Hartman, p. xxvi.

16. Lathrop, *English Translations*, p. 98.

17. In A. C. Baugh, ed., *A Literary History of England* (New York, 1948), p. 334.

18. C. S. Lewis, *English Literature in the Sixteenth Century Excluding Drama* (Oxford, 1954), p. 234.

19. Ridley, *The Aeneid of Henry Howard*, p. 32.

20. *Vergilius cum commentariis. Opera Vergiliana antea corrupta et mendosa nunc vero multorum exemplarum collatione in integrum restituta* (Venice, 1519).

21. H. R. Fairclough, *Virgil with an English Translation* (Cambridge, Mass., 1947), I, 443–45.

22. For the effect of humanism on English prose, Ian A. Gordon, *The Movement of English Prose* (Bloomington, Ind., 1966), pp. 73–84, "The Impact of Humanist Latinity." Cf. Emrys Jones, *Surrey*, pp. xiv-xv: Surrey's aim "was to reproduce, as clearly as was consistent with the idiom of an uninflected language, the disposition of sense-masses and the figures of speech of the Latin. . . . The structural unit in Surrey's unrhymed verse is not the line . . . but the phrase or the clause." Surrey's verse "reveals itself as part of an intricate balancing system, composed of varied and yet predictably recurring patterns. It encourages in the reader a sense of mass and momentum" (p. xiii). The matter of prosodic intention requires further comment. In *The Founding of English Metre* (London, 1961), John Thompson argues that in earlier sixteenth-century English verse, meter dominates and voice stress is ignored. Later, English poets learn how to create "maximum tension between the language of the poem and the abstract pattern of the meter" (p. 156). In a rebuttal, Glenn S. Spiegel, "Perfecting English Meter: Sixteenth-Century Criticism and Practice," *JEGP*, 79(1980), 192–209, contends that English critics and poets are scrupulously metrical throughout the century. The case is more complex than either Thompson or Spiegel suggests. Surrey employs strong counterpoint in his *Aeneid*, and Emrys Jones is correct to emphasize the importance of phrase and clause in his blank verse. Surrey, however, *varies his practice in relation to the genre in which he is writing*. This is an illustration of the general principle, inherited from the *ars metrica*, of prosodic decorum. The question is not what English poets do in general, but what they do when using different genres.

23. Douglas's version is given below. The first four lines are impressive—

and Surrey obviously agreed. Later (ll. 10–15) Douglas is weak, and Surrey departs freely:

> Almychty Iuno havand rueth, by this
> Of hir long sorow and tarsum ded, I wyss,
> Hir mayd Irys from the hevyn hess send
> The throwand sawle to lowyss and mak ane end
> Of al the iuncturis and lethis of hir corss;
> Because that nothir of fatis throu the forss
> Nor yit by natural ded peryschit sche,
> Bot fey in hasty furour emflambyt hie
> Befor hir day had hir self spilt,
> Or that Proserpyne the yallow haris gilt
> From hir fortop byreft, or dubbyt hir hed
> Onto the Stygian hellis fludd of ded.
> Tharfor dewy Iris throu the hevyn
> With hir safrom weyngis flaw ful evin
> Drawand, quhar scho went, forgane the son cleir,
> A thousand cullouris of diverss hewys seir,
> And abufe Dydoys hed arest kan:
> "I am comandyt," said scho, "and I man
> Omdo this hayr, to Pluto connsecrate,
> And lowis thi sawle out of this mortale stait."
> Thys sayand, with rycht hand hess scho hynt
> The hair, and cuttis in twa, or that scho stynt;
> And tharwithall the natural heyt outquent,
> And, with a puft of aynd, the lyfe furthwent.

David Coldwell, ed., *Vergil's 'Aeneid' Translated into Scottish Verse by Gavin Douglas* (London, 1951), II, 192.

24. Padelford gives "where as" for Tottel (p. 188), and "whereas" for Hargrave (p. 189).

25. Padelford: Tottel, "therewith al" (p. 188); Hargrave, "therewith all" (p. 189); Rollins and Baker, "therewithal" (p. 519).

26. Tottel's substitution of "kindly" is pointless if "naturall" can be pronounced "nat'ral" (cf. l. 6). From an accentual point of view, the problem of how to scan the third and fourth syllables in the line is intriguing. Should "wyth" receive a full stress or a secondary stress or a minimum stress? Halle and Keyser argue for the integrity of the foot. If so, the best that the syllable can take is a secondary stress if it is to remain iambic. The problem is further complicated by the strong phrase boundary in midfoot between "-wyth" and "al."

27. *Servii grammatici qui feruntur in Vergilio commentarii*, ed. Georg Thilo and Herman Hagen (2 vols., Leipzig, 1923), note on IV, 696: "Difficilisque obitus quia supererat vita ei, que casu, non aut fato aut natura moriebatur: ut 'nam quia nec fato, merita nec morte peribat', id est naturali."

28. Wright, "Wyatt's Decasyllabic Line," pp. 134–35.

CHAPTER VII: JASPER HEYWOOD'S FOURTEENERS

1. For Heywood's life, Henry de Vocht, *Jasper Heywood and His Translations* (Louvain, 1913; rpt. Vaduz, Austria, 1963), pp. vii-xix. In the dedication of *Troas*, Heywood describes Elizabeth's accession as "that thing . . . which to the honour of him and for the wealth of us God hath ordained" (de Vocht, p. 4). See also E. M. Spearing, *The Elizabethan Translations of Seneca's Tragedies* (Cambridge, 1912; rpt. Norwood, Penna., 1978).

2. E. M. Spearing, *Studley's Translations of 'Agamemnon' and 'Medea'* (Louvain, 1913; rpt. Vaduz, Austria, 1963), pp. i-xiii.

3. The standard edition is by T. S. Eliot, *Seneca His Tenne Tragedies* (London, 1927; rpt. Bloomington, Ind., 1966). For general background, F. S. Boas, *University Drama in the Tudor Age* (Oxford, 1914); F. P. Wilson, *The English Drama, 1485-1585*, ed. G. K. Hunter (Oxford, 1969). For Seneca in Europe, Jean Jacquot, ed., *Les Tragédies e Sénèque et la théâtre de la renaissance* (Paris, 1964). For Seneca in England, Werner Habicht, "Sénèque et le théâtre populaire pré-Shakesperien," in Jacquot, ed., *Les Tragédies*, pp. 175-87, and Bruce R. Smith, "Toward the Rediscovery of Tragedy: Productions of Seneca's Plays on the English Renaissance Stage," *Renaissance Drama*, n. s., 9(1978), 3-37. Smith notes performances in Latin of *Hippolytus* at Westminster School in 1546, and, at Trinity College, *Troas* in 1552, *Oedipus* and *Hercules* in 1559, and *Medea* and *Troas* in 1560-61.

4. For Latin comedy in England, Bruce R. Smith, "Sir Amorous Knight and the Indecorous Romans; or, Plautus and Terence Play Court in the Renaissance," *Renaissance Drama*, n. s., 6(1973), 3-27. The earliest references reported by Smith to a performance of a Latin comedy in England is 1510/11, at Cambridge. A comedy by Plautus was performed at court in 1519/20.

5. Henry B. Lathrop, *Translations from the Classics into English from Caxton to Chapman, 1477-1620* (Madison, Wisc., 1933), pp. 142, 309. Thomas Heywood's *The Captives*, written ca. 1624, is based on the *Rudens* of Plautus, ed. Alexander Judson (New Haven, Conn., 1921).

6. Lathrop, *Translations*, pp. 16-20, 29-31, 91, 223, 291, 309.

7. Ibid., p. 291.

8. *Tenne Tragedies*, ed. Eliot, II, 3-4.

9. Quotations here and below from *Thyestes* are from *The Seconde Tragedie of Seneca Entituled Thyestes* (London, 1560). I have printed the lines as continuous. They are always broken in the quartos into lines of eight and six syllables because of the small size of the page; however, Newton prints them as continuous. See also the excellent modern-spelling edition by Joost Daalder, *Thyestes: Lucius Annaeus Seneca, Translated by Jasper Heywood (1560)* (London, 1982), pp. 7-21.

10. Studley, ed., Spearing, pp. 17, 22. Heywood's translation is "so excellently well done . . . it semeth me no translation but even *Seneca* him selfe to speke in Englysh." The *Medea* begins with the announcement, "Lo Senec

crounde wyth Lawrell leafe / in England now appeares / Medea pende with hawtye style / noe Englysh Meetre weares."

11. Although there are errors in Tottel's printing, the edition is not as corrupt as Heywood's protests would suggest. John Day, printer of the 1570 edition of *Gorboduc*, makes the same complaint about the printer of the first (1565) edition of that play.

12. Leicester Bradner, *The Poems of Queen Elizabeth I* (Providence, R. I., 1964). The Seneca chorus is on pp. 16–18. Bradner estimates (p. xiv) that Elizabeth translated Boethius's *Consolation* in 1593 and the Plutarch and part of Horace's *Ars poetica* in 1598. The *Hercules* manuscript is in the Bodleian Library. It is "a very free paraphrase . . . one-third of the first thirty-one lines have no parallel in the Latin" (p. 80). "We know she was making translations of other Latin classics in the first decade of her reign, and perhaps this [Seneca] should be put among them" (p. 80). See also Caroline Pemberton, *Queen Elizabeth's Englishings* (London, 1899).

13. Pemberton, *Englishings*, judges the *Ars poetica* "above her [Elizabeth's] power" (p. xi). Perhaps she realized this fact and gave it up in midcourse. It is, at any rate, incomplete.

14. Cf. Studley's Latin poem against Zoilus, ed. Spearing, p. 11.

15. J. E. Bernard, Jr., *The Prosody of the Tudor Interlude* (New Haven, Conn., 1939), p. x.

16. Ibid., pp. 201–10.

17. Ibid., p. 3

18. Ibid., p. x.

19. A survey of the plays turns up a variety of verse forms. Dialogue is normally in fourteeners, though decasyllabic quatrains are sometimes used. The choruses are varied. The most common feature is the tendency to use decasyllabic verse. Here the authors are probably seeking an English equivalent for lines that are shorter than the *iambicum trimetrum* of the Latin dialogue. But the imitation goes further. Just as Seneca varies the meters of his choruses, the translators frequently (though not always) vary the rhyme schemes of the choral passages. In *Hercules furens*, the first chorus is in quatrains, the second in rhyme royal, the third in poulter's measure, and the fourth in double quatrains. In *Troas* the first chorus has refrain lines. In *Thyestes* the chorus at the end of act 3 concludes with a metrically short line unique to the play:

> suche friendship fynde with godds yet no man might,
> That he the morowe might be sure to lyve.
> the god our things all tosst and turned quight
> Rolles with a whirle wynde.

The first line of act 4 is, "What whirlwinde may me headlong drive. . . ." The translations also include occasional octosyllabic and Alexandrine couplets (*Agamemnon*), and adaptations of Chaucer's Monk's Tale stanza (*Troas*).

20. See the review of the question by H. A. Kelly, "Tragedy and the Per-

formance of Tragedy in Late Roman Antiquity," *Traditio*, 35(1979), 21–44. The foremost proponent of the declamation theory is Otto Zwierlein, editor of the Oxford edition of Seneca's plays and author of *Die Rezitationsdramen Senecas* (Meisenheim am Glan, 1966). Cf. the authors cited by Zwierlein, pp. 10–11, for the contrary position. Kelly appears to believe (pp. 42–44) the plays were written with the possibility of stage performance in mind. On the opposite side, see J. A. Tarrant, ed., *Seneca's 'Thyestes'* (Atlanta, 1985), pp. 13–15.

21. Cf. *Tenne Tragedies*, ed. Eliot, I, 187.

22. *L. Annaei Senecae tragoediae . . . explanate diligentissime tribus commentariis* (Paris, 1514). The commentaries are by Badius Ascensius, Daniele Gaetano, and Bernardino Marmita. This text was edited by Erasmus. The quotation from *Thyestes* begins fol. XLr. Several renaissance texts print *extrahit* for *abstrahit* in line 1.

23. Both de Vocht (*Heywood*, p. xxix) and Daalder (*Thyestes*, p. xlii) remark on the involuted word order. Daalder writes that Heywood "considered the word order of the Latin to have merit as such. . . . The Renaissance clearly experimented very much more than our own time with the possibility that the syntax and vocabulary of English might be enriched by Latinizing."

24. As demonstrated by Daalder, *Thyestes*, pp. 83–88. Heywood also referred to the notes in the edition by Badius Ascensius (Paris, 1514).

25. Jakob Schipper, *A History of English Versification* (Oxford, 1910; rpt. New York, 1971), pp. 126–27.

26. Bernardino observes in a note to this passage "Hic est *cantus* Thyestis qui est in conviviis" (italics added). For comment on Seneca's versification, see the edition by Tarrant, pp. 27–33.

27. The Latin passage was recognized as an especially complex and affecting moment. Note especially the expressive repetition of *prohibet* in the Latin. In the 1514 edition (fol. XLr):

> . . . miseri
> Tempora omnes dimitte notas,
> Redeant vultus ad laeta boni. . . .
> Quid me revocas: festumque vetas
> Celebrare diem? quid flere iubes
> Nulla surgens dolor ex causa?
> Quis me prohibet flore decenti
> Viniere comam? prohibet: prohibet.
> Vernae capiti fluxere rosae: . . .

28. Heywood's choruses are beyond the scope of the present study because English drama did not adopt the chorus. They can also, however, be brilliantly poetic; e.g., the following bit from the first chorus of *Hercules furens*:

> The fading starres now shyne but selde in sighte
> In stipye skye, night overcome with day

Plucks in her fyres, while spronge agayne is light.
The day starre drawes the clersome bemes their waye,
The ycye signe of haughtye poale agayne,
With seven starres markt, the Beares of Arcadye,
Do call the light with overturned mayne.

29. *Thyestes*, Daalder, p. lxii.

CHAPTER VIII: GORBODUC AND DRAMATIC BLANK VERSE

1. Text of *Gorboduc* in J. Q. Adams, ed., *Chief Pre-Shakespearean Dramas* (Boston, 1924), pp. 503–35. All later quotations from *Gorboduc* are from this text, which is based on the Day edition of 1570, in preference to the modern-spelling text by Irby Cauthen, *Gorboduc* (Lincoln, Neb., 1970). I have, however, benefited in many important ways from Cauthen's discussion of the play.

2. E. W. Talbert, "The Political Import and the First Two Audiences of *Gorboduc*," in *Studies in Honor of DeWitt T. Starnes* (Austin, Tex., 1967), p. 99.

3. See *Gorboduc*, ed. Cauthen, pp. xvii–xix.

4. For Seneca's influence on *Gorboduc*, Paul Bacquet, "L'imitation de Sénèque dans 'Gorboduc,'" in Jean Jacquot, ed., *Les Tragédies de Sénèque et la théâtre de la renaissance* (Paris, 1964), pp. 153–73. In general Bacquet tends to find more evidence for Senecan influence than, for example, Wolfgang Clemen, *English Tragedy before Shakespeare: The Development of Dramatic Speech*, tr. T. S. Dorsh (London, 1961), p. 59: "The majority of speeches in Seneca's plays are essentially a medium of rage or despair, or intense emotion of some other kind. In *Gorboduc*, however, only a few scenes, indeed only a few speeches, have strong feelings as their basis." Consequently (p. 60) *Gorboduc* is *less* dramatic than any of Seneca's plays. In *The Tudor Play of the Mind* (Berkeley and Los Angeles, 1978), pp. 249–59, Joel B. Altman takes the position that *Gorboduc* is Senecan in spite of its chronological plot, lack of stichomythia, and homiletic choruses. Altman, however, considers a Senecan play to be essentially a "sophistic construction carefully designed to invoke a wide range of intellectual and emotional responses" (p. 231). The essential Senecan legacy to the Elizabethans is a fondness for rhetorical declamation and a penchant (p. 255) for arguing cases pro and con, both of which features are evident in *Gorboduc*.

5. Moody Prior, *The Language of Tragedy* (New York, 1947), suggests (p. 29), "The few examples of blank verse before *Gorboduc* . . . appear to have had epic in mind, and, in fact, English dramatic blank verse shows occasional marks of its epic origin for some time. The blank verse of *Gorboduc*, however, seems to have been designed as an adaptation to the characteristics of the English language of the tragic meter and style of Seneca." This ignores the

impact of Italian arguments about *versi sciolti* on the versification—questionable in view of the dumb shows and other evidences of Italian influence.

6. See *Gorboduc*, ed. Cauthen, pp. xvii-xix. Among the features of *Gorboduc* that Prior (*Language*, pp. 30-32) considers prominent are repetition, balance of adjective and noun units in the first and the second half of the line, *sententiae*, use of formal debates, and "almost complete absence of metaphor." Clemen (*English Tragedy*) also stresses "continual parallelism of half-lines and line endings" (p. 65) and adds that the verse is so regular that it is monotonous.

7. Clemen appears to believe the orations are judicial (i.e. forensic; *English Tragedy*, p. 63). They are deliberative. They are in the form of political council and deal with future action. Forensic oratory is delivered in a court and concerns what has been done in the past. Cf. *Rhetorica ad Herennium*, ed. Harry Caplan (Cambridge, Mass., 1954), I, 2, II, 1-7, III, 1-9.

8. Talbert, "Political Import," pp. 89-115.

9. Clemen, *English Tragedy*, p. 67.

10. Marvin T. Herrick, *Italian Comedy in the Renaissance* (Champaign, Ill., 1960), pp. 65-98. Still very useful for the subject is R. W. Bond, *Early Plays from the Italian* (Oxford, 1911), esp. pp. xl-lxv. More recently, David Orr, *Italian Renaissance Drama in England* (Chapel Hill, N.C., 1970). Orr is generally more cautious about asserting Italian influence than earlier scholars.

11. Marvin T. Herrick, *Comic Theory in the Sixteenth Century* (Champaign, Ill., 1964), p. 219.

12. Cintio, *Discorsi di M. Giovambattista Giraldi Cinthio* (Venice, 1554), pp. 49-50.

13. Bond, *Early Plays*, p. lxxxv.

14. Ibid., p. lxxxix.

15. Text in *Chief Pre-Shakespearean Dramas*, ed. Adams, pp. 367-84.

16. This, however, needs further examination.

17. *Chief Pre-Shakespearean Dramas*, ed. Adams, p. 425.

18. How regular and by what criteria? A strongly classical approach to the songs might find the songs imitations of iambic dimeter.

19. Gascoigne's plays are reprinted in Bond's *Early Plays*.

20. Text in *Chief Pre-Shakespearean Dramas*, ed. Adams, pp. 536-67.

Chapter IX: Heroic Experiments

1. For Grimald, Le Roy Merrill, *The Life and Poems of Nicholas Grimald* (New Haven, Conn., 1925); for Turberville, F. S. Boas, ed., *The Heroical Epistles of Ovid* (London, 1928). Ten of the heroical epistles are in poulter's measure, five in fourteeners, and six in blank verse. Thomas Norton's use of blank verse for a few lines of Vergil in his translation of Calvin's *Institutes* (1561) should also be noted.

2. Gascoigne learned from Horace that Lucilius is an archaic poet. His blank verse is intentionally archaic and quite unlike Surrey's or even Turberville's. In it the influence of Langland's *Piers Plowman* mixes exotically with classical concepts of satire. See William L. Wallace, ed., *George Gascoigne's 'The Steele Glas' and 'The Complainte of Phylomene'* (Salzburg, Austria, 1975), pp. 27–44. Also Stanley R. Maveety, "Versification in *The Steele Glas*," *SP*, 60(1963), 166–73, who argues that the medieval element in the verse—e.g., its tendency to revert to a four-stress accentual line—is dominant.

3. See Susan B. Snyder, *The Divine Works and Weeks of Guillaume de Salluste Sieur Du Bartas*, tr. Joshua Sylvester (2 vols., Oxford, 1979). Also George C. Taylor, *Milton's Use of Du Bartas* (Cambridge, Mass., 1934).

4. From the preface to the 1558 edition, in Hyder Rollins and Herschel Baker, eds., *The Renaissance in England* (Boston, 1954), p. 521. See also Henry B. Lathrop, *Translations from the Classics into English from Caxton to Chapman, 1477–1620* (Madison, Wisc., 1933), p. 108. There is no modern edition of Phaer. Phaer completed nine books before his death. Thomas Twyne finished the translation and published all twelve books in 1573.

5. Rollins and Baker, *Renaissance in England*, p. 522.

6. Ibid., p. 520. The phrase "I sing" is incorporated into the line preceding this one which translates the brief pseudo-Vergilian introduction usually included in Renaissance editions.

7. *Aeneid*, tr. Phaer and Twyne (1584), fol. Dii v. Phaer's style was examined in the nineteenth century by Eduard Brenner, *Thomas Phaer, mit besonderer Berüksichtigung seiner Aeneis Uebersetzung* (Heidelberg, 1893). Brenner notes especially Phaer's tendency to expand his original, his lack of elevation, and his uncertain vocabulary.

8. J. C. Smith and E. de Selincourt, eds., *Spenser: Poetical Works* (Oxford, 1966), p. 611.

9. Edward Arber, ed., *Richard Stanyhurst: Translation of the First Four Books of the 'Aeneis' of P. Virgilius Maro* (Westminster, 1895), p. vii.

10. Ibid., p. xviii.

11. Ibid., pp. xviii-xix. Bishop Hall devotes the sixth satire of the first book of *Virgidemarium* (1597) to Stanyhurst, making him an example of absurd affectation in language: "If *Iove* speake English in a thundering cloud, / *Thwick thwack* and *Rif raf* rores he out aloud" (ibid., p. xx).

12. Thomas Warton, *History of English Poetry* (London, 1840), III, 323.

13. *Stanyhurst*, ed. Arber, p. 4.

14. Ibid., p. 8.

15. Ibid., pp. 11–16.

16. Ibid., p. 17.

17. And was equally ridiculous to Hall in 1597: "*Manhood and garbroiles shall he chaunt* with chaunged feete."

18. *ECE*, ed. Smith (cited ch. 1, n. 20), II, 177–78.

19. Allardyce Nicoll, ed., *Chapman's Homer* (New York, 1956), I, 504,

preface to the 1598 edition of the first seven books of the *Iliad*. Chapman's Neoplatonic sources are discussed by F. L. Schoell, *Etudes sur l'humanisme continental en Angleterre* (Paris, 1926).

20. *Chapman's Homer*, ed. Nicoll, I, 507.

21. Ibid., pp. 548–49. Cf. "To the Reader," I, 17: "Not to follow the number and order of the words but the materiall things themselves . . . and to clothe and adorne them with words and such a stile and force of Oration as are most apt for the language into which they are converted."

22. Ibid., p. 549.

23. Ibid., p. 10.

24. Ibid., pp. 509, 523. For discussion of Chapman's style, George de F. Lord, *Homeric Renaissance: The Odyssey of George Chapman* (New Haven, Conn., 1956), pp. 127–67.

25. Cf. Lord, *Homeric Renaissance*, pp. 161–67.

26. *Chapman's Homer*, ed. Nicoll, II, xi. The conclusion is fully supported by Lord, *Homeric Renaissance*, p. 128:

> The distinctive style of the *Odyssey* does not inhere . . . in one or two particular features but in the particular way in which Chapman combined all of the elements of poetry. The enjambed decasyllabic couplets, the long verse paragraphs, what a recent Milton scholar calls "the systematic deformation of logical word-order, the abundance of parenthetical and subordinate clauses, the use of anacoluthon, and the particular blend of common words with neologisms, compound epithets, and Latinate words," operate together to create a highly individual style.

The *Odyssey* couplet, says Lord (p. 130), is "so enjambed that it might as well be blank verse."

27. For the influence of the Pléiade, W. L. Renwick, *Edmund Spenser: An Essay on Renaissance Poetry* (London, 1925), pp. 44–52, 82–93, etc.

28. For Marot and Spenser, see especially Annabel Patterson, "Re-Opening the Green Cabinet: Clément Marot and Edmund Spenser," *ELR*, 16(1986), 44–70.

29. Bernard Weinberg, *A History of Literary Criticism in the Italian Renaissance* (Chicago, 1961), II, 1152–53, lists the various editions of the *Discorsi*. For the *Discorsi* of 1594, *Torquato Tasso: Prose*, ed. Francisco Flora (Milan, 1935), pp. 320–539.

30. *Tasso*, ed. Flora, pp. 352–54.

31. Ibid., pp. 478–79.

32. Ibid., pp. 533–34.

33. Ibid., p. 478.

34. Ibid., pp. 495–98.

35. Josephine W. Bennett, *The Evolution of the Faerie Queene* (Chicago, 1942).

36. Cf. Weinberg, *History*, II, 954–1073.

37. *Poetical Works*, ed. Smith and de Selincourt, pp. 407–8.

38. Cf. Ronald Horton, *The Unity of the 'Faerie Queene'* (Athens, Ga., 1978).

39. Emma F. Pope, "The Critical Background of the Spenserian Stanza," *SP*, 24(1926), 31–53, finds English analogues for the *Faerie Queene* stanza, but opts for the influence of terza rima and Italian madrigal stanzas. Leicester Bradner, "Forerunners of the Spenserian Stanza," *RES*, 4(1928), 207–8, notes that there are two nine-line stanzas in Tottel that have rhyme schemes close to Spenser's, although they do not end with Alexandrines. Theodore Maynard, *The Connection between the Ballade, Chaucer's Modification of It, Rime Royal, and the Spenserian Stanza* (Washington, D.C., 1934), pp. 107–27, argues in favor of rhyme royal and notes that Sir Thomas More wrote rhyme royal ending with an Alexandrine.

40. This passage was usually included in renaissance editions of Vergil on the authority of Donatus and Servius. The Latin is as follows:

> Ille ego, qui quondam gracili modulatus avena
> carmen, et egressus silvis vicina coegi
> ut quamvis avido parerent arva colono,
> gratum opus agricolis; at nunc horrentia Martis. . . .

Translated by Fairclough: "I am he who once tuned my song on a slender reed, then, leaving the woodland, constrained the neighboring fields to serve the husbandmen, however grasping—a work welcome to farmers: but now the shocks of Mars [and arms and the man, I sing. . .]."

41. "The Wisdom of the Ancients (1609)," in Sidney Warhaft, ed., *Francis Bacon: A Selection of His Works* (Toronto, 1965), p. 277.

42. In *Critical Essays of the Seventeenth Century*, ed. J. E. Spingarn (rpt. Bloomington, Ind., 1957), I, 6.

43. Ibid., p. 9.
44. Ibid., p. 31.
45. Ibid., pp. 52–53.
46. Ibid., p. 210.
47. Ibid., p. 155. Note also the frontal attack on Bacon, p. 177.
48. Ibid., II, 1.
49. Ibid., pp. 31–53, 54–76.
50. Ibid., p. 6.
51. Ibid., p. 19.
52. Ibid.
53. Ibid., pp. 32–33.
54. Ibid., p. 67.
55. Ibid., p. 62.
56. Ibid., p. 59.
57. Ibid., p. 65.
58. Ibid., p. 57.

Chapter X: Speech and Verse

1. F. E. Halliday, *The Poetry of Shakespeare's Plays* (London, 1954), p. 15. For a suggestive analysis of the dramatic potentialities of Shakespeare's verse, see the chapter "Speaking the Speech," in J. L. Styan, *Shakespeare's Stagecraft* (Cambridge, 1967), pp. 141–71. Among important modern studies of Shakespeare's prosody are Dorothy L. Sipes, *Shakespeare's Metrics* (New Haven, Conn., 1968), and Marina Tarlinskaja, *Shakespeare's Verse: Iambic Pentameter and the Poet's Idiosyncrasies* (New York, 1987). George T. Wright's *Shakespeare's Metrical Art* was not available as the present book was being prepared for press. See, however, his article "The Play of Phrase and Line in Shakespeare's Iambic Pentameter," *SQ*, 34(1983), 133–58. For evaluation of current trends, T. V. F. Brogan, "Shakespeare's Command of His Medium of Verse: New Work at Last," *Style*, 21(1987), 464–75. The approach taken here differs from traditional metrical approaches in its focus on *opsis* and the actorly element in dramatic dialogue. I believe this approach accords with the emphasis of classical and renaissance theory on the fact that dramatic dialogue is "like speech" and "biotic." Further sixteenth-century evidence is offered below in the section of this chapter titled "Renaissance Comments on Actors and on Acting."

2. Keir Elam, *The Semiotics of Theatre and Drama* (London, 1980), p. 209.

3. *Aristotle's 'Poetics': A Translation and Commentary for Students of Literature*, tr. and ed. Leon Golden and O. B. Hardison (Gainesville, Fla., 1981), p. 34.

4. Elam, *Semiotics*, pp. 74–75, 158–59.

5. Gerald Else, *Aristotle's Poetics: The Argument* (Cambridge, Mass., 1957), pp. 233–34.

6. Ibid., p. 486. Else translates Aristotle's *kai tois schemassin* as "with the patterns [of speech]." The more common translation is "with gestures." That is, the poet who uses gestures as he writes will develop a sense of speech in performance that will transfer to his dialogue. Else's "patterns" are (p. 490) "the forms of statement: command, prayer, threat, question, etc." In other words, they are precisely the forms of syntax that contribute to making the dialogue "actorly." Modern speech act theory considers the most important element of any utterance "the *illocutionary* act: the act performed *in* saying something, such as asking a question, ordering someone to do something, promising, asserting the truth of a proposition, etc." (Elam, *Semiotics*, p. 159). What Aristotle calls *schemata* in the *Poetics*, speech act theory calls "illocutionary acts." For more detail on the contemporary background of the term, J. L. Austin, *How To Do Things with Words* (Cambridge, Mass., 1962), and John Searle, *Speech Acts: An Essay in the Philosophy of Language* (Cambridge, 1969).

7. Heinrich Keil, ed., *Grammatici Latini* (7 vols., Leipzig, 1857–80), I, 482.

8. Coburn Freer, *The Poetics of Jacobean Drama* (Baltimore, 1981), pp. 28–61.

9. *To Gentlemen Students of Both Universities*, in Nashe, *Works*, ed. R. B. McKerrow and F. P. Wilson (Oxford, 1958), III, 311–12.

10. Greene, *A Groatsworth of Wit* (London, 1923), p. 45. Cf. "The complaint of Levinus Lemnis," *The Touchstone of Complexions*, tr. Thomas Newton (1576), sig. G5, about actors who "measure rhetorike by their peevish rhythmes." Also the preface to Thomas Middleton's *A Mad World My Masters*, which points out that the play has "no bumbasted or fustian stuff, but every line weighed as with a balance, and every sentence placed with judgment and deliberation." By 1640 there was a trend favoring drama in prose or at least in verse that is not heavily "poetic." Middleton, *Works*, ed. A. H. Bullen (London, 1885), III, 251. Ben Jonson translates the advice of Horace to the would-be tragedian by saying that if he would move audiences he "must throu by / His Bumbard-phrase, and foot-and-half-foot words: / 'Tis not enough the labouring Muse affords / Her Poems beauty, but a sweet delight / To wake the hearers minds, still to the plight." In *Complete Poetry of Ben Jonson*, ed. W. B. Hunter, Jr. (Garden City, N. Y., 1963), pp. 281–82.

11. *Virgidemarium*, in *Collected Poems*, ed. A. Davenport (Liverpool, 1949), p. 14.

12. Freer, *Poetics*, p. 32.

13. *Timber, or Discoveries*, in *Critical Essays of the Seventeenth Century*, ed. J. E. Spingarn (rpt. Bloomington, Ind., 1957), I, 23.

14. *Apology for Poetry*, in *ECE*, ed. Smith (cited in ch. 1, n. 20), I, 159–60.

15. *The Malcontent*, ed. M. L. Wine (Lincoln, Neb., 1964), pp. 4–5.

16. *Theatrum triumphans* (London, 1670), pp. 34–35.

17. Prologue to *The Comicall Gallant*, in John Dennis, *Critical Works*, ed. Edward Niles Hooker (Baltimore, 1943), II, 391. Freer remarks (*Poetics*, p. 32), "What Dennis offers is a definition of dramatic poetry that splits poetry and drama." If so, Aristotle and Sidney made the same error.

18. *Critical Works*, ed. Hooker, II, 4–5.

19. *Ludus literarius: Or the Grammar School* (London, 1612), p. 213.

20. *Apology for Actors*, sig. C4r.

21. Bertram Joseph, *Elizabethan Acting* (1st ed., London, 1951), pp. 77, 81, 123, 125.

22. Bertram Joseph, *Elizabethan Acting* (2nd ed., London, 1964), p. 100. Throughout this edition Joseph compares Elizabethan acting with the style recommended by Stanislavski; e.g., pp. v–vi: "Rhetorical delivery at school meant that boys were required to act naturally, as if they really were the persons they represented. . . . The rhetorician who followed Quintilian tapped the resources of his emotional life by methods used in the modern theatre and advocated by Stanislavski."

23. *A Short Discourse of the English Stage*, in *Critical Essays of the Seventeenth Century*, II, 95.

24. For a traditional analysis of this verse, John Bakeless, "The Mighty Line," in *The Tragicall History of Christopher Marlowe* (Cambridge, Mass., 1942), II, 173–204.

25. *Tamburlaine*, in *The Complete Works of Christopher Marlowe*, ed. Fredson Bowers (Cambridge, 1981), I, 79.

26. Eugene Waith, "Marlowe's Herculean Hero," in John Russell Brown, ed., *Christopher Marlowe: A Casebook* (London, 1982), pp. 87–113. For *Hercules Oetaeus*, esp. pp. 106–8. See also Eugene Waith, *The Herculean Hero* (London, 1962).

27. E.g., John Russell Brown, "Marlowe and the Actors," in *Christopher Marlowe: A Casebook*, pp. 51–69, and Clifford Leech, *Christopher Marlowe: Poet for the Stage*, ed. Anne Lancashire (New York, 1986), pp. 199–218, "The Acting of Marlowe and Shakespeare." Cf. Harold F. Brooks, "Marlowe and the Early Shakespeare," in Brian Morris, ed., *Christopher Marlowe* (London, 968), pp. 93–94: "Tucker Brooke's verdict was once orthodox: that Marlowe never learnt to integrate poetry and drama. . . . The more recent critics have demonstrated his sense of the theatre."

28. Herbert Hartman, ed., *The Fourth Boke of Virgill* (Purchase, N. Y., 1933), p. 34.

29. *The Tragedie of Dido, Queene of Carthage*, ed. Bowers, I, 54.

30. *Pharsalia*, ed. Bowers, II, 282 (ll. 98–106).

31. This does not mean that the *Pharsalia* has no passages that are close to speech. Heroic verse can move toward speech just as dramatic speech can move toward the heroic norm. There is an edge of cynicism in Lucan that is nicely conveyed by a diction that verges at times on the colloquial. Marlowe catches this quality nicely in a passage when Rome appears in a dream to Caesar:

> And staring, thus bespoke: what mean'st thou *Caesar*?
> Whether goes my standarde? Romans if ye be,
> And beare true harts, stay heare: this spectacle
> Stroake *Caesars* hart with feare.
> (ll. 192–95)

Lucan's exposition could often be transferred without change to a drama. For example, the following description of the portents of disaster at Rome remind one of descriptions of similar portents in the first act of Shakespeare's *Julius Caesar*:

> The flattering skie gliter'd in often flames,
> And sundry fiery meteors blaz'd in heaven;
> Now spearlike long; now like a spreading torch:
> Lightning in silence, stole forth without clouds,
> And from the northern climat snatching fier
> Blasted the Capitoll.
> (ll. 528–33)

32. *Tamburlaine*, ed. Bowers, I, 84 (ll. 160–67).

33. Brown, "Marlowe and the Actors," pp. 51–69.

34. *Tamburlaine*, ed. Bowers, I, 86 (ll. 33–43). I omit the stage direction—"Takes off shepheards cloak"—which Bowers gives in brackets after "Lie here ye weedes. . . ."

35. Morris Halle and Samuel Keyser, *English Stress: Its Form, Its Growth, and Its Role in Verse* (New York, 1971), pp. 169–74.

36. Several writers have commented on the passage, among them, W. A. Armstrong, *Marlowe's 'Tamburlaine': The Image and the Stage* (Hull, 1966), p. 16, Bowers, ed., *Works*, I, 86, and Felix Bossonet, *The Function of Stage Properties in Christopher Marlowe's Plays* (Bern, 1980), p. 15. Bossonet offers (pp. 12–37) extremely useful and persuasive evidence of Marlowe's awareness of the stage throughout this most "poetic" of plays. His analysis of the scene under discussion is that "Tamburlaine throws off his shepherd's mantle, revealing a magnificent suit of armour. Beneath it, there is a battle-axe that Tamburlaine takes in his hand and brandishes aloft." There is no way of deciding how the scene in question should be staged. Many ways will work. To me, it seems more likely that Tamburlaine picks up his armor than that he has been wearing it all along.

37. The dates of all of Marlowe's works are conjectural. The problem of development is further complicated by the fact that the text of *Doctor Faustus* is corrupt, and *The Massacre at Paris* is evidently the work of several hands. *Dido* is early, perhaps done at Cambridge for student performance. *Tamburlaine* was written by 1587, and *Edward II* around 1582. *Faustus* is probably fairly close to *Tamburlaine*. If so, Marlowe's development as a writer of actorly blank verse is impressively rapid. The most recent attempt at a chronology is that by Leech, *Christopher Marlowe: Poet for the Stage*. Leech offers tentative dates (p. 23; justification on pp. 219–22). Before 1587: Ovid's *Elegies*, Lucan, *Pharsalia*, *Dido*. 1587: *Tamburlaine* parts 1 and 2. 1588–89: *Faustus*. 1590–91: *Edward II*. 1591–92: *The Massacre at Paris*, *The Jew of Malta*. 1592–93: *Hero and Leander*.

38. *Doctor Faustus*, ed. Bowers, II, 225–27 (ll. 1937–82).

39. Frederick S. Boas, *The Works of Thomas Kyd* (Oxford, 1901), p. 6 (I, i, 63–69).

40. Ibid., p. 26 (II, iii, 24–30).

41. Ibid., p. 39 (III, ii, 1–11).

42. F. P. Wilson, *Marlowe and the Early Shakespeare* (Oxford, 1953), p. 108. This opinion is now standard. See Harold F. Brooks, "Marlowe and the Early Shakespeare," in Morris, ed., *Christopher Marlowe*, esp. pp. 65–77. The traditional view is outlined by Bakeless, *Tragicall History*, II, 205–67.

43. Wilson, *Marlowe and the Early Shakespeare*, pp. 121–22.

44. See the discussion of the prosody of the "play within a play" in G. R. Hibbard, *The Making of Shakespeare's Dramatic Poetry* (Toronto, 1981), pp. 18–19.

45. Richard Mulcaster, *Positions* (1581), ed. R. H. Quick (London, 1888),

p. 58, urges children to recite "either *Iambicke* verse, or *Elegies*, or such numbers which with their currant carie the memorie on." Cf. Sidney's *Apology*, in *ECE*, I, 182–83:

> Now, that verse farre exceedeth Prose in the knitting up of the memorie, the reason is manifest; the words . . . beeing so set as one word cannot be lost but the whole worke fails: which accuseth it selfe, calleth the remembrance back to it selfe, and so most strongly confirmeth it. . . . But the fitness [verse] hath for memory is notably proved by the delivery of Arts: wherein . . . the rules chiefly necessary to bee borne away are compiled in verse.

Chapter XI: True Musical Delight

1. T. S. Eliot, "Marlowe," in *Collected Essays, 1917–1932* (New York, 1932), p. 100. Cf. also "Milton I (1936)," in *On Poetry and Poets* (New York, 1957), pp. 156–64, and "Milton II (1947)," pp. 165–83.

2. Ezra Pound, *A B C of Reading* (New York, 1960), pp. 18–23, 63.

3. Eliot, "Milton I," pp. 157–61. Eliot uses Satan's address to his followers at the beginning of the rebellion in heaven (V, 772–84) as an example of a speech in which "the arrangement is for the sake of musical value, not for the significance."

4. F. T. Prince, *The Italian Element in Milton's Verse* (Oxford, 1954), ch. 2 (pp. 34–57). W. B. Hunter, "The Sources of Milton's Prosody," *PQ*, 27(1949), 125–44, argues conversely that the two key influences are the translation of DuBartas by Sylvester and hymnody.

5. Roland Frye, *Milton's Imagery and the Visual Arts* (Princeton, 1978). Cf. esp. the review (pp. 9–19) of "Milton's Visual Imagination and the Critics."

6. The standard study is John Hollander, *The Untuning of the Sky* (Princeton, 1961). See also Mortimer Frank, "Milton's Knowledge of Music: Some Speculations," in *Milton and the Art of Sacred Song*, ed. J. Max Patrick and Roger H. Sundell (Madison, Wisc., 1979), pp. 83–98, for comment on Milton's familiarity with seventeenth-century music and the possible implications for his poetry of the move from polyphony to *stile rappresentativo* (i.e., *stile recitativo*). For the possible influence of hymnody, Hunter, "Sources of Milton's Prosody." The performance background is reviewed by Elsie Jorgens, *The Well Tun'd Word: Musical Interpretations of English Poetry, 1579–1651* (Minneapolis, Minn., 1982). No critic has attempted an analysis of the relation between music and style in Milton's thought comparable to Mario Pazzaglia's *Il Verso e l'arte della canzone nel 'De vulgari eloquentia'* (Florence, 1967).

7. R. D. Havens, *The Influence of Milton on English Poetry* (Cambridge, Mass., 1922).

8. Texts in *John Milton: Complete Poems and Major Prose*, ed. Merritt Y. Hughes (New York, 1957). In "Of Education," pp. 630–39, Milton outlines

a curriculum that culminates in reading the "organic arts" of logic, rhetoric, and poetics. He contrasts the poetic arts with "the prosody of a verse, which they could not but have hit on before among the rudiments of grammar." This sentence has created problems for commentators for whom prosody is not a trivial but a challenging art. Milton does not mean to be condescending to the art of prosody; he is merely commenting on the place where it comes in the curriculum. I believe that the word "organic" should be interpreted here in relation to the medieval-renaissance tradition locating rhetoric and poetics along with dialectic in the *Organon*. If so, "organic" means "related to the *Organon*," not "skillfully organized." "Poetic arts" refers to topics like the function of poetry, the three manners of imitation, characterization, and verisimilitude. These are normally beyond prosody, which is a part of grammar rather than part of the *Organon*. After the famous remark that poetry is "more simple, sensuous, and passionate" than prose, Milton advocates reading the critics: "I mean not heere the prosody of a verse . . . ; but that sublime art which in Aristotle's *Poetics,* in Horace, and the Italian commentaries of Castelvetro, Tasso, Mazzoni, and others, teaches what the laws are of a true epic poem, what of a dramatic, what of a lyric, what decorum is, which is the grand masterpiece to observe." *Reason of Church Government,* ed. Hughes, pp. 667–69; and *Samson Agonistes,* pp. 549–50.

9. *Poetics* in Aristotle's '*Poetics*': *A Translation and Commentary for Students of Literature,* tr. and ed. Leon Golden and O. B. Hardison (Englewood Cliffs, N.J., 1968), p. 44 (1459b35–36). S. H. Butcher, *Aristotle's Theory of Poetry and Fine Arts* (rpt. New York, 1951), p. 97, translates: "Once the material has been introduced, and an air of likelihood imparted to it, we must accept it in spite of the absurdity. Take even the irrational incidents in the *Odyssey*. . . . How intolerable these might have been would be apparent if an inferior poet were to treat the subject. As it is, the absurdity is veiled by the poetic charm with which the poet invests it." Cf. Gerald Else, *Aristotle's Poetics: The Argument* (Cambridge, Mass., 1957), pp. 621–31.

10. Aristotle's '*Poetics,*' p. 46 (1460a34–b2).

11. *A Defence of Ryme* (1603), in *ECE,* ed. Smith (cited ch. 1, n. 20), II, 359.

12. *Preface to Gondibert* (1650), in *Critical Essays of the Seventeenth Century,* ed. J. E. Spingarn (rpt. Bloomington, Ind., 1957), II, 21–22.

13. Ibid., II, 23.

14. *An Apology for Poetry,* in *ECE,* I, 202–4. Cf. O. B. Hardison, Jr., "The Two Voices of Sidney's *Apology for Poetry,*" ELR, II (1972), 83–99.

15. *Conversations,* in *Critical Essays of the Seventeenth Century,* I, 214.

16. *Advancement of Learning,* bk. 2, in ibid., p. 5.

17. *History of the Royal Society,* in ibid., II, 118.

18. *Answer to Davenant's Preface,* in ibid., p. 59. Compare Davenant's comment (II, 25) on inspiration: "Yet to such painfull Poets some upbraid the want of extemporary fury, or rather *inspiration,* a dangerous word, which

many have of late successfully us'd; and *inspiration* is a spiritual Fitt, deriv'd from the ancient Ethnick Poets, who then, as they were Priests, were Statesmen too . . . and as their well dissembling of inspiration begot them reverence then equall to that which was paid to the Laws, so these who now profess the same fury may perhaps by such authentick example pretend authority over the people." Cf. also in ibid., III, 292–98, George Granville's "Essay upon Unnatural Flights in Poetry" (1701).

19. Cf. C. M. Webster, "The Satiric Background of the Attack on the Puritans in Swift's *A Tale of a Tub*," *PMLA*, 50(1935), 210–23.

20. Wm. H. Hudson, ed., *Dramatic Poesy and Other Essays of John Dryden* (rpt. London, 1950), pp. 51–52. Neander concludes—somewhat prematurely, as things turned out—that blank verse is "properly but measured prose" and "at most . . . but a poetic prose, a *sermo pedestris*." Both the equation of blank verse with prose and the use of the ancient rhetorical term *sermo pedestris* invite further historical analysis.

21. Preface to the *Rival Ladies* (1664), ibid., pp. 187–88.

22. Gilbert Murray, *The Classical Tradition in Poetry* (New York, 1957), p. 87.

23. *Essays of Dryden*, ed. Hudson, p. 54. Among the "errors" cited by Davenant in Tasso's poetry are "his Councell assembled in Heaven, his Witches Expeditions through the Air, and enchanted Woods inhabited with Ghosts. For though the elder Poets, which were then the sacred priests . . . compounded the Religion of Pleasure and Mysterie . . . Yet a Christian Poet, whose Religion little needs the aids of Invention, hath less occasion to imitate such Fables as meanly illustrate a probable heaven . . . and make a resemblance of Hell out of the Dreams of frighted Women." *Critical Essays of the Seventeenth Century*, II, 5.

24. *Essays of Dryden*, ed. Hudson, p. 58.

25. Ann Ferry, *Milton's Epic Voice: The Narrator in 'Paradise Lost'* (Cambridge, Mass., 1963), p. 18.

26. *John Milton*, ed. Hughes, p. 210. For background, see Morris Freedman, "Milton and Dryden on Rhyme," *HLQ*, 24(1960/61), 337–44, and A. M. Clark, "Milton and the Renaissance Revolt against Rhyme," in *Studies in Literary Modes* (Edinburgh, 1946), pp. 104–41.

27. *Essays of Dryden*, ed. Hudson, p. 51.

28. Edward Weismiller, "Studies of the Verse Forms of the Minor English Poems," in *A Variorum Commentary on the Poems of John Milton*, ed. A. S. P. Woodhouse and Douglas Bush, vol. 2, pt. 2 (New York, 1972), p. 1017. Cf. also vol. 4 (*Paradise Regained*) (1975), pp. 268–80. Robert Bridges, *Milton's Prosody* (rev. ed., Oxford, 1921); Prince, *Italian Element* (p. 131), whose quarrel with Bridges (p. 137) is that he does not accept the implications of the syllabic prosody that he himself so brilliantly uncovered. S. E. Sprott, *Milton's Art of Prosody* (Oxford, 1953), p. 5.

29. Cf. George A. Kellog, "Bridges' *Milton's Prosody* and Renaissance Metrical Theory," *PMLA*, 68(1953), 268–85.

30. Bridges, *Milton's Prosody*, pp. 18, 35. Cf. George Saintsbury, *History of English Prosody*, I, 173. Morris Halle and Samuel Keyser (*English Stress: Its Form, Its Growth, and Its Role in Verse* [New York, 1971], p. 141) agree that renaissance poets did not pronounce the elisions that they claimed by right of poetic license and prove this with a bit of dialogue from Tirso de Molina in which the meter calls for elision but the division of speakers makes the elision impossible. The argument works for Spanish and Italian; it is less applicable to renaissance French.

31. Prince, *Italian Element*, p. 144.

32. Christopher Ricks, *Milton's Grand Style* (Oxford, 1963), p. 31. Prince, *Italian Element*, pp. 112–49, examines Milton's figures of diction in detail and in relation to the prescriptions given in Tasso's *Discorsi del poema eroico* (1587).

33. The dependence of *Paradise Lost* on inspiration is documented in the extensive literature on Milton's invocations and need not be further documented here. It may, however, be useful to note two earlier passages that relate to heroic inspiration. The first is from *Elegy VI*, written to Diodati by Milton at age 21: "Diis etenim sacer est vates, divumque sacerdos, / Spirat et occultum pectus et ora Iovem." The second is from *Reason of Church Government*, where Milton speaks of extraordinary poetic abilities (ed. Hughes, p. 669): "The abilities, wheresoever they be found, are the inspired gift of God rarely bestowed, but yet to some (though most abuse) in every nation; and are of the power beside the office of a pulpit, to inbreed and cherish in a great people the seeds of virtue and public civility." Milton sees the epic poet in the line of poet-prophets who are chosen by God to lead His people to new understanding: "Some I have chosen of peculiar grace / Elect above the rest; so is my will" (*PL*, III, 183–84).

34. *Paradise Lost*, ed. Hughes, XII, 514.

35. *The Complete Poetry of Ben Jonson*, ed. W. B. Hunter, Jr., (Garden City, N.Y., 1963), pp. 166–67.

36. Alexander Gil, *Logonomia Anglica* (1619), ed. Bror Danielsson and Arvid Gabrielson (Stockholm, 1972), p. 127: "Quia numerus poeticus, et ordo syntaxeos non semper conveniunt; et poeta necessario observandus est uterque numerus; et rythmi causa frequentior est in tropis et temporis in hyperbato; aliquando etiam ad synchesin cogitur."

37. Campion, *Observations*, *ECE*, II, 331.

38. Daniel, *Defence of Ryme*, ibid., p. 365.

39. Gil, *Logonomia*, p. 141. "At odiosa sunt (inquis) perpetua homoioteleuta: minuunt enim sermonis maiestatem."

40. Daniel, *Defence of Ryme*, *ECE*, II, 382.

41. Carl W. Cobb, "Milton and Blank Verse in Spain," *PQ*, 42(1963), 264–67. Cobb points out that the two candidates best known today, Juan Boscan

and Garcilaso de la Vega, were hardly recognized for their blank verse experiments in Spain and would almost certainly not have been known in that connection by Milton. Perez was probably known to Milton only because he is mentioned as an experimenter in unrhymed verse by Roger Ascham in *The Scholemaster* (*ECE*, I, 30).

42. *John Milton*, ed. Hughes, p. 669.

43. Tr. Benjamin Jowett, *The Basic Aristotle* (New York, 1941), pp. 1314–15.

44. *ECE*, II, 329.

45. Cf. the review by Weismiller, *Variorum*, vol. 4 (1975), pp. 333–35. Broadbent thinks Milton's phrase refers to "iterative rhetorical structures." James Whaler, *Counterpoint and Symbol: An Inquiry into the Rhythm of Milton's Epic Style* (Copenhagen, 1956), is still a useful discussion of the larger rhetorical effects of Milton's verse.

46. Cf. *Second Defense*, ed. Hughes, pp. 830–31: "When, therefore, I perceived that there were three species of liberty which are essential to the happiness of social life—religious, domestic, and civil; and as I had already written concerning the first, and the magistrates were strenuously active in obtaining the third, I determined to turn my attention to the second, or the domestic species."

47. Morris Freedman, "Dryden's 'Memorable Visit' to Milton," *HLQ*, 18(1955), 99–108.

48. *John Milton*, ed. Hughes, pp. 109–10.

Index

Inclusion of footnotes has been selective. A few footnotes that treat specific topics in detail have, however, been included.

Abbregé de l'art poétique françois. See Ronsard, Pierre de
Absalom and Achitophel, 261
Absalom. See Watson, Thomas
Absurd *(to alogon)*, 261
Académie de Poesie et de Musique, 69–70
Accademia della nuova poesia Toscana, 89
Accent, 82, 106–9, 115, 120, 135, 139–40, 142–44, 160, 187–89, 219
Accent (acute, circumflex, grave), 5, 97, 107–8
Accent (in rhyme) 12, 13, 51, 54, 57, 59–60, 82, 118
Accent (speech-accent), 3–4, 10, 14, 109–10, 113, 189, 227–29. *See also* Construction; Illocution
Accentual foot meter, 7–8, 109, 121
Accentual meter (Latin), 39, 41, 43–46, 120–21, 290 n68
Accentual-alliterative prosody, 6–7, 106, 160–64
Achilles' shield. See Chapman, George
Acolastus. See Palsgrave, John
Action (in iambic verse) 25, 36, 228, 287 n50, 288 n51
Actorly dialogue, 157, 158–60, 162, 165–67, 169, 177, 182, 185, 193, 227–28, 230–34, 243–45, 247–51, 256, 323 n36

Acutus, 5, 97, 107–8
Adagia. See Erasmus, Desiderius
Adam of St. Victor, 48, 50, 52
Advancement of Learning. See Bacon, Francis
Aelius Aphthonius, 30
Aeneid: trans. Gavin Douglas, 128–29; trans. Thomas Phaer, 197–203; trans. Richard Stanyhurst, 203–66; trans. Surrey, 127–47. *See also* Vergil
Aeterne rerum conditor, 44
Agamemnon, 148, 157–58
Aigu, 5, 97, 107–8
Alamanni, Luigi, 20, 86, 88, 90, 130
Aldus Manutius, 102
Alexandreis. See Gualtharius, Phillip
Alexandrine, 9, 10, 11, 16, 46, 62, 65–66, 112, 119, 120, 142, 156, 186, 188, 189, 191, 217, 219
All for Love. See Dryden, John
Alliteration, 6–7, 16, 138, 160, 161, 162, 164, 169–70, 199, 200, 208, 209, 214
Allyn, Edward, 241
Ambitus. See Period
Ambrose, Saint, 40
Ambrosian hymns, 43–45, 50
Anacreontic, 32
Anceps, syllable, 33

Ancient versus medieval cultural forms, 63–70, 94–97, 122–24, 214–15
Andria. See Terence
Aneau, Barthelémy, 67, 68, 124
Antonio da Tempo, 72, 76, 78, 82
Antony and Cleopatra, 181
Aphthonius, 177
Apocope. See Metaplasm
Apology for Actors. See Heywood, Thomas
Apology for Poetry. See Sidney, Sir Philip
Aquilano, Serafino. See Serafino Aquilano
Aquinas, St. Thomas, 123
Arator, 40
Arcadia. See Sidney, Sir Philip
Archilochus, 36, 37
Areopagus, 112
Aretino, Pietro, 182
Ariosto, Lodovico, 76, 78, 86, 87, 104, 149, 182, 193–94, 195, 214, 224
Aristides Quintilianus, 31
Aristotle, 21, 23–24, 26, 36, 38, 61, 68, 81, 83, 85, 87, 88, 103, 117, 155, 227–30, 238, 257, 261, 265, 273
Aristotle's Poetics, 229
Arnault Daniel, 75
Ars dictaminis, 55
Ars major. See Donatus, Aelius
Ars metrica, 23–42, 59, 66, 68, 69, 72, 97, 98, 102, 105, 108, 117, 131, 134, 136, 153, 182, 183, 195, 222, 228, 241, 259, 260
Ars poetica. See Horace
Ars rithmica, 25, 43–58, 72
Ars versificatoria, 56
Arsis (in metrical foot), 32, 34, 35, 108
Art de dictier. See Deschamps, Eustache
Art of English Poetry, 8
Art poétique, 263–64
Art poétique françoys. See Sebillet, Thomas
Art poétique d'Horace. See Peletier, Jacques
Arte of English Poesie. See Puttenham, George
Arte of Rhetorique. See Wilson, Thomas
Articulus, 28
Artis grammaticae libri III. See Diomedes

Ascensius, Badius. See Badius Ascensius
Ascham, Roger, 20, 43, 94–96, 98, 103–5, 110, 141, 152, 203, 204, 206, 212, 262, 268, 269
Astrophil and Stella. See Sidney, Sir Philip
Attridge, Derek, 7, 98, 131
Aubrey, John, 276
Augustine, Saint, 21, 25, 38–39, 42, 50, 141

Bacon, Roger, 123
Bacon, Sir Francis, 80, 219, 263, 275
Badius Ascensius, 39, 61, 101, 131, 133, 158, 230
Baïf, Jean-Antoine de, 64, 68, 69–70, 113, 116
Baker, Richard, 238
Baldus, 76
Baldwin, William, 151, 197
Bale, John, 155, 172
Ballad, 73, 154, 156, 214, 222
Ballade, 15, 59, 62, 64, 69, 83, 111, 213
Ballata, 83
Barrio, Antonio Garcia, 25, 26–27
Baum, Paull, 17
Bavand, William, 151
Bede, Venerable, 39–42, 44, 45, 46, 107, 123
Bembo, Pietro, 20, 76, 77, 78, 81, 86, 90, 129
Beowulf, 43
Bernard, Richard, 149
Bernard, J. E., Jr., 154, 155, 183
Beroaldus, Philippus, 133
Beza, Theodore, 196
Bibbiena, Cardinal (Bernardo Dovizi), 182 .
Biotic verse, 36, 238
Blank verse, 62, 123, 127–47, 173, 181, 193, 195, 196, 197, 206, 211, 257, 262, 265, 266, 267–69, 272, 275
Blunderville, Thomas, 151
Boccaccio, Giovanni, 19, 76, 77, 78, 79, 80, 83, 86, 92, 215, 224
Boileau, 263–64
Bond, R. W., 183
Book of the Courtier. See Castiglione, Baldessar

Borghesi, Bernardino, 88
Bowcutt, Priscilla, 129
Bradner, Leicester, 152
Breath (= *Spritus*; prosodic term), 5, 97
Brenner, Eduard, 202
Brevissima institutio seu ratio. See Lily, William
Bridges, Robert, 13, 17, 268–69, 274
Brinsley, John, 98–101, 105, 109, 110, 203, 239, 269
Brooke, Tucker, 132
Brown, John Russell, 246
Brunetto Latini, 72
Buchanan, George, 103
Buckhurst. See Sackville, Thomas
Burbage, Richard, 240
Burger, Michel, 46
Bysshe, Edward, 8

Cadence, 12, 57, 118, 120, 221, 279 n8, 293 n34
Caesura, 9, 10, 11, 13, 15, 37, 38, 54, 60, 61, 62, 66, 74, 98, 111, 119, 124, 134, 136, 137, 138, 140, 142, 159, 160, 162, 174, 178, 188, 200, 208, 246; classical forms defined, 37; French forms defined, 9–10
Calandria, 182
Calvin, John, 151, 171
Camerata, of Florence, 70
Campaspe, 195
Campion, Thomas, 22, 69, 90, 116–17, 122–24, 212, 271–72, 274, 307 n70
Canace. See Speroni, Sperone
Cantelène de sainte Eulalie, 53
Canterbury Tales. See Chaucer, Geoffrey
Cantica, 37
Cantilevered verse, 154, 156, 183–84, 188, 190, 256
Canzone, 72, 73, 74, 80, 83, 207
Carlino, Gioseffo, 4
Caro, Annibale, 90–91, 259
Cassaria. See Ariosto, Lodovico
Cassidy, Edwin, 130
Cassirer, Ernst, 94
Castellano. See Trissino, Giangiorgio
Castelvetro, Lodovico, 261

Castiglione, Baldessar, 20, 76, 77–78, 79, 81, 96, 171
Cauda, 75
Caudata, 58
Caxton, William, 128
Cecil, William, 150
Certayn Notes of Instruction. See Gascoygne, George
Cervantes, Miguel de, 215
Cesano. See Tolomei, Claudio
Chapman, George, 197, 203, 206–12, 217, 222, 224, 265, 274
Chaucer, Geoffrey, 4, 8, 15, 16, 19, 54, 58, 59, 60, 81, 92, 104, 106, 107, 111, 119, 128, 131, 204, 214, 216, 219, 269
Chaucer's prosody, 279 nn27, 28
Chaucer's Prosody. See Robinson, Ian
Chaucer's Verse. See Baum, Paull
Cheke, Sir John, 20, 95
Chevalier, Jean-Claude, 4
Chiabrera, Gabriello, 90
Cicero, Marcus Tullius, 21, 42, 60, 70, 77, 99, 105
Cinna. See Corneille, Pierre
Cintio, Giraldi, 86–89, 124, 183, 184, 193, 216
Circonflexe, 5, 97, 107–8
Circumflexus, 5, 97, 107–8
City of God. See Augustine, Saint
Claritas, 111
Clarity, 111
Classical Theory of Composition, 4
Clausula (= sentence unit), 21, 28
Clausulae (= rhythmic termination), 28, 29, 48, 51, 55, 99, 292 n15
Clemen, Wolfgang, 181
Clerk, John, 131
Clizia. See Machiavelli, Niccolò
Collocatio. See Construction
Colloquia. See Erasmus, Desiderius
Colon, 48, 119, 134
Coltivazione. See Alamanni, Luigi
Comedy, 23, 26, 36, 37, 41, 55, 62–63, 64, 65, 73, 81, 83, 90, 101, 102, 103, 116, 117, 118, 148–49, 182–95; in prose, 87, 182, 183, 193–95
Comic style, 37, 153, 182

Comic verse, 287 nn49, 51
Comma, 28, 48, 119
Commodian, 45, 51
Common meter, 31, 154
Composite poem, 57
Composition. *See* Construction
Confessions. *See* Augustine, Saint
Conner, Jack, 17, 18
Conpositio. *See* Construction
Constitutive function of verse, 25, 95, 259
Constructio. *See* Construction
Construction, 3, 4, 12, 28, 29, 66, 73–75, 83–84, 97, 99, 110, 119, 122, 129, 132, 134, 136, 137, 161, 164, 169, 185, 199, 202, 203, 206–10, 212, 215, 242, 245, 258, 260–70, 277 n2, 282 n21
Contre-rejet, 11
Corneille, Pierre, 11
Coup. *See* Caesura
Couple, 53, 59
Couplet (heroic), 123, 208–12, 262, 265–66
Couplet. *See* Decasyllable; Fourteener
Cowley, Abraham, 270
Coxe, Leonard, 206
Cross rhyme, 54, 115, 123
Crystal, David, 4, 14, 19
Cursus, 21, 51

Daadler, Joost, 169
Dactyl, 32, 34, 37, 38, 50, 116, 121, 134
Dactylic hexameter. *See* Hexameter
Dametas (= tolomei), 89
Daniel, Samuel, 90, 122–24, 262, 265, 268, 270, 271
Dante Alighieri, 4, 9, 11–12, 18, 19, 71–76, 77, 80, 82, 83, 124, 141, 214, 275
Davenant, William, 123, 197, 219–25, 262–63
Davideis, 270
Davies, Sir John, 259
Day-Owen Edition of Surrey, 130–32, 136–47, 196, 197, 198
De arte metrica. *See* Bede, Venerable
De duplici copia. *See* Erasmus, Desiderius
De emendata structura, 4

De inventione. *See* Cicero
De la Taille, Jacques, 68, 69
De lingua Latina. *See* Varro
De musica. *See* Augustine, Saint
De pueri instruendis. *See* Erasmus, Desiderius
De ratione studii. *See* Erasmus, Desiderius
De vulgari eloquentia. *See* Dante Alighieri
Death of Zoroas. *See* Grimald, Nicholas
Débat, 184, 186
Decasyllable, 8, 10, 13, 18, 46, 58, 62, 65, 66, 74, 112, 115, 119, 123, 131, 136, 137, 139, 146, 156, 168, 174, 175, 186, 197, 198, 208, 210–12, 221, 222, 224, 269
Dechamps, Eustache, 22
Decorum, 38, 60, 83, 87, 103, 186, 205, 289 n58
Defence of Ryme. *See* Daniel, Samuel
Deffence et illustration. *See* DuBellay, Joachim
DeMedici, Ippolito, 72, 88, 90, 130
DeMedici, Lorenzo, 76
Demetrius Phalarion, 84
Dennis, John, 238
Deschamps, Eustache, 9, 58–63, 92, 260
Despautarius, Joannes, 4, 102
Diaeresis, 98, 110, 134, 188. *See also* Metaplasm
Dial of Princes, 150
Dialogo delle lingue. *See* Speroni, Sperone
Dic nobis Maria, 52
Dido Queene of Carthage. *See* Marlowe, Christopher
Didone. *See* Cintio, Giraldi
Diegetic poetry, 228
Diesis, 75
Diiambus, 32, 82, 102, 161
Diomedes (4th-cen. grammarian), 25, 28, 30, 35–39, 41, 42, 102, 230
Dionysius of Halicarnassus, 29, 33
Dipodic foot, 32, 82, 102, 161
Discorsi del arte poetica. *See* Tasso, Torquato
Discorsi del poema erico. *See* Tasso, Torquato
Discorsi intorno al comporre... *See* Cintio, Giraldi

Discorso in cui si dimostra..., 86–87
Discourse of English Poetrie. *See* Webbe, William
Discourse on the Eucharist, 155
Discoveries. *See* Jonson, Ben
Dispositio, 177–78
Diverbia, 37
Divine Comedy. *See* Dante Alighieri
Doggerel verse, 183–84
Dolce, Lodovico, 76, 193
Don Quixote, 215
Donatus, Aelius, 5, 25, 29, 39, 82, 97, 102
Donatus, Tiberius Claudius, 133
Donne, John, 260
Dorat, Jean, 63, 69
Douglas, Gavin, 128, 135, 137, 141, 142, 146, 198, 199, 205
Dragonetti, Roger, 73
Drama, 226–57
Dramatic verse like speech. *See* Poetry, like speech
Drant, Thomas, 112, 152, 203
Drummond, William, 220, 263
Dryden, John, 222, 256, 265, 266, 268, 269, 270, 276
DuBartas, Guillaume, 197
DuBellay, Joachim, 20, 60, 61, 62, 63–64, 65, 67, 69, 80, 81, 88, 111, 124, 213
Dudley, Robert, 150

E.K. (Writer of Glosses to *Shepheardes Calender*), 212–13
Eclogues, of Mantuan. *See* Mantuan
Eclogues. *See* Vergil
Ecthlipsis, 98, 102, 201. *See also* Metaplasm
Edwards, Richard, 152
Elam, Keir, 226, 230
Elegy, 23, 26, 29, 32, 36, 39, 40, 47, 59, 62, 64, 65, 66, 73, 89, 98, 117, 118, 214
Eliot, T. S., 258–60, 274
Elision. *See* Metaplasm
Elizabeth I, 94, 148, 150, 152, 171–72, 181
Elizabethan acting, 239–40
Else, Gerald F., 229

Empedocles, 24, 35, 36
Emphasis, 105–6
Enargia, 84, 85, 134, 172, 178, 179, 259
Enchiridion. *See* Hephaestion
Endymion. *See* Lyly, John
Eneydos, 128
English Prosody from Chaucer, 17, 18
English Stress, 17
Enjambment, 11, 15, 29, 40, 134, 135, 136, 137, 162, 169, 174, 185, 200, 201, 202, 208, 209, 212, 215, 218, 265, 272
Enthusiasm, 264, 266
Enthymeme, 177
Epic, 25, 26, 29, 32, 36, 38, 63, 64, 66–67, 84, 88, 89, 98, 103, 116, 117, 123, 127–47, 131, 196–225, 258–76
Epic caesura. *See* Caesura
Epic style, 197
Epic verse, 288 n53, 289 n62
Epicoene. *See* Jonson, Ben
Erasmus, Desiderius, 4, 93, 98, 100, 101, 124, 152, 155, 215
Esoteric humanism, 93–94, 101, 127, 152, 206
Ethiopian History. *See* Heliodorus
Etrenes de poëzie fransoeze. *See* Baïf, Jean-Antoine de
Etymologiarum, 40
Euphony, 28
Euripides, 23–24, 149, 152, 193
Evardus Alemannus, 55
Evidentia. *See* Enargia
Exoteric humanism, 93–94
Explanatio, 111

Faerie Queene. *See* Spenser, Edmund
Fairclough, H. R., 133–34, 201
Famous Victories of Henry V, 195
Faral, Edmond, 72
Farce, 184
Fenolossa, Ernest, 258
Fenyo, Jane K., 116
Ferry, Anne, 266, 270
Fescennine verse, 31
Ficino, Marsilio, 275
Figure (in classical verse), 33, 35, 37
Figures: of diction, 27, 29, 74, 99, 122, 134, 229, 282 n21; of thought, 29, 134

Filtostato. See Boccaccio, Giovanni
Fisher, John, 17
Flecknoe, Richard, 240
Fletcher, Giles, 20
Fletcher, Phineas, 20
Flora, Francesco, 91
Flora. See Alamanni, Luigi
Flores poetarum, 99
Flowers for Latin Speaking. See Udall, Nicholas
Folengo, Teofilo, 76
Foot, 7–8, 10, 13, 17, 18–19, 31–35, 38, 40, 57, 59, 61, 75, 82, 90, 98, 102, 104, 106, 109, 115, 120–21; classical (Donatus), 32–35, 285 n35; English (George Gascoigne), 108–10; Italian (Trissino), 82; medieval (John of Garland), 57; as rhyme, 57; as stanza, 75; as syllable, 13, 17, 59, 115
Founding of English Metre, 109
Foure P. P. See Heywood, John
Fourteener, 111, 115, 119, 141, 146, 156, 158, 160–70, 173, 197, 198, 200, 202, 204–10, 214, 245, 253–54, 275
Franciade. See Ronsard, Pierre de
Freer, Coburn, 236–38
French prosody, 277 n5
French verse-art. See Scott, Clive
Frons, 75
Frontinus, 75
Frye, Roland, 259

Gascoigne, George, 7, 105–12, 114, 115, 148–49, 182, 193–95, 196, 214, 224, 256
Gelli, Giambattista, 76
Genius and Writings of Shakespeare, 238
Geoffrey of Vinsauf, 56
Georgics. See Vergil
Gerusalemme liberata. See Torquato Tasso
Gil, Alexander, 108, 258, 271–72, 308 n85
Gnapheus, Guilelmus, 101
Golding, William, 118, 203, 206
Gondibert. See Davenant, William
Googe, Barnabe, 151
Gorboduc, 149, 151, 152, 157, 171–82, 315 n4. *See also* Sackville, Thomas

Grammar and prosody, 30–35, 281 n18
Grammatical theory of prosody, 282 n18
Grand style. *See* Style, three styles
Gravis, 5, 97, 107–8
Gray, Thomas, 223
Greene, Robert, 204, 237
Greene, Thomas, 67
Grimald, Nicholas, 70, 152, 183, 196
Gryphius, Sebastian (editor of Seneca), 161
Gualtharius, Phillip, 196
Guarino da Verona, 93
Guillaume de Lorris, 68

Haec domus aulae, 49
Hagar, Alan, 128
Hall, Bishop Arthur, 203
Hall, Joseph, 237
Halle, Morris, 17, 248
Halliday, F. E., 226
Hamlet, 165, 233–34, 254
Handbook (of Prosody). *See* Hephaestion
Hardie, W. R., 26
Harding, D. W., 4, 14, 19
Hargrave Manuscript of Surrey, 130, 139, 142, 146
Hartmann of St. Gall, 45
Harvey, Gabriel, 13, 112–14, 190, 203–4, 213
Heliodorus (grammarian), 30, 31, 117
Hendecasyllable, 46, 71, 74, 75, 83, 87, 89, 119
Henry V, 246
Hephaestion (grammarian), 25, 30–31, 37
Herbert, William, 150
Hercules Oetaeus, 148, 152, 157–58
Hercules furens, 148, 150, 157–58
Hero and Leander. See Marlowe, Christopher
Heroic couplet. *See* Couplet (heroic)
Heroic elevation. *See* Epic
Heroic style. *See* Epic
Heroic verse. *See* Hexameter
Heroical Epistles of Ovid, 196
Herrick, Marvin T., 182
Herrick, Robert, 22
Hexameter, 24, 25, 26, 32, 33, 34, 35, 37,

38, 40, 46, 47, 51, 83, 88, 98, 104, 113, 114, 146, 188, 197, 198, 200, 203, 205, 224, 268
Heywood, Jasper, 110, 148–70, 171, 173, 197, 208, 227, 245, 252
Heywood, John (father of Jasper), 148, 154, 183, 184–86
Heywood, Thomas, 239
Higgins, John, 149
Hippolytus, 148, 157–58
Histoire de la syntaxe, 4
History of English Versification. See Schipper, Jakob
Hobbes, Thomas, 221, 223–24, 264
Hoby, Sir Thomas, 79, 96, 171
Holy Weeks, 197
Homer, 21, 22, 26, 29, 40, 42, 61, 66, 85, 116, 207, 217, 221, 227, 228; *Iliad* (tr. George Chapman), 206–10; *Odyssey* (tr. George Chapman), 210–12
Homoeoteleuton 47, 113
Hopkins, John, 171
Horace (Q. Horatius Flaccus), 30, 31, 35, 36, 37, 38, 39, 55, 58, 61, 62, 63, 64, 65, 66, 68, 72, 83, 92, 97, 101, 103, 114, 131, 152, 198, 220, 228, 230, 261, 262, 264, 274
Hudibras, 261
Humanism and style, 310 n22
Hunt, T., 149
Hymnes. See Ronsard, Pierre de

Iambic (licensed), 37, 104, 182, 188
Iambic dimeter, 43–45, 98
Iambic hexameter, 120
Iambic pentameter, 9, 18, 55, 116, 174
Iambic rhyme, 51
Iambic trimeter, 23, 32, 34, 39, 41, 82, 86, 98, 102–3, 113, 116, 157, 161, 173, 187, 193
Iambic verse, 23, 25, 26, 31, 34, 36, 37, 39, 41, 50, 57, 59, 86, 87, 88, 98, 103, 109, 114, 116–17, 122, 123, 156–57, 159, 161, 183, 187–88, 189, 191, 237
Iambus, 32, 34, 43, 82, 103, 113, 115, 116, 121
Ictus, 31, 33, 43, 57, 104, 108, 285 n37
Iliad. See Homer

Illocution, 176, 179, 192, 227, 228, 229, 232, 236, 242–43
Imagination, 219
Imitation, 12, 26, 36, 71, 73, 85, 92, 94, 117, 142, 154, 160–61, 172, 195, 215, 220, 227–28, 230, 257
Inkhorn terms, 105, 180, 204
Inspiration, 223, 259–60, 264–65, 270–71, 325 n18, 326 n33
Institutes. See Calvin, John
Institutio oratoria. See Quintilian
Instructiones. See Commodian
Interlude, 154
Irrational (*to alogon*), 261, 262, 271
Isidore of Seville, 40
Iso of St. Gall, 48
Isocrates, 30
Italia liberata. See Trissino, Giangiorgio
Italian Elements in Milton's Verse. See Prince, F. T.

Jean de Meun, 68
Jephtha, 103
Jerome, Saint, 40, 42
Jeu de saint-Nicolas, 9–10
Jocasta. See Gascoigne, George
Johan Johan. See Heywood, John
John of Garland, 55–58, 72, 75, 269
Jones, C. W., 41
Jones, Emrys, 128
Jonson, Ben, 20, 22, 195, 219, 220, 231, 237, 240, 241, 262, 263, 271
Joseph, Bertram, 239–40
Juan de Jauregui, 273
Juba (grammarian), 30
Jubilus, 47–48
Julius Caesar, 231
Juvenal, 61

Kalendrier des bergers, 213
Kellog, George, 268
Kendall, C. B., 39
Keyser, Samuel J. See Halle, Morris
King John. See Bale, John
Knight, G. Wilson, 255
Kyd, Thomas, 92, 173, 195, 251–54
Kyffin, Maurice, 149

INDEX / 335

Laborintus, 55
Lancelot, Claude, 8
Lathrop, Henry, 128, 132
Latinitas, 27, 28, 35, 64, 82, 105, 111, 124, 199, 262, 282 n19
Le Fèr, Pierre, 60
Lee, Nathaniel, 123, 256
Legrande, Jacques, 60
Leonine rhyme, 15, 51, 54, 59
Leoninus, 49–50
Lesclarissement de la langue francoyse. See Palsgrave, John
Levis, 5, 97, 107–8
Lewis, C. S., 132
Liber hymnorum. See Notker Balbulus
Libro del Cortegiano. See Castiglione, Baldessar
Liburnio, Niccolò, 130
Licenciate iambic, 37, 104, 182, 188
Lillo, George, 256
Lily, William, 93, 97–98, 100–101, 106, 116, 303 n12
Linacre, Thomas, 4
Livy (Andronicus Livius), 75
Logonomia Anglica. See Gil, Alexander
London Merchant, 256
Lote, Georges, 47, 50, 51, 53
Lucan (M. Annaeus Lucanus), 75, 146, 221, 244
Lucretius (T. Lucretius Carus), 35, 36
Ludus literarius. See Brinsley, John
Lydgate, John, 119
Lyly, John, 195
Lyric caesura. See Caesura

Mac Flecknoe, 261
Machiavelli, Niccolò, 76, 182
Madagascar. See Davenant, William
Magnificence (aesthetic term), 215, 216, 219, 266
Magnificence (play). See Skelton, John
Maître Pathelin (French farce), 68
Malcontent, 238
Malherbe, François de, 11, 68
Mallius Theodorus, 38, 39
Malof, Joseph, 8
Mandragola. See Machiavelli, Niccolò

Maniere de faire vers en françois. See de la Taille, Jacques
Manner of imitation, 36
Mantuan (Baptista Spagnuoli), 152, 213
Manual of English Meters, 8
Map, Walter, 123
Marcus Tullius Cicero's Death. See Grimald, Nicholas
Mario Pazzaglia, 72
Marius Victorinus, 25, 30, 39
Marlowe, Christopher, 92, 132, 146, 157, 173, 195, 206, 211, 237, 241–51, 253–54, 258, 275
Marot, Clément, 61, 62, 63, 67, 69, 70, 81, 213–14
Marriage of Wit and Science. See Redford, John
Marston, John, 238
Marvell, Andrew, 276
Mason, John, 150
Matthew of Vendôme, 56
Mazzoni, Jacopo, 124
Measure, 9–10, 15, 48, 107, 115, 119, 124
Medea, 148, 157–58
Medwall, Henry, 183
Mellin de Saint-Gelais, 60, 61, 70
Memory, 257
Menaechmi. See Plautus
Menaphon. See Greene, Robert
Metamorphoses. See Ovid
Metaplasm, 9, 10, 14, 27, 30, 40, 62, 69, 97, 98, 110, 113, 117, 200, 201, 259, 271, 283 nn24, 25
Meter (prototype) 31, 37, 284 n30
Metrikoi, 24
Metrum, 45, 122
Meyer, Wilhelm, 46, 53
Michele, Agostino, 86–87
Midsummer Night's Dream, 254
Miles gloriosus. See Plautus
Milton, John, 4, 13, 16, 17, 20, 22, 90, 91, 108, 123, 132, 139, 146–47, 169, 182, 197, 217, 258–76, 324 n8
Milton's Prosody. See Bridges, Robert
Mimetic (vs. diegetic) poetry, 228
Minturno, Sebastiano, 216, 261

Mirandula, Octavianus, 99
Mirror for Magistrates, 151, 171, 197
Mirror image (for drama), 231–32
Modes (of music), 26
Modulatio, 45
Molinet, Jean, 60
Molza, Francesco, 86
Mora (quantitative unit of measure of time). *See* Time
Morality play, 62, 65, 69, 187
More, Henry, 264
More, Sir Thomas, 155
Morgante Maggiore, 215
Mors Ciceronis, 196
Murray, Gilbert, 265
Music and poetry, 21–22, 26–27, 43–55, 56, 58–59, 66–67, 69, 72, 75, 115, 118, 119, 258–76, 281 n8, 297 n5, 324 n6
Musica mensurabilis, 50, 292 n19
Musica plana, 50
Musical Encyclopedia, 31
Musical modes, 273
Muzio, Girolamo, 76, 84

Nashe, Thomas, 204, 236
Natural Emphasis, 17
Nature of the 4 Elements. See Rastell, John
Nevyle, Alexander, 148, 150, 151, 157
Newton, Thomas, 148, 149, 157
Nicoll, Allardyce, 210
Norberg, Dag, 41, 51
Norden, Eduard, 47
North, Thomas, 150
Norton, Thomas, 114, 149, 151, 152, 171–82, 196, 253
Note on the verse of *Paradise Lost*, 267–76
Notker Balbulus, 47, 51
Novum organum. See Bacon, Francis
Nuce, Thomas, 148, 150, 156
Number 13, 32, 53, 102, 107, 114, 115, 117, 118, 274, 276
Nunc vos, o socii, 49

Observations in the Arte of English Poesie. See Campion, Thomas
Octavia, 148, 157–58

Odyssey. See Homer
Oedipus, 148, 157–58
Old Testament (as poetry), 26, 40, 42
Old Wive's Tale, 195
Olive. See DuBellay, Joachim
Olivier, Sir Laurence, 233–35
On Nature. See Empedocles
On Schemes and Tropes. See Bede, Venerable
On Style, 84
Opsis, 227, 228–29
Oratio, 177–78
Orbecche. See Cintio, Giraldi
Orchestra, 259
Order, 28–29, 99, 105, 110, 136, 164, 199, 298 n10
Ordo Ciceronianus. See Order
Ordo artificialis. See Order
Ordo grammaticus. See Order
Ordo naturalis. See Order
Ordo rhetoricus. See Order
Ornate style, 28, 29
Orosius, 75
Othello, 181, 235, 255
Ottava rima, 15, 88, 146, 207, 214, 215, 216–17, 224
Ovid, 63, 75, 99
Owen, William. *See* Day-Owen Edition

Padelford, F. M., 130
Palengenius (Pier Angelo Manzolli), 151, 152
Pallavicino, Cosimo, 89
Palsgrave, John, 101–3, 183, 186
Paradise Lost. See Milton, John
Paraphrase of the New Testament. See Erasmus, Desiderius
Parisiana poetria. See John of Garland
Pasquier, Etienne, 68
Patterson, W. F., 60, 68
Paulinus of Nola, 41, 42
Pazzaglia, Mario, 73
Peele, George, 195
Peletier, Jacques, 60, 61, 63, 64–65
Perez, Gonzalo, 273
Peri Bathos, 256
Peri syntheseos. See Dionysius of Halicarnassus

Period, 28, 30, 48, 119, 133–34, 137–38, 142, 145, 164, 180, 215, 218
Perotinus, 49–50
Pes. See Foot
Peter Martyr, 155
Petrarca, Francesco, 12, 20, 71, 73, 76, 77, 78, 79, 80, 86, 104, 123, 129, 215
Phaer, Thomas, 118, 151, 196–203, 204, 206, 210, 217
Pharsalia. See Lucan
Philosophy of Symbolic Form, 94
Phocas, 102
Phoenissae. See Euripides
Phrase, 28
Piccolomini, Alessandro, 88
Piccolomini, Bartolomeo, 130
Piers Plowman, 7, 43
Piez. See Foot
Pigna, Giovanni Battista, 124, 216
Plato, 36, 61, 219, 228
Plautus, T. Maccius, 88, 103, 116, 148–49, 182, 186, 189, 195, 230
Pléiade theory, 63–67
Pliny (Caius Plinius Secundus), 75
Poetic license. See Metaplasm
Poetic (vs. biotic) verse, 36
Poetica. See Trissino, Giangiorgio
Poetices libri septem. See Scaliger, Julius Caesar
Poetics of Jacobean Drama, 236–38
Poetics. See Aristotle
Poetria nova, 56
Poetry and music. See Music and poetry
Poetry: as imitation of action, 24, 117–18, 228–29, 232, 238; like speech, 23–25, 36, 39, 86, 87, 100, 117, 157, 167, 173, 175, 181–82, 228, 253; as verse, 24, 35, 68, 72, 118
Poliziano, Angelo, 76
Pomponazzi, Pietro, 79–80
Pope, Alexander, 265
Poulter's measure, 107, 111, 146, 187
Pound, Ezra, 256
Powell, Thomas, 151
Praise of Folly. See Erasmus, Desiderius
Prince, F. T., 17, 269–70
Priscian, 28, 30, 34, 74, 102

Probus, 133
Progymnasma scholasticum. See Stockwood, John
Progymnasmata, 177
Proportion, 55–58, 115, 119–20, 124, 207, 215, 216–17
Prose (for comedy), 87, 182, 183, 193–95
Prose (for tragedy), 86, 87, 256
Prose della volgar lingua. See Bembo, Pietro
Proses. See Sequence
Prosodia promptissima, 100
Prosodia, 24, 92, 96, 97, 114, 116, 119
Prosodic systems: accentual, 41, 135–45; accentual-alliterative, 6–7, 106, 160–64; accentual foot meter, 7–8, 109, 121; accentual-Latin, 44–46, 268 n1, 290 n68; accentual-syllabic, 46–63, 92–124; English Renaissance, 13–19, 92–124; English versus French, 106–12, 160–62, 174, 191, 213–15, 219, 248, 268–69, 279 nn24, 27; English versus Latin, 104–11, 112–22, 159–64, 169, 189, 191–92, 208 n29, 213; Italian versus French, 11–12, 17, 19–20, 72–74, 139, 145–46; quantitative, 7, 32–35, 41, 204–5, 274; syllabic, 8–13, 46–63, 72, 102, 107, 118, 127, 135–45, 274; syllabic-Latin, 46–55
Prosper of Aquitaine, 41
Prototype meters, 31, 37, 284 n30
Prudentius, 41, 42
Psalms, 69, 111
Psychomachia. See Prudentius
Pulci, Luigi, 215
Purcell, Henry, 261
Puttenham, George, 13, 111, 117, 118–22, 124, 205, 307 n83

Quantitative prosody, 7, 32–35, 41, 204–5, 274
Quantitative verse: English, 112–17; French, 68–70; Italian, 89–90
Quatrain, 13, 44, 45, 57–58, 115, 119, 123, 154, 156, 168–69, 185, 221–25
Quatre traites de poésies, 8
Question of language, 63, 71–72, 76–79, 124

Qui regis sceptra, 51
Quintil Horatian. *See* Aneau, Barthelémy
Quintilian, Marcus Fabianus, 21, 33, 105
Quintilianus, Aristides, 31

R. R., Master in Arts, 99
Raleigh, Sir Walter, 119
Ralph Roister Doister. See Udall, Nicholas
Rastell, John, 149, 154, 183
Rationalism (and prosody), 221–25
Recherches de la France, 68
Redford, John, 154, 183
Rejet, 11
Republic. See Plato
Res et verba, 80, 94, 263
Res Metrica, 26
Resolution, 32, 33
Respublica (Anon.), 155
Reynolds, Henry, 220
Rhetorica ad Herennium, 12, 28, 38, 60, 72, 73, 177
Rhyme, as an aspect of rhythm, 56, 63, 82, 107, 120, 269
Rhyme, 12–13, 15, 17, 46, 51, 54, 59, 61, 64, 65, 72, 75, 82, 83, 84, 87–88, 95–96, 104, 111, 116, 118, 119, 120–21, 123, 124, 169, 192, 208, 212–13, 215, 216–17, 224, 259, 262, 265, 267, 268, 270, 271–72, 275, 278 n19
Rhyme royal, 15, 59, 107, 131, 154, 156, 187, 214, 216
Rhythm, 4, 12, 14, 21, 28, 30, 31–32, 33, 35, 41, 82, 138, 247, 286 n41, 287 n48
Rhytmikoi, 24
Ricchi, Agostino, 85
Richard III, 254
Richardson, David, 128
Ricks, Christopher, 270
Riding rhyme, 111
Ridley, Florence, 128–29, 132
Rime Équivoque, 55, 59, 64
Rime Léonine, 15, 51, 54, 59
Rime Riche, 54, 55, 59–60, 66
Rime Suffisante, 54, 55
Rime Toscane. See Alamanni, Luigi
Rimes Croisées, 54
Rimes Plates, 54

Rithmus, 45, 56, 122
Rival Queens. See Lee, Nathaniel
Roaf, Christina, 87
Robinson, Ian, 17
Romance, 61, 78, 212–19
Romeo and Juliet, 254
Ronsard, Pierre de, 64, 65–67, 68, 69
Rood, T., 149
Rosmunda, 87
Royal grammar. *See* Lily, William
Ruccelai, Giovanni, 87
Rules, for quantitative poetry: French, 68; Italian, 89–90
Russell, Francis, 150

Sackville, Thomas, 6, 149, 151, 152, 171–82, 196, 253
Saintsbury, George, 17
Sannazaro, Jacopo, 213
Sapphic, 32, 35, 40, 46, 51, 58, 98
Satire, 26, 37, 39, 64, 117, 118, 130, 288 n54
Saturnian meter, 31
Scaglione, Aldo, 4
Scaliger, Julius Caesar, 68–69, 118, 220
Scazon, 32, 37, 39, 102
Schemata dianoias, 29, 134
Schemata lexeos. See Figures of diction
Schipper, Jakob, 9, 161
Scholemaster. See Ascham, Roger
Scott, Clive, 3, 5, 10
Scotus, Duns, 123
Sdrucciolo, 12, 87, 182, 238
Sebillet, Thomas, 60–63, 65, 111
Second rhetoric, 60, 65, 70, 107, 214
Sedulius, 40
Sei primi libri del Eneide. See Zoppio
Semiotics of Theatre and Drama. See Elam, Keir
Senarius, 66, 83, 88, 102, 161, 187, 188–89, 190, 191–92. *See also* Iambic verse
Seneca (plays performed in Latin), 157–58
Seneca, L. Annaeus, 92, 148–70, 172, 177–78, 185, 227–28, 241, 251, 254, 315 n4
Septenarius, 31, 102

Sequence, 21, 41–42, 47–54, 55, 75, 292 n14
Serafino Aquilano, 20, 76, 81, 130
Servius, 25, 30, 39, 102, 133, 146
Sette giornate del mondo creato. See Tasso, Torquato
Shakespeare's verse, 320 n1
Shakespeare, William, 132, 149, 157, 173, 182, 186, 226–57, 261, 272–73
Shaped verse, 120
Shelley, Percy Bysshe, 26
Shepheardes Calender. See Spenser, Edmund
Shorte Introduction of Grammar. See Lily, William
Sic voluntatis integrae, 45
Sidney, Sir Philip, 9, 12, 13, 17, 112, 117–18, 119, 124, 128, 190, 238, 263
Similiter cadens. See Cadence
Simmons, Samuel, 267
Simone, Franco, 63
Sirma, 75
Skelton, John, 155, 156, 172, 213
Smetius, 100
Sonnet, 62, 64, 65, 72, 80, 83, 111, 112, 129
Sophocles, 23, 116
Sophonisba. See Trissino, Giangiorgio
Sopplimenti musicali, 4
Spectacle, 227, 228–29
Speech: organization, 177–78; as speeches, 176–82; techniques of persuasion, 177; three kinds of oration, 177–78
Spelling, reform of, 78, 90, 113, 204
Spenser, Edmund, 7, 16, 19, 20, 27, 112–14, 123, 190, 197, 203, 212–19, 221–22, 261, 262, 266, 269, 270
Spenserian stanza, 146, 216–17, 319 n39
Speroni, Sperone, 63, 79–80, 87
Spiritus, 5, 97
Spondaic rhyme, 51
Spondanus (Jean de Sponde), 210
Spondee, 32, 34, 35, 37, 38, 57, 59, 116, 121, 134, 174
Sprat, Thomas, 263
Stanyhurst, Richard, 114, 121, 197, 203–6, 217–18

Stanza, 12, 15, 52–53, 54, 57–58, 60, 61, 72, 75, 83, 111, 119–20, 124, 207, 216–18, 221, 224
Statius, Publius Papinius, 12, 75, 88
Steele Glas. See Gascoigne, George
Sternhold, Thomas, 171
Stevenson, William, 155, 186
Stichomythia, 157, 165–66
Stockwood, John, 29, 100
Strange News. See Nashe, Thomas
Straunge metre (= foreign meter), 131–32, 207
Stress (= word accent), 6, 8, 17, 18, 109, 113–14, 138, 154, 174
Studley, John, 148, 150, 151, 152
Style (three styles), 29, 38, 55, 73–74, 297 n4
Substitution, 34, 110, 134, 174, 189
Summa artis rithmici. See Antonio da Tempo
Supposes. See Gascoigne, George
Suppositi. See Ariosto, Lodovico
Surrey, Henry Howard, Earl of, 88, 104, 110, 114, 118, 127–47, 173, 179, 182, 183, 196, 198, 199, 208, 210, 217, 224, 242–43, 244, 254, 267–68, 269, 274
Swift, Jonathan, 264
Syllabic meter (Latin), 46–58
Syllabic prosody, 8–13, 46–63, 72, 102, 107, 118, 127, 135–45, 274
Sylvae. See Statius
Sylvester, Joshua, 197
Synaeresis. See Metaplasm
Synaloepha, 9, 30, 40, 54, 98, 102, 134, 160, 200, 202. See also Metaplasm
Syncope, 113, 137, 142, 144, 146, 200. See also Metaplasm
Syntaxis. See Despauterius, Joannes
Syntaxis. See Construction
Synthesis. See Construction
Syzygiae (composite feet), 32

Tale of a Tub, 264
Tamburlaine. See Marlowe, Christopher
Tasso, Torquato, 88, 90, 91, 147, 215–16, 221, 222, 259, 266, 269, 273
Tempest, 255, 261

Tempus, 5, 32, 33, 35, 97
Tenne Tragedies (of Seneca). *See* Newton, Thomas
Terence (Publius Terentius Afer), 3c, 88, 92, 103, 116, 149, 155, 182, 186, 188, 195, 230
Terentianus (grammarian), 30, 102
Terza rima, 71, 80, 82, 83, 84, 129, 214, 275
Teseida. See Boccaccio, Giovanni
Tesor, 72
Theatrum triumphans, 238
Thebias, 148, 157–58
Thesis (prosodic term), 32, 34, 35
Thibault de Courville, Joachim, 69–70
Things and words, 80, 94, 263
Thomas, Duke of Norfolk, 130
Thompson, John, 109
Thyestes, 148–70
Time (= *Tempus*; classical unit of measure), 5, 32, 33, 35, 97
Titus Andronicus, 254
Tolomei, Claudio, 76, 86, 89, 90, 112, 113, 273
Tone (= *Tonus*; classical term for tonal accent), 5, 97, 106, 108
Tottel, Richard, 127, 129, 130, 132, 139, 146, 151, 171, 183, 196, 198, 206
Toxophilus. See Ascham, Roger
Tragedy, 23, 26, 36, 37, 55, 62, 64, 65, 66, 73, 81, 83, 84, 86, 87, 88, 90, 103, 114, 116, 117, 118, 123, 148–82; tragic style, 37, 62, 85–88, 116–17, 153, 156–57, 169, 179, 181
Tragedy in prose, 86, 87, 256
Traugott Lawler, 55
Tre libri di arte poetica. See Muzio, Girolamo
Treatise of Nobility, 131
Tre trianni, 85
Trionfi. See Petrarca, Francesco
Trissino, Giangiorgio, 71, 72, 77, 78, 81–86, 87, 88, 90, 91, 124, 130, 184, 193, 217, 273
Tristia. See Ovid
Troas, 148, 150, 157–58
Tully. *See* Cicero, Marcus Tullius

Turberville, George, 196
Turn (= *Volta*), 75
Twyne, Thomas, 203

Udall, Nicholas, 149, 155, 184, 186–93

Vaquelin de la Fresnaye, Jean, 68
Varchi, Benedetto, 76, 90
Varro, M. Terentius, 31, 37, 105, 262
Vellutello, Alessandro, 85
Venerable Bede. *See* Bede, Venerable
Vergil, 12, 33, 36, 38, 42, 61, 62, 64, 66, 67, 75, 88, 89, 90, 91, 92, 100, 127–47, 197–206, 213, 214, 221, 239
Vers mesurées, 62, 69
Versi, et regole de la nuova poesia Toscana. See Tolomei, Claudio
Versi sciolti, 13, 72, 74, 76, 81, 83, 84, 85, 86, 87, 88, 89, 90, 91, 147, 173, 193, 224, 259, 275
Versus, 45, 75
Victorinus. *See* Marius Victorinus
Vie de saint Alexis, 11, 18
Vittorino da Feltre, 93
Volta, 75
Vulgaria Terentii, 149

W.W. (tr. of Plautus; probably William Warner), 149
Waith, Eugene, 241
Warton, Thomas, 204
Watson, Thomas, 95, 103, 104, 113
Watton, Henry, 150
Webbe, William, 96, 114–16, 117, 124, 213
Weismiller, Edward, 17, 268
Well-Weighed Syllables. See Attridge, Derek
Wheel of Vergil, 38, 73, 289 n60
Whole Works of Homer. See Chapman, George
William of Lô, 48
William of Occam, 123
Wilson, F. P., 254
Wilson, Thomas, 20, 105
Winter's Tale, 255
Wipo, chamberlain to Henry III, 52

Wisdom of the Ancients. See Bacon, Francis
Woods, Susanne, 17
Words and things, 80, 94, 263
Words into Rhythm. See Harding, D. W.
Wright, George T., 146
Wyatt, Sir Thomas, 22, 60, 70, 110, 118, 129, 130, 146, 154, 183

Ylverton, Christopher, 151

Zodiakus vitae. See Palengenius
Zoilus, 152
Zoppio (Niccolò d'Aristotile), 88, 130
Zyma vetus expergetur, 52–53